The advancement of social theory requires an analytical approach that systematically seeks to explicate the social mechanisms that generate and explain observed associations between events. These essays, written by prominent social scientists, advance criticisms of current trends in social theory and suggest alternative approaches. The mechanism approach calls attention to an intermediary level of analysis, in between pure description and storytelling, on the one hand, and grand theorizing and universal social laws, on the other. For social theory to be of use for the working social scientists, it must attain a high level of precision and provide a toolbox from which middle-range theories can be constructed.

Contributors: Raymond Boudon, Tyler Cowen, Jon Elster, Diego Gambetta, Peter Hedström, Gudmund Hernes, Timur Kuran, Thomas C. Schelling, Aage B. Sørensen, Arthur L. Stinchcombe, Richard Swedberg, and Axel van den Berg.

SOCIAL MECHANISMS

STUDIES IN RATIONALITY AND SOCIAL CHANGE

Editors: Jon Elster and Michael S. McPherson

Editorial Board:
Fredrik Barth
Amartya Sen
Arthur L. Stinchcombe
Bernard Williams

Edited by
Peter Hedström and Richard Swedberg
Stockholm University

SOCIAL MECHANISMS

An Analytical Approach to Social Theory

CAMBRIDGE
UNIVERSITY PRESS

CAMBRIDGE UNIVERSITY PRESS
Cambridge, New York, Melbourne, Madrid, Cape Town, Singapore,
São Paulo, Delhi, Dubai, Tokyo, Mexico City

Cambridge University Press
The Edinburgh Building, Cambridge CB2 8RU, UK

Published in the United States of America by Cambridge University Press, New York

www.cambridge.org
Information on this title: www.cambridge.org/9780521596879

First published 1998
Reprinted 2004, 2005

A catalogue record for this publication is available from the British Library

Library of Congress Cataloguing in Publication Data
Social mechanisms : an analytical approach to social theory / edited
by Peter Hedström, Richard Swedberg.
p. cm. - (Studies in rationality and social change)
Includes index.
ISBN 0-521-59319-0. - ISBN 0-521-59687-4 (pbk.)
1. Sociology - Methodology. 2. Social systems. I. Hedstrilm,
Peter. II. Swedberg, Richard. III. Series.
HM24.S54426 1997
301'.01-dc21   97-11413
                                    CIP

ISBN 978-0-521-59319-9 Hardback
ISBN 978-0-521-59687-9 Paperback

For James S. Coleman and Robert K. Merton

Contents

Acknowledgments

We gratefully acknowledge financial support from the following sources: the Bank of Sweden Tercentenary Foundation, the Tore Browaldh Foundation for Scientific Research and Education, and the Swedish Council for Research in the Humanities and Social Sciences. This support enabled us to hold a lively symposium on the theme of social mechanisms at The Royal Academy of Sciences in Stockholm, during June 6–7, 1996. We also would like to thank the participants at this symposium, in particular Andrew Abbott, Mario Bunge, Ronald Burt, Michael Hannan, Michael Hechter, Daniel Klein, Peter Marsden, Robert K. Merton, Charles Tilly, and Harriet Zuckerman.

We owe a special debt to Christofer Edling, Fredrik Liljeros, Rickard Sandell, Lotta Stern, and Cecilia Swedberg, whose help in organizing the symposium was invaluable. The personnel at the Royal Academy of Science kindly assisted us in all possible ways. Rickard Sandell helped out in putting together the final version of the manuscript. We are also very grateful to Elizabeth Neal at Cambridge University Press, who helped to see this volume into press with customary skill and professionalism. Finally, Amos Tversky was scheduled to have participated in the symposium, but sadly passed away before it took place.

Stockholm
November 1996

Contributors

RAYMOND BOUDON is Professor of Sociology at the University of Paris-Sorbonne (Paris IV).

TYLER COWEN is Professor of Economics at George Mason University.

JON ELSTER is Robert K. Merton Professor in the Social Sciences at Columbia University.

DIEGO GAMBETTA is Professor of Sociology at Oxford University.

PETER HEDSTRÖM is Professor of Sociology at Stockholm University.

GUDMUND HERNES is Minister of Health in Norway.

TIMUR KURAN is Professor of Economics and Faisal Professor of Islamic Thought and Culture at the University of Southern California in Los Angeles.

THOMAS C. SCHELLING is Professor of Economics at the University of Maryland at College Park.

AAGE B. SØRENSEN is Professor of Sociology at Harvard University.

ARTHUR L. STINCHCOMBE is Professor of Sociology at Northwestern University.

RICHARD SWEDBERG is Professor of Sociology at Stockholm University.

AXEL VAN DEN BERG is Professor of Sociology at McGill University.

1. Social mechanisms: An introductory essay

PETER HEDSTRÖM AND RICHARD SWEDBERG

Introduction

The main message of this book is that the advancement of social theory calls for an analytical approach that systematically seeks to explicate the social mechanisms that generate and explain observed associations between events. It might appear obvious that every social theory, worthy of its name, should be explanatory. But upon closer examination, it turns out that what often goes under the rubric of social theory, should more properly be viewed as conceptual or sensitizing schemes, and not as explanatory theory proper.[1] Much of modern social theory has a tendency – just like the Parsonianism of yesterday – to label, relabel, and to describe rather than to explain.[2] In the case of sociological theory, our main concern in this essay, a sustained focus on explanatory social mechanisms would allow sociological theory to re-connect with what we consider to be its most promising and productive era – namely, middle-range sociology of the kind that Robert Merton and Paul Lazarsfeld tried to develop at Columbia University after World War II.[3]

This essay is an extended and revised version of Hedström and Swedberg (1996b). We wish to thank Mario Bunge, Mark Granovetter, Barbara Hobson, Ole-Jørgen Skog, Arthur Stinchcombe, Cecilia Swedberg, Michael Tåhlin, and Lars Udehn for their useful comments. We owe special thanks to Carl-Gunnar Janson for his detailed written comments, and to Alejandro Gil-Villegas and Aage Sørensen for the valuable background information they provided.

[1] In an insightful article by someone who has devoted most of his academic career to general social theory, Göran Therborn (1991:178) notes: "Absent or marginal to currently prevailing general sociological theorizing is any ambition to explain." See also Jeffrey Alexander's plea in the *Handbook of Sociology* that more attention should be given to "discourse" and less to "explanation" (Alexander 1988:78–81).

[2] That Parsons had a similar problem to explain, rather than to describe and relabel, is clear. See, for example, George Homans's statement from the early 1960s, with explicit address to Parsons, Shils, and Smelser, that "much modern sociological theory seems to me to possess every virtue except that of explaining anything" (Homans 1961:7).

[3] The two best introductions to middle-range sociology are, in our opinion, Robert Mer-

The mechanisms-based approach to social theory should not be confused with a purely descriptive approach that seeks to account for the unique chain of events that lead from one situation or event to another. All proper explanations explain the particular by the general, and as will be demonstrated later, there are general types of mechanisms, found in a range of different social settings, that operate according to the same logical principles. Our vision of an explanatory sociology contains an ensemble of such fundamental mechanisms that can be used for explanatory purposes in a wide range of social situations.

In this chapter, we will describe how the concept of mechanism has been used in the social sciences, especially sociology. We will discuss the explanatory status and importance of social mechanisms, the characteristics of analytical sociology, and the relationship between variable-based and mechanism-based approaches. Thereafter we will illustrate our notion of a general social mechanism with reference to the work of Robert Merton, James Coleman, and Mark Granovetter. The essay ends with a typology of such social mechanisms and a brief guide to the other chapters of the book.

On the use of the concept of mechanisms in the social sciences

An interesting aspect of the mechanism approach is its interdisciplinarity. As an example of this, we refer to contemporary biology.[4] According to

ton's essay "On Sociological Theories of the Middle Range" and Raymond Boudon's short article "What Middle-Range Theories Are" (Merton 1967; Boudon 1991).

[4] In modern physics, the term "mechanism" is not used, but many of the explanations are mechanism based. The reason for not using the term itself is of a historical or accidental nature and has to do with the fact that in physics the word "mechanism" is connected to the scientific world view of the 17th century (e.g., Dijksterhuis 1986). It should also be remembered that in the 19th century, thermodynamics popularized the notion of a system, which is broader than that of "mechanism/machine" and allows the analyst to choose the environment of the system according to the purpose of the study. The attempt to conceptualize all phenomena according to the elementary laws of mechanics became impossible after the emergence of field physics in the middle of the 19th century. The 17th-century notion of mechanism spread from physics and astronomy to a number of sciences – such as chemistry and biology – where the term "mechanism" is still used, though with different meanings. The Cartesian notion that organisms can be conceptualized as machines turned out to be very useful, and it became central to a new biological philosophy called "mechanism," which is usually contrasted to that of "vitalism" or the doctrine that life cannot be reduced to mechanics (e.g., Beckner 1967). In the 19th century, the term "mechanism" was

Francis Crick, who shared the Nobel Prize in 1962 for his discovery of the molecular structure of DNA, 20th century biologists prefer to think in terms of "mechanisms" and not "laws." The reason for this is that the notion of "laws" is generally reserved for physics, which is the only science that can produce explanations based upon powerful and often counterintuitive laws with no significant exceptions. "What is found in biology is *mechanisms*, mechanisms built with chemical components and that are often modified by other, later, mechanisms added to the earlier ones" (Crick 1989:138).

In the social sciences, the prevalence of explicitly stated mechanism-based explanations vary widely between the disciplines. These types of explanations are rarely used (explicitly) in history, sometimes in sociology, and quite frequently in economics and psychology. Particularly in cognitive psychology, the notion of mechanism plays a key role. To cite a well-known work, "The information-processing approach [in cognitive psychology] assumes that perception and learning can be analyzed into a series of stages during which particular components ('mechanisms') perform certain transformations or recoding of the information coming into them" (Bower 1975:33).

Economists often see themselves as thinking in terms of mechanisms, as opposed to sociologists and historians, who are believed to be more interested in social institutions. Schumpeter, for example, writes that "by economics – or, if you prefer, 'economics proper' – we denote the interpretive description of economic mechanisms that play within any given state of those institutions [studied by economic sociology], such as market mechanisms" (Schumpeter 1989:293). The one mechanism that economists relate most of their analyses to – their master mechanism, so to speak – is the market. That the market can be seen as a "mechanism" goes back to the 18th century, when economics (via, e.g., Adam Smith) became influenced by the Newtonian–Cartesian worldview, and it has become so self-evident to contemporary economists that the market is a mechanism, that they often use the terms "market" and "market mechanism" synonymously.

Much of neoclassical economics in the 20th century can be understood as an attempt to explain ever more aspects of the economic process

disconnected from the metaphor of the machine and instead became linked to that of the system.

through the mechanism of the market: production as well as consumption and distribution. The notion of mechanism is furthermore implicit in the idea of equilibrium, as Tyler Cowen points out in his survey of the use of mechanisms in economics (Chapter 6). It is worth noting that economists' talents for thinking in terms of mechanisms often only becomes clear to non-economists when they go beyond the traditional boundaries of their discipline. Examples of this can be found in Albert Hirschman's *Exit, Voice, and Loyalty* (1970) and even more so in Thomas Schelling's *Micromotives and Macrobehavior* (1978).[5]

As economists gradually have expanded the boundaries of their discipline to include a range of topics traditionally considered the domain of sociologists, such as the family and organizations, the difference between the disciplines to an increasing extent have come to concern the types of theories being used. One such difference, but by no means the only one, centers exactly on the importance attributed to explanatory mechanisms. Comparing labor market sociology with labor economics, Aage Sørensen (1990) has noted that most labor market sociologists think of theory

> as having to do with which variables should be included in the equations and how these variables relate to other variables – and not as something which is about which mechanisms produce the observed associations in the variables. This is where there is a huge difference between sociological research and economic research in this area; and the difference is very much to the disadvantage of the sociologist. (308)

The use of mechanisms in sociology

Sociology, as we noted earlier, lags behind economics and many other sciences when it comes to explicitly formulated mechanism-based theories. The term "mechanism" is quite common in sociological works and has a long history, but it is nearly always used in a casual everyday sense. As an illustration of this tendency, we cite what is in all likelihood its earliest

---

[5] The problem that Hirschman addresses has to do with what happens when an organization (including a firm) begins to decline. According to Hirschman, two "mechanisms of recuperation" are usually triggered off in this situation, one that is discussed primarily in economics ("exit") and one that is focused on primarily by political scientists ("voice"). Schelling's *Micromotives and Macrobehavior* is the classic in the area of social mechanisms. The essay on segregation ("Sorting and Mixing: Race and Sex") is the most famous, but we also would like to draw attention to Schelling's attempt to produce a catalogue of social mechanisms in "Thermostats, Lemons, and Other Families of Models."

use in sociology. In 1905 Albion Small published a textbook in sociological theory, *General Sociology*, in which he had included a list of the most important sociological concepts. Among Small's examples were "society," "social structure," "social status," and "social mechanism" (Small 1905:401–2). Nowhere in the text of his work, however, does Small explicate the concept of social mechanism in a serious manner.

Small's concept of a social mechanism is, as in today's sociology, used in a casual everydayish way. Robert Merton's term for this type of use is "proto-concept," and he explains its meaning in the following manner: "a proto-concept is an early, rudimentary, particularized, and largely unexplicated idea . . . ; a concept [on the other hand] is a general idea which once having been defined, tagged, substantially generalized, and explicated can effectively guide inquiry into seemingly diverse phenomena" (Merton 1984:267).

Among the sociological classics, the term "mechanism" is rarely used, even if the idea itself is present.[6] Among the best-known examples is the mechanism that *The Protestant Ethic* is centered around, more precisely the way that ascetic Protestantism at one point in history led to changes in people's economic behavior. Thanks to a believer's conversion to ascetic Protestantism, to recapitulate Weber's argument, he or she began to set a religious premium on a certain type of behavior, the unintended consequence of which was a novel norm for how to act in economic questions.[7] The works of Simmel and Durkheim similarly contain a number of important mechanisms. Simmel's use of *tertius gaudens* is one example of this, as is Durkheim's analysis of the way that the balance between individual and group affects the suicide rate.

An explicit use of the concept of "mechanism" does not seem to have emerged in sociology until after World War II. In our opinion the most suggestive discussion of the concept is to be found in the writings of Robert Merton, who brought together the idea of mechanism with that of

---

[6] Weber, for example, rarely used the term "mechanism" ("Mechanismus") except in his analysis of bureaucracy, where it is more or less synonymous with "machine" (Weber [1921–2] 1978:961, 967, 988; Weber as cited in Marianne Weber 1975:416–17). In *Zwischenbetrachtung*, Weber makes the following statement, which sums up the situation brought about by Descartes and Newton: "The tension between religion and intellectual knowledge definitely comes to the fore wherever rational, empirical knowledge has consistently worked through to the disenchantment of the world and its transformation into a causal mechanism [*kausalen Mechanismus*]" (Weber 1946:350; emphasis added).

[7] For a discussion of this and many other mechanisms in Weber's work, see Richard

middle-range theorizing (Merton 1967).[8] Merton firmly rejected all attempts to develop general systems of sociological theory and advocated instead that sociological theory should deal with "social mechanisms." The point is to locate a middle ground between social laws and description, Merton said, and "mechanisms" constitute such a middle ground.

In *Social Theory and Social Structure*, Merton defines social mechanisms as "social processes having designated consequences for designated parts of the social structure" and argues that it constitutes the main task of sociology to "identify" mechanisms and to establish under which conditions they "come into being," "fail to operate," and so on (Merton 1968:43–44). Merton briefly discusses concrete mechanisms that determine reference groups, create dissonance, and articulate role-sets.[9] In our opinion the most important contribution of his essay, however, is the view of mechanisms as elementary building blocks of middle-range theories.

After the demise of the Columbia School, there has been little serious discussion in sociology of mechanism-based theorizing. There exists only one exception, as far as we know, when it comes to a general meta-theoretical discussion within sociology, and that is a recent article by Arthur Stinchcombe: "The Conditions of Fruitfulness of Theorizing about Mechanisms in Social Science" (1991, revised version 1993). In this article, Stinchcombe correctly observes that "we do not have a sufficiently supple armory of mechanisms for making social science theory" (Stinchcombe 1993:24). He defined the concept of mechanism in the following way:

Mechanisms in a theory are defined here as bits of theory about entities at a different level (e.g., individuals) than the main entities being the-

Swedberg, *Max Weber and the Idea of Economic Sociology* (forthcoming, Princeton University Press).

[8] Merton's work on middle-range theory goes back to his critique of Parsons at the 1947 meeting of the American Sociological Association (see Merton, 1948). Also, Parsons discussed the concept of mechanism, especially in his work from the early 1950s (see, e.g., Parsons 1951:201–325, Parsons and Shils 1951:125–49). Parsons's view, however, was marred by his functionalism as well as by his attempts at grand theory, and the function of social mechanisms was basically reduced to that of maintaining the social system when this was threatened in some manner. As Lars Udehn has pointed out to us, George Lundberg also uses the concept of social mechanisms in *Foundations of Sociology* (1939). Lundberg argued for a common-sense approach to the notion of mechanism, often with functionalist overtones.

[9] To this can be added a few other more general mechanisms that were to emerge from Merton's own work as well as from Columbia Sociology in general: the two-step model of communication, the self-fulfilling prophecy, the Matthew Effect, and the diffusion mechanism of *Medical Innovation* (Coleman, Katz, and Menzel 1966).

orized about (e.g., groups), which serve to make the higher-level theory more supple, more accurate, or more general. (Stinchcombe 1991:367)

The examples that Stinchcombe uses to illustrate his definition include maximizing individuals (on the lower level) who create a market through their actions (on the higher level) and molecules (on the lower level) that under certain conditions turn into gas (on the higher level).

What Stinchcombe is talking about are indeed important types of mechanisms, but there also exist other types of mechanisms, as we will suggest below. A much broader, as well as more differentiated, concept can be found in the work of Jon Elster, who has clearly done more than anybody else to advance mechanism-based theorizing in the 1980s and 1990s.[10]

The explanatory importance of social mechanisms

The core argument of this chapter is that the identification and analysis of social mechanisms is of crucial importance for the progress of social science theory and research. But what exactly is a mechanism, and why should we focus on mechanisms rather than on statistical associations or other forms of relationships between the entities of interest?

It is far from trivial to provide a precise yet sufficiently general definition of a social mechanism that captures the essence of the concept. As suggested by Harré (1970), one key defining characteristic of an explanatory mechanism is the function it performs in an explanatory account. Assume that we have observed a systematic relationship between two entities, say I and O. In order to explain the relationship between them we search for a mechanism, M, which is such that on the occurrence of the cause or input, I, it generates the effect or outcome, O. The search for mechanisms means that we are not satisfied with merely establishing systematic covariation between variables or events; a satisfactory explanation requires that we are also able to specify the social "cogs and wheels" (Elster 1989:3) that have brought the relationship into existence. As Schelling emphasizes in Chapter 2, a mechanism can be seen as a systematic set of statements that provide a plausible account of how I and O are linked to one another.

---

[10] Many of Elster's ideas are distinctly summarized in the chapter entitled "Mechanisms" in *Nuts and Bolts for the Social Sciences* (1989:3–10), but the reader is also referred to the more detailed discussion in many other works (see, e.g., Elster 1989, 1991, 1992, 1993).

This view of causal explanations differs in important respects from the classic covering-law model as advocated by Carl Hempel and his followers (see Hempel 1942, 1962). According to Hempel, an explanation of an event entails subsuming the event under a general law. A satisfactory explanation therefore must specify the general covering law and the conditions that make the law applicable in the specific case.[11] According to Hempel, deterministic laws are quite unlikely in the social and the historical sciences. The "laws" that can be invoked in the social sciences are instead of a probabilistic nature (i.e., they state that the occurrence of a particular event will come about with such and such probability if certain specified conditions are at hand).

Since this form of explanation simply entails applying a general law to a specific situation, the insights offered by the exercise are directly proportional to the depth and robustness of the "probabilistic law." If this law is only a statistical association, which is the norm in the social and historical sciences according to Hempel, the specific explanation will offer no more insights than the law itself and will usually only suggest *that* a relationship is likely to exist, but it will give no clue as to *why* this is likely to be the case. For these reasons, we are inclined to agree with von Wright's position that it is better "not to say that the inductive-probabilistic model [of Hempel] explains what happens, but to say only that it justifies certain expectations and predictions" (von Wright 1971: 14).

The covering-law model provides justification for the use of "black-box" explanations in the social sciences because it does not stipulate that the mechanism linking *explanans* and *explanandum* must be specified in order for an acceptable explanation to be at hand. This omission has given leeway for sloppy scholarship, and a major advantage of the mechanism-based approach is that it provides (or encourages) deeper, more direct, and more fine-grained explanations. The search for generative mechanisms consequently helps us distinguish between genuine causality and coinci-

[11] Hempel (1942) uses the example of an automobile radiator cracking during a cold night to illustrate the logic of his proposal. The general laws cited in the explanation would need to refer to how the pressure of water changes with changes in temperature and volume, and the specific circumstances referred to would be conditions such as the temperature during the night and the bursting pressure of the radiator. A proper explanation has been proposed if, and only if, the proposition about cracking of the radiator can be logically deduced from the sentences stating the laws and the specific circumstances.

dental association, and it increases the understanding of why we observe what we observe.

The role that the search for mechanisms plays in distinguishing between spurious and real associations can be illustrated by the recent controversy surrounding possible health effects of electromagnetic fields. Some epidemiological studies have found an empirical association between exposure to electromagnetic fields and childhood leukemia (see Feychting and Ahlbom 1993). However, the weight of these empirical results are severely reduced by the fact that there exists no known biological mechanism that can explain how low-frequency magnetic fields could possibly induce cancer (ORAU 1992). According to Bennett (1994), it is furthermore extremely unlikely that a mechanism will ever be found, because such a mechanism would have to violate well-established physical principles. The lack of a plausible mechanism increases the likelihood that the weak and rather unsystematic empirical evidence reported in this epidemiological literature, simply reflects unmeasured confounding factors rather than a genuine causal relationship (Hedström 1994a).

The distinction between black-box explanations and mechanism-based explanations can be illustrated in more general terms with the following example, which is adopted from the work of Bunge (1967). Assume that we have observed a systematic (nonrandom) relationship between two types of events or variables, I and O. The way in which the two sets of events or variables are linked to one another is expressed with the mechanism, M:

$$I \longrightarrow \boxed{M} \longrightarrow O$$

What characterizes a black-box explanation is that the link between input and output, or between *explanans* and *explanandum*, is assumed to be devoid of structure, or, at least, whatever structure there may be is considered to be of no inherent interest (perhaps because it cannot be observed or because O can be predicted even though the mechanisms linking I and O are unknown).

In sociology the most systematized form of black-box explanation can be found in the so-called causal modeling approach (see Duncan 1975), which will be discussed more fully later. In the causal-modeling tradition, the explanatory "mechanism" simply is a regression coefficient linking I and O, and this regression coefficient (if the model includes all relevant variables) is supposed to describe the causal influence of I upon O. The approach advocated here does not rest with describing the strength and the form of the relationship between the entities of interest but addresses a further and deeper problem: how (i.e., through what process) was the relationship brought about?[12]

Consider the example of poisoning. It would be possible to estimate the parameters of an equation describing the relationship between the intake of, say, strychnine and the risk of dying. If the model had the correct functional form, we might even have established a "covering law" of the dose-response relationship, which could be used for predicting the likely outcomes of other occurrences of strychnine intake. But as long as we have not specified the mechanisms that link strychnine intake to morbidity and mortality, the explanation is clearly wanting. By pointing to how strychnine inhibits the respiratory centers of the brain and to the biochemical processes responsible for this paralysis, we provide a mechanism that allows us not only to describe what is likely to happen but also to explain why it is likely to happen (see Bunge 1967).

It is important to note that the mechanisms referred to in the foregoing discussion are mechanisms of some generality, and it is this generality that gives them their explanatory power. Simply making up an ad hoc story tailored to a specific case does not constitute an acceptable explanation. Even moderately talented journalists are able to make up these sorts of ad hoc stories, and, as Arthur Stinchcombe once noted, "a student [of sociology] who has difficulty thinking of at least three sensible explanations for any correlation that he is really interested in should probably choose another profession" (Stinchcombe 1968:13). Serious, noncommonsensical explanations require mechanisms of some generality.

One line of sociological research that illustrates the shortcomings of black-box explanations is research on class and its individual correlates. In empirically oriented sociology, individuals' class belonging has become a popular explanation for various individual-level phenomena such as income (e.g., Kalleberg and Berg 1987) and health (e.g., Townsend and

---

[12] It should be emphasized that the distinction between "black boxes" and "mechanisms" to some extent is time-bound. In the words of Patrick Suppes (1970:91): "From the standpoint of either scientific investigation or philosophical analysis it can fairly be said that one man's mechanism is another man's black box. I mean by this that the mechanisms postulated and used by one generation are mechanisms that are to be explained and understood themselves in terms of more primitive mechanisms by the next generation."

Davidson 1990). The concept of class might be useful for descriptive purposes where it serves as a shorthand for various aspects of individuals' socioeconomic living conditions, and research in this tradition has produced informative empirical research describing the living conditions of different "classes." Whether the empirical exercise of relating variables describing class and income or class and health also has an explanatory value – in the deeper sense of saying something about why we observe what we observe – is much more doubtful since it does not explicate the causal mechanisms that generated the relationship.

Despite the common sociological rhetoric of describing class as a "determinant" of various individual traits and behaviors, class in and of itself obviously cannot influence an individual's income or health. A "class" cannot be a causal agent because it is nothing but a constructed aggregation of occupational titles. A statistical association between "class" and income, or "class" and health, tells us that individuals from certain "classes" have lower incomes or worse health than others, but it says nothing about why this is the case. To answer such questions, it is necessary to introduce and explicate the generative mechanisms that might have produced the observed differences in average income or health between the occupational groups that the researchers have assigned to different "classes." A statistical "effect" of a class variable in contexts like these is essentially an indicator of our inability to specify properly the underlying explanatory mechanisms. The worse we do in specifying and incorporating the actual generative mechanisms into the statistical model, the stronger the "effect" of the class variable will appear to be.

Methodological individualism

Mechanism-based explanations usually invoke some form of "causal agent" (Bhaskar 1978) that is assumed to have generated the relationship between the entities being observed. It is by explicitly referring to these causal agents that the relationship is made intelligible. In the natural sciences, causal agents come in a variety of forms such as organic reactions in chemistry and natural selection in biology. In the social sciences, however, the elementary "causal agents" are always individual actors, and intelligible social science explanations should always include explicit references to the causes and consequences of their actions.[13] This principle of methodological individualism is intimately linked with the core idea of the mechanism approach: Understanding is enhanced by making explicit the underlying generative mechanisms that link one state or event to another, and in the social sciences, actions constitute this link.

It is useful to distinguish between a strong and a weak version of methodological individualism. The strong version of the doctrine only accepts "rock-bottom" explanations (i.e., explanations that include no references to aggregate social phenomena in the *explanans*). The weak version of methodological individualism takes the same ontological position as the strong version but accepts for the sake of realism nonexplained social phenomena as part of the explanation (see Udehn 1987).

Although the search for rock-bottom explanations usually is intellectually challenging and intriguing, the strategy often is likely to be of limited use when it comes to explaining concrete social phenomena. The reason for this has been aptly described by David Lewis:

> Any particular event that we might wish to explain stands at the end of a long and complicated causal history. We might imagine a world where causal histories are short and simple; but in the world as we know it, the only question is whether they are infinite or merely enormous. (1986:214)

Since many essential elements of sociological explanations – such as legal rules, social institutions, and productive capacities – are the results of long and intricate historical processes, these sorts of elements must either be ignored and a world of short and simple causal histories be assumed, which to us seems unacceptable as a general rule, or they must be endogenized, which seems unrealistic given the current state of social theory. In contrast to areas such as moral philosophy and normative economic theory, where the strong individualistic program is essential, for an empirical science like sociology, state-of-nature stories appear to be of restricted use.

The weak version of methodological individualism agrees with the strong version in assuming that all social institutions in principle can be explained by only the intended and unintended consequences of individuals' actions. But faced with a world consisting of causal histories of

---

[13] For the sake of clarity, it should be noted that we also include "intentions" among the possible "causes" of individual action.

nearly infinite length, in practice we can only hope to provide information on their most recent history.[14] The weak version of methodological individualism, therefore, is more apt in our view for the construction of explanatory theory. By taking certain macro-level states as given and incorporating them into the explanation, the realism and the precision of the proposed explanation is greatly improved. From what we have just said, it is also clear that the use of methodological individualism in sociology differs in one respect from the way in which it normally is used in, say, economics and psychology: The action being analyzed is always action by individuals that is oriented to the behavior of others.[15]

The primacy of the analytical

It also is important to recognize that mechanisms, in the natural as well as in the social sciences, usually are unobserved analytical constructs. Weinberg (1993) emphasizes the important role that unobserved analytical entities have played in physics. For example, the existence of both the electron and the neutrino were conjectured and their role in various physical processes were usefully theorized, long before they actually were observed. Similarly, the social sciences routinely postulate the existence of unobserved explanatory mechanisms. Assumptions of intentions, discounting, and preferences have proven to be extremely useful analytical devices even though they never have been observed. Mechanisms, as Gudmund Hernes so forcefully argues in Chapter 4, are analytical constructs that provide hypothetical links between observable events.

The key characteristic of an analytical approach is that it proceeds by first constructing an analytical model of the situation to be analyzed (an "ideal type"). This theoretical model is in principle constructed in such a way that it includes only those elements believed to be essential for the problem at hand. The target of the theoretical analysis, then, is this model

---

[14] Alfred Marshall ([1920] 1986:644), when discussing the use of abstract reasoning in economics, advanced a similar argument regarding the necessity of short chains of deductive reasoning.

[15] See Weber's well-known definition of sociology: "Sociology . . . is a science concerning itself with the interpretive understanding of social action and thereby with a causal explanation of its course and consequences. . . . Action is 'social' insofar as its subjective meaning takes account of the behavior of others and is thereby oriented in its course" (p. 4 in *Economy and Society: An Outline in Interpretative Sociology*. Trans. Ephraim Fischoff et al. Berkeley: University of California Press [1921–22] 1978).

and not the reality that the model is intended to explain. However, to the extent that the theoretical model has been constructed in such a way that it incorporates the essential elements of the concrete situation, the results of the theoretical analysis will also shed light on the real-world situation that the model is intended to explain. Or, as Schumpeter (1908:527–8) once put it, when the tailor is good, the coat will fit.

Much of current sociological theorizing appears to be guided by a disbelief in the value of analytical abstractions and by a corresponding belief in the possibility of providing theoretical accounts of what happens as it actually happens. No one would dispute the attractiveness of this position if it were possible to realize, but accounting for something ''as it actually happens'' is always problematic and is reminiscent of Ranke's by now outdated and naive historicist position that history always should be analyzed ''wie es eigentlich gewesen'' (Ranke [1824] 1885:vi). Simply describing all the events, microscopic and macroscopic, that take place in a room during one second would – if it were technically possible – take centuries, and this very fact is the main reason for the necessity of an analytical approach. Even in the most trivial description of a social situation, we are forced to be highly selective about which events to include and which events to exclude from the description; this choice, implicitly or explicitly, is guided by our prior belief about the essential elements of the situation. Thus even the most detailed descriptive accounts are always ''models'' of concrete social situations, and these descriptive models will always distort reality by accentuating certain aspects of the situation and by ignoring others. An important implication of this, as Hernes emphasizes in his chapter, is that the alternative to a specific model never can be no model at all but is always an alternative model. Or in Hernes's colorful language, ''models are to social science what metaphors are to poetry – the very heart of the matter'' (Hernes 1979:20).

The distinction between a complex social reality and an intentionally simplified analytical model of this reality seems to have been lost in many sociological discussions of social theory. The standard sociological critique of analytical theory focuses on the realism of its assumptions. Criticism of this sort – which basically entails pointing out that theories intentionally built upon empirically inaccurate or incomplete assumptions indeed are built upon empirically inaccurate or incomplete assumptions – appears somewhat redundant. Criticizing an analytical model for lack of realism is a common instance of the logical fallacy, which consists of mistaking the abstract for the concrete – what Whitehead ([1925] 1948: 52) called "The Fallacy of Misplaced Concreteness." The choice between the infinitely many analytical models that can be used for describing and analyzing a given social situation can never be guided by their truth value, because all models by their very nature distort the reality they are intended to describe. The choice must instead be guided by how useful the various analytical models are likely to be for the purpose at hand.

The belief in explanations that provide accounts of what happens as it actually happens has pervaded the sociological literature for decades and has produced an abundance of detailed descriptive narratives but few explanatory mechanisms of any generality. It is through abstractions and analytical accentuation, however, that general mechanisms are made visible. But these abstractions also distort by their very nature the descriptive account of what actually happened, by accentuating certain aspects of the situation and by ignoring others. Francis Crick's characterization of the process through which good biological theories are arrived at is in our opinion equally valid for the social sciences: "To produce a really good biological theory one must try to see through the clutter produced by evolution to the basic mechanisms lying beneath them" (Crick 1989:138).

Variables versus social mechanisms

The widespread use and knowledge of survey analysis and the statistical techniques needed for analyzing such data have clearly improved the ability of sociologists to describe social conditions and to test sociological theories. But, as emphasized by Sørensen in Chapter 10, the increasing use of these techniques has also fostered the development of a variable-centered type of theorizing that only pays scant attention to explanatory mechanisms. Coleman (1986) aptly described this type of sociology as a form of "individualistic behaviorism." The guiding principle behind this type of theorizing – usually referred to as "causal-modeling" – is the notion that individual behavior can and should be explained by various individual and environmental "determinants," and the purpose of the analysis is to estimate the causal influence of the various variables representing these determinants.[16]

[16] The affinity between behaviorism and structural equation modeling was also noted by O. D. Duncan himself: "In [structural equation] models that purport to explain the behavior of individual persons, the coefficients [of the structural equation] could well take the form

According to Coleman, this emphasis on "causal" explanations of behavior represented a considerable change from the type of explanatory account used in the earlier tradition of community studies: "One way of describing this change is to say that statistical association between variables has largely replaced meaningful connection between events as the basic tool of description and analysis" (Coleman 1986:1327–8). In the causal-modeling tradition, variables and not actors do the acting (Abbott 1992).[17]

The tension between a variable-centered causal approach to sociological theorizing and a generative view emphasizing the importance of social mechanisms came to the fore in an exchange between Robert Hauser and Raymond Boudon in the mid-1970s. The context of this exchange was a review by Hauser of Boudon's (1974) book on education and inequality. In this book, Boudon developed a theoretical model that he hoped would make intelligible a number of apparent paradoxes reported by empirical research on social mobility. Hauser suggested numerous changes to Boudon's model, but the main message of his article was a strong disbelief in the very idea that had motivated Boudon to write the book (i.e., that an important distinction should be made between statistical and theoretical models, and that theoretical models are needed to explain the results of an empirical analysis):

> Boudon dismisses several standard representations of the mobility process as being "basically statistical." I can only guess what this means
> – perhaps that they are rich in formal properties or that sampling distributions of their parameters are known. Neither of these properties strikes me as undesirable, and these models do have coherent and intuitively meaningful interpretations relative to the mobility process. (Hauser 1976:923)

of units of response per unit of stimulus strength; the structural equation is, in effect, a stimulus–response law" (Duncan 1975:162–3).

[17] Throughout his career, Coleman was a strong proponent of a generative view of causality, and he often expressed serious doubts about the usefulness of the type of causal analysis referred to previously. In *Introduction to Mathematical Sociology*, he wrote: "Note, however, that there is nowhere the proposal simply to engage in curve fitting, without an underlying model which expresses a social process. If the data happen to fit a simple curve, this may provide an economical statement of the data, in terms of the one or two parameters of the distribution curve. But if there is no underlying model with a reasonable substantive interpretation, little has been gained by such curve fitting" (Coleman 1964:518).

Boudon responded by noting that descriptive models of the sort advocated by Hauser are undoubtedly useful for many purposes but that their usefulness for causal analysis is considerably more restricted than assumed by Hauser. According to Boudon, understanding normally is achieved not by the means of descriptive statistical models but through theoretical models that show the abstract *logic* of the process being analyzed. In order to understand this logic, Boudon argued, "we must go beyond the statistical relationships to explore the generative mechanism responsible for them" (Boudon 1976:117). As he expressed it in a different context,

> Causal analysis does not explain the [statistical] chart. It simply summarizes it. *Understanding* a statistical structure means in many cases building a generating theory or model . . . that includes the observed empirical structure as one of its consequences. (Boudon 1979:51–2)

So where does this leave us? We do not wish to suggest that quantitative empirical research is of minor importance for the sociological enterprise. Quite the contrary: Quantitative research is essential both for descriptive purposes and for testing sociological theories. We do, however, believe that many sociologists have had all too much faith in statistical analysis as a tool for *generating* theories, and that the belief in an isomorphism between statistical and theoretical models, which appears to be an integral feature of the causal-modeling approach, has hampered the development of sociological theories built upon concrete explanatory mechanisms.

Over the last few years, one can discern a movement away from the "hard-core" position represented by Hauser. Nevertheless, the way in which quantitative sociologists still allocate their time and intellectual energy between statistical and theoretical modeling reveals a strong preference for description and testing of hypotheses formulated by others, and they rarely show any serious intellectual commitment to developing the theoretical foundation of the discipline themselves. As suggested by Stinchcombe (1993:27–8), sociologists in the multivariate modeling tradition still "make only rhetorical use of the language of mechanisms."

Social mechanisms: Some selected examples

In order to concretize the idea of a general social mechanism underlying a range of different social phenomena, we will briefly examine three well-known theories in sociology – the self-fulfilling prophecy (Robert Merton), network diffusion (James Coleman), and threshold-based behavior (Mark Granovetter) – and we will suggest that they all are founded upon the same basic *belief-formation mechanism.*

The self-fulfilling prophecy is one of the most famous of all mechanisms-based theories in sociology and was formulated in 1948 by Robert Merton in a seminal article (Merton [1948] 1968). The basic idea is that an initially false definition of a situation evokes behavior that eventually makes the false conception come true (Schelling discusses numerous examples of such processes in Chapter 2). The key example that Merton uses to illustrate his argument is a run on a bank. If a rumor of insolvency somehow gets started, some depositors will withdraw their savings. Their withdrawal will strengthen the belief in the rumor, partly because the withdrawals actually may hurt the financial standing of the bank, but more importantly because the act of withdrawal in itself signals to others that something indeed might be wrong with the bank. This produces even more withdrawals, which further reduces the trust in the bank, and so on. Because of the operation of this mechanism, even an initially sound bank may go bankrupt if enough depositors withdraw their money in the (initially) false belief that the bank is insolvent.

The study of network diffusion processes currently is a vigorous area of sociological research (cf. Burt 1987; Marsden and Podolny 1990; Strang and Tuma 1993; Hedström 1994b). To a considerable extent, this line of research has been inspired by Coleman, Katz, and Menzel's classic study of the diffusion of a new drug (see Coleman, Katz, and Menzel 1957 1966). Their main finding was that physicians' positions in various professional networks influenced the diffusion process, particularly during the period immediately after the new drug had been introduced on the market. Their explanation for this finding is reminiscent of Merton's argument about the self-fulfilling prophecy:

> Why should these sociometric ties to colleagues who have used the drug be influential during the first months of the drug's availability, but not later? One possible answer lies in the greater uncertainty about the drug that must have prevailed when it was new. . . . We know from work in the tradition of Sherif that it is precisely in situations which are objectively unclear that social validation of judgments becomes most important. More generally, this explanation implies that a doctor will be

influenced more by what his colleagues say and do in uncertain situations, whenever and wherever they may occur, than in clear-cut situations. (Coleman, Katz, and Menzel 1957: 268–9)

The core of their argument is consequently that networks are important because information about innovations, in this case a new drug, diffuse through them, and that an individual's propensity to adopt the innovation is influenced by what others do, particularly when there is a great deal of uncertainty about the true value of the innovation.

Our final example is Granovetter's threshold theory of collective behavior (see Granovetter 1978; Granovetter and Soong 1983). Granovetter argued that an individual's decision whether or not to participate in collective behavior often depends in part on how many other actors already have decided to participate. He further argued that actors differ in terms of the number of other actors who already must participate before they decide to the same, and he introduced the concept of an individual's "threshold" to describe this individual heterogeneity. An actor's threshold denotes the proportion of the group which must have joined before the actor in question is willing to do so, and an important qualitative result of Granovetter's analysis was that even slight differences in thresholds can produce vastly different collective outcomes (see also Schelling 1978, for a similar analysis).

Granovetter gives a range of examples of threshold-based behavior, but the following example illustrates particularly well the logic behind this sort of conditional behavior:

Suppose you are in an unfamiliar town and enter an unknown restaurant on Saturday evening at seven o'clock. Whether or not you decide to take a meal there will depend in part on how many others have also decided to do so. If the place is nearly empty, it is probably a bad sign – without some minimal number of diners, one would probably try another place. (Granovetter 1978:1438–9)

The reason that the number of visitors at the restaurant is likely to influence an individual's choice of restaurant is that in situations of uncertainty, the number of diners constitute a signal about the likely quality of the restaurant, and this signal may be decisive for the individual's choice of action.

In order to more clearly see the logical structure of the arguments advanced by Merton, Coleman, and Granovetter, it is useful to adopt a slightly more formalized language. Let

P_{it} = propensity of individual i to perform the act being analyzed at time t (e.g., withdrawing savings from the bank, adopting a new drug, visiting a restaurant, or joining an organization for collective action), and

b_{it} = the strength of individual i's belief in the value or necessity of performing the act in question at time t.

Merton, Coleman, and Granovetter all assume that individuals are goal directed and that an individual's propensity to perform the act being analyzed is an increasing function f of the individual's belief in the value of performing the act: $P_{it} = f(b_{it})$. However, the core mechanism that gives Merton's, Coleman's, and Granovetter's analyses their counterintuitive appeal, concerns the ways in which they assume that individuals' beliefs are being formed. More specifically, their proposed mechanism states that individual i's belief in the value or necessity of performing the act is a function of the number of other individuals who performed the act at time $t - 1$. Merton's bank customers based their judgments about the solvency of the bank on the number of other customers withdrawing their savings from the bank; Coleman's physicians based their evaluations of the possible effect of the new drug on the doings of their colleagues; and Granovetter's restaurant visitor based his/her decision on the number of diners already in the restaurant. That is, they all assumed that

$$b_{it} = g(n_{t-1})$$

where n_{t-1} = number of individuals performing the act time $t - 1$, and g is an increasing function.

Inserting this expression into the former one, we arrive at $P_{it} = f[g(n_{t-1})]$, which suggests that an individual's propensity of withdrawing savings from the bank, adopting a new drug, visiting a restaurant, or joining an organization for collective action is an increasing function of the number of other individuals who already have performed the same act.

The main difference between the three theories considered here centers on the function g, which provides the fine-grained details of the link between b_{it} and n_{t-1}, and the details of this link will influence the aggregate dynamics of the system.[18] But the core characteristic of these theories that gives them their nonobvious character and appeal is the general *belief-formation mechanism* which states that the number of individuals who perform a certain act signal to others the likely value or necessity of the act, and this signal will influence other individuals' choice of action. It is this belief-formation mechanism that is at the heart of the self-fulfilling prophecies of Merton, the network effects of Coleman, and the bandwagon effects of Granovetter. On the fundamental level of mechanisms, the run on the bank, the prescription of the drug, and the emergence of the collective movement, all are analogous.[19]

Social mechanisms: A typology

As several authors in this book point out, explanations of most concrete social events or states require resort to several elementary mechanisms; one is not enough. Sometimes these mechanisms counteract one another, and sometimes they work together. In any case, the multiplicity of mechanisms makes it important to introduce some kind of typology that sorts them in a meaningful way. The one we shall present here takes its departure from James Coleman's (1986) well-known model for how to conceptualize collective social action, the so-called macro-micro-macro model. The three different types of social mechanisms in our typology are summarized in Figure 1.1.

The general thrust of this model is that proper explanations of change and variation at the macro level entails showing how macro states at one point in time influence the behavior of individual actors, and how these actions generate new macro states at a later time. That is, instead of analyzing relationships between phenomena exclusively on the macro level, one should always try to establish how macro-level events or conditions affect the individual (Step 1), how the individual assimilates the impact

---

[18] Coleman assumed that *g* was a function of the sociometric ties, Granovetter assumed that it was a function of individual thresholds, and Merton left the functional form unspecified. When mechanisms are expressed in mathematical language, they appear as functions transforming variables. These functions can be distinguished from one another on the basis of their functional form and their parameter values. See Hernes (1976).

[19] In addition to this belief-formation mechanism, there are, of course, other action and transformation mechanisms that are involved in Merton's, Coleman's, and Granovetter's analyses, but these mechanisms are commonplace and tangential to the core processes they analyze. See Hedström's Chapter 12 in this volume for a more detailed analysis of this type of mechanism.

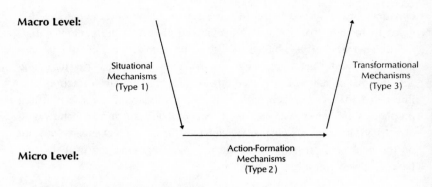

Figure 1.1. A typology of social mechanisms.

of these macro-level events (Step 2), and how a number of individuals, through their actions and interactions, generate macro-level outcomes (Step 3). This way of conceptualizing social action lends itself in a very natural way to a typology of mechanisms: macro-micro mechanisms, micro-micro mechanisms, and micro-macro mechanisms – and a few words will be said about each of these.[20]

The actor in the first two types of situations is a single individual, and the mechanism is internal (and in this sense "psychological" or "social-psychological"); in the third type, there are a number of actors, and the mechanism is typically external (and "social"). The following description of what a mechanism is (by Diego Gambetta in Chapter 5 of this book) captures the essence of the first two types of mechanisms, which focus on single pieces of behavior: "[Mechanisms are] hypothetical causal models which make sense of *individual* behavior [and] have the form 'given certain conditions K, an agent will do x because of [mechanism] M with probability p.' " Stinchcombe's earlier cited definition of mechanisms as mediating between lower and higher levels, however, focuses more directly on social interaction and on the consequences of social action. This is also true for Thomas Schelling's definition (in Chapter 2): "A social

---

[20] The logic of Coleman's argument also suggests that any kind of continuous social action can be conceptualized as a long chain of successive macro-micro-macro transformations, where, in many cases, only the peaks, so to speak ("macro-macro"), are visible to the researcher – but where the analytical point is precisely to explain this cumulative social action as a result of a large number of macro-micro-macro transitions.

mechanism is a plausible hypothesis, or set of plausible hypotheses, that could be the explanation of some social phenomena, the explanation being in terms of interactions between individuals, or individuals and some social aggregate.''

The first of the three types of mechanisms covers the macro-to-micro transition, in Coleman's terminology, and following a suggestion of Stinchcombe (1993), we shall call it a *situational mechanism*. The individual actor is exposed to a specific social situation, and this situation will affect him or her in a particular way. Erving Goffman's (1963) work on behavior in public places and Karl Popper's form of situational analysis (cf. Popper, 1994) have these sorts of mechanisms at their core. The belief-formation mechanism discussed previously, opportunity-generating mechanisms such as White's (1970) vacancy chains, and preference-formation mechanisms such as those expressed in the idea of reference groups (see Merton and Rossi 1968; Boudon 1988) are prototypical examples of general social mechanisms that in a systematic and reasonably precise way link a social structure or other macro-sociological event or states to the beliefs, desires, and opportunities of some individual actor.

The second type of mechanism is to be located at the micro level, and we refer to it as an *action-formation mechanism*. This type of mechanism shows how a specific combination of individual desires, beliefs, and action opportunities generate a specific action. A plurality of psychological and social-psychological mechanisms operate at this level. General decision theories as well as more specific theories such as Leon Festinger's (1957) theory of cognitive dissonance and George Ainslie's (1992) on discounting illustrate different types of action mechanisms.

The third type of mechanism covers the micro-to-macro transition, and we propose to call it a *transformational mechanism*. Here a number of individuals interact with one another, and the specific mechanism (which differs depending on the nature of the interaction) shows how these individual actions are transformed into some kind of collective outcome, be it intended or unintended. Several of the theories mentioned elsewhere in this book – Schelling's tipping model, standard game-theoretic models such as the tragedy of the commons, and neoclassical market models – are examples of transformational mechanisms.

Brief summary

We have argued that the notion of social mechanism is essential to social theory in general and to sociological theory in particular, and it is now time to conclude with a more formal definition of a social mechanism. The mechanism approach, as we see it, can be characterized by the following four core principles:

1. Action
2. Precision
3. Abstraction
4. Reduction

The first of these principles – explanations based on *actions* – means, among other things, that it is actors and not variables who do the acting. A mechanism-based explanation is not built upon mere associations between variables but always refers directly to causes and consequences of individual action oriented to the behavior of others. A corollary to this principle states that there exist no such things as "macro-level mechanisms"; macro-level entities or events are always linked to one another via combinations of situational mechanisms, action-formation mechanisms, and transformational mechanisms (i.e., all macro-level change should be conceptualized in terms of three separate transitions: macro-micro, micro-micro, and micro-macro).[21]

The second principle – explanatory *precision* – captures the essence of middle-range sociology and expresses the idea that sociology should not prematurely take on broad-sweeping and vague topics or try to establish universal social laws (which are unlikely to exist in any case). It should instead aim at explanations specifically tailored to a limited range of phenomena. This limited range is not synonymous with some small area of society; the same mechanism can often be found in many places in society.

The third principle – *abstraction* – expresses the idea that effective theorizing is not possible without a prompt elimination of irrelevant factors and a sharp focus on the central issue. Whereas this process is well un-

---

[21] In addition to these basic characteristics of social mechanisms, the ideal mechanism, it seems to us, should also be simple and nonobvious.

derstood in economics, it is much less so in sociology. It is through abstraction and analytical accentuation that general social mechanisms are made visible.

The last of the four principles that characterize the mechanism approach – what we call *reduction* – is equivalent to the general reductionist strategy in science of opening up black boxes, and always striving for narrowing the gap or lag between input and output, cause and effect. A mechanism-based explanation seeks to provide a fine-grained as well as tight coupling between *explanans* and *explanandum*.

A general social mechanism can now be defined in the following way:

A social mechanism is an integral part of an explanation which (1) adheres to the four core principles stated previously, and (2) is such that on the occurrence of the cause or input, *I*, it generates the effect or outcome, *O*.

But even if definitions like this may be useful, it deserves to be pointed out that the essence of the mechanisms approach is to be found in a special *style of theorizing* rather than in any specific definition of what a social mechanism is. This style can be roughly characterized by a focus on middle-range puzzles or paradoxes for which precise, action-based, abstract, and fine-grained explanations are sought.

Brief overview of the book

The remaining chapters in this book roughly fall into three categories. First, a few general chapters discuss the defining characteristics and advantages of a mechanisms-based approach in the social sciences. Thomas Schelling explains with characteristic elegance and clarity how social mechanisms operate and how they can be used to explain different types of social dynamics (Chapter 2). The emphasis in the two following chapters in this section is somewhat different. Jon Elster notes that mechanisms abound in the works of Montaigne, Tocqueville, and in proverbs (Chapter 3). He also argues that social mechanisms are characterized by the fact that they are easily recognizable causal patterns that are triggered under generally unknown conditions. In this respect, they differ from laws, which state that given certain initial conditions, an event of one type (the cause) will always produce an event of another type (the effect). Gudmund Hernes addresses the same problematique as Elster but sug-

gests an alternative way of approaching it (Chapter 4). A social mechanism, according to Hernes, is perfectly general because mechanisms
belong to the realm of the abstract. However, mechanisms can be of limited applicability, Hernes argues, if they describe few real-life processes
realistically.

The second category essays are more specific in nature yet still of a
general character. Diego Gambetta, for example, uses some empirical research to illustrate the point that social mechanisms often operate together in specific concatenations (Chapter 5). Tyler Cowen looks at
economics and argues that it is a science of social mechanisms. He pays
particular attention to the problem of indeterminacy that arises when
multiple equilibria exist (Chapter 6). Timur Kuran, an economist as
Cowen, discusses mechanisms involved in preference falsification and
also points to a number of mechanisms that can come into play when an
actor has contradictory values (Chapter 7). Raymond Boudon argues that
in a rational-choice type of analysis, all black boxes can in principle be
eliminated and all mechanisms laid bare – but only if the analysis is
broadened to include normative beliefs (Chapter 8). One of the examples that Boudon uses to illustrate his argument comes from Tocqueville, one of the most explicitly mechanisms-oriented classics of the
social sciences.

The third category essays are all written by sociologists and either deal
with specific sociological problems or attempt to survey the current state
of sociology. Axel van den Berg analyzes a number of so-called general
theories – as can be found in the works of Jeffrey Alexander, Pierre Bourdieu, Anthony Giddens, and Jürgen Habermas – and argues that all of
them are marred by their lack of precision and their unsystematic attention
to the role of social mechanisms in explaining concrete social phenomena
(Chapter 9). Aage Sørensen criticizes a different tendency in today's sociology – the obsession with statistical models and the neglect of the need
to develop sociological models mirroring the social mechanisms and their
role in social change (Chapter 10). Arthur Stinchcombe analyzes three
different categories of actors – elite universities, enterprises, and nation
states – and shows how they all exemplify the workings of one and the
same mechanism: monopolistic competition (Chapter 11). Finally, Peter
Hedström examines social mechanisms of imitative behavior, paying particular attention to the role of rational bases of imitative behavior (Chapter 12).

References

Abbott, A. 1992. What Do Cases Do? Some Notes on Activity in Sociological Analysis. Pp. 53–82 in C. C. Ragin and H. S. Becker (eds.), *What is a Case? Exploring the Foundations of Social Inquiry*. Cambridge: Cambridge University Press.

Ainslie, G. 1992. *Picoeconomics: The Strategic Interaction of Successive Motivational States within the Person*. Cambridge: Cambridge University Press.

Alexander, J. C. 1988. The New Theoretical Movement. Pp. 77–102 in N. Smelser (ed.), *Handbook of Sociology*. London: SAGE.

Beckner, M. O. 1967. Mechanism in Biology. Pp. 250–2 in Vol. 5 of P. Edwards (ed.), *The Encyclopaedia of Philosophy*. New York: Macmillan and The Free Press.

Bennett, W. R. Jr. 1994. *Health and Low-Frequency Electromagnetic Fields*. New Haven: Yale University Press.

Bhaskar, R. 1978. *A Realist Theory of Science*. Sussex: The Harvester Press.

Boudon, R. 1974. *Education, Opportunity, and Social Inequality*. New York: Wiley.

Boudon, R. 1976. Comment on Hauser's Review of *Education, Opportunity, and Social Inequality*. *American Journal of Sociology* 81: 1175–87.

Boudon, R. 1979. Generating Models as a Research Strategy. Pp. 51–64 in R. K. Merton, J. S. Coleman, and P. H. Rossi (eds.), *Qualitative and Quantitative Social Research: Papers in Honor of Paul F. Lazarsfeld*. New York: The Free Press.

Boudon, R. 1988. The Logic of Relative Frustration. Pp. 245–67 in M. Taylor (ed.), *Rationality and Revolution*. Cambridge: Cambridge University Press.

Boudon, R. 1991. What Middle-Range Theories Are. *Contemporary Sociology* 20: 519–22.

Bower, G. H. 1975. Cognitive Psychology: An Introduction. Pp. 25–80 in W. K. Estes (ed.), *Handbook of Learning and Cognitive Processes*. New York: Wiley.

Bunge, M. 1967. *Scientific Research*. Volume 3 in *Studies of the Foundations, Methodology, and Philosophy of Science*. Berlin: Springer-Verlag.

Burt, R. S. 1987. Social Contagion and Innovation: Cohesion versus Structural Equivalence. *American Journal of Sociology* 92:1287–1335.

Coleman, J. S. 1964. *Introduction to Mathematical Sociology*. New York: The Free Press.

Coleman, J. S. 1986. Social Theory, Social Research, and a Theory of Action. *American Journal of Sociology* 91:1309–35.

Coleman, J. S. 1990. *Foundations of Social Theory*. Cambridge, MA: Harvard University Press.

Coleman, J. S., E. Katz, and H. Menzel. 1957. The Diffusion of an Innovation among Physicians. *Sociometry* XX:253–70.

Coleman, J. S., Elihu Katz, and Herbert Menzel. 1966. *Medical Innovation*. Indianapolis: Bobbs-Merril.

Crick, F. 1989. *What Mad Pursuit: A Personal View of Scientific Discovery*. London: Penguin Books.

Dijksterhuis, E. J. 1986. *The Mechanization of the World Picture: Pythagoras to Newton*. Princeton: Princeton University Press.

Doll, R., and R. Peto. 1981. *The Causes of Cancer*. Oxford: Oxford University Press.

Duncan, O. D. 1975, *Introduction to Structural Equation Models*. New York: Academic Press.

Elster, J. 1983. *Explaining Technical Change: A Case Study in the Philosophy of Science*. Cambridge: Cambridge University Press.

Elster, J. 1989. *Nuts and Bolts for the Social Sciences*. Cambridge: Cambridge University Press.

Elster, J. 1991. Patterns of Causal Analysis in Tocqueville's *Democracy in America. Rationality and Society* 3(3):277–97.

Elster, J. 1992. *Local Justice: How Institutions Allocate Scarce Goods and Necessary Burdens*. New York: Russell Sage Foundation.

Elster, J. 1993. *Political Psychology*. Cambridge: Cambridge University Press.

Festinger, L. 1957. *A Theory of Cognitive Dissonance*. Stanford: Stanford University Press.

Feychting, M., and A. Ahlbom. 1993. Magnetic Fields and Cancer in Children Residing Near Swedish High-voltage Power Lines. *American Journal of Epidemiology* 138:467–81.

Ghins, M. 1990. Méchanisme. Pp. 1582–3 in S. Auroux (ed.), *Les Notions Philosophique – Dictionnaire*. Paris: Presses Universitaires de France.

Giddens, A. 1987. *Social Theory and Modern Sociology*. Stanford: Stanford University Press.

Gladwell, M. 1996. The Tipping Point. *New Yorker* June 3:32–8.

Goffman, E. 1963. *Behavior in Public Places: Notes on the Organization of Gatherings*. New York: The Free Press.

Goldthorpe, J. H. 1996. The Quantitative Analysis of Large-scale Data Sets and Rational Action Theory. *European Sociological Review* 12:109–26.

Granovetter, M. 1978. Threshold Models of Collective Behavior. *American Journal of Sociology* 83:1420–43.

Granovetter, M. 1982. Review of Christopher Jencks et al., *Who Gets Ahead? The Determinants of Economic Success in America. Theory and Society* II:257–62.

Granovetter, M., and R. Soong. 1983. Threshold Models of Diffusion and Collective Behavior. *Journal of Mathematical Sociology* 9:165–79.

Hamlin, C. 1990. *A Science of Impurity: Water Analysis in Nineteenth Century Britain*. Bristol: Adam Hilger.

Harré, R. 1970. *The Principles of Scientific Thinking*. Chicago: University of Chicago Press.

Harré, R. 1984. *The Philosophies of Science.* 2nd ed. Oxford: Oxford University Press.

Hauser, R. M. 1976. Review Essay: On Boudon's Model of Social Mobility. *American Journal of Sociology* 81:911–28.

Hedström, P. 1994a. Magnetic Fields and Cancer Risks: Should Recent Epidemiological Results be a Cause of Concern? *Occasional Paper Series.* Department of Sociology, Stockholm University.

Hedström, P. 1994b. Contagious Collectivities: On the Spatial Diffusion of Swedish Trade Unions, 1890–1940. *American Journal of Sociology* 99:1157–79.

Hedström, P. Forthcoming. Rational Choice and Social Structure: On Rational-Choice Theorizing in Sociology. In B. Wittrock (ed.), *Social Theory and Human Agency.* London: Sage.

Hedström, P., and R. Swedberg. 1996a. Rational Choice, Empirical Research, and the Sociological Tradition. *European Sociological Review* 12:127–46.

Hedström, P., and R. Swedberg. 1996b. Social Mechanisms. *Acta Sociologica* 39: 281–308

Hempel, C. G. 1942. The Function of General Laws in History. *Journal of Philosophy* 39: 35–48.

Hempel, C. G. 1962. Explanation in Science and in History. Pp. 9–33 in R. G. Colodny (ed.), *Frontiers of Science and Philosophy.* Pittsburgh: University of Pittsburgh Press.

Hernes, G. 1976. Structural Change in Social Processes. *American Journal of Sociology* 82:513–47.

Hernes, G. 1979. Om bruk av Økonomiske Modeller i sosiologien. *Sosiologi i Dag* 4:19–39.

Hirschman, A. O. 1970. *Exit, Voice, and Loyalty: Responses to Decline in Firms, Organizations, and States.* Cambridge, MA: Harvard University Press.

Homans, G. C. 1961. *Social Behaviour: Its Elementary Forms.* London: Routledge & Kegan Paul.

Humphreys, P. 1991. Review of Jon Elster, *Nuts and Bolts for the Social Sciences. Philosophy of the Social Sciences*, 21(March):114–21.

Kalleberg, A., and I. Berg. 1987. *Work and Industry: Structures, Markets, and Processes.* New York: Praeger.

Karlsson, G. 1958. *Social Mechanisms: Studies in Sociological Theory.* Stockholm: Almquist & Wicksell.

Kiser, E., and M. Hechter. 1991. The Role of General Theory in Comparative-historical Sociology. *American Journal of Sociology* 97:1–30.

Lazarsfeld, P., B. Berelson, and H. Gaudel. 1944. *The People's Choice.* New York: Columbia University Press.

Lewis, D. 1986. *Philosophical Papers*, ii. Oxford: Oxford University Press.

Lieberson, S. 1985. *Making it Count: The Improvement of Social Research and Theory.* Berkeley: University of California Press.

Lundberg, G. A. 1939. *Foundations of Sociology.* New York: Macmillan.

Marsden, P. V., and J. Podolny. 1990. Dynamic Analysis of Network Diffusion

Processes. Pp. 197–214 in H. Flap and J. Weesie (eds.), *Social Networks through Time*. Utrecht: ISOR.

Marshall, A. [1920] 1986. *Principles of Economics*. 8th ed. London: Macmillan.

Merton, R. K. 1948. Discussion [of Talcott Parsons, "The Position of Sociological Theory"]. *American Sociological Review* 13:164–8.

Merton, R. K. [1948] 1968. The Self-fulfilling Prophecy. Pp. 475–90 in *Social Theory and Social Structure*. New York: The Free Press.

Merton, R. K. 1967. On Sociological Theories of the Middle Range. Pp. 39–72 in *On Theoretical Sociology*. New York: The Free Press.

Merton, R. K. 1984. Socially Expected Durations: A Case Study of Concept Formation in Sociology. Pp. 262–83 in W. W. Powell and R. Robbins (eds.), *Conflict and Consensus*. New York: The Free Press.

Merton, R. K., and A. S. Rossi. 1968. Contributions to the Theory of Reference Group Behavior. Pp. 279–334 in *Social Theory and Social Structure*. New York: The Free Press.

ORAU. 1992. *Health Effects of Low-Frequency Electric and Magnetic Fields*. Oak Ridge Associated Universities Panel. Washington, D.C.: U.S. Government Printing Office.

Oxford English Dictionary. 1989. Mechanism. Pp. 536–7 in vol. IX. Oxford: Clarendon Press.

Parsons, T. 1951. *The Social System*. New York: The Free Press.

Parsons, T., and E. Shils (eds.). 1951. *Toward A General Theory of Action*. Cambridge: Harvard University Press.

Pawson, R. 1989. *A Measure for Measures: A Manifesto for Empirical Sociology*. London: Routledge.

Popper, K. R. 1994. Models, Instruments, and Truth: The Status of the Rationality Principle in the Social Sciences. Pp. 154–84 in K. R. Popper, *The Myth of the Framework: In Defence of Science and Rationality*. London: Routledge.

Ranke, von. L. [1824] 1855. *Geschichten der romanischen und germanischen Völker von 1494 bis 1514*. 3rd ed. Munich: Duncker & Humblot.

Sayer, A. 1984. *Method in Social Science*. London: Hutchinson.

Schelling, T. C. 1978. *Micromotives and Macrobehavior*. New York: W. W. Norton.

Schumpeter, J. 1908. *Das Wesen und der Hauptinhalt der theoretischen Nationalökonomie*. Munich: Duncker & Humblot.

Schumpeter, J. A. 1989. *Essays on Entrepreneurs, Innovations, Business Cycles, and the Evolution of Capitalism*. New Brunswick: Transaction Publishers.

Small, A. 1905. *General Sociology: An Exposition of the Main Development in Sociological Theory from Spencer to Ratzenhofer*. Chicago: University of Chicago Press.

Sørensen, A. B. 1990. Interview. Pp. 303–15 in R. Swedberg, *Economics and Sociology*. Princeton: Princeton University Press.

Stinchcombe, A. L. 1968. *Constructing Social Theories*. Chicago: University of Chicago Press.

Stinchcombe, A. L. 1991. The Conditions of Fruitfulness of Theorizing about Mechanisms in Social Science. *Philosophy of the Social Sciences* 21(3):367–88. (See also Stinchcombe 1993).

Stinchcombe, A. L. 1993. The Conditions of Fruitfulness of Theorizing about Mechanisms in Social Science. Pp. 23–41 in A. Sørensen and S. Spilerman (eds.), *Social Theory and Social Policy: Essays in Honor of James S. Coleman*. Westport, CT: Praeger. (This paper is identical, save for a few items, to Stinchcombe 1991).

Strang, D., and N. Brandon Tuma. 1993. Spatial and Temporal Heterogeneity in Diffusion. *American Journal of Sociology* 99:614–39.

Suppes, P. 1970. *A Probabilistic Theory of Causality*. Acta Philosophica Fennica, Fasc. XXIV. Amsterdam: North-Holland.

Swedberg, R. 1996. Analyzing the Economy: On the Contribution of James S. Coleman. Pp. 313–28 in J. Clark (ed.), *James S. Coleman*. London: The Falmer Press.

Swedberg, R. Forthcoming. *Max Weber and the Idea of Economic Sociology*. Princeton: Princeton University Press.

Therborn, G. 1991. Cultural Belonging, Structural Location and Human Action: Explanation in Sociology and in Social Science. *Acta Sociologica* 34:177–91.

Townsend, P., and N. Davidson. 1982. *Inequalities in Health: The Black Report*. Baltimore: Penguin Books.

Udehn, L. 1987. *Methodological Individualism*. Ph.D. diss. Uppsala: Dept. of Sociology, Uppsala University.

von Wright, G. H. 1971. *Explanation and Understanding*. Ithaca: Cornell University Press.

Weber, Marianne. 1975. *Max Weber: A Biography*. Trans. Harry Zohn. New York: Wiley.

Weber, Max. [1921–2] 1978. *Economy and Society: An Outline of Interpretive Sociology*. Ed. G. Roth and C. Wittich. Trans. Ephraim Fischoff et al. 2 vols. Berkeley: University of California Press.

Weber, M. 1946. *From Max Weber: Essays in Sociology*. Trans. and ed. H. Gerth and C. Wright Mills. New York: Oxford University Press.

Weber, Max. 1949. *The Methodology of the Social Sciences*. Trans. and ed. E. A. Shils and H. A. Finch. New York: The Free Press.

Weinberg, S. 1993. *Dreams of a Final Theory: The Search for the Fundamental Laws of Nature*. London: Vintage.

White, H. C. 1970. *Chains of Opportunity: System Models of Mobility in Organizations*. Cambridge: Harvard University Press.

Whitehead, A. N. [1925] 1948. *Science and the Modern World: Lowell Lectures, 1925*. New York: New American Library.

2. Social mechanisms and social dynamics

THOMAS C. SCHELLING

In the various chapters of this book, social mechanisms are contrasted with theories, laws, correlations, and black boxes. There is near consensus on a hierarchy that has "mere" correlations at the bottom, with laws higher up. Laws that are black boxes (i.e., opaque as to how they work) are, even if fully reliable like the law of gravity, less helpful than laws that work transparently. Theories have less status than laws if the laws are well established and the theories not; theories built on established laws, like the theory of planetary motion, are at the summit.

A pervasive question for social phenomena is the role, or the exclusive role, of "methodological individualism," the notion that the ultimate unit of analysis is a rational, or at least a *purposive*, individual. For some of the authors here, any social phenomenon that can not be reduced to the behavior (choices) of individuals is a black box and therefore unsatisfactory. There is some notion that what is inside a black box must be a social mechanism, or several social mechanisms.

What, though, are social mechanisms, and where do they fit? And are social mechanisms little things, big things, or great big things? Did Keynesian theory constitute a social mechanism; is the arms race a social mechanism; is inflation a social mechanism? Or is giggling such a mechanism, or yawning, or the propagation of gossip? On the relation of social mechanisms to theories, I propose that a theory may comprise many social mechanisms, but also a social mechanism may comprise many theories. And a particular issue that arises is whether a social mechanism can be purely mathematical. That may depend on what "purely" means, as I shall propose in a moment.

I propose – and I believe I am paraphrasing Hedström and Swedberg in their introductory essay – that a social mechanism is a plausible hypothesis, or set of plausible hypotheses, that could be the explanation of some social phenomenon, the explanation being in terms of interactions between individuals and other individuals, or between individuals and some social aggregate. (I interact with an individual if I change lanes when his front bumper approaches within five feet of my rear bumper; I interact with a social aggregate when I adjust my speed to the average speed on the highway.) Alternatively, a social mechanism is an *interpretation*, in terms of individual behavior, of a model that abstractly reproduces the phenomenon that needs explaining.

Let me illustrate by means of a phenomenon that is well described, that follows a recognizable pattern, and that fits a simple curve. According to Marchetti, Meyer, and Ausubel (1996:25), "Literally thousands of examples of the dynamics of populations and other growth processes have been well modeled by the simple logistic. Classic examples include the cumulative growth of a child's vocabulary and the adoption of hybrid corn by Iowa farmers." The authors proceed to show that life expectancy, fertility rates, and infant mortality conform nicely to a logistic pattern over time for virtually every country or region of the world.

The logistic for their purpose is defined as a trajectory of increase or decrease over time in a variable that is subject to upper or lower limits (including zero), with the rate of increase (or decrease) being proportional both to the value of the variable itself and to the difference between the value of the variable and the upper or lower limit. Specifically, if X embarks, from a very small initial value, on a growth trajectory, subject to an upper limit L, the *rate of increase* of X is proportionate to X times $(L - X)$ [i.e., $dX/dt = aX(L - X)$]. The curve is the familiar ogive, sigmoid, or S-curve.

This is not yet a social mechanism, but it invites interpretation. Marchetti et al.'s analysis of population involves some speculative analysis of what individual behavior underlies these fertility and mortality rates. I say they do not yet have a social mechanism not because their interpretations are speculative and far from substantiated but because they are incomplete. If they were complete, I'd say they had presented a social mechanism that *could be* the explanation. Without their speculative interpretation, they have a fascinating black box. Something is going on. Someone might propose a "law" on the basis of enough instances; indeed, if we look at children's vocabularies, Iowa farmers, Finnish and Egyptian fertility, and "thousands of examples," we might formulate a law not limited to population growth. But it would be a law without a mechanism, until we had the mechanism. (And probably, for many of those examples, various mechanisms have been identified, or can be.)

Let me now propose another logistic curve, with an underlying interpretation. A new author publishes a highly successful first novel. Sales data are gathered on a monthly basis. Over the course of 3 years, sales follow a logistic path, growing exponentially at first, then passing an inflection point, and declining exponentially until the leftover copies are remaindered. We compare that pattern with other works of fiction, biography, and history and find a lot of logistic curves, enough so that publishers and bookstores get familiar with the S-curve.

Can we think of a social mechanism that accounts for these dynamics? Of course we can. People who read the book, if they like it, *they* talk about it, some people more than others; the more people who read the book, the more people there are to talk about it. Some of the people they talk to buy the book; if they like it, they talk about it. Talk is proportionate to the number of people who have read the book; if all talk is equally effective, the number talking about it grows exponentially. But there is a limit to the number of people likely to be recruited; eventually most of those who would be interested have already heard of the book, maybe bought it, and when they want to talk about it find that there's hardly anybody left who hasn't already heard about it. If there were initially L potentially interested readers, and N have now read it and want to talk about it, and everybody who has read it meets and talks about it with n out of the L per week, there will be $N \times n \times L$ contacts per week, with $N \times n \times (L - N)$ of them potentially productive, and N will grow logistically.

If we began with the sales data as I described, I would call the process I just described a social mechanism. It may be false – the underlying reason for the shape of the curve may be altogether different – but it is a mechanism that can account for what we observed. Furthermore, it may be a mechanism we can attempt to verify or disconfirm.

We might call the mechanism I described (but probably not the fertility–mortality mechanism of Marchetti et al.) a "contagion" model. Or a "recruitment" model. We can modify it in several ways. One is to consider only the recent recruits to N to be contagious (i.e., to still talk about the book). In our formula for $dN/dt = Nn(L - N)$, we replace N with the integral of dN/dt from $t - x$ to t, where x is the mean period of contagion. During the early near-exponential growth period, the difference will not much affect the shape of the growth curve, and the final result will have much the same shape. We can also let L change over time in a contagion model if we now interpret it as a disease model and let some of the potential susceptibles learn to take precautions.

The disease analogy is valuable here. A former student of mine, a physician, worked in a public health clinic in Africa for several years, long enough to notice that the demand for free measles vaccination came in great waves. He grew curious and studied what was going on. At the peak of a measles epidemic, mothers brought their babies over great distances to be vaccinated; the vaccination worked, the epidemic was shortly ended, and all the living babies were immune to measles either from vaccination or from surviving the disease. Then no epidemic could take hold until the stock of nonimmune newborns had reached "critical mass," in which each sick infant could infect, on average, more than one additional infant. Then the disease would begin to take off, but mothers were not motivated to carry their infants long distances until they became acutely aware of neighbors' babies dying of measles. Then the vaccination boomed again. This model included critical mass, the logistic phenomenon, and two "contagions" – the measles contagion, and the contagious transmission of alarm. Its parameters were population density, birth rate, periods of incubation and infectiousness specific to measles, and speed of transmission of alarming information.

The question whether a social mechanism can be purely mathematical, raised earlier, I think I have answered. The S-shaped logistic curve is not a social mechanism, but it can be generated by a social mechanism, and it can be given a specific interpretation as a social mechanism. And I believe that the social mechanism we found underlying our mathematical model (or that we guessed was underlying the model), like most social mechanisms, may suggest other phenomena to which our model is pertinent. It is easy to assimilate our fiction-sales phenomenon to the Iowa farmers' adoption of hybrid corn, but less easy to analogize to the underlying social mechanism for children's vocabulary. And once one sees how the logistic-generating differential equation, $dN/dt = aN(L - N)$, can account for Iowa corn and romantic novels, it is no surprise that "thousands of examples" of logistic-shaped growth processes have been discovered.

Of course, the logistic shape will necessarily be only an approximation to the empirical data, and there may be other differential equations that can generate approximations to the data. The *fact* of a good fit does not alone confirm the conjectured underlying mechanism, and there may be a family of mechanisms of which the contagion model is only one. A sine curve may decently mimic a logistic curve, and if the variable that appears to be exhausting its limit is capable of reversal – unlike the novel, which probably won't come back on the used-book market – we may want to hold judgment until we are sure it is approaching an asymptote and not a wavecrest.

Here is where "pure" mathematics can contribute to the study of social mechanisms. Note that exponential growth itself can reflect a social mechanism; in an infinite population, the $(L - N)$ term never becomes binding, and the logistic curve never reaches that inflection point. We can easily think of social mechanisms that lead to pure exponential growth; having babies is one. Can a simple differential equation generate either exponential growth or sine waves, according to initial conditions or parameter values? How simple can it be?

Ecologists have studied predator–prey relations and found cycles; linear second-order differential equations – derived from a pair of first-order linear equations – are sufficient. Studying the *form* of the equation can suggest what to look for in a social mechanism and can help us to see how the same mechanism might account for either exponential growth or cycles (see the appendix at the end of this chapter).

Before introducing some other social mechanisms, I want to advert to the discussion of what one can do with social mechanisms that one cannot do with "mere correlations," or, perhaps more aptly, "curve fitting." A distinction is often made between *prediction* as the goal of science (and as the "test" of a theory), and *explanation* (i.e., a better understanding of what is going on, a more satisfying place to stop). I think there are at least three other advantages of having a grasp of the social mechanism that lies behind the regularity in behavior.

One is that exceptions to the familiar regularities may be identified with, for example, particular parameter values. An instance is in the contagion model if only those recently infected (recruited) perform the recruitment function. In ordinary exponential growth, $N(t)$ is proportionate to $N(t) - N(t - p)$, with p being here interpreted as the (constant) period that an infected individual remains infectious; the rate of growth is still exponential but slower. (We could also make some allowance for an "incubation" period between infection and infectiousness, which would work in the same direction.) But since ultimately the exponential growth gets damped by the approach to the population limit, it can turn out that a very short period of infectiousness leads to an S-curve that does not approach the population limit. If we compare, say, diseases and find that some show S-curves that peter out and others go on to approach the original limit, knowing something about the mechanism lets us know what to look for – incubation period, period of infectiousness (unlimited with HIV), and perhaps some fraction of the sick quarantined – to explain the differences and verify the mechanism itself.

A second advantage of knowing the mechanism is the possibility of intervention. For example, in the measles case, the number actually sick – not the number that has cumulatively contracted the disease – is probably what the mothers observe. A more rapid growth in N, the number who have already contracted the disease, will be associated with a larger $N(t)$ $- N(t - x)$, the number currently sick. Paradoxically, accelerating the epidemic can accelerate the vaccination rate and reduce the ultimate cumulative number of infants who contract the disease and, of course, the number who die. Other interventions, such as publicity, might be suggested. Since our measles epidemic is only a metaphor for social mechanisms that display the same underlying generative process, there may be varieties of interventions to consider once we have the underlying mechanism and some appreciation of the most influential parameters.

A third advantage is that once we see the mechanism, how it works, and maybe its mathematical shape, we have a kind of template that may fit other phenomena. True, we want to avoid what my colleague Robert Solow described as what a person does who gets a new electric drill for Christmas – go around looking for holes that need to be drilled – but if measles and sales of fiction respond, maybe we can find similar shapes and forms underlying the number of voters supporting Ross Perot during the 1992 election campaign, the number of people who procure microwave ovens, or the number of young people in America who went into science and engineering post-Sputnik. (And we want to beware of concluding too soon that the curve is logistic rather than sinusoidal, or something in between. Once we have a bit of insight into what *might* be the underlying mechanism, we know something about what to look for.)

And it is important to recognize that there often are whole families of social mechanisms, differing from each other significantly, that apply to similar-appearing phenomena, just as there are phenomena that appear similar but reflect wholly different mechanisms. Jon Elster has often called attention to the fact that the eagle, the pterodactyl, and the sparrow have wings, and bats have wings, and flying fish have wings, but the evolutionary mechanisms may unite the pterodactyl, the eagle, and the sparrow but not the bat or the flying fish. Measles, especially its etiology, and flying fish are a far cry from what we might explain as a "social mechanism," but the *models* of the mechanisms may sometimes unite them. In my teaching, I always spend some time on the ordinary household thermostat as a generator of cyclical behavior that helps one to understand what kinds of ingredients in a model – social, mechanical, biological, even psychological – may produce key characteristics of a phenomenon. (Long ago, when I smoked, I found that I kept running out of matches; upon reflection, it seemed that after a match famine I scrounged matches at every chance, to build up a safe inventory, then relaxed and used up all my matches, and had to survive another famine and start scrounging again, somewhat like the mothers responding to the measles cycle. This might qualify as a "psychological mechanism.")

To illustrate what I mean by "families" of mechanisms – what I once called "families of models" – mechanisms that produce similar results, and enjoy similarities but also differences, I shall offer a number of examples of the kind of things often called "self-fulfilling prophecies." A somewhat better term would probably be "self-realizing expectations," with prophecies being only one source of the expectations.

Here are some examples. If people expect a coffee shortage, there will be a coffee shortage. If people believe that only the careless split infinitives, only the careless will split infinitives. If people believe that the only women who smoke on the street are streetwalkers, the only women who smoke on the street will be streetwalkers. If people believe the Harvard department of economics will always attract the best faculty, the Harvard department will always attract the best faculty. If men believe they will be conspicuous without neckties, they will be conspicuous without neckties. If people believe neighbors invariably develop hostility toward each other, neighbors will develop hostility toward each other. If young men believe they needn't learn to cook because the women they marry will have learned how to cook, and if young women believe young men believe that, then young men needn't learn to cook. If people believe it will be hard to get spare parts for Korean-manufactured automobiles, it will be hard to get spare parts for Korean-manufactured automobiles. If scientists, engineers, and international-business people believe that English is bound to become the unique common language of science, engineering, and international business, English will become the language of scientists, engineers, and international-business people. If people believe that nobody with a southern accent can get the party nomination for the U.S. presidency, then nobody with a southern accent can get the nomination. If everybody believes you have to go early to get a seat, you'll have to go early to get a seat. If gunfighters know that when two gunfighters meet on the street they will both draw, and the first to draw will probably kill the other, then when two gunfighters meet they will draw, and the first to draw will probably kill the other. If people believe that only men and women looking for sexual partners go to singles bars, only men and women looking for sexual partners will go to singles bars. If people believe the bank is insolvent, it already is. If people believe that nobody can win a lottery twice, nobody will win a lottery twice. And if people believe that someone recently very popular in social life is on the way out, he or she is on the way out.

These propositions all have, or would have if I eliminated a little variety in the formulation, the same syntactical form. They all invite exploration for underlying mechanisms. Any one of them, I think you will agree, could be true; most of them could also be false. Some of them share a mechanism: Coffee shortage, the insolvent bank – we could have mentioned the stock market – and going early to get a seat all look to me like the same principle. A few – the smoking prostitutes, the frequenters of singles bars – look like powerful coercive conventions: Women who like to smoke who are not prostitutes will feel the privation when walking at night, and somebody who wants to use the telephone may feel unwelcome or conspicuous in the singles bar. The split infinitive and the necktie appear to be similar; the cooking case could be seen either as a coercive convention or as a socially convenient rule of coordination, since there may be advantages to the division of labor and skills, and in monogamous societies, any other rule specifying which member of a marital pair should learn to cook (e.g., alphabetical) would prove confusing and inefficient. The mechanism behind the inability of the southern accent to get nominated may be twofold: No one wants to waste a vote in the primaries, and no one wants to contribute to the campaign fund of a certain loser; without those votes in the early primaries and without those campaign funds, the case is hopeless.

I'm sure not only that there are thousands of such (possibly true) propositions about self-realizing expectations but that there are, at least, dozens or scores of different mechanisms underlying them. I've never seen a catalogue. If given the opportunity, I'd like to offer a prize to whoever – decided by common consent – provides the richest menu of self-realizing expectations. More than that, I'd like to see the beginning of a catalogue of social mechanisms. And for teaching, I would like to see a catalogue of unexpected or anomalous observed behaviors that test and exercise students' skills in solving the puzzles, conceiving of (potential) social mechanisms.

There is, in these chapters, much discussion of "laws" in the social sciences – what laws are, and how they relate to mechanisms or to correlations. We don't have many recognized laws in my discipline, economics – in recent years, what might earlier have been identified as empirically established "laws" have come to be referred to as "stylized facts." But I want to introduce a kind of law that plays a great role in physics, mechanics, genetics, and chemistry, that plays a great role in demography, that plays an unrecognized role (i.e., unrecognized as "law") in economics, and that, though less pervasive, probably has application to sociology and all the disciplines interested in social mechanisms.

I shall introduce this kind of law by introducing two similar-sounding statements, each of which might qualify as a law, one of which would be a law of behavior of the kind that might be recognized in social theory, and the other a law of the kind to which I want to call attention. Here are the two statements:

1. When the average speed on the Autobahn increases, most drivers will drive a little faster.
2. When most drivers drive a little faster, the average speed on the Autobahn increases.

Alternatively,

1. When the noise level at a reception goes up, most people will speak a little louder.
2. When most people at a reception speak a little louder, the noise level goes up.

In each of these pairs, the first is a proposition about behavior, a falsifiable hypothesis. In each, the second proposition is not about behavior: It follows from the definition of "average speed," or "noise level." There are, especially in economics, less obvious identity relations of this kind, usually arrived at by combining two or more statements that are necessarily, identically, true. The mathematical analogy is the pair,

$$aX + bX^2 = Y \quad \text{and} \quad aX + bX^2 = X(a + bX).$$

The first is true only for certain values of X, the second independently of the value of X. In economics, identities of this kind are often called "accounting identities," and they show up in national-income accounting, foreign-transactions accounting, and monetary-system accounting. In demography such an accounting statement would be, for example: In a monogamous society, the number of blacks married to whites is equal to the number of whites married to blacks (as long as we are consistent in the definitions of "whites," "blacks," and "married").

These accounting statements often provide the "feedback loop" in a social mechanism. For example, suppose that the first of the foregoing behavioral statements is found to be approximately true, and that people tend

1. to each have his or her own preferred average speed, to which he or she would conform if it were the actual average, and
2. when the average speed differs from their preferred average, to drive at a speed midway between their preferred average and the actual average (i.e., they accommodate partway to the actual average). If the average is 65, and one's preferred average is 55, one drives 60; if preferred speed is 75, one drives 70.

Suppose now that the average speed on our highway has settled down to where everybody is comfortable (i.e., driving midway between the average and his or her own preferred speed) and the average is 65. Half the people suddenly undergo a change in preference: Preferred average for these people goes up by 20 mph. What will happen to the average? Initially, those whose preferred average has increased by 20 mph will drive 10 mph faster. If they were already driving 60, their preferred average must have been 55; now it is 75, and they raise their speed to 70. If they were already driving 75, their preferred average must have been 85; now it is 105, and they will increase their speed to 85. And so on. Since half the drivers raised their speeds by 10 mph, the average must have gone up by 5, to 70.

But it doesn't stop there. Everybody – those whose preferences changed and who raised their speeds, and those who didn't – now experience an average greater by 5 mph than it used to be, so they will *all* raise their speeds by 2.5 mph. And there it goes again: Now they all accelerate another 1.25 mph, and so on until the average is 75. Those whose preferences changed are now driving 15 mph faster than before, the rest 5 mph faster.

I imputed an especially simple formula for each driver's chosen speed, linear in the actual and preferred averages; as a result, it turns out that the equilibrium average is simply the average of the preferred speeds. But at least that simple formulation shows the "feedback" effect; those who raise the average pull the others along with them, and pull each other, too. The same mechanism can underlie college grade inflation, restaurant tipping, loudness of dormitory record players, and sometimes legislators' willingness to vote for unpopular measures.

I devoted a chapter entitled "The Inescapable Mathematics of Musical Chairs" to these ineluctable logical propositions in an earlier work (Schelling, 1978) and do not want to repeat myself much. But a couple of examples may illustrate. I said, "A fact of some significance is that in a monogamous population the difference between the numbers of unmarried women and unmarried men is the same as the difference between the numbers of women and men" (Schelling, 1978:56). I probably should not have said "fact." A fact is usually something that could be true or false and has to be verified; the assertion in that statement follows logically from the definitions of "men," "women," "unmarried," and "monogamous." I added:

And if we count the women and men over some common age of eligibility for marriage, the percentage difference between the two in a stable population will be the percentage difference in life expectancies at that age. If women live longer or marry earlier there will be more eligible women than men. There will be the same number more of eligible unmarried women than unmarried men. The ratio of unmarried women to unmarried men will be larger, the more people are married. If women begin to marry at seventeen and (as in the United States) have a life expectancy of another sixty years, and men at twenty-one with a life expectancy of fifty, in a stationary population adult women will exceed men in the ratio 60:50. If one-fifth of the men are unmarried, one third of the women will be. If women marry three years earlier and live seven years longer than men, women will average ten years longer divorced or widowed than men. (Schelling, 1978:56)

Some of these (logical) propositions are instantly, or almost instantly, obvious. When Garrison Keillor refers to Lake Woebegone as "where all the children are above average," nobody fails to smile; he could as well say "where all the people give more at Christmas than they receive." It is almost, but not quite, as obvious that if you count all the black neighbors of all the white people in a city, you already know how many white neighbors the black people have. But when there is a great "selling wave" on the stock market, indicated by a decline in average values and heavy turnover, intelligent-sounding people on public radio discuss such questions as where all the money is going that people are taking out of the stock market, apparently unaware that every share sold must have been purchased.

All such logical propositions that I know of are quantitative. They are therefore common in economics, demography, and epidemiology. (Proportionately more people die in the United States from noninfectious diseases than they did 50 years ago but not because noninfectious diseases have become more deadly.)

Peter Hedström and Richard Swedberg hoped, in organizing this book, to influence the entire discipline of sociology (and anthropology, political science, and social psychology) to take more interest in social mechanisms, in their discovery and explication, in their typology, in basic mechanisms, and in their variants and offspring. I believe all the authors join in that wish. What we need is to exploit some social mechanisms that will accomplish that. Probably the first step is to achieve critical mass. If, with this book, we have succeeded in that, perhaps we can look forward to healthy logistic growth.

Appendix

Consider two first-order differential equations involving X and Y, each growing or declining as a function of both of their current values (X' denotes the current rate of change of the value of X):

1. $X' = A + BX + CY$
2. $Y' = a + bY + cX$

Differentiating 1, we get:

3. $X'' = BX' + CY'$

Substituting 2 into 3, we get:

4. $X'' = BX' + Ca + CbY + CcX$

If we multiply 1 by b and subtract it from both sides, we eliminate the term in Y, and get:

5. $X'' = (Ca - bA) + (B + b)X' + (Cc - Bb)X.$

The same may be done for Y''; the resulting equation in terms of Y' and Y will have corresponding coefficients (from the symmetry of the coefficients in 5).

If we "solve" this equation, we find five possible modes of behavior:

1. If either of the two coefficients, $(B + b)$ or $(Cc - Bb)$ is positive, X and Y will monotonically grow exponentially.
2. If both are negative, and $(B + b)^2/4 > -(Cc - Bb)$, X and Y will converge monotonically on equilibrium values.
3. If $(Cc - Bb)$ is negative, but $(B + b)^2/4 < -(Cc - Bb)$, X and Y will cyclically (sinusoidally) converge on equilibrium values if $(B + b)$ is negative,
4. will cyclically (sinusoidally) diverge exponentially if $(B + b)$ is positive, and
5. will display a uniform sine curve if $(B + b)$ is zero.

References

Cesare Marchetti, Perrin S. Meyer, and Jesse H. Ausubel. 1996. "Human Population Dynamics Revisited with the Logistic Model: How Much Can Be Modeled and Predicted?", *Technological Forecasting and Social Change*, 52, 1–30.

Schelling, Thomas C. 1978. *Micromotives and Macrobehavior*. New York: W. W. Norton and Company.

3. A plea for mechanisms

JON ELSTER

Introduction

Are there lawlike generalizations in the social sciences? If not, are we thrown back on mere description and narrative? In my opinion, the answer to both questions is No. The main task of this essay is to explain and illustrate the idea of a *mechanism* as intermediate between laws and descriptions. Roughly speaking, mechanisms are *frequently occurring and easily recognizable causal patterns that are triggered under generally unknown conditions or with indeterminate consequences.* They allow us to explain but not to predict. An example from George Vaillant gives a flavor of the idea: "Perhaps for every child who becomes alcoholic in response to an alcoholic environment, another eschews alcohol in response to the same environment" (Vaillant 1983, p. 65). Both reactions embody mechanisms: doing what your parents do and doing the opposite of what they do. We cannot tell ahead of time what will become of the child of an alcoholic, but if he or she turns out either a teetotaler or an alcoholic, we may suspect we know why.

Although the bulk of this essay concerns the use of mechanisms in the social sciences, the idea has wider application. In her claim that "the laws of physics lie," Nancy Cartwright uses the following illustration:

Last year I planted camellias in my garden. I know that camellias like rich soil, so I planted them in composted manure. On the other hand,

I am grateful to Nancy Cartwright, G. A. Cohen, Robyn Dawes, Dagfinn Føllesal, Peter Hedström, George Loewenstein, Richard Posner, Nils Roll-Hansen, Bernt Stigum, and the late Amos Tversky for comments on an earlier version of this essay. I also benefited from comments by the participants in the conference on "Mechanisms" in Stockholm in June 1996, notably by my discussant Arthur Stinchcombe. A fuller version of the present essay is presented in my *Alchemies of the Mind* (forthcoming).

the manure was still warm, and I also know camellia roots cannot take high temperatures. So I did not know what to expect. But when many of my camellias died, despite otherwise perfect care, I knew what went wrong. The camellias died because they were planted in hot soil. . . .

So we have an explanation for the death of my camellias. But it is not an explanation from any true covering law. There is no law that says that camellias just like mine, planted in soil which is both hot and rich, die. To the contrary, they do not all die. Some thrive; and probably those that do, do so *because* of the richness of the soil they were planted in. We may insist that there must be some differentiating factor which brings the case under a covering law: in soil which is rich and hot, camellias of one kind die; those of another thrive. I will not deny that there may be such a covering law. I merely repeat that our ability to give this humdrum explanation precedes our knowledge of that law. On the Day of Judgment, when all laws are known, these may suffice to explain all phenomena. But in the meantime we do give explanations; and it is the job of science to tell us what kinds of explanations are admissible. (Cartwright 1983, pp. 51–2)

Cartwright's example relies on what I shall call *type B mechanisms*. Briefly defined, they arise when we can predict the triggering of two causal chains that affect an independent variable in opposite directions, leaving the net effect indeterminate. I contrast them with *type A mechanisms*, which arise when the indeterminacy concerns which (if any) of several causal chains will be triggered. An example from the natural sciences of type A mechanisms can be taken from fear-elicited behavior in animals.[1] Environmental stimuli can trigger one of three mutually incompatible fear reactions: fight, flight, or freeze. We know something about the conditions that will trigger these reactions. Thus "in response to a painful shock, animals will typically show increased activity, run, jump, scream, hiss or attack a suitable target (e.g., another animal) in their vicinity; but, in response to a stimulus associated with shock, the animal will most likely freeze and remain silent. The brain mechanisms that mediate these two kinds of reactions are quite distinct" (Gray 1991, p. 244). But although we can identify the conditions that trigger freeze versus either fight or flight, we do not know which will trigger fight versus flight. "Rather than

[1] I am indebted to Nils Roll-Hansen for suggesting this example.

thinking in terms of two systems for reaction to different classes of punishment, it makes better sense to imagine a single fight/flight mechanism which receives information about all punishments and then issues commands *either* for fight *or* for flight depending on the total stimulus context in which punishment is received" (ibid., p. 255). But to say that the independent variable is "the total stimulus context" is equivalent to saying that the two responses are triggered under "generally unknown conditions." Cartwright's example and the flight–fight example provide robust instances of mechanisms in the natural sciences.

In developing the idea of a mechanism, I shall proceed as follows. In the following section, I provide a more precise definition of the notion of a mechanism. In the third section, I discuss some pairs of psychological mechanisms in more detail. In the fourth section, I indicate how these elementary mechanisms may form building blocks in constructing more complex explanations. In the fifth section, I discuss some conditions under which it may be possible to move beyond the ex post identification of mechanisms to predictive statements ex ante. The final section offers a few conclusions.

Explaining by mechanisms

Let me begin by clearing up a terminological ambiguity. In *Explaining Technical Change*, I used the term "mechanism" in a sense that differs from the one adopted here (1983a). In that work, I advocated *the search for mechanisms* as more or less synonymous with the reductionist strategy in science. The explanation of cell biology in terms of chemistry or of chemistry in terms of physics are strikingly successful instances of the general strategy of explaining complex phenomena in terms of their individual components. In the social sciences, this search for mechanisms (or for "microfoundations") is closely connected with the program of *methodological individualism* – the idea that all social phenomena can be explained in terms of individuals and their behavior.

In that earlier analysis, the antonym of a mechanism is a *black box*. To invent an example at random, suppose somebody asserted that unemployment causes wars of aggression and adduced evidence for a strong correlation between the two phenomena. We would hardly accept this as a lawlike generalization that could be used in explaining specific wars unless we were provided with a glimpse inside the black box and told *how* unemployment causes wars. Is it because unemployment induces political leaders to seek for new markets through wars? Or because they believe that unemployment creates social unrest that must be directed toward an external enemy, to prevent revolutionary movements at home? Or because they believe that the armament industry can absorb unemployment? Although many such stories are conceivable, some kind of story must be told for the explanation to be convincing, whereby "story" I mean "lawlike generalization at a lower level of aggregation."

In the present analysis, the antonym of a mechanism is a scientific *law*. A law asserts that given certain initial conditions, an event of a given type (the cause) will always produce an event of some other type (the effect). For example, if we keep consumer incomes constant, an increase in the price of a good will cause less of it to be sold ("the law of demand"). Again, we may ask for a story to support the law. One story could be that consumers maximize utility. Gary Becker (1962) showed, however, that the law of demand could also be supported by other stories (e.g., that consumers follow tradition, as far as possible, or even that they behave randomly).

In more abstract terms, a law has the form "If conditions C_1, C_2, ... C_n obtain, then always E." A covering-law explanation amounts to explaining an instance of E by demonstrating the presence of C_1, C_2 ... C_n. At the same abstract level, a statement about mechanisms might be "If C_1, C_2 ... C_n obtain, then sometimes E." For explanatory purposes, this may not seem very promising. It is true, for instance, that when there is an eclipse of the moon, it sometimes rains the next day, yet we would not adduce the former fact to explain the latter. But consider the idea that when people would like a certain proposition to be true, they sometimes end up believing it to be true. In this case, we often do cite the former fact to explain the latter, relying on the familiar mechanism of wishful thinking.

This is not a lawlike phenomenon. Most people entertain some beliefs that they would like to be false. Ex ante, we cannot predict when they will engage in wishful thinking – but when they do, we can recognize it after the fact. Of course, the mere fact that people adopt a belief that they would like to be true does not show that they have fallen victim to wishful thinking. Even if the belief is false or (more relevantly) inconsistent with information available to them, we cannot infer that this mechanism is at work. To draw that conclusion, more analysis is needed. Is this a regular pattern in their behavior? Do they often stick to their beliefs even as evidence to the contrary becomes overwhelmingly strong? Do they seem to be strongly emotionally attached to their beliefs? Can other hypotheses be discarded? By standard procedures of this kind, we can conclude, at least provisionally, that wishful thinking was indeed at work on this particular occasion. In doing so, we have offered an explanation of why people came to hold the belief in question. The mechanism provides an explanation because it is *more general* than the phenomenon that it subsumes.

In my earlier terminology, going from a black-box regularity to a mechanism is to go from "If *A*, then always *B*" to "If *A*, then always *C*, *D*, and *B*." In this perspective, mechanisms are good because their finer grain enables us to provide better explanations. Understanding the details of the causal story reduces the risk of spurious explanations (i.e., of mistaking correlation for causation). Also, knowing the fine grain is intrinsically more satisfactory for the mind. (On both points, see Elster 1983a, Ch. 1.) On the view set out here, the move from theory to mechanism is from "If *A*, then always *B*" to "If *A*, then sometimes *B*." (Because fine grain is desirable in itself, I also urge the further move to "If *A*, then sometimes *C*, *D*, and *B*.") In this perspective, mechanisms are good only because they enable us to explain when generalizations break down. They are not desirable in themselves, only *faute de mieux*. Yet because the best is so hard to attain, it can easily become the enemy of the good. The "plea for mechanisms" is not an argument against lawlike explanations, only against the idea that when such explanations fail – which they usually do – we must fall back on narrative and description.

Mechanisms often come in pairs. For instance, when people would like the world to be different from what it is, wishful thinking is not the only mechanism of adjustment. Sometimes, as in the story of the fox and the sour grapes, people adjust by changing their desires rather than their beliefs (Elster 1983b). But we cannot make a lawlike statement to the effect that "Whenever people are in a situation where rational principles of belief formation would induce a belief that they would like to be false, they either fall victim to wishful thinking or to adaptive preference formation." To repeat, most people entertain some beliefs they would like to be false. Or take another pair of mechanisms: adaptive preferences versus counteradaptive preferences (sour grapes versus forbidden fruit). Both phenomena are well known and easily recognizable: Some people prefer what they can have, while others tend to want what they do not or cannot have. Yet it would be absurd to assert that all people fall in one of these two categories. Similarly, some people are conformists, some are anticonformists (they always do the opposite of what others do), and some are neither.

When the paired mechanisms, as in most of the examples given so far, are mutually exclusive, they are what I called *type A mechanisms*. Yet paired mechanisms can also operate simultaneously, with opposite effects on the dependent variable. Even when the triggering of these mechanisms is predictable, their net effect may not be. These are what I call *type B mechanisms*. For an example, consider the impact of taxes on the supply of labor:

> A high marginal tax rate lowers the opportunity cost or "price" of leisure, and, as with any commodity whose price is reduced, thereby encourages people to consume more of it (and thus do less work). But, on the other hand, it also lowers peoples' incomes, and thereby may induce them to work harder so as to maintain their standard of living. These two effects – the substitution and income effects, in economists parlance – operate in opposite directions, and their net effect is impossible to predict from theory alone. (Le Grand 1982, p. 148)

As in Cartwright's camellia example, the separate effects are robust propensities, but the net effect is more contingent. The *indeterminacy* associated with mechanisms can, therefore, take two forms. With type A mechanisms, we may not be able to predict whether they will be triggered; with type B mechanisms, we may not be able to assess the net effect of two opposing mechanisms.

A further distinction may be made between cases in which the two opposing mechanisms are triggered simultaneously by the same cause, and cases in which one is triggered by the other.[2] I shall refer to these as mechanisms of type B_1 and B_2, respectively. A paradigm case of a B_2 mechanism is the "opponent-process system" (Solomon and Corbit 1974). An initial experience of pleasure or pain, when terminated, instead of bringing the subject back to the preexperience baseline state, generates an oppositely signed experience of pain or pleasure. Euphoria and withdrawal in drug addiction illustrate the pleasure–pain sequence. The pain–

---

[2] An application of this distinction of Marx's theory of the falling rate of profit is in Elster (1985, pp. 123–4).

pleasure sequence is illustrated by the relief a woman experiences upon learning that her fear of cancer was ungrounded.

I have asserted that we cannot tell, in general, when a given mechanism will be triggered or, in the case of several mechanisms that operate simultaneously or successively, what their net effect will be. In doing so, I may appear to dismiss a large psychological literature demonstrating the operation of these mechanisms under specific conditions. Consider, for instance, the availability and representativeness heuristics (Tversky and Kahneman 1974). For each of these mechanisms, it is possible to specify conditions under which it will predictably come into play. Yet this set of sufficient conditions, which can be realized in experimental situations, may not often appear in real-life cases. Knowing that C_1, C_2 ... C_4 are sufficient for X to occur and D_1, D_2 ... D_5 are sufficient for Y to occur does not help us to predict what will happen in the presence of C_1, C_3, D_2, D_4. If we know that "If C_1, then sometimes X" and "If D_4, then sometimes Y," we should be ready for either effect. In fact, in some conditions, both the availability and representativeness heuristics are observed:

> When in a game there is a 50% chance of winning, people expect that a small number of rounds will also reflect this even chance. This is only possible when runs of gains and losses are short: a run of six losses would upset the local representativeness. This mechanism may explain the well-known gamblers' fallacy: the expectation that the probability of winning increases with the length of an ongoing run of losses. The representativeness heuristic predicts that players will increase their bet after a run of losses, and decrease it after a run of gains. This is indeed what about half the players at blackjack tables do. ... But the other half show the reverse behavior: they increase their bets after winning, and decrease them after losing, which is predicted by the availability heuristic. After a run of losses, losing becomes the better available outcome, which may cause an overestimation of the probability of losing. [The] repertoire of heuristics predicts both an increase and decrease of bet size after losing, and *without further indications about conditions that determine preferences for heuristics, the whole theoretical context will be destined to provide explanations on the basis of hindsight only.* (Wagenaar 1988, p. 13, italics added)

To summarize, I am not advancing explanation by mechanisms as an ideal or a norm. Explanation by laws is better – but also more difficult, usually too difficult. Moreover, as will be clear by now, I am not suggesting that mechanisms can be identified by formal conditions analogous to those that enter into the formulation of laws. "If p, then sometimes q" is a near-useless insight. Explanation by mechanisms works when and because we can identify a particular causal pattern that we can recognize across situations and that provides an intelligible answer to the question, "Why did he do *that*?"

Some elementary mechanisms

In this section, I offer a more systematic discussion of some elementary or atomic mechanisms. The purpose of the discussion is to demonstrate the range and power of mechanism reasoning. I am not trying to prove any particular thesis, only to persuade the reader of the fruitfulness of the approach. I first consider two type A mechanisms and then two type B mechanisms.

Adaptive preferences versus wishful thinking

In Festinger's theory of cognitive dissonance (Festinger 1957, 1964; Wicklund and Brehm 1976), dissonance is stipulated to arise when a person holds two or more "cognitions" that are inconsistent with one another. Here, cognitions include not only ordinary factual beliefs but also consciously held values as well as mental representations of the choices or behaviors of the subject. The notion of inconsistency is based on "expectations about what goes with what . . . built up on the basis of past experience, including notions of logical relations, cultural mores, and learned empirical correlations among events" (Festinger and Bramel 1962, p. 255). Thus if a person has just bought a car of brand X, the expectation is that he will not believe brand Y to be better. Or to take another famous paradigm of dissonance research, if a subject is asked to write an essay giving arguments for abortion and chooses to do so even if the rewards are small, expectations are thwarted by learning that he is actually strongly against abortion.

Dissonance reduction (or avoidance) takes place by changing or blocking some of the dissonant cognitions, and sometimes by adding new ones. In spite of certain ambiguities in Festinger's original formulations, the process has to be thought of as unconscious. In the car example, for instance, dissonance can be avoided by reading ads for the car one has just bought and avoiding reading ads for other brands. These behaviors cannot proceed from conscious choices for the purpose of reducing dissonance, for if one *knew* that the ads were read or avoided to bolster one's confidence in the choice one had just made, no bolstering could take place. Somehow, one "just gravitates" toward the behaviors that confirm the wisdom of the choice. The dissonance-reducing change in the essay-writing example is even more obviously constrained to be unconscious. When subjects are unable to tell themselves that the behavior is justified by their lack of choice or by a high reward, they reduce their dissonance by adopting a more favorable attitude toward the view they defended.

In an important special case, dissonance is generated by the presence of a desire that X be the case and a belief or suspicion that X is not the case. There are (at least) five possible outcomes. (1) People can try to modify the world to make X be the case. (2) They can accept the fact that the world is not as they want it to be. (3) The beliefs may change so that they acquire a firm belief that X is in fact the case. (4) The desires may change so that they cease to desire that X be the case. (5) The desires may be changed so that they come to desire that X not be the case ("sour grapes"). Of these, (1), (2), and (3) may represent autonomous behaviors or mental processes, governed by the reality principle rather than the pleasure principle. In particular, (4) may result from autonomous character planning such as has been advocated by Stoics, Buddhists, and others. By contrast, (3) and (5) are escape mechanisms that operate at an unconscious level.

As far as I know, nothing is known about when dissonance reduction takes the form of wishful thinking (3) and when it appears as adaptive preference formation (5). Note that each reaction, although valuable in easing short-term tension, has undesirable – and different – long-term consequences. If the wishful thinking leads to the formation of false beliefs about the world, as it usually although not necessarily does, acting on these beliefs can have bad consequences. Adaptive preferences tend to overshoot by a kind of psychic momentum that carries them beyond mere indifference into aversion (Veyne 1976, p. 312; Mora 1987, p. 72). The point I want to make is that it *matters* which of the two functionally equivalent mechanisms is triggered, because each of them has further, different consequences over and above that of reducing the tension.

Spillover, compensation, and crowding out

In an essay "How to profit from one's enemies," Plutarch observes "that a man is farthest removed from envying the good fortune of his friends or the success of his relatives, if he has acquired the habit of commending his enemies, and feeling no pang and cherishing no grudge when they prosper." This illustrates what I shall call *the spillover effect*: envy of one's enemies tends to induce envy of one's friends. A few pages later he notes that "since all human nature bears its crop of contention, jealousy and envy . . . , a man would profit in no moderate degree by venting these emotions upon his enemies, and turning the course of such discharges, so to speak, as far away from his associates and relatives." This is what I shall call *the compensation effect*: envy of one's enemies immunizes against envy of one's friends.

More formally, the spillover effect is that if a person follows a certain pattern of behavior P in one sphere of his life, X, he will also follow P in sphere Y. The compensation effect is that if he does not follow P in X, he will do so in Y. To these we should add the *crowding-out effect*: If he does follow P in X, he will not do so in Y. If the compensation effect and the crowding-out effect obtain simultaneously, they yield a *zero-sum effect*.[3]

Tocqueville's analyses of American democracy rely heavily on these mechanisms and on their interaction. Rather than reproducing what I have written elsewhere on this topic (Elster 1993, Ch. 4), I shall give some examples from other subject matters and other writers. I begin with an example from discussions of participatory democracy. First, there is the thesis advocated by Carole Pateman (1970): If people participate in decision making at the workplace, they will also become more predisposed to participate in politics. This is the spillover effect. Second, there is what we may call the Oscar Wilde thesis: Even under socialism, Wilde ob-

---

[3] Claims that mental life in general is subject to a zero-sum law amounts to a theory – the "hydraulic theory of the mind" – rather than to a mechanism. It is, moreover, a false theory, as acutely noted by Tocqueville: "It would seem that civilized people, when restrained from political action, should turn with that much more interest to the literary pleasures. Yet nothing of the sort happens. Literature remains as insensitive and fruitless as politics. Those who believe that by making people withdraw from greater objects they will devote more energy to those activities that are still allowed treat the human mind along false and mechanical laws. In a steam engine or a hydraulic machine smaller wheels will turn smoother and quicker as power to them is diverted from the larger wheels. But such mechanical rules do not apply to the human spirit" (Tocqueville 1986, p. 168).

served, the week will only have seven evenings, implying that participation in one sphere will be at the expense of participation in other spheres. This is the crowding-out effect. Third, one might argue that people have a need to participate in joint decision-making processes, so that if they are denied, say, democracy at the workplace, there will be a strong demand for political democracy, and vice versa. This is the compensation effect.

In an article on the organization of leisure, Harold Wilensky (1960) traces what he calls "the compensatory leisure hypothesis" and "the spillover leisure hypothesis" back to Engels's work, *The Conditions of the Working-Class in England in 1844*. The first states that the worker who is alienated at work compensates by active and energetic leisure activities; the second that "he develops a spillover leisure routine in which alienation from work becomes alienation from life; the mental stultification produced by his labour permeates his leisure." Rather than assuming that the one or the other mechanism is true always and everywhere, we may conjecture that some individuals are subject to the first and others to the second, or that the same individual cycles between the two. A conjunction of the two mechanisms might offer a more satisfactory account than either of them taken separately.

So far I have considered spillover and compensation as intrapersonal mechanisms of attitude formation. The last few remarks suggest, however, that one may enlarge the perspective to consider how similar effects may be at work in interpersonal relations. When young aristocrats and young elite commoners are educated together, the compensation effect may dampen the dueling tendencies of the former while the spillover effect may enhance those of the latter (Billacois 1990, p. 136). Another example is provided by individual donations to charity. A spillover-like mechanism is that embodied in the *norm* of fairness: If others give more, I should give more, too (Elster 1989, p. 187 ff.; Sugden 1984). A compensation-like mechanism arises from more outcome-oriented utilitarian reasoning: If others give more, my contribution matters less so that I can give less (Elster 1989, p. 46 ff.; Margolis 1982). I will return to this example shortly.

Contrast effect versus endowment effect

In the mid-1980s, Amos Tversky suggested (personal communication) that past experience has a dual effect on present welfare. On the one hand, there is an endowment effect: A memory of a good experience is a good memory, the memory of a bad one a bad memory. Hence a good past tends to improve the present, a bad past to make it worse. On the other hand, there is a contrast effect: A good experience in the past tends to devalue less good experiences in the present, and a bad event in the past will similarly throw the present into favorable relief. A meal at a superlatively good French restaurant may cause one to enjoy later meals at French restaurants (and perhaps at other restaurants, too) less than one would otherwise have done. Conversely, there is nothing like recovery from illness to make you appreciate a normal state of health.[4]

Given the existence and regular operation of these two mechanisms, we can ask several questions. First, there is a mechanism of type B_2: If a positive or negative experience triggers a negative or positive contrast effect (and assuming no endowment effect), will the net effect be positive or negative? This question has been much discussed ever since it was recognized that "if the best can come only rarely, it is better not to include it in the range of experiences at all" (Parducci 1968, p. 90).[5] Second, there is a mechanism of type B_1: What is the net effect, mediated by contrast and endowment, of experiences at an earlier time on welfare at a later time? This was the question identified by Tversky. Third, combining the first two questions, we might ask about the net effect of the initial experience on welfare overall, either as discounted to the earlier time or without discounting. In a given case, the net effect on later welfare might be negative (a negative contrast effect being stronger than a positive endowment effect), but the net effect on overall welfare might still be positive (the positive utility from the experience itself offsetting the negative net effect at the later times). To my knowledge, nobody has studied the third and more important question.

In a study of the second question, Amos Tversky and Dale Griffin (1991) assume that the contrast effect, unlike the endowment effect, re-

---

[4] These phenomena should not be confused with the opponent-process mechanism (see section 2). In that process, an initial positive experience generates a later negative experience independently of whatever other events may transpire. In the presently discussed case, the subsequent effects depend on later events. If all my later meals are taken in superlatively good French restaurants, the contrast effect will not operate.

[5] Conversely, he argues that "The ideal lower end-point might be a strong electric shock, unbearable, but quickly over. The shock would have to be readministered occasionally, whenever it dropped from the context or whenever its memory ceased to be dreadful" (Parducci 1984, p. 16).

quires some similarity between the present and the past. The superlative French meal will not, for instance, tend to devalue a meal in a Chinese restaurant. In this specific case, that assumption seems reasonable. If, however, we imagine a man in prison dwelling miserably on how it felt to be free or a recovering patient enjoying his improved health, we do not need to stipulate a contrast between specific types of experience. Given this assumption and the high susceptibility of judgments of similarity to framing effects, they note that "one should find ways to treat the positive experiences of the past as different from the present" (ibid., p. 299). They also note, however, that people may not have much freedom in the framing of hedonic events. I will return to that issue in the fifth section, "From mechanisms to laws."

The bulk of Tversky and Griffin's study is devoted to an analysis of net effects in specific experimental situations. Although they assert that their predictions were confirmed, this turns out to mean mainly that if the past events were dissimilar from the present ones, there was no contrast effect. In addition, they note that the principle of loss aversion suggests a prediction (which was confirmed) that the negative contrast effect following a high payoff will be larger than the positive contrast effect following a low payoff (ibid., p. 305). They do not, however, offer any prior reasons for believing that the contrast effect will dominate the endowment effect or vice versa when both operate. It turns out that in one of their two experiments the endowment effect was stronger, whereas in the other, the two effects were of roughly equal strength. Although loss aversion is cited as an explanation for the difference between the two experiments, no explanation is given for the results obtained in any one of them.

Later, George Loewenstein and I (Elster and Loewenstein 1992) generalized Tversky's idea to a larger variety of experiences. In addition to endowment and contrast effects that arise from one's own past experiences, we identified similar effects that arise from the anticipation of one's future experiences, from other people's experiences, and from merely imagined or counterfactual experiences. Because the term "endowment" does not fit these other contexts, we used "consumption effect" as the more general term. To some extent, we also addressed the question of the net effect. We noted that in interpersonal comparisons there is a transition from a dominant consumption effect to a dominant contrast effect that occurs at the point of equality (Loewenstein, Thompson, and Bazerman 1989). We also noted the absence of a contrast effect when the future is expected to be worse than the present. In other cases, however, the net effect remains indeterminate. It is an open question, for instance, whether the consumption effect of daydreaming can offset the contrast effect.[6]

Consumption and contrast effects are not the only results of interpersonal comparisons. Abraham Tesser (1991) compares the painful contrast effect (or envy) with a pleasurable "reflection effect," basking in the reflected glory of a superior individual. Because both envy and reflected glory depend on our closeness to the other person, they will wax and wane together, the net effect being in general indeterminate.[7] In one of his experiments, Tesser found that the two effects were of approximately equal magnitude, with zero net effect *as far as pleasure or pain goes*. Yet this finding does not imply that this condition is equivalent to one in which the subject and the comparison person are equal, in which case both effects would be zero. The latter condition would produce not only zero net pleasure or pain but also zero arousal. Tesser found, however, that the subjects in the former condition did experience arousal, as evidenced in their enhanced ability to perform simple tasks and decreased ability to perform complex tasks. I return to some methodological implications of this finding in the final section of the chapter.

Desires and opportunities

Actions are caused by desires and opportunities. But the explanation of behavior need not stop there. We may go one step further and inquire into the causes of the causes. In some cases, the desires are caused by the opportunities. In others, desires and opportunities have a common cause in an antecedent variable. I shall discuss both cases, with reference to the "Tocqueville effect" in the explanation of revolutionary behavior. In a dynamic version, the effect says that discontent with existing conditions increases when conditions improve. The static version is that discontent

---

[6] See Elster (1997, Ch. IV. 1) for some comments on daydreaming. Note that in daydreaming, the consumption effect comes first and the contrast effect later, upon return to reality. If people discount the future, therefore, they might indulge in daydreaming, therefore even if on balance it makes them worse off.

[7] According to Ben-Ze'ev (1992, p. 568), "Achievements of those very close to us evoke pride *rather than* envy when these achievements are . . . connected with us in such a manner that we can share the credits they bestow" (my italics). Thus he asserts, in my terminology, that closeness is the triggering variable in a type A mechanism. Tesser, by contrast, asserts that closeness is part of a set of conditions that induce both pride and envy in a type B mechanism. A priori, one cannot tell who is right – or whether both might sometimes be.

is greater when conditions are better. Although Tocqueville (1955, p. 176) runs the dynamic and the static effects together, they are clearly distinct; either might exist without the other.[8] I first discuss the dynamic and then the static effect.

The standard account of the dynamic Tocqueville effect is probably that when opportunities increase, aspiration levels increase even faster, making for more discontent. The idea lacks, I think, the compelling simplicity one would want to have in a mechanism. More satisfactory is Tocqueville's idea that "the mere fact that certain abuses have been remedied draws attention to the others and they now appear more galling" (1955, p. 177). Also, economic progress makes for more occasions for abuse, by bringing more individuals into contact with the inefficient state administration (ibid., pp. 178–9). Moreover, as suggested by Hirschman and Rothschild (1973, p. 46), economic progress that is not accompanied by ascent along other dimensions may create a frustrating state of status incongruence.

The possibility of telling different fine-grained stories to support the dynamic Tocqueville effect illustrates the move from "If A, then sometimes B" to "If A, then sometimes C, D, and B" (see the second section of this chapter). Whichever of the stories we prefer, it seems clear that the dynamic Tocqueville effect may but not need to go together with a net increase in discontent. After all, economic satisfaction may offset the frustration caused by dealings with state bureaucrats or by status incongruence. Tocqueville does not offer a theory to the effect that economic progress invariably causes revolution but rather an argument to the effect that it may do so. The status-incongruence version shows this especially clearly. While economic progress satisfies one desire, it creates another and leaves it unsatisfied. The net effect of an increase in opportunities on satisfaction and on the desire for further change can go either way.

Consider next the static effect – the relationship between hardship and change. I have suggested elsewhere (Elster 1985, pp. 352–3) that necessity may be not only the mother of invention but also an obstacle to invention. Although invention requires motivation, which is stimulated by necessity, it often requires resources that may be lacking in situations of hardship. A similar two-pronged argument applies to collective action, and more specifically to revolutionary behavior. Revolutions are rarely caused by extreme hardship, because people living at subsistence conditions have to

---

[8] See Elster (1989, p. 68) for a similar distinction in the analysis of wage bargaining.

spend all their time simply staying alive. They may have the desire for change but no opportunities to effect it. Conversely, those well-off may have the opportunities but not the desire. In between, there may be a range of incomes that have a positive net effect – mediated by desires and opportunities – on the propensity to engage in revolutionary behavior. Although the static Tocqueville effect cannot be monotonic throughout the whole income range, the tendency for middle peasants to be more revolutionary than landless peasants indicates that it may be monotonic in the lower part of the range. Even in that range, however, the sign of the net effect is in general indeterminate, although the sign of the first derivative is not.

The static and dynamic effects may obviously be combined. When people grow richer, their frustration may increase; at the same time, their increased wealth may give them the resources to do something about their dissatisfaction. I now proceed to a more general discussion of such cases.

Molecular mechanisms

In this section, I go beyond elementary or atomic mechanisms to molecular mechanisms, both at the intrapersonal and the interpersonal levels. The usefulness of the mechanism approach is, I believe, particularly apparent in the analysis of complex psychic and social phenomena. The purpose is to illustrate and stimulate the imagination rather than to argue for any specific thesis.

The idea of molecular intrapersonal mechanisms can be illustrated by the following example. Suppose that you have been with a lover for a while but that he or she decides to break off the relationship. Because of the contrast effect, there will be an initial reaction of grief. You may then observe your mind play the following trick on you: To reduce the pain of separation, you redescribe your lover to yourself so that he or she appears much less attractive. This, obviously, is a case of sour grapes, or adaptive preference formation. You then notice, however, that the endowment effect is also affected. By degrading the other, you can no longer enjoy the memory of the good times you had together. In fact, you will feel like a fool thinking back on the relationship you had with an unworthy person. To restore the good memories, you have to upvalue the other, but then, of course, the grief hits you again.

The exact course of events will depend on the relative strength of the different mechanisms at work. Just as people "may vary in the degree to which their reactions are dominated by endowment or by contrast" (Tversky and Griffin 1991, p. 298), they may also differ in their susceptibility to adaptive preference formation. A person dominated by the contrast effect and highly vulnerable to the sour grapes mechanism will initially be very miserable and then quickly overcome the grief. A person dominated by the endowment effect will not suffer so much in the first place. Others may be miserable for a long time, and still others may experience cycles of misery and relief. And if we add counteradaptive preference formation to the range of mechanisms, even more possibilities come into play. Such interplay of mechanisms is the stuff of novels and of everyday life. Perhaps it is time for the social sciences to consider them?

Tocqueville relies heavily on molecular interpersonal mechanisms. In the *Ancien Régime*, he plays on both the compensation effect and the spillover effect in his explanation of the radical character of the French Revolution. Because of the lack of political freedom under the old regime, "the political ferment was canalized (*refoulé*) into literature, the result being that our writers now became the leaders of public opinion and played for a while the part which normally, in free countries, falls to the professional politician" (Tocqueville 1955, p. 142): This is the compensation effect. Later, "when the time came for action, these literary propensities were imported into the political arena" (ibid., p. 147): This is the spillover effect.

Another Tocquevillian example concerns the relation between religion and politics. If a society has a democratic political organization, does that make it more or less likely to be strongly religious? On the one hand, there is a *compensation effect*: "I doubt whether man can support complete religious independence and entire political liberty at the same. I am led to think that if he has no faith, he must obey, and if he is free he must believe" (Tocqueville 1969, p. 444). In other words, when people's need for authority is not satisfied in politics, they seek it in religion. On the other hand, there is a *spillover effect*. "Men who live in times of equality find it hard to place the intellectual authority to which they submit, beyond and outside humanity. . . . One can anticipate that democratic peoples will not easily believe in divine missions, that they will be quick to laugh at new prophets, and that they will wish to find the chief arbiter of their beliefs within, and not beyond, the limits of their kind" (ibid., p. 435). Here, the argument is that the lack of authority in politics tends to undermine religious authority rather than support it. As noted previously, there is no need to see these analyses as contradicting each other. In fact, their conjunction may provide a better explanation of the fate of religion in democratic societies than either does separately.

A common theme in *Democracy in America* is that the flaws of democracy can be overcome by more democracy; democracy secretes the antidotes to its own diseases. An important special case of this argument stipulates that democracy may reduce the desire of the citizens to do what democracy allows them to do. We have just seen that religion may be an endogenous product of democracy, through the compensation effect. Religion, in turn, will limit the desires of the citizens in a way that may counteract the greater opportunities for licentious or dangerous behavior that democracy offers them. Thus "while the law allows the American people to do everything, there are things which religion prevents them from imagining and forbids them to dare" (ibid., p. 292). The argument does not allow us, however, to conclude anything about the net effect. If the opportunity set is greatly expanded and the desires only weakly restrained, the net effect of democracy may be to increase rather than to reduce the incidence of the behavior in question. The two pairs of mechanisms are summarily represented in Figure 3.1: *If* the influence of democracy on religion is mediated by the compensation effect rather than the spillover effect, democratic societies will be religious. *If* the negative effect of democracy on desires (mediated by religion) is strong enough to offset the positive effect of democracy on opportunities, democratic citizens will behave moderately.

From mechanisms to laws

Although it is difficult to establish laws in the social sciences, that goal will always, for better or for worse, continue to guide scholars. In this section, I discuss some ways of going beyond mechanisms to lawlike statements.

Eliminating spurious mechanisms

In some cases, the presence of two opposed mechanisms may be an artifact of social perception. Consider "Like attracts like" versus "Opposites attract each other." These apparently opposed proverbs may in fact turn out

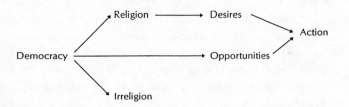

Figure 3.1. Mechanisms for interaction of democracy and religion

to be different versions of the same claim – analogous to the glass that is both half-full and half-empty. If people's curiosity and thirst for novelty is triggered by options that are neither very similar to nor very dissimilar from one's present state (Middleton 1986), their marital choices might be uniquely guided by the search for an optimal difference between their spouse and themselves (Byrne and Kurmen 1988). Depending on the perspective, that difference might be seen as closer to similarity or to dissimilarity, giving rise to the two opposed proverbs.

The point can also be put in a slightly different way. If attractiveness is an inversely U-shaped function of novelty or similarity, each of the two opposing mechanisms might simply describe different parts of the curve. "On the rising point of such a curve, increased liking is held to result from increases in the independent variable (e.g., unexpectedness, complexity). Ultimately, some optimal level is reached, whereafter increases in the independent variable are held to give rise to reductions in liking. Thus, up to a point, 'the more the merrier,' after which, 'one can never have too much of a good thing' " (Ortony, Clore, and Collins 1988, p. 166).

Predicting mechanisms from outcomes

I have been assuming that mechanisms shape outcomes, but it may also be the other way around. Consider again donations to charity. Earlier, I identified two mechanisms that can be summarized as "Give much when others give much" and "Give little when others give much." An indeterminacy then arises if we are unable to predict which individuals in which situations will be subject to the one or the other reaction. We could, however, look at the problem the other way, and assume that people (1) would like to give as little as possible but (2) would also like to tell a story (i.e., cite a mechanism) to others and to themselves that justifies small donations. We can then predict that small donations by others will trigger the fairness mechanism and large donations, the utilitarian mechanism. The outcome is the same in both cases (viz. small donations). This identity obtains not because different motivations yield the same outcome (as in Becker's argument) but because people adopt the motivation that will yield the desired outcome.

This example is a bit awkward, because if donations are always going to be low, it is not clear that there could ever be an occasion for releasing the utilitarian mechanism. In other examples that I now proceed to cite, this difficulty does not arise. Let me first cite a Jewish joke about anti-Semitism.

Ignace Paderewski, Poland's post–World War I premier, was discussing his country's problems with President Woodrow Wilson:

> "If our demands are not met at the conference table," he said, "I can foresee serious trouble in my country. Why, my people will be so irritated that many of them will go out and massacre the Jews."
>
> "And what will happen if your demands are granted?" asked President Wilson.
>
> "Why, my people will be so happy that they will get drunk and go out and massacre the Jews." (Telushkin 1992, p. 112)

Similarly, studies of gambling have "found that, like . . . winners, losers increased the riskiness of subsequent bets" (Greenberg and Weiner 1966, reported in Cornish 1978, p. 17). If you win, you can afford to take bigger risks; if you lose, you increase the odds to recoup your losses. It is also significant that in the Twenty Questions developed by Gamblers Anonymous to help problem gamblers diagnose themselves, all the following appear:

- After losing, do you feel you must return as soon as possible and win back your losses?
- After you win, do you have a strong urge to return and win more?
- Do arguments, disappointments, or frustrations create within you an urge to gamble?
- Do you have an urge to celebrate any good fortune by a few hours of gambling?

Other addictive behaviors, such as smoking or drinking, have similar features: They are triggered by bad news or bad moods as well as by good news and by good moods. In either case, "This calls for a drink" or "This calls for a cigarette" is cited as the justification for indulging one's craving.

Amos Tversky and Eldar Shafir (1992) conducted a series of experiments that are also relevant in this connection. One of them, which is related to gambling, finds that a majority of subjects assert that they will accept a second gamble if they won in a prior gamble *and* if they have lost in a prior gamble; however, only a minority say they will accept a second gamble if they do not know whether they will have won or lost in the first. As they observe, this is a violation of the sure-thing principle, which states that if x is preferred to y knowing that event A obtained, and if x is preferred to y knowing that A did not obtain, then x should be preferred to y even when it is not known whether A obtained. Their explanation for the observed violation of this principle is cognitive, not motivational. But at least in the gambling example – and assuming that the subjects like the thrill of gambling and do not only think in financial terms – a motivational explanation could also be possible. If one really wants to gamble but knows that it is not a good idea, one needs an excuse, a reason, a story to justify doing so. Winning will provide one story, losing will provide another, but ignorance does not. One cannot decide to accept the gamble by telling oneself that whatever happens in the first gamble, one *will have* an excuse for continuing, because that is not how excuses work. They are not planned ahead of time; rather, one observes the situation when it arises and finds a reason in it to do what one wants to do.

To the extent that mechanisms provide one with excuses for doing what one would like to do, we can predict which mechanism will in fact be triggered under which conditions. The effect is a little bit like "hedonic framing." The hypothesis of hedonic framing states that "people edit gambles in a way that would make the prospects appear most pleasant" (Thaler and Johnson 1990, p. 53). In other words, hedonic framing involves a preference-based choice among different ways of describing the same situation. Similarly, the would-be minimizer of charitable donations compares the fairness mechanism and the utilitarian mechanism and settles for the one that allows him to donate as little as possible, consistently with his need to retain his self-respect. In both cases, the comparison and choice would have to take place unconsciously: One cannot *decide* to trick oneself in these ways. A difference between the two effects can be brought out by citing an objection to hedonic framing: "Imagine you had just received an unexpected gain of $50. This could be hedonically reframed

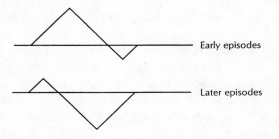

Figure 3.2. Dominance of main and opponent effects over time.

into two gains of $25, but why stop there? Why not 50 gains of $1?''
(ibid., p. 56). By contrast, the hedonic manipulation of mechanisms as
excuses is limited by the small number of stories that are available.

Identifying the triggers

Consider "Absence makes the heart grow fonder" versus "Out of sight,
out of mind." La Rochefoucauld pointed to a possible triggering factor
that would explain when the one or the other mechanism would be observed: "Absence lessens moderate passions and intensifies great ones, as
the wind blows out a candle but fans up a fire" (Maxim #276). Here, the
generalizing strategy is to identify a particular aspect of the *situation* that
allows us to predict which mechanism will be triggered. Similarly, Tversky and Griffin show that the endowment effect dominates the contrast
effect when the present event differs qualitatively from the past one. With
regard to the opponent-process effect (see the second section of this chapter), Solomon argues that the main effect dominates in the initial episodes,
and the opponent effect in later episodes. In addiction, for instance, euphoria initially dominates withdrawal, which then comes to dominate in
later stages (see Figure 3.2).

In other cases, we might be able to point to properties of the *individual*
that allow us to predict the triggering of a particular mechanism. As Tversky and Griffin also mention, some individuals may be more sensitive to
the contrast effect than to the endowment effect, and perhaps we might
be able to identify them on the basis of other properties. Yet if Walter
Mischel (1968) is right in his claim that there is little intrapersonal, cross-
situational consistency, such differences might themselves be situation-

specific. Moreover, the behavior might not be rigidly fixed to a given type of situation. If Tocqueville is right in arguing that people have a need for a sphere in which they are independent and also for a sphere in which they are subject to authority, which sphere serves which need may be a somewhat arbitrary matter.

A more ambitious strategy for anchoring mechanisms in laws relies on catastrophe theory. When I gave a talk on this topic some years ago, I cited various pairs of opposed mechanisms – sour grapes versus forbidden fruits, the attraction of likes versus the attraction of opposites, conformism versus anticonformism. Normal Schofield then remarked in the discussion that this kind of *bifurcation* is exactly what one would expect in cusp catastrophe models. In these models, the surface describing the behavior of a dependent variable as a function of two independent variables folds in on itself in a cusp. Within a certain range, a given constellation of the independent variables is thus consistent with several values of the dependent variable. Moreover, these values tend to be far apart from each other, corresponding to the polarized nature of mechanisms.

More recently, Abraham Tesser and John Achee (1994) have developed this argument more systematically. They observe that in many social situations, the function relating the independent variables to the dependent variable is two-valued rather than one-valued; hence the distribution of behaviors is bimodal rather than unimodal. Jack Brehm's (1966) theory of "reactance," for instance, is based on the premise that social pressure can decrease as well as increase conformity. John Roemer's (1985) idea of the "psychology of tyranny" is also relevant here. The tyrant induces fear in his subjects but also hatred. The former makes them less likely to rebel, the latter more likely. Tesser and Achee argue, however, that the indeterminacy disappears once we go beyond state variables and introduce path dependence or hysteresis:

Dissonance theory provides a very nice psychological model for hysteresis. Assume that one's disposition is consonant with engaging in the behavior and that undergoing negative social pressure is dissonant with engaging in the behavior; one's disposition is dissonant with not engaging in the behavior, and the presence of negative social pressure is consonant with not engaging in the behavior. If one starts out high on the behavior in the face of strong social pressure, then as one's disposition decreases, dissonance increases. To reduce the dissonance, one will look for additional cognitions to support the behavior. Hence the behavior will tend to remain high even in the face of a decreasing disposition. On the other hand, starting with strong social pressure and low levels of behavior, increasing one's disposition will increase dissonance. To reduce the dissonance, one will look for additional cognitions to support not engaging in the behavior. Hence the behavior will remain low even though the disposition is increasing. (Tesser and Achee 1994, p. 104)

The model has several further implications. In the first case, as the disposition continues to decrease in the face of strong social pressure, there will come a point when the person switches from engaging in the behavior to not engaging in it. In the second case, as the disposition continues to increase, there will come a point when the person switches from not engaging in the behavior to engaging in it. Moreover, the level of disposition at which the first switch occurs is lower than the level at which the second occurs. A person who has adopted an unpopular opinion will need to see a lot of the evidence for it fritter away before he gives it up, whereas an uncommitted person will need a lot of evidence for it before adopting it. Finally, a given combination of social pressure and disposition can lead to high as well as low engagement in the behavior, depending on where the person initially started up.

Many of the arguments offered by Tesser and Achee are tantalizingly similar to the ideas I have been developing here. It may indeed turn out to be the case that pairs of opposed mechanisms correspond to different parts of the cusp surface. In that case, we could use knowledge of the past behavior of the individual to go beyond mechanisms and predict what he will do. This would still fall short of the ideal of science, which is to predict and explain using state variables only. Appealing to past values of the variables in order to explain behavior in the present is intrinsically unsatisfactory (Elster 1976). Although we would prefer to explain in terms of the traces left by the past in the present rather than in terms of the past itself, this approach would at least provide a determinate explanation.

Yet ultimately I think the two approaches are quite different. Consider the following discussion of two opposed reactions to social pressure:

J. W. Brehm suggested the presence of a motive to maintain one's freedom to behave as one wishes. This countermotive to conformity is termed *reactance*. There is now a substantial body of literature documenting the operation of this motive. In one study, for example, Heil-man gave subjects on the streets of New York the opportunity to sign a petition for an issue they mildly endorsed. In the course of the inter-action, some of the subjects learned that someone else believed that people should not be allowed to sign such petitions. This latter group was more likely to sign the petitions than were subjects who were not exposed to this social pressure. So, sometimes social pressure encour-ages contrary behavior. (Tesser and Achee 1994, pp. 103–4)

In this approach, the contrary of conformism is behaving as one wishes, or nonconformism. In my thinking about mechanisms, the contrary of conformism is anticonformism – doing the opposite of what others do or try to get you to do. Elsewhere I have described these antonyms of con-formism as its external and internal negation respectively (Elster 1993, Ch. 2). The person who stands up to pressure, and disregards what others think if he believes he is right, is autonomous. As La Bruyère observed, however, "there is equal weakness in opposing the mode and in embracing it" (*The Characters* XIII.11). The person who always does the opposite of what others do or want him to do is as heteronomous – dependent on others – as the conformist is (Elster 1983b, pp. 23, 67). In the catastrophe model, the opposite of adaptive preference formation would presumably be the absence of any causal influence of the feasible set on the prefer-ences. In my approach, the antonym is counteradaptive preference for-mation. Although the catastrophe model may be capable of explaining when we do or don't bend to pressure, it does not seem capable of ex-plaining why we sometimes bend over in the opposite direction.

A plea for disaggregation

When opposing explanation by mechanisms to explanation by laws, I have assumed that the latter is invariably deterministic. Much social science, however, relies on statistical explanation, a procedure notoriously plagued by many conceptual difficulties. One cannot use statistical explanation to account for individual cases, although it is often used in that way. Also, in this mode of analysis, it is particularly difficult to distinguish causation from correlation. I believe the mechanism approach provides yet another reason why statistical explanations tend to be weak and unreliable.

Suppose that a scholar decides to study the dependence of donations to charity on the amount of money donated (and known to be donated) by other people, and that there turns out to be very little correlation. It might be tempting to conclude that people do not really take account of how much others give when deciding how much to give themselves. An alternative explanation might be that the population consists of two roughly equal-sized groups, one motivated by the norm of fairness and one motivated by more utilitarian considerations. On this account, *everybody* would look to others before deciding how much to give but would differ in the way the decisions of others affect their own. To uncover the presence of these two opposed mechanisms (nonlawlike tendencies), one has to go to a lower level of aggregation and look inside the black box.

This perspective suggests a reinterpretation of the Mischel's findings. Contrary to what would be implied by a universal spillover effect, people who are altruistic, aggressive, or impulsive in one context (e.g., work) do not systematically behave the same way in other settings (e.g., the family). It does not follow, however, that there is no causal relationship operating across contexts. It might be the case that what we observe is the net effect of spillover and compensation. Suppose, for instance, that we found a relatively weak correlation between individual rates of time discounting across different activities or for different goods. The explanation might be that for some individuals the habit of foresight spills over from one sphere to other spheres, whereas for others the demands of self-control are so strenuous that when they achieve it in one part of their life they have to give themselves a break elsewhere.

Similarly, it has often been observed that human beings are subject to two very strong desires: the desire to be like others and the desire to differ from others, conformism and anticonformism. If some individuals are strongly dominated by the former desire and others by the latter, the aggregate effect might be very weak, suggesting that people are mostly autonomous rather than heteronomous. Theories of voting behavior, for instance, have identified both an underdog mechanism and a bandwagon mechanism (Simon 1954). Those subject to the former tend to vote for the candidate who is behind in preelection polls, whereas those subject to the latter vote for the front-runner. With many voting for the underdog, the frontrunner might lose, and vice versa. If the two types are more evenly mixed, there might be no noticeable net effect, so that the polls would be good predictors of the actual vote. The lack of influence of polls on voting in the aggregate does not show, however, that individuals are unaffected by the polls. The neutral aggregate could mask a homogeneous population of neutral individuals – or a heterogeneous population of individuals who are all strongly affected but in opposite directions.

George Vaillant (1983, p. 65) observes that in the aggregate, "there is no evidence that [various mediating factors] statistically increase the risk of alcohol abuse in children if they are not biologically related to the alcoholic family member." Yet, as he goes on to say in the statement cited in the opening paragraph of this chapter, this weak aggregate effect could mask two strong, oppositely directed effects at a less aggregate level. If that is in fact the case, strategies of intervention might be justified that would be pointless if children were never or rarely driven to alcoholism because their parents drink. This is perhaps the most important implication of the argument. For research purposes, the disaggregate approach may be too expensive or otherwise impractical. For purposes of public policy, however, identification of subgroups may be crucial.

The plea for disaggregation also has consequences for the interpersonal case. In the third section of this chapter, "Some elementary mechanisms," I discussed Tesser's findings that the conjunction of the contrast effect and the reflection effect may yield an emotional state that is neutral as far as pleasure and pain goes. To predict behavior, however, we may need to know the strength of each mechanism, not only their net effect. Type B mechanisms within individuals may neutralize each other, as may type A mechanisms across individuals, but that does not allow us to infer that they are absent. Nor can we assume that the net effect is all that matters for prediction or intervention.

References

Becker, G. 1962. "Irrational behavior and economic theory," *Journal of Political Economy* 70, 1–13.
Ben-Ze'ev, A. 1992. "Envy and inequality," *Journal of Philosophy* LXXXIX, pp. 551–81.
Billacois, F. 1990. *The duel.* New Haven: Yale University Press.
Brehm, J. 1966. *A theory of psychological reactance.* New York: Academic Press.
Byrne, D., and K. Kurmen. 1988. "Maintaining loving relationships," in R. J. Sternberg and M. L. Barnes (eds.), *The psychology of love.* New Haven: Yale University Press.

Cartwright, N. 1983. *How the laws of physics lie*. Oxford University Press.
Cornish, D. B. 1978. *Gambling: A review of the literature and its implications for policy and research*. London: Her Majesty's Stationery Office.
Elster, J. 1976. "A note on hysteresis in the social sciences," *Synthese* 33, 371–91.
Elster, J. 1983a. *Explaining technical change*. Cambridge University Press.
Elster, J. 1983b. *Sour grapes*. Cambridge University Press.
Elster, J. 1985. *Making sense of Marx*. Cambridge University Press.
Elster, J. 1989. *The cement of society*. Cambridge University Press.
Elster, J. 1993. *Political psychology*. Cambridge University Press.
Elster, J., and G. Loewenstein. 1992. "Utility from memory and anticipation," in G. Loewenstein and J. Elster (eds.), *Choice over time*. New York: Russell Sage.
Festinger, L. 1957. *A theory of cognitive dissonance*. Stanford University Press.
Festinger, L. 1964. *Conflict, decision and dissonance*. Stanford University Press.
Festinger, L., and D. Bramel. 1962. "The reactions of humans to cognitive dissonance," in A. J. Bachrach (ed.), *Experimental foundations of clinical psychology*. New York: Basic Books.
Gray, J. A. 1991. *The psychology of fear and stress*. Cambridge University Press.
Greenberg, M. E., and B. B. Weiner. 1966. "Effects of reinforcement history upon risk-taking behavior," *Journal of Experimental Psychology* 71, 587–92.
Hirschman, A., and M. Rothschild. 1973. "The changing tolerance for income inequality in the course of economic development," *Quarterly Journal of Economics* 87, 544–65.
Le Grand, J. 1982. *The strategy of equality*, London: Allen and Unwin.
Loewenstein, G., L. Thompson, and M. Bazerman. 1989. "Decision making in interpersonal contexts," *Journal of Personality and Social Psychology* 57, 426–41.
Margolis, H. 1982. *Selfishness, altruism and rationality*. Cambridge University Press.
Middleton, E. 1986. "Some testable implications of a preference for subjective novelty," *Kyklos* 39, 397–418.
Mischel, W. 1968. *Personality and assessment*. New York: Wiley.
Mora, G. F. de la. 1987. *Egalitarian envy*. New York: Paragon House.
Ortony, A., G. L. Clore, and A. Collins. 1988. *The cognitive structure of the emotions*. Cambridge University Press.
Parducci, A. 1968. "The relativism of absolute judgments," *Scientific American* (December), 84–90.
Parducci, A. 1984. "Value judgments," in J. R. Eiser (ed.), *Attitudinal judgment*. New York: Springer.
Pateman, C. 1970. *Participation and democratic theory*. Cambridge University Press.
Roemer, J. 1985. "Rationalizing revolutionary ideology," *Econometrica* 53, 85–108.

Simon, H. 1954. "Bandwagon and underdog effects in election predictions," *Quarterly Journal of Economics* 69, 99–118.

Solomon, R., and J. Corbit. 1974. "An opponent-process theory of motivation," *Psychological Review* 81: 119–45.

Sugden, R. 1984. "Reciprocity: The supply of public goods through voluntary contribution," *Economic Journal* 94, 772–87.

Telushkin, J. 1992. *Jewish humor*. New York: Morrow.

Tesser, A. 1991. "Emotion in social comparison processes," in J. Suls and T. A. Wills (eds.), *Social comparison*. Hillsdale, N.J.: Lawrence Erlbaum.

Tesser A., and J. Achee. 1994. "Aggression, love, conformity, and other social psychological catastrophes," in R. R. Vallacher and A. Nowak (eds.), *Dynamical systems in social psychology*. New York: Academic Press.

Thaler, R., and E. Johnson. 1990. "Gambling with the house money and trying to break even," *Management Science* 36, 643–660, cited after the reprint in R. Thaler, *Quasi-Rational economics*. New York: Russell Sage.

Tocqueville, A. de. 1955. *The Old Regime and the French Revolution*. New York: Anchor Books

Tocqueville, A. de. 1969. *Democracy in America*. New York: Anchor Books.

Tocqueville, A. de. 1986. *"The European revolution" and correspondence with Gobineau*. Gloucester, Mass.: Peter Smith.

Tversky, A., and G. Griffin. 1991. "Endowment and contrast in judgments of well-being," in R. Zeckhauser (ed.), *Strategy and choice*. Cambridge, Mass.: M.I.T. Press.

Tversky, A., and D. Kahneman. 1974. "Judgment under uncertainty," *Science* 185, 1124–30.

Tversky, A. and E. Shafir. 1992. "The disjunction effect in choice under uncertainty," *Psychological Science* 3, 305–9.

Vaillant, G. 1983. *The natural history of alcoholism*. Cambridge, Mass.: Harvard University Press.

Veyne, P. 1976. *Le pain et le cirque*. Paris: Seuil.

Wagenaar, W. A. 1988. *Paradoxes of gambling behaviour*. Hillsdale, N.J.: Lawrence Erlbaum.

Wicklund, R. A., and J. Brehm. 1976. *Perspectives on cognitive dissonance*. Hillsdale, N.J.: Lawrence Erlbaum.

Wilensky, H. 1960. "Work, careers, and social integration," *International Social Science Journal* 12, 543–60.

4. Real virtuality

GUDMUND HERNES

Inhabitants of two worlds

It is a widespread misconception that social science is about human beings. This is a fallacy that brings to mind the riposte of Henri Matisse when a critic assailed one of his works with the words "This is not a woman – a woman cannot look like that!" To which Matisse responded: "This is not a woman. It is a painting depicting a woman!" By the same token social scientists may counter if someone asserts that what they describe does not resemble real people: "We do not paint persons – we paint images of persons." For sociologists are inhabitants of two worlds: one that is made for them and one that is made by them – one which they construct in order to figure out the one in which they live; they interpret the world they inhabit. By a powerful metaphor, sociologists do so by constructing "mechanisms." A mechanism is a set of interacting parts – an assembly of elements producing an effect not inherent in any one of them. A mechanism is not so much about "nuts and bolts" as about "cogs and wheels" (cf. Elster, 1989) – the wheelwork or agency by which an effect is produced. But a mechanism or inner workings is an abstract, dynamic logic by which social scientists render understandable the reality they depict.

Hence a mechanism like, say, the logic of a Prisoner's Dilemma is perfectly general. It is not the case, as Elster (1991: 7–8) maintains, that social mechanisms, as opposed to laws, only have limited generality. But a mechanism from the social sciences may have *limited applicability*, in the sense that it represents or portrays few – indeed, in some cases no – life processes realistically. All social science models are not equally good, and it is "goodness of fit" that is the measure by which we decide whether a model is plausible, or, put differently, whether what is conceivable (the abstract model) is reasonable (depicting real-world phenomena properly). The goodness of fit is determined by comparing implications of the mechanism with the facts.

At the same time, there is a fundamental difference between the natural and the social sciences. A "law of nature" lays claim to general validity (e.g., gravity is a universal force). A single counterexample is often sufficient to refute a "law of nature": If one apple does not fall, the law of gravity is out. In contrast mechanisms in the social sciences lay no such claim. They are constructs that may or may not fit real-life situations or serve to interpret real-life pursuits and phenomena.

Moreover, the insights natural scientists acquire do not affect the phenomena they describe – nature is there to be known but is itself impervious to knowledge. The knowledge won by social scientists, on the other hand, diffuses to people who then may change their behavior as a consequence. High consumption of margarine or animal fats increases the probability of cardiovascular disease; this is a law of nature. But knowledge about this connection leads to consumption of low-fat milk and lean meat; that is a fact of life. Indeed, the models *of* social phenomena that social scientists construct in the abstract may become models *for* social relations in real life.

Hence the point of constructing mechanisms is that their general logic may be applicable to many different situations. They are what James S. Coleman (1964: 516 ff.) called "sometimes-true theories" (i.e., general models that can adequately account for the results or regularities that obtain in some specific cases):

> Thus none of these [theories] is absolutely or unilaterally true; *any* of them can be true in a specific instance. The problem in any given application is to know *which* of the many [theories] is followed in this case. . . . They are not theories to be confirmed or disconfirmed in general, but only confirmed or disconfirmed in specific applications. As a result, they are not theories which explain "how people behave"; they are theories or models which describe how people behaved in this or that circumstance. . . . It goes without saying that the model becomes a theory whenever the social process parallels the [mechanism] which generated the model. . . . [The tactic proposed is this:] that one fruitful line of development, particularly in the area of social processes described above, will not be to ask what is *the* theory of a certain kind

of behavior, or what are *the* postulates which correctly describe a general area of behavior. The tactic proposed here is to set about developing and applying a number of sometimes-true theories which relate consequences to postulates, and which may adequately describe behavior in a given situation. (1964: 517 ff.)

In this chapter, I will first argue that mechanisms or sometimes-true theories are inherent in any social science explanation. Second, mechanisms are more or less densely interjected into explanations even when the authors are not aware of them. Third, mechanisms are combined and connected into machinery (i.e., into greater assemblies when more complex phenomena are to be accounted for). Finally, I will discuss some general characteristics of social science mechanisms or models.

Wasps and social structure

In the summer of 1990, Norwegian media reported that women more often than men were stung by wasps. For a sociologist, man's interactions with animals – even insects – are intriguing, because even such encounters are molded by social organization. To understand social life, not only beasts but also insects may be brought back in. For example, a classic study in statistics proved that the number of deaths from horse kicks in the Prussian army was a purely random phenomenon – that they were bona fide accidents – even though the *rate* or parameter governing the number of mishaps in a given year had a specific, socially determined value (Bortkiewicz, 1897). And this value surely reflected aspects of the Prussian social structure at the time, such as the size of a cavalry, norms of bravado, the experience of soldiers in associating with horses and hence the degree of mechanization of farming, and so on. So when we learn that women in Norway are more prone to be stung by wasps, we are clearly onto some portentous information about the Norwegian social structure.

What could possibly explain the skewed sex ratio in wasp bites?[1] Here are four conceivable explanations.

---

[1] It is interesting to note that much that goes under the name of "causal analysis" stops at this point (e.g., when it was established a solid correlation between some independent and dependent variables). It is then argued, for example, that education, sex, age, socioeconomic status, and so on "explain" a certain amount of the variation in a dependent variable. The claim here is that only when such correlations or path coefficients are established does the

1. *The Rambo theory:* Women are a more *tender* species than men. Boys don't cry. For a real man it would be disgracefully effeminate to call a doctor for a dinky distress. Whoever saw Rambo whack a gnat or Kung Fu chop a fly?
2. *The outdoors theory:* Women spend more *time* in the open air than men, walking their babies and playing with their children. In the great outdoors, they have their involuntary dates with the stinging beasts.
3. *The hysteria theory:* Women are more *hysterical* than men. They jump up on a chair when they see a mouse. And they wave their hands frantically when a wasp comes by, hence agitating them so that they attack in defense. Men are more stoic and do not ruffle the wasps. Women typically produce their own tormentors and are in this sense self-made victims.
4. *The scent theory:* Women use more hairspray and *perfumes.* The fragrances are pleasurable to those who wear them. Moreover, not only do they entice men; they also function as fleurissants and pheromones, which beguile wasps, but which then sting because they become all aroused and then aggrieved when they discover that the bouquet stems not from flowers and react to frustration by aggression.

Now that we have these possible explanations, the next question becomes: How can we decide which, if any, is most tenable? The answer is that we try to do the explanations in by their consequences, kill them off by drawing implications from them and by checking whether these implications square with the facts.

Take the first explanation: *If* it is the case that women are a more tender species, *then* women in general should be less tolerant of pain than men. Does this square with facts that we can research? Does it, for example, square with suffering the pains of childbirth? Are there any psychological experiments supporting the thesis? Do other medical records show that women more promptly than men check painful symptoms of the same afflictions with their doctors? If we answer such questions in the negative (i.e., if the implications of the tenderness thesis do not correspond to the

fun begin. Indeed, what the "explanatory" variables "explain," they explain only insofar as they correspond to a process produced by a model.

facts – "are not verified," "supported by the evidence," or "borne out") then the explanation is rejected or eliminated.

This is, in general, the logic of research: (1) arresting an observation, (2) providing a line-up of candidates for explanation, (3) drawing implications from them, (4) checking the evidence (i.e., checking these implications against the facts), and (5) eliminating those explanations that are not supported (cf. Stinchcombe, 1968). I will not pursue the logic of research further here but rather focus on the second step: providing explanations by forging mechanisms or constructing models.

A *mechanism* is an intellectual construct that is part of a phantom world which may mimic real life with abstract actors that impersonate humans and cast them in conceptual conditions that emulate actual circumstances. A mechanism like a *model* is a stripped-down picture of reality; it is an abstract representation that gives the logic of a process that *could* have produced the initial observation. At the same time, this imagined world may seem vividly real; indeed, it is a conceptual copy that enables us to understand the real world. Reality presents itself to us, but we have to *represent* it in order to *make sense of it*. Mechanisms are the virtual reality of social scientists. But it is the stuff of which the world of the social scientist is made: This artificial, manmade world of mechanisms is real – real virtuality.

To argue this point more thoroughly, let me return to the four explanations of the skewed relation between gender and wasp stings and try to lay bare their logical structure.

Humanoids in action

The first explanation – that women are more tender than men – is based on the assumption of a gender-related capacity, the capacity to withstand pain. That is, implicitly in the argument is a *model of man* that distinguishes between *actors of two kinds*. There is a simple characteristic that cuts between them.

Stripped down to its essentials, the crucial point in this explanation of reported wasp stings are two logical prototypes: *Sissies* and *Huskies*. (I use capital letters to indicate that they are logical constructs and not real persons.) These creatures of the imagination can be further characterized. The Sissies are fragile crybabies. The Huskies are rough and robust and spurn cuts and bites. The Sissies quickly feel ill and promptly run off to doctors. The Huskies have to be dragged to the hospital, and they get there only when they are so weakened by illness or injury that they can put up no resistance.

Note also that the Sissies and the Huskies both are placed in the *same imaginary environment*. They meet the same number of wasps, and the wasps have no preference for either type; indeed, the Wasps of the mechanism are also imaginary – just a crucial part of a constructed environment. In other words, the social structure within which the two types of actors operate is homogenous, and Sissies and Huskies are exposed to the same number of imaginary bites.

This is the mechanism or abstract explanatory logic. *Empirically* the explanation assumes that more real-life women than men are Sissies and more real-life men than women are Huskies – hence the differences between the sexes. Empirically (the argument runs) tenderness is a gender-related characteristic. Therefore we do not get a perfect correlation between sex and reported bites. Some men are Sissies, and some women Huskies. In other words, our empirical referents, men and women, are *faulty representatives* of our theoretical concepts, Sissies and Huskies.

In this sense we are in Plato's cave: In our theoretical world, relations between actors' characteristics and responses to bites are tight. However, real-life women and real-life men are only shadows or imperfect pictures of our beautiful logical creatures. Humans are, so to speak, substitutes, alternates, or stand-ins who fill the positions and exercise the functions of the abstract Actors. Just as Hamlet can be more or less well impersonated by humans, so can Huskies be more or less well impersonated by ordinary men.

This point can be illustrated by a fourfold matrix (Table 4.1). Our logically constructed actors with crisp attributes look like humans along a key dimension; we could call them "Humanoids." But in a sense, they are too good intellectually to be true in reality. The real world does not fall into such neat categories. So across the columns we have the theoretically constructed actors, the Humanoids, "Sissies" and "Huskies." Along the rows we have the real-life women and men. The sizes of the circles indicate the empirical distribution over the theoretical concepts. Put differently, when we use mechanisms to explain social phenomena, living persons, men and women, serve as *proxies* for our theoretical concepts.

Table 4.1. *Degree of correspondence between the logically constructed actors − the Humanoids − and real-life persons*

		Logically constructed actors − Humanoids	
		Sissies	Huskies
Real-life persons	Men	o	O
	Women	O	o

But then real-life men and women are imperfect representatives of the Humanoids. Real men may not be Real Men.

To take another example: In mechanisms we often encounter the construct "Rational Actors." They are, in a sense, theoretical Stuntmen, who perform feats and actions too heroic or too fantastic, too demanding or too difficult, for ordinary humans to perform. Since it is inconceivable that mortals can accomplish the stunts (e.g., to carry out stupendous calculations in no time) we conceive of nonmortals or Humanoids − *dei ex machina* − to make our mechanisms work. In other words, social life is about humans, and social science about their imaginary doubles.

Here we also see why we in the social sciences often obtain low correlations in our empirical studies. Our theoretical world in this case looks like the top part of Figure 4.1. We have a solid relationship between our theoretical concepts and the outcomes of the process: Sissies report bites, and Huskies do not. However, what intervenes between the Humanoids and the outcomes are the human look-alikes. Hence everything gets fuzzy, and the fuzzier representatives the real life persons are, the lower the correlations, even if the mechanism has much going for it.

What has been illustrated here is a key point in measurement theory. Previously I argued that the Rambo mechanism assumes that tenderness is a sex-*related* characteristic. It is precisely because it is merely sex-*related* that we get low correlations. There are some phenomena that are sex-*specific*, such as the capacity to bear children. In those cases, the theoretical concepts are near identical to the observables, and then of course the correlations rise when the theory holds.

There is one more point to be made here: The higher the correlation between theoretical constructs and real-life proxies, the more *valid* the

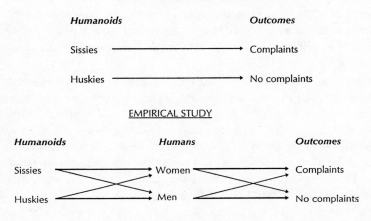

CONCEPTUAL MECHANISM

Humanoids   *Outcomes*

Sissies ────────────→ Complaints

Huskies ────────────→ No complaints

EMPIRICAL STUDY

Humanoids   *Humans*   *Outcomes*

Sissies   Women   Complaints

Huskies   Men   No complaints

Figure 4.1. The difference between relations in a conceptual model and the results in an empirical study. Actor-based model.

empirical identification between theoretical constructs and real-life representatives. However, often the sources of our data pose practical problems. For example, with respect to the Rambo theory of wasp bites, doctors and hospitals do not pigeonhole patients into "Sissies" and "Huskies," whereas they scrupulously catalog their gender. We are, therefore, as social scientists, often constrained by administrative routines to use imperfect proxies of our theoretical constructs. Hence we are frequently stuck with categories such as "whites" and "blacks" or "white collar" and "blue collar" and so forth, which are too fuzzy to make for good logical mechanisms. In a sense, the more down to earth the terms are, the poorer the mechanisms we get.

Consequently, to pursue the Rambo theory of wasp bites, we would get a better test if we could sort real-life persons into two groups that better correspond to the Humanoids Sissies and Huskies, since real-life men and women mix them up. In practical studies, such advice is often left as "suggestions for further research." However, from the point of view of constructing mechanisms, the crux of the argument here is the *assumptions about the actors*: that they are of *two kinds*, and that the *difference between them is the mechanism which produces the end result*. Sissies and Huskies are attacked to the same extent by the wasps – it is the *differential response of the different types of actors that produces the outcome.* In other words, a broad class of social science explanations consists of those mechanisms that produce their results by differentiating between types of actors that act or react in different ways. The differences between the actors is the agency of the mechanism.

The logic of this explanation illustrates a generic point about social models: In contrast to models in physics, for example, *some assumptions about actors must always be made.* The Humanoids we construct can be of quite different kinds, simple or complex, more or less stylized. However, even when they are just a flat silhouette of colorful real-life persons, they must be sharply enough defined to portray the clear-cut essentials that we believe operate in the process we want to explain. (I will return to "default models of man" or "collapsed actors.")

Even though the Rambo theory focuses on only two static types of actors, we could expand on the topic by asking: How are Sissies and Huskies produced? The reference to norms of masculinity, Rambo and Kung Fu, suggests one direction in which one might move: toward the social structure that produces particular kinds of Humanoids. However, I shall leave the Sissies and Huskies at this point – as is done in many kinds of social models.[2] Instead we shall move on to another of the explanations of wasp bites suggested earlier, precisely because it illustrates another generic type of mechanism.

Social structure and hazard

The second explanation for the higher frequency of female stings was that women spend more *time* in the open air than men, walking their babies and playing with their children. In contrast to the actor-based explanation, there is here no assumption made about sex differences. Basically all the *actors* here are assumed to be *of one kind.* What counts is not *what* you are but *where* you are. In this sense, the model is, so to speak, actor blind – once you are in the outdoors, wasps are nondiscriminating. There is no difference between them in *reaction*; there is only a difference in *exposure.*

---

[2] A much used pair of actors are Consumers and Producers/Firms in microeconomic theory. Another logical prototype in economic theory is that of the Entrepreneur, which is assumed to have an identifiable set of abstract traits distilled from real-life persons. Theories of entrepreneurship take these logical Actors as their agent mechanism.

In the actor-based Rambo model, the environment or structure that the different actors face is the same. Now, in this structure-based model, the actors are all the same, but different subgroups of them may be placed in structurally different environments. In other words: even though the actors are assumed to be all alike, they can be located in different slots in the social structure (i.e., they can be in different *states*). And different consequences flow from these different states.

If we extract the essence of the outdoors model, the abstracted social structure is for the purpose of this explanation divided into two states: *Sanctuaries* and *Danger Zones*. In the former, whoever is there is off limits to wasps. In the latter, whoever is there is in jeopardy.

Now *actors* can be distributed over the states in a random fashion. And different *proportions* may be apportioned to the two states by some random mechanism. In many schools, this happens when pupils are assigned to different class teachers, with different consequences for their academic achievements. In either case, it is not who you are but where you end up that decides what happens to you.[3]

But actors may also be filtered and funneled to the states by some extraneous criterion. By extraneous is meant that this criterion does not affect the consequences of being *in* the states, although it may affect assignment *to* those states. One such criterion could be sex. That is, we introduce a *sorter* that assigns different proportions of men and women to the states (i.e., Danger Zones and Sanctuaries). In this case, the states are outdoors where there are many wasps (Danger Zones) and indoors where there are no or few wasps (Sanctuaries). Actors are identical in response but are differentially sorted to different states.

So the logic of the explanation is this: Since more women than men (sorter) are outdoors (state), they get bitten more. It has nothing to do with female tenderness or other attributes that might distinguish them from

---

[3] In Durkheim's work on suicide, religious states produce differential risks of taking one's own life (i.e., the explanation is primarily structural). Put differently, into what state you were born determines the hazard to which you are exposed. Of course, one of the standard plots of sociological explanations is that different types of actors are allocated to different positions (e.g., by social mobility). Here one can, for example, characterize the types of actors by their social origins ("Father's SES") to explore the effect on their own social location ("Son's SES"). The point of the mechanism is to explain to what extent where you end up is determined by where you come from. But the actors themselves are, by the definition introduced later, collapsed, in the sense that they are not purposive. Mobility, in terms of the model, is something that happens to them, not something they explicitly seek. Of course, a model of mobility could add such a mechanism of purposive action.

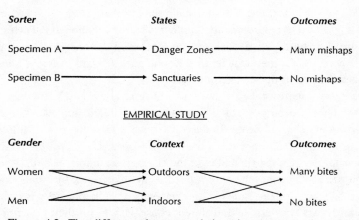

Figure 4.2. The difference between relations in a conceptual model and the results in an empirical study. Structural model.

men, such as their being more hysterical (cf. explanation 3). What happens to them is their lot – the predicament that falls upon those who are assigned to the Danger Zones.

Other sorters than sex might be used. For example, a higher proportion of blue collar workers are assigned to the outdoors (Danger Zones), or those living in rural areas. *If* the thesis about differential exposure holds, *then* these groups should have higher rates of bites.

In this case, then, we have *a model of the social structure* consisting of two parts: the *states* that actors can be in and their associated consequences, and the *sorter* that assigns actors to these states. Hence we can summarize the logic of a structure-based explanation as in Figure 4.2. This general logic of structural explanations is used for many different phenomena: work accidents accounted for by industrial hazards (states) and allotment of different specimens to those states (sorter), entry into marriage, status attainment, and so on. There are also other kinds of structural models, which I will not go into here.

Two further points can be made. Some sorters function as *scramblers* (i.e., they increase the randomness in assignments to states). For example, when entering the United States, airline passengers are sorted by two criteria: by class (first-class passengers are let out first, then business class, and finally tourist class), and they are sorted by nationality (citizens and noncitizens). But then they are scrambled by seating arrangement; your place in line in front of the immigration officer is more or less random within each of these subgroups. Sometimes the social structure is modified in the direction of more sorting (e.g., streaming in schools) and sometimes in the direction of more scrambling (equalization of the sexes).

There is a second, more important point, however. In *complex* social models, we usually *combine* more elaborate assumptions about actors than that they are all alike in the relevant respect. Rather than different actors facing the same environment or the same actors facing different environments, different actors are sifted to different environments. For example, we could assign Sissies to Danger Zones and Huskies to Sanctuaries and would then expect even greater differences in reported bites. Or if these two types were apportioned to the states in different proportions, we would have to try to sort out what was the relative effect of actor attributes and structural factors. An example of such a sorting mechanism is found in Marx's chapter 14 on manufacture in *Capital*, where he describes that once a division of labor has been established, personnel is recruited to crafts according to their most prominent skills – being a blacksmith requires different capacities from those of a goldsmith, as does those of a discus thrower from those of a ballerina.

In this simple example of wasp bites, the logic of two types of explanations has been reviewed. The two other explanations – the hysteria theory and the scent theory – can be examined in a similar fashion.

Dense explanations

Hedström and Swedberg have argued that

> the prevalence of mechanism-based explanations vary widely between the disciplines. These types of explanations are rarely used in history, sometimes in sociology, and quite frequently in economics and psychology. (1996: 6)

I do not think that it is so much the *prevalence* as the *explicitness* of models that varies between disciplines. There are more pronounced differences in traditions in the *specificity* and *preciseness* of mechanisms than in the *extent of use* of mechanisms in explanations.

Mechanisms may be densely packed and combined in explanations even when authors are unaware of or do not make them explicit. Some years ago, the Norwegian historian Andreas Holmsen wrote in his *History of Norway* about Viking graves:

> The sudden affluence in the graves must have had a certain correlate in the actual living conditions. The findings cannot reasonably be interpreted in any other way than that both the general level of living, the quantity of tools, and, above all, the richness of iron was increased in the Viking age. A direct manifestation of a higher prosperity is also provided by the skeletons, which show growing body height. (1961: 109)

These three sentences encompass at least four models or mechanisms, as follows.

1. *Sociology of religion*: Nordic religion was such that increased prosperity expressed itself in greater offerings to the gods. In other words, a specific assumption is made about the actors' belief systems: Gods should receive their proportional share of riches. One could conceive of an alternative: When times are adverse, the gods must be placated (i.e., there is an inverse proportionality between fortune and fearing). But this may perhaps be rejected on account of the knowledge of Old Norse religion and of the climatic conditions at the time (Holmsen touches on this possibility). In any case, the explanation is made in terms of an actor-based mechanism.
2. *Biology*: Here the assumption is that improved nutrition for the same group of actors manifests itself as increased body height (i.e., an actor-based biological mechanism). Again another sociobiological mechanism is possible: During the Viking ages, the seafarers brought home women of a different, taller stock who mothered taller children. They later turn up in graves.
3. *Stable class structure*: Holmsen assumes that there is a *general* improvement in living conditions of all actors, and that a certain proportion of them are later found in graves. However, one can imagine a different mechanism:
   a. There were actors of two (or more) kinds: the upper class and the lower class.
   b. The cleavage between them increased (i.e., the structural inequality between different class positions became more pronounced).

   c. On the whole, only graves from the upper classes have been
      found.
   Hence the inference that there was a "general" improvement in living conditions is invalid, as the improvement only took place in the
   upper class.
4. *Statistical representativeness*: The final mechanism that Holmsen's
   argument is based on is that the graves that have been found are a
   representative sample of the graves from the different time periods.
   In other words, he assumes that social practice at the time or ar-
   cheological practice today have not biased the sample.

The point of this exercise is to highlight that even simple statements
which explain social phenomena are densely packed with mechanisms
with implicit assumptions about actors and structure. This also becomes
evident when mechanisms are combined into machinery – into more complex explanations of social phenomena.

Two worlds – One language?

Initially I argued that social scientists are inhabitants of two worlds: one
that they populate and one that they ponder, one that they mold and one
that they model. A problem with identifying the logical mechanisms inherent in their modeling is nicely illustrated by the example taken from
Holmsen: that the same language often is used for both activities. That is,
the same everyday terms are used both in the construction of mechanisms
and in the social processes that they are to represent and mirror.

   Some disciplines choose to construct a distinct language and even separate symbols for phenomena in the real world and for mechanisms in the
phantom world that they use to represent it. For example, in probability
theory, language distinctions are made as shown in Table 4.2. Likewise,
we talk of estimates and parameters, and we use Latin letters for the former
and Greek letters for the latter. In standard microeconomic theory, we talk
of Rational Actors in the phantom world and of persons in the real world.
We can also talk about Corporate Actors, which correspond to, say, corporations.

   In the social sciences, however, even in economics, the two worlds often
get mixed up because the same nomenclature is used for phenomena both
in the real world and in the conceptual world of the theorist: We may use

Table 4.2. *Examples of the two languages of probability theory*

Real world	Model
Random experiment	Probability model
Simple result	Simple event
List of simple results	Event set
Long run frequency	Probability

the term "consumers" when we mean real people who buy goods and "Consumers" in the distinct sense used in microeconomic theory. We use the term "firms" for both actual businesses and for the abstract entities maximizing profit in our conceptual analyses, and so forth.

Since our language mixes up the two worlds, it also tends to mix up our thinking about them – and hence hamper the formulation of mechanisms which may help us understand the goings on in the real world. Or to put it sharply: If sociologists are to comprehend what takes place in the real world, they have to forget about it and transfer themselves to another place – to the never-never-land of phantom actors (who are the opposite numbers of real people) lodged in intangible structures (which are the counterparts of concrete social arrangements). Hence we should cultivate and become fluent in the separate languages of the two worlds, as well as in the translation between them.

This may also help prevent social theorizing being lured or captured by the language of other disciplines, such as the language of statistics. If we unwittingly surrender to the lingo of "variables," "correlations," and so on, we are diverted from the construction of explanations based on mechanisms. For example, if we find a positive correlation between education and openness toward immigrants and let it rest at that, we are in a sense abdicating as social scientists. One possible explanation could be to argue that education broadens minds (i.e., changes the *nature of the actors*). Another mechanism could be formulated in terms of relative deprivation (e.g., when immigrants are given the same incomes by the state as those of low education who must work for it, they react with anger against the intruders). Those of high education are not touched by this since they earn higher incomes. The point is simply that the work of the theorist begins when the correlation is established and a mechanism to account for it is needed.

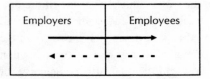

Figure 4.3. Flows between employers and employees.

Mechanisms and combination into machinery

In this section, I first want to describe four mechanisms that are related to competition in the market.

1. A simple use of a market mechanism is to explain how the number or relative size of two types of actors shifts as the mechanism unfolds. The model can take as its point of departure a structural-assumption situation of pure competition. Second, it could be based on an assumption of differential profitability of different firms. The mechanism then works to make the least profitable firms go bankrupt. Hence what starts out as a pure competition over time moves toward monopolization with fewer firms dominating the market. At the same time, this would convert former employers in noncompetitive firms to employees in firms that survive. Even though some new entrepreneurs might move the other way, the size of the arrows in Figure 4.3 indicate the drift over time toward fewer employers and more employees. Depending on the specific assumptions made, the theoretical end result may either be some oligopolistic equilibrium or monopolistic competition. In any case, the population size of the two groups shifts in favor of the employees.

2. Another use of the market mechanism as a generating force follows directly from the first: If we start out with many firms with relatively few employers of each, and the firms are reduced in number but the employers still obtain work, it follows that the average number of employers of each firm will increase.

   On this mechanism of *concentration* can be grafted another mechanism combining *cognition, communication, and action* on the part of the employees. The basic argument would be that when workers are concentrated they observe their own situation in that of the others. It enables them to communicate easily and enter into manifold relations, which can also be used as side payments to overcome the free-rider problem. In other words, similarity of structural position begets not just commonality of cognitions but also coincidence of concerns (i.e., a common identity as well as a common interest). And closeness of location generates a community of fate and begets communications and a community for action.

3. A third use of the market mechanism is to ask what happens to the wage rate of the employees over time when their firms are subject to competition and employers to population growth. Classical political economists (e.g., Smith, Malthus, and Ricardo) discussed this topic, and Lasalle coined what he termed "the iron law of wages": that although the growth of capital could periodically outstrip the growth of population, population growth itself was responsive to wages above the subsistence level and would hence reduce wages to that level. Here two mechanisms are combined: that of competition and that of population growth, interacting in such a way that wages will approach starvation levels. Again, a model combining the two mechanisms can be formalized in a straightforward manner. In short, competition can be used to describe how competition generates exploitation.

4. A fourth use of the market mechanism is to analyze what kinds of skills employers seek in their employees. One possible mechanism is as follows. Competition forces employers to produce at the lowest possible cost (i.e., with the cheapest, hence least specialized, workers). Hence they will replace specialists with machines.

   Specialization, however, is an impediment to the development of solidarity among workers. But when the division of labor is reduced, workers structurally become more alike – in hierarchical position, type of work, and remuneration. The objective change in situation is followed by a subjective change in sentiment, by the process Durkheim called "mechanical solidarity." That is, uniformity of social conditions translates into comradeship and potential for collective action. Note that in this case employers not only change the *conditions* of their employees but also that these changed conditions change the *character* of the employees.

The purpose of presenting these different mechanisms is not to show simple, though classical, examples of mechanisms with competition as the agency. The point is to show that they can be *combined*. This was done by Marx in his theoretical machinery for how revolutionary potential builds up: He identified *who* the revolutionary actors (workers) would be and then argued that they would become the great *majority* in industrial societies. Furthermore, he showed *how* collective action would be spurred by concentration and communication. He demonstrated *why* they would act from exploitation and deprivation, and why they would act *together* due to equalization and solidarity. Marx himself summarizes the whole argument in two sentences – to my mind one of the most beautiful and succinct statements combining a whole set of social mechanisms:

> But with the development of industry the proletariat not only increases in number; it becomes concentrated in greater masses, its strength grows, and it feels that strength more. The various interests and conditions of life within the ranks of the proletariat are more equalized, in proportion as machinery obliterates all distinctions of labor, and nearly everywhere reduces wages to the same low level. (Marx and Engels, 1978 [1848]:480)

Marx's analysis was very sophisticated in that it focused on aggregate, organizational, psychological, and social phenomena and developed a model of how they would simultaneously change as a consequence of market competition. Analytically separate mechanisms were joined in more complex social machinery and operated simultaneously. Or put differently, simple models were used as modules in theory construction. Weber did much the same thing in *The Protestant Ethic and the Spirit of Capitalism* (cf. Hernes, 1989).

Note that Marx uses actors with complex attributes:

- They are *rational actors* pursuing their interests.
- They are *cognitive actors* who *learn* in a changing environment.
- They are *emotional* actors whose sentiments change as a consequence of their shifting social location.

Note also that we do not need all three attributes in each of the four mechanisms described. For example, we do not need them all for a mechanism for changing the ratio between employers and employees, but we do in the mechanism for the development of the latter's solidarity.

It is often stated that humans are complicated creatures. Here we see that to each human there may correspond a whole family of Humanoids: purposive actors, abstracted workers with differential skills of which they may be deprived, agents with the capacity for cognition and learning, for frustration and aggression, agents constituted of multiple actors such as Id, Ego, and Super-Ego, and so on. In order to keep track of our interpretations and explanations as social scientists, the different mechanisms should be kept analytically distinct, assumptions about abstract actors made explicit, and postulates about conceptual structures made plain.

Finally it should be noted that although Marx used terms from everyday language – such as *workers* and *competition* – he nevertheless did not describe a particular social situation or unique historical process. He depicted a general logic, an interacting set of mechanisms. But the whole point of Marx's machinery as combination of mechanisms was that it *may* be used to disentangle, describe, and explain many particular courses of events. (That he mixed up the logic of the machinery with historical necessity is another matter.) In short, the machinery is perfectly general, and it may have fairly wide applicability; indeed, it may be a "many-times-true" theory. On the other hand, *if* not all mechanisms in fact are operative the way Marx assumed, we may use the machinery with those mechanisms switched off, so to speak, to explain why revolutionary potential did *not* build up (cf. Hernes, 1991).

Elements of social mechanisms

Mechanisms in social science have two sets of abstract elements. The first construct is the specification of *actors* (i.e., the identification of what *model of man* or Humanoid is to be assumed) (i.e., the *casting* of the mechanism by stand-ins for humans). The other set is the assumed structure they are placed in or type of scene on which the Humanoids operate (i.e., the *staging* of the mechanism by the guide rails along which the actors can move.) The point of the construction of the mechanism is to work out its systemic effects (i.e., the *plotting* – what happens to the actors or to the structure as a consequence of their combination). It is precisely this combination of elements – actor assumptions, structure assumptions, and how they create a logical dynamic – which distinguishes a social mechanism from a number of other phenomena, such as covering laws, mere correlations, and so forth.

Actor assumptions

Actors or Humanoids are typically identified by the answers given to four questions:

1. *What do they want?* This may be specified in terms of preferences and purposes (e.g., in the manner done in microeconomic theory with utility functions and the like). More complex Humanoids with contradictory inclinations, or even multiple selves, can be postulated. Sometimes the actors retain constant preferences throughout; sometimes it is assumed that these can change. Different actors can have different preferences or different awareness of their preferences, which may provide interesting opportunities for plotting.
2. *What do they know?* By the most heroic assumptions, the actors may possess "perfect information" (i.e., they are fully informed about all relevant conditions that can affect their choices). However, knowledge can be treated as a changeable, or something that can be acquired, as in various models of learning. Beliefs may be uncertain or firm, tentative or unshakable, wrong or superstitious. A special case of particular interest is models of cognitive conflicts. Different actors may have different amounts of relevant knowledge, or different possibilities for learning, for example, which may provide interesting opportunities for plotting.
3. *What can they do?* Actors can have different capacities and abilities. For example, it is assumed of "rational actors" that they all have unlimited capabilities for instantaneous calculations. In models of educational attainment, actors are assumed to have different aptitudes that impinge on their results. What actors can do may be insufficient for the tasks at hand – but can also be postulated to be malleable. Whether such capacities are assumed to be intelligence, dexterity, or skill, they can also be differentially distributed among all or subgroups of actors, which again opens opportunities for different kinds of plots.
4. *What are their attributes?* Such attributes may be effects of causal processes, such as their sex or race, or being infected by a disease

or immunized by a vaccine. Some such attributes of actors are ineradicable; others can be changed voluntarily or involuntarily. However, the characteristics of actors often are *not* specified. For example, in a journal of theoretical economics, it is rather deviations from standard assumptions about Rational Actors that are stated. Otherwise the traits of the professional archetypes or the "usual suspects" are taken for granted.

In one sense, the answers to the four questions about actors posed previously correspond to methodological individualism. Nevertheless, methodological individualism is not the same as assuming *purposive* or *rational* actors, although they constitute powerful agents in a wide array of mechanisms.

Some mechanisms are based rather on what could be dubbed "collapsed actors." That is, in one subset of mechanisms, actors are *subjects*, originators of actions. In another subset, they are, in addition, the *objects* of actions, in the sense that they are recipients of consequences. This subject–object relationship is crucial in some types of mechanisms (e.g., in models of learning by doing). However, there is also a subset of mechanisms where the actors are just objects. In models of contagion, for example, infection is clearly not something we would ordinarily assume that rational actors *strive for*. Rather it is something that *happens to* them. Nevertheless a standard diffusion model with the infection rate being proportional to the number of haves and have-nots is a perfectly legitimate mechanism to apply. However, another mechanism for learning *that* contagion is loose and infection may be curbed can, of course, be grafted onto the simple diffusion model to make a more complex machinery.

Structure assumptions

The typical questions that can be asked about the other set of elements, the structure or the staging, are as follows:

1. *What are the states actors can be in?* Such states can be positions or roles that can be taken, the number of other actors, the number or relations they can enter, and the like. Such states can also be the alternatives they confront, options they face, or constraints they encounter. Some of these states are collective properties, such as

norms, rules, or laws. A key question will usually be whether such states remain constant or whether they are subject to change.

2. *What are the correlatives of these states?* For instance, what are the wages drawn from different kinds of jobs, the authority or status associated with a given position, the attention or external pressure directed toward a role irrespective of its incumbent, and so forth? In other words, the whole opportunity structure – the rewards and responsibilities, the rights and burdens – are structural correlates of different kinds of states.

3. *What are the distributional characteristics of actors as distinct from their individual manifestations?* For example, gender is an individual attribute, whereas the sex ratio is a structural characteristic, as is age distribution in population models. Similarly, crime rates are structural characteristics, which in some mechanisms may be taken as premises for individual choices and hence in turn be affected by them. Such distributional characteristics are all properties not of individuals but of populations.

Social mechanisms

A social mechanism is a device for combining actors with a given set of characteristics ("casting") with a particular social structure ("staging") in order to infer what outcomes will result ("plotting"). Simple mechanisms may lodge different types of actors in the same structural condition or environment, as was illustrated previously by the use of Sissies and Huskies. Or they may put the same kind of actor in different environments as in Sanctuaries and Danger Zones. They can also start off a group of actors with initial endowments – be it bundles of goods or control over issues – that are different from that which they desire, and then explore what kind of equilibrium state is reached if exchange is allowed.

Default models and collapsed actors

Some mechanisms are structurally robust in that they basically take it for granted that the structure will overwhelm the actors whatever assumptions are made about them. For example, it is a common observation that affairs and divorces have increased with increasing participation of women in the labor force. One mechanism to account for this is the changing opportunities for extramarital affairs as the composition of the labor force changes, as follows.

Actor assumptions:

- Actors are of two kinds, Men and Women, who may engage in affairs.
- The propensity to engage in affairs – frailty – is constant.

Structure assumptions:

- Environments vary in the number of potential *couples* who may engage in affairs.

From this follows that the maximum number of couples who can engage in affairs is largest when the numbers of the two kinds of actors, Men and Women, are most equal.

To *apply* this set of assumptions as a mechanism to account for affairs in firms, we would argue as follows. As the *proportion* of both sexes becomes more *equal*, the number of *potential couples* is *maximized*. For example, in a firm with 10 employees:

- No couples can form if all are recruited from either sex,
- 9 couples can form if *one* employee is from the opposite sex, and
- the maximum 25 couples can potentially form when there are 5 of each sex.

In this simple model of the social distribution of temptations, one could ignore the actors, so to speak, and expect that the more numerous temptations, will lead to more transgressions – "other things being equal," as the saying goes. In this case, Ben Franklin best describes the logic of the mechanism: "Keep yourself from the opportunity and God will keep you from the sin" – with the added observation that a changing social structure may, so to speak, create a social Danger Zone where opportunity knocks.

The point of this example is to illustrate that for some *structure-oriented* mechanisms what could be called *collapsed actors* are assumed. That is, no specific assumptions are made about what the actors want, know, or have, aside from being of two kinds (male and female). They are reduced to the barest of essentials: two types with one propensity. No intentions are specified, and by default all are assumed more or less equal – attractiveness, age, and civil status do not enter the mechanism.

The mechanism *can* be elaborated, however, to include such aspects and thereby make it "more realistic." It can be refined by further specifications. For example, one could differentiate among subgroups that have different propensities. The simplest elaboration would be to distinguish between Philanderers and the Purehearted (inspired by the English proverb that states "Good men, like good women, never see temptation when they meet it") and setting the propensity of the former at some larger value and of the latter at zero. This could then be used to mirror the behavior of puritans and mortal flesh. But the groups of actors could also be further specified (e.g., by assumptions about purposive actors seeking salvation and avoiding certain proscribed actions).

There are a large number of such structure-oriented mechanisms (i.e., mechanisms based on collapsed actors) circulating among social scientists. One example is Alex Bavelas's explication of systemic effects of different communication structures. Another is the general model of the population pyramid, where probabilities of survival from one age group to the next and age-specific birth rates serve as a kind of conceptual shorthand for "actors" in this structure-oriented model.

Similarly there are some *actor-oriented* mechanisms that produce the same outcomes irrespective of the structural conditions in which the actors are placed. One example could be mechanisms of aging. Such mechanisms could also be elaborated by structural additions to the mechanism (e.g., by "sorters" that place actors of different ages in different positions).

Models of change

Several of the mechanisms already illustrated describe not just differences in what happens to actors depending on their type or their social location but also social change. This was the case with all the simple mechanisms of the effects of competition: shift in the relative numbers of employers and employees, concentration, exploitation, and leveling of skills that illustrate social change of different kinds.

It is important to note that some of these mechanisms generate *structural* change, such as change in the number of employees or in their remuneration. Others generate *actoral* change, such as the change in actors' cognition, sentiments, or actions. Hence we can expand our theoretical concern and ask:

1. What does the assignment of different types of actors to different states *do to the actors*? For example, will putting Sissies in Danger Zones make them into Huskies? Will sending effeminate adolescents to the Marine Corps make them into Real Men? Will exposure to initiation tests (in "Hell Week") make greenhorns into strongly bonded veterans? Will study abroad broaden minds? Will exposure to capitalism change Russian communists?
2. What will the assignment of different types of actors to different states *do with the structure*? For example, will Sissies try to reduce objective risks? Will Huskies introduce killer bees for the fun of it? Will women in the Army change its ambiance? Will liberals appointed to the Supreme Court change the constitution? Are minorities recruited to positions of power coopted, or do they push for affirmative action rules?
3. What *does what the actors do with the structure in turn do to themselves*? For example, will Sissies manage to modify risks and this accomplishment enhance their fortitude? Will an organization train recruits in such a way that they transform the organization? Will a religious awakening wrought by a charismatic leader be transformed into a routinized church? Will ballet not just recruit lithe youngsters but also shape them in predictable ways?

These three questions are the typical questions asked in *models of social change*. The structure may change actors, their hearts and minds. The actors may change the structure, its positions and possibilities. And actors may react to conditions of their own making, by an echo effect from an edifice of their own making, so to speak. Sometimes they get caught by what they have wrought; sometimes they do not master the world they have made.

But if such observations are to become social science, they have to be translated into mechanisms, which can be of four types, given in Table 4.3. The types of phenomena in the upper left box can be illustrated by both the mechanism's wasp bites (Figures 4.1 and 4.2): The first distinguishes between two types of actors in the same environment, and neither the actors nor the structure in which they are haunted change. The same

Table 4.3. *Types of mechanisms of social change*

		Does the structure change?	
		No	Yes
Do the actors change?	No	Aggregate effects	Structural effects
	Yes	Actoral effects	Dialectical effects

holds for the second mechanism, with actors who visit Sanctuaries or Danger Zones: They are not changed by the experience.

When we moved to the market mechanisms derived earlier, however, we also moved to models of social change. The first, second, and fourth market mechanisms generate structural changes. According to the first, the ratio between the two types of actors shifts, which is a structural (distributional) characteristic even though it is mediated by individual actors. Likewise the change in the size distribution of firms is a structural change, and it transforms the *conditions* for collective action by the changing potential for communication and organization by overcoming the free-rider problem. Finally the leveling of skills of employees changes the structure of the labor market. In its bare essentials, the first mechanism – that the ratio of the two types of actors shifts – implies no change of the actors themselves. The change described by the mechanism is purely structural in terms of the assumptions made. *Concentration* leads not just to structural change, however, but to a cognitive change as well: Employees come to see themselves as equal to those treated in the same manner by the employers – i.e., a marxist version of the looking-glass self since the workers "take the role of the capitalist and see the nexus between the 'I' and the 'we' among workers" (Hernes, 1991: 240). The structural change expressed in a lower wage rate also translates into change of the actors – to new sentiments due to greater absolute and relative deprivation and hence to heightened emotional potential for collective action. Finally the fourth mechanism – that employers become objectively more alike by the structural leveling of skills – also has a counterpart in actors' cognition and sentiment (i.e., in producing a solidarity based on both common interest and mutual empathy).

When we depict mechanisms where actors change the structure in ways which in turn change them (i.e., when actors react to conditions of their own making), we can in a meaningful and precise manner talk of "dialectical models" (cf. Hernes, 1976). Clearly the marxist machinery recounted earlier falls into this category. Capitalists seek to maximize profits, but by their efforts entire sections of their kind are precipitated into the Proletariat, who grow into an immense majority. Not only do Capitalists concentrate the means of production in a few hands; they also concentrate and organize Workers in large units. By depressing Workers' incomes, and by exploiting Workers and dispossessing them of their skills and subsistence, Capitalists deprive them absolutely and relatively and thereby incite them to collective action.

At the same time, there are many partial mechanisms embedded in this marxist machinery – for example, unanticipated consequences of purposive social action (Merton, 1936), such as when Marx writes: "The advance of industry, whose involuntary promoter is bourgeoisie, replaces the isolation of the laborers, due to competition, by their revolutionary potential, due to association" (1978 [1848]: 474). The by-product of Capitalists pursuing their own interests is an undermining of their own position.

Dialectical models often are based on such counterproductive effects when actors do not master the world they have made. But they may also be based on mechanisms where actors are changed in a more helpful way, as when actors make new structures that in turn provide new opportunities for learning. Models of scientific advance are often of this kind.

Conclusion

Social scientists are commuters between two worlds: the world they make and the world they mirror. The purpose of the intellectual constructs that constitute social mechanisms is to account for what goes on in real social life. But then actor assumptions, structure assumptions, and their interactions have to be made explicit in order to explain both constancy and continuity as well as innovation and change. The true magic of the phantom world of mechanisms is that it may lift the fog over and make transparent the world in which we live.

References

Bortkiewicz, Ladislaus von. 1897. *Das Gesetz der kleinen Zahlen.* Leipzig: Teubner.

Coleman, James S. 1964. *Introduction to Mathematical Sociology*. Glencoe: The Free Press.

Elster, Jon. 1989. *Nuts and Bolts for the Social Sciences*. Cambridge: Cambridge University Press.

Elster, Jon. 1991. "Patterns of Causal Analysis in Tocqueville's *Democracy in America*." *Rationality and Society* 3 (3): 277–97.

Hedström, Peter, and Richard Swedberg. 1996. "Social Mechanisms: Their Theoretical Status and Use in Sociology." Stockholm University, Department of Sociology. Working Paper No. 27.

Hernes, Gudmund. 1976. "Structural Change in Social Processes." *The American Journal of Sociology*, 82: 513–47.

Hernes, Gudmund. 1989. "The Logic of The Protestant Ethic." *Rationality and Society*, 1, 123–62.

Hernes, Gudmund. 1991. "The Dilemmas of Social Democracies: The Case of Norway and Sweden." *Acta Sociologica*, 34: 239–60.

Holmsen, Andreas. 1961. *Norges historie*. Oslo: Universitetsforlaget.

Marx, Karl. 1906. *Capital. A Critique of Political Economy*. New York: The Modern Library.

Marx, Karl, and Friedrich Engels. 1978 (1848). "The Manifesto of the Communist Party." Pp. 469–500 in Robert C. Tucker (ed.), *The Marx-Engels Reader*. New York: W. W. Norton.

Merton, Robert. 1936. "The Unanticipated Consequences of Purposive Social Action." *American Sociological Review* 1: 894–904.

Stinchcombe, Arthur L. 1968. *Constructing Social Theories*. New York: Harcourt, Brace and World.

5. Concatenations of mechanisms

DIEGO GAMBETTA

Introduction

I take "mechanisms" to be hypothetical causal models that make sense of *individual* behavior. They have the form, "Given certain conditions K, an agent will do x because of M with probability p." M refers either to forms of reasoning governing decision making (of which rational choice models are a subset) or to subintentional processes that affect action both directly (as impulsiveness) or by shaping preferences or beliefs.

Two other meanings may be attached to "mechanisms," as suggested by Hedström and Swedberg in Chapter 1 of this volume. The first refers to models of *interaction* among individuals that generate particular social outcomes (the micro-to-macro case in their terminology). We construct these models to explain social phenomena such as markets, inequality, institutional performance, collective action, and so forth. Interaction models are predicated on individual-level mechanisms. The Prisoner's Dilemma, for instance, predicts a suboptimal solution by assuming self-interested and rational agents. If people cooperate when the hypothetical mechanism predicts they should not, as many experiments in social psychology have found (cf., e.g., Thaler 1994, Ch. 2), one is forced to search for other mechanisms. The second meaning refers to "macro" conditions that, via a given individual mechanism, can affect, say, beliefs or desires and, through those, behavior. Once again, these models are predicated on individual-level mechanisms. If an increase in opportunities for upward mobility leads to an increase in the number of people who feel *more* rather than less frustrated with the promotion system, we have a puzzling cor-

I would like to thank for their helpful and insightful comments John Alcorn and the Social-Science Reading Group at Trinity College, Hartford, and the editors of this book, Peter Hedström and Richard Swedberg.

relation. The search is then open for the individual-level mechanism that can best make sense of it (as I will show later in an example).

To avoid confusing levels of analysis and using "mechanism" as a loose umbrella term, we ought to distinguish between individual mechanisms proper and the processes by which these are both triggered by social conditions (macro-micro) and generate social outcomes (micro-macro). The latter should be called something else, perhaps just "models." "Mechanisms" in the sense adopted here refer to those minimal assumptions about agents' make-up that we require to deduce how they both interact with one another and respond to external conditions.

The family of individual mechanisms identified by social scientists as relevant to their models is large and growing: instrumental rationality; focal points; biased inferential processes; cognitive dissonance reduction; self-validating beliefs such as distrust; emotions such as envy; passions such as *amour propre*; evolved dispositions toward altruism, sex, or children; special cognitive quirks like the endowment effect, and so on. (A catalogue of mechanisms, which Schelling suggests in Chapter 2 of this volume, would indeed be of great value.)

The individual-level mechanism, which travels wider and lighter than any other through the jungle of social phenomena, is, I suspect, rationality in its barest adaptive version.[1] It works like this. Assume that an agent has certain preferences. Do not waste time making sense of them ("de gustibus non est disputandum"). Then work out what is the best strategy to satisfy those preferences at the minimum cost. You can then deduce a set of testable behavioral hypotheses. In this way, you can explain a wide variety of social phenomena. You can explain *how* Frederick and Rosie West went about kidnapping, raping, and murdering an as yet unknown number of young women in Gloucester, England, as well as *how* members of Amnesty International or the bursars of Oxbridge Colleges go about investing the assets of their institutions. To work out *why* the murderous couple had those appalling preferences or why some people work hard for altruistic purposes is an altogether tougher task. It is, by contrast, quite straightforward to understand that in order not to be caught (preference) the former (1) kidnapped only women fleeing from their family whose whereabouts were unknown to others, and (2) chose to live in a road with

---

[1] In terms of generality and parsimony, the evolutionary model may well be superior, and could even make sense of the wide diffusion of adaptive rationality itself, but I will not consider it here.

lots of Bed & Breakfasts where no one paid much attention to people coming and going. We can also easily understand why the couple hunted for victims traveling in their car *together* – "in this way we did not scare them," they declared. Rationality and sanity do not always go together. The motives of Amnesty and the Oxbridge bursars are no doubt altruistic, to make money for their cause and college; still, they will behave like any other investor out to make as much money as possible. They will endeavor to choose the best ways, with some moral limitation, to invest the money entrusted to them. Not only will a rational choice explanation be parsimonious and generalizable; it will also be the end of the story. Once intentions are posited, we as social scientists do not need to look further for yet more fine-grained mechanisms.

This line of research is of great value: Why posit a cumbersome "model of man" when a simpler one will do? In order to explain many social phenomena, we do not need to assume special features of agents psychology. There is no need to invoke the Oedipus complex to explain why a mafioso is, as it were, dead keen on his reputation. However, if our interest lies not as much in proving the power of any particular mechanism as in explaining social phenomena as they manifest themselves in the world (rather than in controlled experiments), in many cases we have to follow the opposite route – namely, pick our social puzzle and explain as much of it as possible regardless of how many mechanisms it takes. (A grand example of this strategy is provided by Tocqueville in *Democracy in America*.)

Most social phenomena require more than just one mechanism to make sense. Here is an example. Contrary to what one might expect given the vehement antismoking feelings in the United States, the number of people one can observe smoking in the streets of New York City is conspicuously high, and the streets are covered by cigarettes stubs. The puzzle is not so difficult to solve: If smoking is forbidden in offices and frowned upon in private homes, we can predict that the number of people smoking outdoors rather than indoors will increase, and so will the number of cigarette butts left around. This prediction seems intuitively sensible enough. If we "unpack" it, we can see that it rests on no less than three mechanisms, and that the plausibility of the latter sustains that of the model. It assumes that the *social norm* against smoking will be effectively enforced; next, that at least some smokers will not give up their *addiction* but persist in smoking even at the cost of doing it outdoors; third, that throwing stubs away in the street, though not a nice thing to do, is *individually cheaper* than either pocketing it or walking to the nearest garbage can (as well as hard to police). Norm, addiction, and elementary rationality jointly explain the puzzle. If any one of these mechanisms either did not work or were offset by yet other mechanisms, the prediction would fail.

It is not just a matter of piling mechanisms on top of each other, however. Mechanisms interact with one another forming *concatenations of mechanisms*. In this chapter, I give some primitive indication of what the search for such concatenations may yield by using three cameo examples. One refers to the stability of suboptimal institutions – in this case, the Italian academic system. The second example comes from recent research on individual schooling decisions and two puzzles it has raised. The third example is a discussion of the competing mechanisms that can account for the classic puzzle discovered by Stouffer and associates in *The American Soldier*.

In the spirit of a mechanism-oriented scholar, I make no overall claim in this chapter. There is no punch line. I also reverse a common sequence. Rather than working out my theoretical elucubrations about mechanisms and then shopping around for ready-made examples that fit them, I have picked examples that are (to me) substantively interesting to see what they can tell us. Here I follow, suitably paraphrased, Arnold Schwarznegger's injunction: "Illustrate first, think later."

The stability of suboptimal institutions: The Italian academic system

In several sections of the Italian academic world – as no doubt in other academic systems – loyalty toward the "barons" pays off more than independent research. If one plans a career in it, one better follow in the professor's steps, regardless of how well directed these may be, study what he wants one to study, avoid criticizing his work, stick by his side when others criticize his work (especially if the critics happen to be right), and carefully avoid outperforming him. There are many exceptions, especially in those subjects in which merit is less controversially established and academics interact closely with the international scientific community. There is, however, overwhelming evidence that that is typically the case. Given this incentive structure, *elementary and unprincipled rationality* suffices to explain intellectual subservience as the standard response on the part of younger academics. Most of those who end up in that system will have strong incentives to conform.

Over time, there is a further effect that reinforces loyalty: Individuals with a greater propensity to accept supine loyalty are, other things being equal, more likely to be selected by that system. Moreover, since the incentive structure is commonly known, there is also *self*-selection: Candidates with the "right" dispositions will be more likely to seek a career in academia. Notice that the selection effect relies on a different mechanism from rationality: It assumes the existence of prior dispositions, such as intelligence, risk aversion, impulsiveness, integrity or, in this case, independence of mind. It further assumes that such dispositions have a bell-shaped distribution in the population, and that institutions, via the incentive structure, select biased groups: The proportion of people displaying low independence of mind (or low attachment to whatever independence they have) will be overrepresented relative to the proportion in the population as a whole. In time, individuals in those institutions will have both the incentives to conform *and* a greater proneness to be governed by those incentives. Since the system is not impermeable, a number of valuable academics manage somehow to get junior positions in the Italian university. The selection effect hits them later when no promotion or research support will be granted to them. Stuck in those positions for life (all positions are tenured in this system from the start), scholars determined to maintain their integrity suffer particularly disturbing effects. The embitterment caused by the lack of appreciation and the frustration of being passed over by people of lesser merit eat their mental resources away and undermine their resolve. They lose their sense of direction and doubt the quality of their work. The selection effect ultimately strengthens the loyalty of subordinates within that system and thus its internal stability. In conclusion, *rationality and type selection form a concatenation of mechanisms that increases the internal stability of the academic institution.*

Two ancillary mechanisms are also at work in the same direction and enlarge the concatenation:

1. If most people behave supinely, supine behavior comes to be perceived as the norm, and independent behavior is felt as correspondingly more extravagant and thus becomes more costly.

2. If sycophancy is a perfectible skill, rather than being just an "on–off" variable, internal competition will reward those who are better at it; in time, they will gain more influence and socialize newcomers to their art.

That academic structure is not likely to produce a socially optimal outcome. Healthy intellectual competition is curbed. The quality of research is lower. Both the amount and the rate of progress of innovative research are also reduced. However, the set of mechanisms which govern that system sustains the prediction that there will be no internal pressure for change. Quite the contrary, we can expect considerable resistance to change. The selection effect may be more significant in this respect than rationality. Were a supine behavior simply chosen for instrumental reasons, a government could expect to modify the behavior of subordinate academics by increasing the rewards to independent research. This strategy, which may succeed with new generations, will, however, be much more costly to implement among those who have been selected already, because they had no great inclination for independent research to start with. Selection effects can cement bad practices and easily wreck naive policies that focus only on agents rationality when trying to improve the performance of institutions.

We can find similar concatenations shaping other institutions. Whether the effects on the internal stability will be positive or negative, however, depends on the disposition selected. For a mafia member, for instance, there are strong incentives to use violence in certain circumstances. Even the meekest of guys, waking up one day as a mafioso, would be under that pressure. It is also the case, however, that the *type* of individuals who are more inclined to use violence to begin with are both selected and attracted by the mafia. In this case, the outcome is not greater loyalty but greater violence. Violence may in fact turn out to undermine loyalty and the internal stability of the system. Mafiosi have been aware of this problem. On the one hand, they have recruited psychopaths to discharge their nastier tasks; on the other hand, in several instances, they have had them murdered when they were getting out of control.

Returning to the more sedate ways of academia, an optimistic reader may be consoled of the bleak picture just painted by hoping that the competition which lacks between subordinates and barons may still be functioning among peers. Alas, the system of academic loyalty in Italy hinders that, too. This is roughly how it works. The allocation of jobs is centralized, and positions on the selection committees rotate. This has promoted an internal "credit" market: The barons on selection committees at any one time give out positions also to the disciples of absent barons in the expectation that the next time around, when their turn will come to serve on selection committees, they will reciprocate. The barons develop a pact of reciprocity. An interesting consequence follows, as pointed out by Varese (1996) in an article in which he exposes a plagiarist who nests undisturbed in that system: If any one baron destroys another baron's academic reputation, the victim loses the ability to pay back his debts on the academic credit market. Debts and credits are passed on from generation to generation. The professors in credit, therefore, even if they had the soundest of intellectual reasons to pull the rug from under the feet of their debtors, refrain from doing so because in future rounds their pupils would suffer the consequences. "Like banks, professors do not wish the bankruptcy of their creditors" (p. 176).

Once again, *elementary rationality* does much to explain the persistence of that credit market. It is not the whole story, however. Italian academia may be an insulated world. Still, occasional meritocratic bacteria "infect" it. Academics catch them visiting foreign universities or coming intermittently in contact with professions where meritocracy does work. Although mediocre academics, who would lose out from a change, know that from *their* point of view this world *is* optimal and cannot be expected to take reforming action, the professors with greater intellectual clout might conceivably gain from a better system. Still, no great change is in sight, and everyone abides by the rules of reciprocity.

The awareness of better selection criteria has generated no more than subterranean dissatisfaction. To adapt to the demands of the credit system may be rational, but it nonetheless creates a friction, which makes it somewhat painful. Barons must know that in job competitions they act in a way that is neither fair nor efficient.[2] Privately, several among them acknowledge that the system is suboptimal in terms of academic output and unfair to the most deserving scholars. Few among those with a preference for a better state of affairs, however, reveal it publicly, as predicted by

---

[2] The selection effect actually may weaken the awareness for it may preselect candidates so that only mediocre ones will present themselves, and selectors will not have a feeling of directly excluding better ones, because these did not apply in the first place.

Timur Kuran's model (1995). Even professors prone to moralize in other fields refrain from doing so in their own. No one speaks up, and, what is worse, no one seems to like those few who do.

We often think of subintentional mechanisms as an alternative to rationality, whereas this is a case in which they work together: The tension between the rationality of complying with reciprocity and the adherence to fairer and more efficient selective criteria is resolved by way of *cognitive reduction of dissonance*. The outcome is a host of self-serving values that justify internal "honesty" and a norm against "cheating" in job competitions by not returning favors obtained in the past. The public defense of reciprocity is not played on grounds of cynicism (e.g., "that's life and we have to make a living" sort of argument) but on grounds of distorted values that get cited when something perturbs that system. The norm is enforced by ostracism of various sorts, both in the first- as well as in the second-order way.

Notice that the theory of cognitive dissonance reduction predicts further a counterintuitive result: On the one hand, the greater the awareness of the negative aspects of the system, the greater the likelihood of speaking up against it; however, since the greater the awareness, the greater the dissonance, if people do not speak up, the theory predicts the opposite effect – namely, that correspondingly more intense will be the activity to justify the existing arrangements. The paradox is that among the most intelligent Italian academics we can expect both those who are more opposed to the system *and* those who come down more cynically in its defense. Since they have reasons to dislike their practices *more* than others, they are also under greater pressure to rearrange their face-saving beliefs more energetically insofar as they themselves comply with those practices.

This suggests a new constellation of mechanisms: *If individually rational behavior is not right – because it produces suboptimal results of which people are aware, or it inflicts unnecessary pain, or because it is illegal or unfair – those with an interest in adapting to it experience a tension. By cognitive dissonance reduction, this leads to the emergence of self-serving values and beliefs which justify that behavior on grounds other than those of rationality.*

This concatenation manifests itself in a number of variants. Until a few years ago, everyone believed that the Sicilians actively liked the mafia and considered it as a legitimate authority. Cultural relativists, cynics, economists who believe in revealed preferences, Northern Italian racists, corrupt locals, and intellectual Cassandras, all agreed on one thing: This is the way things are, and that nothing could be done or was worth doing. This gravely hampered the fight to eradicate the mafia.

Self-serving values and beliefs created in that way are not deprived of important consequences that at best delay social change and at worst make it outright impossible. They remain, however, a thin veneer. Once change occurs, they evaporate more quickly than expected. As soon as all the most important mafiosi ended up in jail, and the government determination became credible enough to reassure Sicilians that the bosses were not only jailed but were likely to stay there for life, the mood shifted dramatically. Even in villages where the mafia was rife, new left-wing antimafia politicians have been elected and have received much more support than any of the foregoing categories would have predicted.

A very interesting example of the same class is provided by Mackie (1996) for vicious practices, such as footbinding and infibulation. These practices are conventions enforced by a perverse but no less compelling form of rationality: Families, argues Mackie, are afraid of being the first and only ones to stop practicing them for fear their daughters will be penalized in the marriage market. In this particular case, a third mechanism joins the constellation to reinforce the stability of those conventions. Mackie aptly calls it a "belief trap": "a belief that cannot be revised, because the believed costs of testing are too high." Women who practice infibulation are caught in such a trap: "The Bambara of Mali believe that the clitoris will kill a man if it comes in contact with the penis" (ibid.).[3] This mechanism can itself originate from or be retained because of cognitive dissonance reduction in the following way: Should a belief be voiced, even fortuitously, such that it provides an extra reason for complying with a painful convention with which it is painfully rational to comply anyway, this belief is more readily believed without testing. In addition, this belief is more likely to be retained if it happens to be a belief trap. Belief traps should be high on the agenda of mechanism-oriented scholars.

---

[3] A general case of self-enforcing beliefs of some considerable importance is that of complete distrust (see Gambetta 1988).

Individual decision mechanisms in education

The next two examples come from a recent survey of 756 subjects, 14–17 years old, in Piedmont, North West Italy (IRES 1996). A local research institute decided to check, among other things, whether my conclusions in a previous research on individual decision mechanisms in schooling choices still held after 10 years (Gambetta 1987). Here I provide no account of the overall results but pick only two puzzles that emerged during our data analysis.

Case 1

One of my original results was simple yet intriguing: Controlling for many other variables, the probability to stay on at school after the end of compulsory education was negatively correlated with father's age. The effect, calculated through multivariate logistic models, was strong. A subject whose probability to stay on at school given all other variables in the model was 50% decreased to less than 30% if his or her father was older than 64 (Gambetta 1987: 144–50). I had inserted that variable with the following hypothesis in mind: Age is an indicator that income will be declining in the near future. Foreseeing the tightening of economic constraints, families should be more prudent and encourage an early entry in the labor market rather than more school. The underlying mechanism is a simple response to expected economic constraints. Insofar as education is at least partially a consumption good or the credit market is not perfect in supplying loans for investment in education, agents should respond to their income level in deciding how much education to consume or in which to invest.

When we carried out the analysis again on the new data, that result was confirmed. We had a surprise, however. The logit model over the whole sample gave much the same coefficient, showing that children of older fathers do suffer from a considerable disadvantage. However, when we ran separate models by gender, the picture changed: In a classic case of the same mechanism generating opposite effects, our expectation was confirmed for boys but reversed for girls. The father's age shows a significant positive effect on the probability that a girl will choose the *liceo,* the most demanding secondary school. Choosing the liceo amounts to an early commitment to sending the child to university later on, so it is not only demanding in terms of its academic content but also of the number of years one expects to be in education. If, for example, a girl's chances are 50%, an older father pushes them up to 70%.

Clearly the expected effect is stronger than the opposite one, or else the overall model would not have picked it up because the effects would cancel each other out. (Notice that this is often a risk of empirical analysis because one may conclude that there is no effect when there are opposite ones neutralizing each other. A mechanisms-sensitive approach makes such wrong conclusions less likely.) Moreover, the expected negative effect dominates also in the models broken down by social class, and in all four classes – upper, middle, self-employed, and working class – age of the father is, with some variation, a disadvantage.

This result backfired on my original hypothesis. Is age really a proxy for declining income, or is it related to some other mechanism? Father's age seems to trigger greater generosity as well as greater prudence. Are we picking up the effect of an intentional mechanism or of some "behind-the-back" force that affects the disposition for risk taking? A sign that suggests that we may be faced with a mechanism other than straightforward rationality is when we observe that the same cause produces opposite effects. Age can plausibly make one both more worried about the future and more carefree; it can fuel egoism or dampen it. "If I spend a lot of money, what will happen if I fall ill? versus I am not going to need much money now for my pleasures and even less when I am dead, so why not be generous and give the best education to my kid?"

The intriguing question, however, is: Why should gender make a difference as to which of the two extremes age should push? Overall the results of the analysis by gender suggest that education is conceived more instrumentally when it comes to boys. They are on average likely to earn more money than girls when they first enter the labor market, so families forego greater sums by sending boys to school than girls. In order to send a boy to school, therefore, incentives must be stronger. This is shown by two facts: (1) boys in general are less likely than girls to stay on at school after compulsory education; if they decide to stay on, however, (2) boys are more likely than girls to choose the liceo rather than less demanding secondary courses.

In conclusion, age captures rather than a concatenation a bifurcating mechanism – in the sense illustrated by Jon Elster in Chapter 3 of this book – the direction of which is controlled by a third variable, the size of the loss: *The greater the loss incurred, the greater the risk aversion that age produces. But if the loss is minimal, age triggers greater generosity.* This is the best explanation we could think of for our puzzle. How robust this mechanism really is, how far it can travel, can be assessed only by further research on whether age has the same dual effect under comparable conditions.

Case 2

In the same models, we specified another variable: whether a subject had an older sibling who was or had been in higher education. Our hypothesis was that that condition should increase the probability of subjects to stay on at school themselves after compulsory education. The mechanism hypothesized is one of opportunity: Older children at school provide help, guidance, and books to their younger siblings. An older child at school increases the cultural capital on which the family can draw and decreases the education costs for younger siblings. The logit models showed that, other things being equal, this variable did have a strong positive effect as we predicted.

Once again, there was a surprise. This variable had a much greater effect for girls than boys, for whom it was negligible (regardless of the gender of the older sibling, which does not make any difference). This prompted a more elaborate reasoning than we had anticipated. If it were just cultural capital, why should it make a difference only for girls? In fact, it should not. The effect of an older sibling at school could be a proxy for a different mechanism.

Consistently with the overall picture presented in the previous case, the reasoning that underlies a school decision for boys seems different: If they have what it takes, they go to school, or else they are off to work. It does not matter whether an older sibling is at school. When the choice is seen as *instrumental,* there is no reason why the action taken for an older sibling should impinge on the younger one. If one brother turns out to be a great soccer player, this does not make the other brother equally good at it. Suppose, by contrast, that the reasoning were one which valued education as a consumption good. In this case, what we allow an older sibling to consume we can hardly deny younger ones. Families are bound by a *norm of distributive fairness* in what they give to their children. This might explain why it works for girls only. Since for them school may be perceived more as cultural consumption than a means to improve career opportunities, and having sent a girl's older brother or sister to school before, one cannot deny her the same treatment. This suggests a concatenation of mechanisms: *Whether the norm of fairness is applied depends on the value we attach to the good to be allocated. Only if this is perceived as a consumption good will the norm be binding.*[4]

Relative deprivation revisited

In *The American Soldier* (1965), Stouffer and his colleagues discovered one of the most challenging puzzles in sociology. Studying soldiers attitudes in World War II, they found that in the Military Police (MP), where opportunities of becoming an officer were much lower than in the Air Corps, subjects were *more* satisfied with the fairness of the promotion system, irrespective of rank and education. In particular, the less educated officers in the Military Police were found to be extraordinarily highly satisfied. (The reader can find the data in the appendix to this chapter.)

This finding has become a classic. There is a very good reason for this: Were it generalizable, it would mean that better and richer societies with higher opportunities produce a higher proportion of frustrated individuals, and this in turn would affect collective action in those societies. Imaginative social scientists have offered different speculative explanations as to why more opportunities can cause a higher level of discontent with the promotion system. I collected five mechanisms. They can be organized in two ways: according to whether frustration is brought about by a change in expectations or a change in preferences, and by distinguishing whether the change is the result of a rational or a nonrational process. This reorganization yields four possible combinations in which we can fit the five explanations (see Table 5.1).

According to the original researchers, the mechanism which explains that correlation is *relative deprivation:*[5] Officers in the MP shared their

---

[4] I do not have good evidence to say whether a different view of education between boys and girls is itself a rational adaptive response to differential opportunities in the labor market or the result of gender-biased values as to what constitutes a desirable life. Either way, insofar as school is singled out as a consumption good, the norm of fairness is triggered, while it remains dormant if school is perceived as a mere investment.

[5] Here I do not touch on the many questions that this concept has generated. One of the most important ones is: How do people select the group with which to compare themselves? Another question concerns whether feelings of relative deprivation are extended to

Table 5.1. *Mechanisms suggested as explanation of why members of the Military Police were found to be more satisfied with the promotion system than members of the Air Corps.*

	Hopes–expectations	Wants–preferences
Nonrational	Excessive hopes (Merton)	Relative (Stouffer) Emulation effect (Tyler)
Rational	Higher incentive to invest (Boudon)	Release from adaptive preferences (Elster)

privilege with relatively fewer fellow officers; similarly, the men were also more content because they shared the absence of promotion with correspondingly more soldiers like them. The concept of relative deprivation was introduced by Stouffer earlier in the book to explain a number of other intriguing correlations found in *The American Soldier*. It was invoked to explain differences in willingness to serve in the army by age, marital status, and educational attainment. ''The idea is simple, almost obvious, but its utility comes in reconciling data . . . where its applicability is not at first too apparent. . . . Becoming a soldier meant to many men a very real deprivation. But the felt sacrifice was greater for some than for others, *depending on their standards of comparison''* (p. 125, vol. I).

The reason why married men are less willing to serve in the army is partly that they suffer more absolute deprivation, in that they give up more; but the critical additional factor, argues Stouffer, is that there are many unfavorable examples around with which to compare themselves. The first is the unmarried men who were also drafted. The second is that the draft board is considerably more liberal with married men than with single, so those married men who *do* get drafted can see numerous examples of married men who avoid it. A similar argument applies to age. Older men are likely to be further on in their career and are therefore objectively giving up more. They are also likely to be less physically fit, and therefore the army made a greater demand on them. But the objective factors of

the group of people in a similar position (''fraternal deprivation'' in Runciman's definition) or whether they remain confined to personal loss (''egoistical deprivation''), which has a bearing on the potential consequences on collective action. A more general question concerns exactly which psychological conditions are required to set off relative deprivation. See Runciman (1966), Crosby (1976), Olson, Herman, and Zanna (1986), and Masters and Smith (1987).

jobs and health, if they had not persuaded the draft board, turned into subjective grievances when in the army, because of the existence of younger fitter comparisons within the army and of other people similar to themselves whom the draft board had treated more leniently.[6]

The second mechanism (upper left cell in the table) was provided by Merton while elaborating on the explanation of the original researchers. He wrote that a "generally high rate of mobility induced *excessive hopes* among members of the group so that each is more likely to experience a sense of frustration in his present position and disaffection with the chances of promotion" (Merton 1957: 237). Here the mechanism is one of *excessive hopes* that lead more subjects to frustration. This explanation seems different from that of relative deprivation more than Merton himself acknowledged: Frustration does not occur directly because one feels deprived as a result of more people getting a desirable promotion. It emerges indirectly, via excessive hopes, generated by more people being promoted.

Merton did not elaborate on how exactly "excessive" rather than "realistic" hopes result from higher opportunities. A false inference – "if a lot made it, I will too" – could be the source of the process. There is evidence, discussed by Elster (1983), of a cognitive mechanism that leads individuals to bring to the extreme what is objectively possible: If little is objectively possible, people tend to believe that nothing is; at the other extreme, if a lot is possible, people tend to believe that everything is. It is important to point out that Merton's explanation could hold even if we assume a *constant* distribution of preferences for promotion in the relevant population. It suffices that more of those who already entertain that preference will also entertain higher and unrealistic expectations about the

---

[6] Stouffer even tries to make this argument apply to education. By extension of the previous arguments, one would have thought that the objective sacrifice would have been greater for educated people, and that, once in the army, they would be able to see less educated soldiers who had given up less, and people attending college outside the army, and thus feel more aggrieved. In fact, the more highly educated were *more* willing to serve in the army. Instead of a host of simpler explanations (the more highly educated identifying more with the objectives of the war, and so on), Stouffer produces a somewhat tortuous argument. The better educated were probably healthier than the less well educated and therefore would not have such a sense of deprivation when they compared themselves with them. Furthermore Stouffer denies that the objective sacrifice over being forced to leave civilian jobs was greater, since the jobs most commonly granted deferment for were skilled manual jobs and agricultural jobs. Therefore it was the less educated who were most likely to have grievous sources of comparison of friends in civilian life. His final argument is that the better educated would also be less objectively deprived because they were less likely to have parents who were economically dependent upon them.

possibility of fulfilling their ambition. The difference between a change in expectations and a change in preferences is conceptually relevant to distinguish Merton's from the other explanations.

Boudon (1977) provides a different view on how higher opportunities could produce higher frustration (bottom left cell in the table). As in Merton's case, the stress is on a change in expectations; unlike Merton's, the process is held to be rational. Ex ante, subjects would be perfectly rational to have higher expectations when facing higher objective opportunities. More of them are therefore justified to invest in trying to obtain promotion, even if ex post more of them are exposed to frustration and disappointment. Merton and Boudon provide alternative interpretations of basically the same mechanism.

The third explanation (bottom right cell in the table) has been suggested by Elster (1983) as an explicit alternative to those of Merton and Boudon. He argues that "when promotion becomes sufficiently frequent, and is decided on sufficiently universalistic criteria, there occurs a *release from adaptive preferences*" (p. 124). These preferences would be there already but kept dormant by subjects through a process of *sour grapes* in response to the lack of opportunities. Higher opportunities bring about a process of disillusionment relative to one's true preferences, and one finally finds the courage to admit that one actually desires promotion. Irrespective of hopes, frustration could result from the fact that more people would consciously reach a "*new* level of wants" about promotion. Thus it is the silent preferences for promotion to be "excessive," the product of a nonrational process by which constraints shape subjects' tastes "behind their backs."

Finally, the fourth explanation (upper right cell in the table) was put forward by Mark Tyler, a student at Cambridge, England, in the class where the late Cathie Marsh and I taught about this case back in 1985. He suggested a mechanism we called the "emulation effect": The larger the number of people obtaining promotion, the higher the feeling that achievement is essential. Thus, in the MP where promotion is more rare, one attaches a *special* significance to it and does not feel that it is something everyone must achieve. In the Air Corps, on the contrary, the higher promotion rate leads to attach a lower significance to being an officer. But, precisely for that reason, those not promoted suffer more by being passed over.

This is an interesting elaboration of the relative deprivation hypothesis:

Frustration does not occur directly through a feeling of injustice but because if many are promoted, then its lack is more sorely missed. It also differs from Merton's explanation in that the stress is on the change in relative desirability rather than on excessive expectations to fulfil one's desires. There would be more people desiring promotion rather than more of those already desiring it, expecting to be promoted. As in Elster's explanation, the stress here is on a change of preferences. In Elster's case, there seems to be a latent autonomous desire brought to the surface, but in the emulation effect, the desire is socially manipulated. In Elster's case, subjects wants become more transparent, thanks to the fact that higher opportunities dissolve the effects of self-deception. By contrast, the emulation effect works behind subjects' backs.

The mechanisms considered so far can make sense of why those who *do not* obtain promotion tend to be more frustrated if chances of promotion are higher. The striking finding of *The American Soldier,* however, is that those who *do* obtain promotion in the Air Corps tend to be more unsatisfied with the promotion system than those in the MP, where there were lower objective possibilities of being promoted. Three of the five mechanisms previously described – "excessive hopes," "rational investment," and "release from adaptive preferences" – can explain only frustration among the nonpromoted group. Only "emulation" and "relative deprivation" can make sense of both sides of the finding and can account for why the difference in frustration with the promotion system is found among the promoted groups also. If a lot of people obtain something desirable, it becomes both *more* disappointing not to have it and *less* valuable once one has it. This double effect can be accounted for by both hypotheses: A privilege shared with many others can be debased either because of some relative comparison between one's ability and the ability of others or because of the *snob* version of the emulation effect – namely, "If a lot have it, then I do not want it."

On balance, when considered together, the findings suggest that something more than a rational mechanism is at work here and that the mechanisms which could explain only the views of the nonpromoted, interesting as they may be in their own right, are not prima facie as parsimonious as the relative deprivation or emulation mechanisms. Parsimony, however, is a logical rather than a substantive criterion, and more research is needed to adjudicate among these hypotheses. There is a rational reason to test parsimonious hypotheses first, but there is no reason to expect only one mechanism to be at work.

So far we have considered only the effect of army section on the level of frustration with the promotion system. The findings also included two other effects: Satisfaction with the promotion system was found to be positively associated with *rank* (holding army branch and education constant) and negatively associated with *education* (holding rank and branch constant).

Officers, by simply having been made such, could feel happier about the promotion system, given that it acknowledged their personal ability. Correspondingly, privates feel more cynical about officers and the method of *their* appointment, for the simple fact of not being among them, *independently* of the proportion of officers and soldiers. The crucial mechanism reflects a reduction of cognitive dissonance working in both directions: "Whatever reward is bestowed on me must be well deserved" and, obversely, "Whatever reward I fail to obtain is the result of an unfair promotion system."

As for the second finding, subjects with lower education could feel less ambitious and more content, irrespective of their rank. If promoted they have a reason to be very pleased with the system; if not, they have less reason to feel deprived. Correspondingly, more educated subjects have more reason to be dissatisfied when not promoted and, if they are, because they have to share their privilege with officers of lower education. Here the governing mechanism is one of adjusting one's expectations to what is possible given one's point of departure coupled with feelings of relative deprivation.

In conclusion, even if we do not know for sure which specific concatenation of mechanisms is at work here, it is unlikely that *one* mechanism could make sense of *all* the findings and succeed in explaining the sources of dissatisfaction with the promotion system.

Conclusions

Why should we work out the individual-level mechanisms that account for social outcomes? Cannot we rest content with establishing correlations avoiding the cogs and wheels of the causality that brings them about? Several other essays in this collection make a very strong case for this approach, so I shall just mention one reason: Unless we gain some knowledge of mechanisms, we remain at the mercy of social statistics. We can collect an infinite amount of information and do not know what to do with it. We know more and understand less. Mechanisms, as many as they may be, are a minute fraction of all possible social events. Many possible events can be explained by few mechanisms. As Hernes's witty paper forcefully shows (Chapter 4 of this volume), the explanation of even the most ordinary phenomenon is ultimately erected, whether explicitly or implicitly, on individual mechanisms.

Even if in principle we feel happy about this route, how can we be sure that mechanisms differ from armchair theorizing? First, I would like to say a word in favor of the latter. Theoretical imagination may be cheap. Stinchcombe notes that "a student who has difficulty thinking of at least three sensible explanations for any correlation that he is really interested in should choose another profession" (quoted by Hedström and Swedberg in Chapter 1 of this volume). Still, were it really so cheap, why is it that so many sociologists are busy doing social statistics and feeble at the former task? Why, in other words, did they not choose another profession? Introspective imagination and analytical energy are not enough to discriminate scientifically among competing mechanisms but are crucial for the supply of candidates. Give me a good speculative mechanism any day rather than a batch of useless survey data.

In doing sociological analysis, we hypothesize the existence of mechanisms, but we cannot observe them directly. Unlike what happened for genes and atoms, which were first hypothesized and much later actually observed, we are unlikely ever to be in that position. This in itself should not rule out testing as much as it does not rule it out for gravity, which we also cannot observe. Testing via the predicted effects is as good as you can get in many sciences, not just the social sciences. Thus if our empirical research were led by mechanism-based reasoning, we would, rather more quickly than we now expect perhaps, be collectively able to focus on those mechanisms that have the wider and more resilient explanatory power. The only way forward we have is to apply our sociological mechanism kit to more social puzzles, large and small alike, searching for evidence that can tell us how far the mechanisms we postulate can travel. Is it the case, for instance, that with age people become simultaneously *more* fearful of losses and *less* prudent when there is little to lose? Does relative deprivation affect agents by modifying their preferences or their expectations? How do rational choice and type selection interact in different institutions?

By venturing out of the relatively safe shores of rational-choice analysis, we may end up in a dead-end alley, speculating about mechanisms that verge on "ad-hockery." Our models may grow heavier. On the other hand, it is a risk worth taking. Rational-choice analysis, powerful as it is, often ends up modeling obvious aspects of phenomena or enslaving the choice of the phenomena to be explained to the limits of the theory. Its neatness comes at the cost of being of less interest to humans other than rational-choice theorists. A small family of mechanisms has strong qualifications already to engage our attention closely as much as rational-choice analysis has done over the past 20 years. Cognitive dissonance reduction in its several variants, type selection, and belief traps, all are mechanisms that seem to travel well beyond our armchairs. They are worth exploring further, possibly in conjunction with one another. The examples in this chapter show that social puzzles of interest have the annoying tendency of presenting themselves in complicated forms, many times removed from the ideal conditions of a controlled experiment. By isolating the concatenations of mechanisms that govern them, we may much improve our explanatory and predictive apparatus to tackle other social puzzles, even if social "laws" remain out of our reach.

Appendix

The findings of The American Soldier[7]

In Volume I, in the section on social mobility within the army, Stouffer et al. (1965) present a table comparing two different branches of the army at two extremes of the proportion of officers in that branch: the Military Police, which had very few officers, and the Air Corps, which had very many. There are three independent variables – rank, education, and section – all having an effect on a dependent variable – perceived fairness of the promotion system in the army. The three independent variables are themselves interrelated: There are very different proportions in different ranks and different educational groups in the different sections, for example (see

---

[7] The data analysis presented here was carried out in collaboration with the late Cathie Marsh.

Table 5.2. *Questionnaire: Do you think a soldier with ability has a good chance for promotion in the army? Percentage saying "A very good chance"*

	Military Police		Air Corps	
	Not high school grad.	High school grad	Not high school grad	High school grad.
Non-coms	58	27	30	19
	(N = 165)	(N = 241)	(N = 70)	(N = 152)
Privates and PFCs	33	21	20	7
	(N = 707)	(N = 470)	(N = 79)	(N = 123)

Source: MP data from special survey of a representative cross section of MPs, S-107, March 1944. (Base: White men enlisted in the army 1–2 years, continental United States.) Air Corps data are a segment from a representative cross section of all white enlisted men in the United States, S-95, January 1944. (Reported in Stouffer 1965, Vol. 1: 252.)

Table 5.2). To examine the relationships, we must look at percentage differences in the various directions. Consider first the effects of rank. In each case, the officers view the system as fairer than do the privates, yielding the following differences:

Military police: less educated	25
Military police: more educated	6
Air corps: less educated	10
Air corps: more educated	12

In other words, in the Air Corps, the differences between officers and men are the same regardless of whether they are educated or not, but among the MP, the differences between officers and men are much more pronounced among the less educated.

Now turn to the effects of education. Unlike the previous example, here the more educated are more critical of the army, viewing the system of promotion as less fair. But, once again, there are important interactions:

Military police: non-coms	31
Military police: privates	12
Air corps: non-coms	11
Air corps: privates	13

Table 5.3. *Percentage of officers in different categories*

	Not high school grad	High school grad	Total
Military Police	19	34	26
	(*N* = 872)	(*N* = 711)	(*N* = 1583)
Air Corps	47	55	52
	(*N* = 149)	(*N* = 275)	(*N* = 424)

The effect of education is similar throughout except among the MP non-coms, where education has a dramatic effect; the non-coms who are not high-school graduates are very much more supportive of the system of promotion.

Finally, consider the effect of section. Here comes the famous finding: In all groups, those in the Air Corps are more critical of the promotion opportunities than comparable groups in the Military Police, despite the fact that the proportion of officers is much greater in the Air Corps:

Less educated non-coms	28
Less educated privates	13
More educated non-coms	8
More educated privates	14

The effects are more or less of the same amount except for the less educated non-coms, where the effect is huge.

We can summarize the whole table parsimoniously by saying that being an officer, being less educated and being in the Military Police all increase perceptions of fairness in the promotion system. It is important now to be aware of the structure of these two different sections of the U.S. army with respect to the three independent variables (Table 5.3).

There are many fewer officers in the Military Police, but the effect of being a high-school graduate is quite marked: There are approaching double the number of officers among those who have graduated from high school. There are many more officers in the Air Corps; there are even more officers without high school in the Air Corps than there are with high school in the MP. But the difference in proportions between those with high-school education and those without is not so marked. Finally, we should note that the educational composition of the two different sections is very different: two-thirds of the Air Corps are high-school graduates, whereas only 45% of the MP are.

References

Boudon, R. 1977. *Effets Pervers et Ordre Social.* Paris: Presses Universitaires de France.

Crosby, F. J. 1976. A Model of Egoistical Relative Deprivation. *Psychological Review*, 83, 85–113.

Elster, J. 1983. *Sour Grapes.* Cambridge: Cambridge University Press.

Gambetta, D. 1987. *Were They Pushed or Did They Jump? Individual Decision Mechanisms in Education.* Cambridge: Cambridge University Press (paperback edition by Westview Press, 1996).

Gambetta, D. (ed.) 1988. *Trust. Making and Breaking Cooperative Relations.* Oxford: Basil Blackwell.

IRES. 1996. *Le Scelte Scolastiche Individuali.* Torino: Rosenberg & Sellier Editori.

Kuran, T. 1995. *Private Truths, Public Lies: The Social Consequences of Preference.* Cambridge, Mass.: Harvard University Press, 1995.

Mackie, G.1996. "Ending Footbinding and Infibulation: A Convention Account." *American Sociological Review*, 61, 999–1017.

Masters, J. C., and W. P. Smith. 1987. *Social Comparison, Social Justice, and Relative Deprivation.* Hillsdale N.J.: Lawrence Erlbaum

Merton, R. K. 1957. *Social Theory and Social Structure.* New York: The Free Press.

Olson, J. M., C. P. Herman, and M. P. Zanna. 1986. *Relative Deprivation and Social Comparison.* Hillsdale N.J.: Lawrence Erlbaum.

Runciman, W. G. 1966. *Relative Deprivation and Social Justice.* Berkeley: University of California Press.

Stouffer, S. A. et al. 1965 [1949]. *The American Soldier.* New York: Wiley.

Thaler, R. H. 1994. *The Winner's Curse.* Princeton: Princeton University Press.

Varese, F. 1996. Economia di Idee. *Belfagor*, LI, no. 302, 169–85.

6. Do economists use social mechanisms to explain?

TYLER COWEN

Introduction

In interpreting the question "Do economists use social mechanisms to explain?" I focus on the phrase "social mechanisms" rather than on the word "explain." I take the explanatory status of economic science as given and ask whether that enterprise uses social mechanisms. I interpret social mechanisms (defined in greater detail later) as rational-choice accounts of how a specified combination of preferences and constraints can give rise to more complex social outcomes. As we shall see, social mechanisms cover a broader class of cases than do invisible hand mechanisms, a more familiar concept to many economists.[1]

The concept of social mechanism holds importance for both rational-choice sociologists and economists. In sociology the study of social mechanisms serves as a methodological competitor to both more atheoretical approaches and to grand theory building. Analyzing social mechanisms puts sociology firmly in the rational-choice camp and brings it closer to economics and public choice approaches to political science. In economics, a strongly unified discipline in methodological terms, explanation in terms of mechanisms is more widely accepted than in sociology. Nonetheless studying the method of social mechanisms has broader implications for how we think about markets, the epistemological status of economic science, comparing mathematical and nonmathematical approaches to eco-

The author wishes to thank Peter Hedström, Gorge Hwang, Daniel Klein, Timur Kuran, Thomas Schelling, Daniel Sutter, Richard Swedberg, and Alex Tabarrok for useful discussions and comments.

[1] On whether economics is an explanatory science, see, for instance, Hausman (1984), Nelson (1986a, 1986b), and Gibbard and Varian (1978). Green and Shapiro (1994) offer a skeptical view, at least as applied to public-choice theory. On the complementarity of economic and sociological approaches, see Coleman (1994) and Swedberg (1994).

nomics, the link between economics and rational-choice sociology, and some concrete problems in game theory. In this chapter, I hope to draw out some of these broader implications, although I do not seek to present definitive answers.

My treatment sets aside the intentions of the individuals who produce economic theorizing. When we ask economists what they do, we receive many conflicting answers, only some of which cite the concept of mechanism. Economics serves multiple ends, consists of numerous subfields, and invokes a wide variety of methodological devices. I will nonetheless interpret neoclassical microeconomic theory as using and creating social mechanisms, regardless of the intentions of its practitioners. The generation of mechanisms through economic science is a result of human action, even though it is not always the product of direct human design.

The second section of this chapter outlines the concept of social mechanism as used by rational-choice theorists. The third section examines how economics can be interpreted as a science of social mechanisms, presents some examples of economic mechanisms, and distinguishes several kinds of economic mechanisms. I present a unified treatment of formal and nonformal treatments of mechanisms, which I see as essentially similar. I also discuss the difference between mechanisms and invisible-hand mechanisms and consider to what degree mechanisms rely upon the concept of agent intention. The fourth section considers one of the most difficult issues with economic mechanisms, the existence of multiple equilibria, and asks whether economics can escape the problem of complete indeterminacy. The final section offers some concluding remarks about the status of an economic science based on mechanisms.

What is a mechanism?

Citing examples of social mechanisms is easier than producing a rigorous definition that commands unanimous acceptance. Thomas Schelling's (1978) "chessboard" account of segregation provides a classic account of a social mechanism. Each individual wishes to live among a slight majority of his or her race, but the induced reshufflings of residencies may produce complete segregation. Schelling suggests that we play a "segregation game" by rearranging pieces on a chessboard, moving any white or black piece that is surrounded by a strong majority of pieces of the other color. When the reshufflings have been completed, all of the white pieces may end up on one side of the board, and all of the black pieces on the other side. Each individual plans where he or she will live, but no individual plans the extreme degree of segregation that results. The bulk of Schelling's *Micromotives and Macrobehavior* focuses on social mechanisms. Schelling presents a wide variety of ingenious accounts of how social order is established through the interaction of preferences and constraints. His now-classic analyses explain how and why crowds tend to gather in back rows of large auditoriums, the rationale for daylight savings time, and why hockey players, in their desire to appear macho, engage in the collectively self-defeating act of taking off their helmets.[2]

Robert Nozick, in his *Anarchy, State, and Utopia*, discusses "invisible-hand explanations," a concept close to social mechanisms. Nozick's list (1974, pp. 20–1) includes Darwin's theory of natural selection, Schelling's theory of residential segregation, Jane Jacobs's (1961) account of how commerce makes city streets safe, theories of how economic calculation is accomplished in markets, and the Peter principle, which states that individuals rise in an organization to their level of incompetence.[3]

Social mechanisms outline processes through which initial conditions operate through human behavior to produce a final result. The link between initial conditions and results should be somehow insightful or surprising, at least prior to theorizing. An explanation of the following sort does not qualify as a mechanism, or only qualifies in a trivial sense: "John wanted to eat cake. John therefore picked up the piece of cake and ate it." A social mechanism, as I use the term, requires intermediate analytical connections between the final social result and individuals' behavior or intentions.[4]

---

[2] Especially see Schelling's (1978) Chapter three. Two recent books, rife with social mechanisms, are Richard Posner's *Sex and Reason* (1992) and *Aging and Old Age* (1995). For an older work that relies heavily on social mechanisms, see de Tocqueville's *Democracy in America*. In my manuscript *Enterprise and the Arts*, I attempt to outline how mechanisms have worked to influence the creation of artistic products. For a general guide to the use of mechanisms in social science, see Elster (1989). Outside of the social sciences, narrowly construed, I recommend the works of Stephen Jay Gould, a biologist, and Bill James, a sports analyst, for their analyses of mechanisms.

[3] See also the list given in Boudon (1986, pp. 57–8).

[4] Economists use the word "mechanism" in a variety of contexts. General equilibrium theorists refer to Adam Smith's "invisible-hand mechanism," and subfields of social-choice theory and principal-agent theory refer to "incentive mechanisms" (typically a kind of contract, either for voting or for performance). These references do qualify as social mechanisms under my treatment, but they do not define the term.

Just as social mechanisms should involve more than the direct fulfillment of intention, they also should avoid a reliance on sheer accident. If a launched satellite falls from the sky, survives its descent through the earth's atmosphere, and destroys a city block, the event *is* a "result of human action but not of human design," as stipulated by Hume and Hayek. Explaining the destruction of the buildings in terms of the satellite's fall, however, hardly qualifies as an invisible-hand explanation. The interaction between preferences and constraints plays no role in the account. Social mechanisms might explain why the satellite had construction defects in the first place, but the fall of the satellite itself is an accident. Similarly, freaky, miraculous, or extraordinary causal chains do not qualify as nontrivial social mechanisms. Social mechanisms involve general chains of causation that may recur in a class of roughly similar circumstances (Ullmann-Margalit 1978, p. 271).

In sociology Robert Merton promoted the identification of social mechanisms. He defined social mechanisms as "social processes having designated consequences for designated parts of the social structure" (Merton 1968, pp. 43–4). Merton's analysis of self-fulfilling prophecies in scientific research and scientific reputation remain some of the most insightful treatments of social mechanism. Hedström and Swedberg (1995, abstract) refer to mechanisms as "an intermediary level of analysis in-between pure description and story-telling, on the one hand, and universal social laws, on the other."[5] Social mechanisms are distinct from laws, as emphasized by Elster (1989, 1996) and Stinchcombe (1993, p. 31). Social laws suggest that conditions A and B always lead to result C, whereas social mechanisms need not make such a strong claim. Conditions A and B need only lead to result C some of the time. Social mechanisms do not necessarily specify all of the initial conditions in formal detail.

Social mechanisms may be used to explain either the emergence of a phenomenon or its survival over time (Ullmann-Margalit 1978). Schel-

---

[5] Stinchcombe (1993) defines a mechanism as "(1) a piece of scientific reasoning which is independently verifiable and independently gives rise to theoretical reasoning, which (2) gives knowledge about a component process (generally one with units of analysis at a "lower level") of another theory (ordinarily a theory with units at a different "higher" level), thereby (3) increasing the suppleness, precision, complexity, elegance, or believability of the higher-level theory with excessive "multiplication of entities" in it, (4) without doing too much violence . . . to what we know as the main facts at the lower level." See also Ullmann-Margalit (1978, pp. 267–8) and Elster (1989, Ch. 1). Elster (1996, p. 1) defines a mechanism as "frequently occurring and easily recognizable causal patterns that are triggered under generally unknown conditions. They allow us to explain but not to predict."

ling's chessboard example, for instance, can explain how an originally integrated neighborhood might become segregated, once mobility increases. Alternatively, the chessboard example can explain why segregated neighborhoods, with their origins in historical accident, remain segregated, even when residents would prefer some degree of integration.

Economic equilibrium as implicit mechanism

I take rational-choice equilibrium to be the organizing concept of economic theory. "Rational choice" refers to models based on the interaction of preferences and constraints. "Equilibrium" refers to a state of affairs following from given initial conditions. As I use the term, "equilibrium" does not require particular assumptions about perfect information or about how well markets work. Any situation can be defined in terms of an equilibrium, if we specify the constraints properly. An equilibrium is a theoretical construct that represents an explanatory link between initial conditions and final results.[6] Models of economic equilibrium can be redescribed in terms of social mechanisms. Consider the claim that binding price ceilings will create shortages and reductions in the quality of goods offered for sale. The model of this proposition describes a formal equilibrium, and the supply functions contain an implicit account of the relevant mechanism. Once the price is capped, sellers will produce fewer units of output for the market, and they will supply only lower-quality units, in an effort to restore a higher net price.

This account, although it relates a relatively simple economic proposition, describes a social mechanism. The model outlines a process through which initial conditions give rise to a final result – a shortage of the commodity in question. The link between initial conditions and results is general and theoretical rather than the result of direct intention or sheer accident. Nor does the economic model constitute a general social law.

---

[6] My treatment of equilibrium follows the older Chicago School tradition (e.g., Coase, Stigler, Friedman) by describing all states of affairs, whether in models or in the real world, as equilibria; Reder (1982) surveys this tradition. My views on social mechanisms do not require adherence to the Chicago approach, although I find it a useful medium of presentation. Other traditions in economics talk of equilibrium as a state of affairs that is either achieved or not achieved, depending on how well markets work (Fisher 1983). The Austrian, post-Keynesian, and institutionalist schools visualize equilibrium as a concept completely removed from the real world. In their view, equilibrium is never achieved. On the role of equilibrium and other economic constructs in rational-choice sociology, see Coleman (1994).

Price ceilings usually cause shortages, but they do not always cause shortages. If the price ceiling is set sufficiently high above the market clearing price, for instance, it will not bind, and no shortage will result. All equilibrium models can be redescribed as mechanisms in this fashion. Equilibrium models outline a specific set of initial conditions and show how those conditions create general forces giving rise to a final outcome. When economists define an equilibrium, they are producing an *existence theorem* outlining the possible effects of those forces in the real world. An economic equilibrium defines a causal sequence linking a particular series of initial conditions to a particular series of final results.

Economic models of equilibrium rely on filters, local adjustments, and aggregation effects. Mechanisms based on filters imply that some underlying structures or institutions sort events into discrete categories. According to Richard Posner, elderly people tend to have lower discount rates than the young, tend to take better care of their health, and tend to eschew reckless risks. One explanation for these stylized facts relies on a selection effect. Individuals who have high discount rates, take excessive risks, and do not care for their health are less likely to survive to old age (Posner 1995, p. 71).[7]

Mechanisms based on local adjustment specify marginal or incremental changes in behavior rather than sorting. Well-informed voters may increase rather than decrease the incidence of shirking and self-seeking behavior by political candidates. Poorly informed voters may hold a single instance of political transgression very strongly against a candidate, given the overall paucity of their information. Well-informed voters may be more forgiving; even when they hear a piece of negative news about a candidate, the informed voters still know the candidate is relatively close to (or far from) their views. The candidate can get away with more shirking than when voters are poorly informed and attach great weight to any single piece of information. For example, a political candidate must take greater care to speak well when he is around strangers than when he is around close friends (Cowen and Glazer 1996).

---

[7] Darwin's theory of natural selection offers a well-known filter-based mechanism from outside of economics. The rigors of existence sort animals into two categories: those that successfully reproduce, and those that do not. Over time, creatures that have the qualities favoring reproduction will flourish and replace the creatures that do not have those qualities. Dennett (1995) suggests that all mechanisms are ultimately reducible to "Darwin's Dangerous Idea." On different types of mechanisms, see Nozick (1974, p. 21).

Professors sometimes use analogous reasoning in drawing up exams. A professor might induce superior effort by sampling small amounts of information rather than large amounts – that is, by giving an exam with only a single question or a small number of questions. The students, knowing that a bad performance on a single question will be held against them strongly, will cover all bases in their studying. Conversely, if the exam covered all the material of the course, students could achieve an A by studying only 91 percent of the material. For this reason, students who shirk typically prefer comprehensive exams to exams with a very small number of questions.

Mechanisms based on aggregation effects postulate nonlinear consequences for a given act. Automobile mechanics sometimes try to cheat their customers by claiming that a car needs repairs even when it does not. (Typically mechanics are better informed than customers.) When mechanics adopt this strategy collectively, however, it proves self-defeating. Customers are wary of dishonest mechanics and will engage in countertactics. Customers will wait until their car is relatively run down before bringing it to a mechanic. If mechanics will claim that something is wrong with the car in any case, customers will wait until something actually is wrong. Overall mechanics end up with less scope to cheat customers, even though each mechanic tries to cheat customers. Although mechanics do not necessarily gain, customers do lose. Customers will care less for their autos than would otherwise be economically optimal, and we will observe "too many" automobile breakdowns on the street (Taylor 1995).[8]

Does the degree of determinacy matter?

Most economic models tend to be formal, whereas most accounts of social mechanisms (in the narrower or more traditional sense) tend to be looser, based on verbal analysis, or more impressionistic. Sociologists, even of the rational-choice variety, offer a less formal treatment of rationality than do most economists. Even within economics, we find both verbal treatments of mechanisms (e.g., Schelling, Olson, and Hirschman) and mathematical treatments. Unlike mathematical economics, verbal accounts of

---

[8] By assumption we cannot contract with our mechanic to tell us the truth. The mechanic will promise to tell the truth, pocket the payment, and in any case claim that repairs are needed.

mechanisms typically present a result without specifying a fully determinate model.

The formalism of a model or the degree of specificity of the assumptions are not essential features for defining a social mechanism. Any verbal account of a mechanism involves an implicit model or set of assumptions, just as a mathematical model does. The verbal result holds only because of background assumptions that external forces do not interfere with the postulated outcome. In this sense, verbal economics or verbal rational-choice analysis does not avoid the well-known problems with mathematical analysis. The results of verbal analysis are no less contingent upon a wide variety of "unrealistic" assumptions. Similarly, any formal treatment of a mechanism can be translated into a verbal account. We need only leave away some information, keep some assumptions unspecified, and translate the mathematics into verbal analysis.

I downplay the significance of the degree of determinacy in an economic model for three reasons. First, I interpret economic theory as a language that can be translated into other languages in a number of different ways (Quine 1960). Of primary importance is the number and kind of translations available rather than the language we use. Social mechanisms belong to the range of possible translations out of the more narrow economic language of formal model building.

Any claim involving a model of greater determinacy can be translated into a claim of lesser determinacy. To return, for instance, to the distinction between mechanisms and laws, any claim to have discovered a law – "If A, then B." – also implies discovery of a mechanism – "If A, then (at least) sometimes B." The more ambitious concept of a law subsumes the weaker concept of a mechanism. Similarly, a more determinate model, or a model based on a narrower idea of rationality, also subsumes models of lesser determinacy.[9] Second, equilibrium models provide determinate results only within the context of a given model. Once we translate an equilibrium model to a real-world context, we accept a greater degree of indeterminacy. Equilibrium theory tells us only which mechanisms might operate in the world. In reality, we do not know whether dishonest auto-

---

[9] I am not suggesting that the choice of mathematical or verbal method should be a matter of indifference. Rather, I am claiming that both mathematical and verbal accounts are equally social mechanisms. (In my opinion, the relevant difference between mathematical and nonmathematical methods is which is a better tool for *discovering* new ideas at least cost. Once the idea is there, the method of expression is less important.)

mobile mechanics always induce too many automobile breakdowns or whether some other factor (e.g., dealer warranties) intervenes to produce a different result. When we translate the language of the model into the language of the real world, we can say only that the initial conditions of the model create some force operating in favor of the model's final result. Equilibrium models outline possible social mechanisms in bare-bones form and do not eliminate the indeterminacy of real-world explanations.[10]

Third, many economic models contain multiple equilibria. Multiple equilibria reflect the indeterminate nature of mechanisms even within the context of the model (much less when we apply the model to the world). The presence of multiple equilibria shows that A need not always give rise to B, even under a specified set of initial conditions. Multiple equilibria show that formal models of economic equilibrium do not offer degrees of determinism that differ in kind from the degrees of determinism offered by less formal accounts of social mechanisms.

Contracts and intended versus unintended consequences

The concept of transaction costs, as explicated by Coase (1960), allows us to classify economic events into two categories: outcomes generated by encompassing contracts and externalities not covered by contract. In the latter case, either no contract is present at all or the relevant contract is incomplete and does not remedy the externality.

In some accounts, contracted-for outcomes are called "intended" or "planned," and the outcomes that agents do not contract for, or externalities, are called "unintended." The distinction based on contracts, however, supersedes this earlier dichotomy between intended and unintended consequences, found most prominently in Merton (1936) and Hayek (1973–9) but dating back to Smith, Ferguson, and the Scottish Enlightenment. Social mechanisms do not require that we penetrate and classify the potentially ambiguous dimension of agent intention.

Richard Vernon (1979), in his insightful polemic against the concept of unintended consequences, questions the ability of the social theorist to classify mechanisms on the basis of agents' intentions. Need the agent intend the act only, or must the agent have intended the entire series of

---

[10] On this interpretation of equilibrium theory, see the works of Alan Nelson, such as Nelson (1986a, 1986b). For a commentary on Nelson, see Rosenberg (1986). Gibbard and Varian (1978) is also relevant.

consequences associated with the act? Vernon gives the example of an insane surgeon who does not *intend* to kill a patient but only intends to remove the man's heart. Is the death of the patient an intended or an unintended consequence? Any treatment of this issue will require resolution of the difficulties involved with the sense-reference distinction, as discussed in analytical philosophy (see Levy 1985). Similarly, every action has extensive unintended consequences at a fine enough level of description. If I drive a nail into a piece of wood, for instance, I do not intend the exact resulting pattern of splintering (Vernon 1979, p. 67).

Consider the Schelling segregation mechanism in this context. Is the resulting segregation an intended or unintended consequence? Does the answer depend upon whether some agents actively desire to create full segregation, whether agents know that their collective actions will lead to segregation, or whether agents are entirely unaware of the mechanism? How fine a description of the final outcome must agents intend, in order to support a classification of the mechanism as an intended or unintended consequence? Focusing on contracts rather than on intentions eliminates the need to provide definitive answers to these questions.

Taking sufficient care with language and classification might, in principle, dissolve the conundrums surrounding intention. Nonetheless, economic mechanisms do not require that we resolve difficult issues in the philosophy of language, and they do not require an airtight distinction between intended and unintended consequences. The Schelling mechanism rests upon the interdependencies of residency decisions across individuals – an unambiguous positive fact – regardless of how we answer the questions about intention posed previously.

Some economists, especially of the positivist Chicago variety, have found the concept of intention to be an embarrassment for economics. Armen Alchian (1950) argues that the hypotheses of profit and utility maximization can be derived through an evolutionary mechanism, without reference to the intentions of agents. Gary Becker (1962) argues that budget constraints will enforce downward-sloping demand curves in the aggregate, even when individual agents are irrational or behave randomly. I read these authors as wishing to abolish the idea of intended consequences altogether and to base all economic propositions on unintended consequences and mechanisms. Even if these arguments succeed, however, I find the Coasian approach superior. The concepts of contracts and transaction costs render nugatory the distinction between intended and unintended consequences, without recourse to complex evolutionary arguments or without invoking extreme versions of positivism.[11]

Are mechanisms invisible-hand mechanisms?

I propose limiting the concept of the invisible hand to market failures, and classifying market successes as instances of the visible hand, or perhaps more appropriately, visible hands. In the Schelling explanation of neighborhood segregation, whites end up on one side of the town, and blacks end up on the other side. Although no individual lives anywhere but the place of his or her choosing, the overall pattern of segregation is unintended and contrary to individual preferences. Undesired segregation comes about because we cannot arrange the appropriate compensating transfers to prevent clustering behavior. The "invisible hand" arises through the effect of one residence decision upon the marginal returns to other residency decisions. Individuals are led, as if by an invisible hand, to create a segregated pattern of residence. We can properly speak of Schelling's account not only as a mechanism but also as an invisible-hand mechanism.

The invisible-hand feature of an explanation or mechanism, such as Schelling's, relies upon market imperfections. When markets are perfect, the so-called invisible hand is not invisible at all; all relevant welfare consequences are the subject of deliberate contract. Consider the Arrow-Hahn-Debreu general equilibrium model, where transactions costs are zero and all mutually beneficial exchanges are consummated. The Coase theorem holds and all relevant externalities are internalized through contract. Any problem that affects welfare, from the availability of fresh bread to neighborhood integration, can be solved by market exchange. The Schelling mechanism cannot arise, as individuals favoring integration would compensate some group members to preserve racial balance and live in neighborhoods in which they are a minority.

To the extent that markets are perfect, all social mechanisms can be reduced to versions of the following claim: "John and Mary wanted X and Y, and therefore contracted to bring X and Y about." We might claim that the overall pattern of welfare maximization is unintended, but all

[11] For one criticism of Alchian's evolutionary arguments that profit-maximizers will survive and dominate, see Schaffer (1989).

economic events have been determined by contract, either implicitly or explicitly. An invisible hand has operated only in the trivial sense. Considering larger numbers of people does not change the nature of the mechanism, given that even large numbers can interact and transact costlessly, by assumption. Market outcomes, insofar as markets are perfect, aggregate many visible hands through the contracting process but do not involve an invisible hand. All of the aggregate effects are controlled and intended, and only the abstract pattern can be treated as unintended. The Schelling segregation example, with imperfect markets, differs. The mechanism specifies a real influence on behavior – the interdependence of residence decisions – that is not controlled by contract or a visible hand.

For these reasons, Adam Smith's famous invisible-hand metaphor is inappropriate for the operation of a successful market economy. Insofar as markets are complete, the hand is visible and operates through contract. Insofar as markets are imperfect, the hand is invisible but does not produce desired outcomes. Forces such as the Schelling segregation mechanism will operate. Market failures, and not the market successes, provide the clearest illustrations of an invisible hand.[12]

The position defended here comes close to some views expounded by libertarian rationalist Murray Rothbard, although I reject Rothbard's conclusions about the universal efficacy of the market. Rothbard identifies the market with the visible hand and denies the relevance of the distinction between intended and unintended consequences. Within libertarian circles, Rothbard is well known for criticizing the Hume-Smith-Hayek account of "unintended consequences." Whereas Alchian and Becker attempt to dispense with the concept of intention, Rothbard enthrones intention. Rothbard sees the order of the market as consciously designed by individuals rather than as the result of a "spontaneous order," as suggested by Hayek.

Rothbard senses correctly that the invisible-hand concept should be as-

---

[12] To introduce one complication, in some "second-best" instances markets do well (although they do not achieve a first-best outcome) precisely because markets are imperfect. It may be for the better, for instance, that consumers cannot bribe a polluting monopolist to expand output. In these cases, we are explaining some of the benefits of imperfect markets in terms of an invisible hand. Similarly, the benefits of markets may consist of uninternalized external benefits, interdependencies, and increasing returns to specialization rather than the direct operation of contracting and the price system. In those cases, we may again have recourse to "invisible-hand" explanations of market success. If we read Adam Smith as presenting this latter account of the virtues of markets, rather than a more neoclassical approach, the metaphor of the invisible hand still may apply to market activity, albeit in a different manner than economists usually mean.

sociated with market failure. His libertarian ideology therefore induces him to go further and rule out the idea of an invisible hand altogether. Rothbard (1977) rejects the possibility of market failures arising through negative externalities or unintended consequences. Given Rothbard's attempt to explain social reality solely in terms of intention, then unintended consequences, by definition, cannot create decisive problems for the market order. In contrast with this view, I regard invisible-hand explanations as perfectly valid, even if I do not associate them with contractual market exchange.[13]

Game theory and the vast multiplicity of equilibria

The predominance of imperfect contracting, strategic behavior, and game-theoretic interdependencies in invisible-hand explanations opens up a can of worms for the status of mechanism in economics. Recent developments in game theory have raised the question of whether economic mechanisms of these kinds involve any determinacy at all.

Models with multiple equilibria have become increasingly common in economics, especially with the advent of game theory. Game theory has grown from an exotic topic to a staple mode of reasoning in most economic fields. Models with strategic interaction and imperfect contracting often give rise to more than one equilibrium, or even to an entire continuum of equilibria. If my behavior depends upon what I expect from you, and your behavior depends upon what you expect from me, multiple solutions usually will obtain. In a wide variety of games, game theorists have outlined entire arrays of mutually consistent strategies, depending upon what the players expect from each other (Kreps 1990, Ch. 14).

In macroeconomic models, entrepreneurs may choose high levels of output if and only if they expect other entrepreneurs to do the same (Murphy, Shleifer, and Vishny 1989). These models have a high-output equilibrium and a low-output equilibrium. In monetary models, fiat money

---

[13] Rothbard's (1977) theory of "demonstrated preference" implies that we can only speak meaningfully of preferences that are observable in a marketplace setting. In his view, economists cannot speak of unfulfilled preferences for a public good in a market setting. The relevant preference has not been demonstrated. Not only is the entirety of the market the result of human planning, but all (meaningful) plans end up being translated into results. Rothbard's views on this issue, of course, represent an extreme minority within the economics profession. See, however, Cordato (1992) for support. Not surprisingly, Rothbard was enamored of conspiracy theories in the political realm.

Table 6.1

		Player 2	
		C	NC
Player 1	C	5, 5	−3, 8
	NC	8, −3	0, 0

typically can take on a multitude of real values, again depending upon what economic agents expect (Kareken and Wallace 1980). In industrial organization models, the pricing and output decisions of firms will depend upon the conjectures they hold about each others' behavior, again leading to multiple equilibria. The economic mechanisms discussed in this chapter, insofar as they involve strategic behavior, will be characterized by similar indeterminacies.[14] The multiperiod prisoner's-dilemma game provides a clear illustration of multiple equilibria. Kreps (1990, p. 504) presents the game specification with an indefinite number of plays, where C and NC stand for "cooperate" and "not cooperate," respectively (Table 6.1). Game theorists typically define equilibrium in terms of the Nash concept. An equilibrium is a Nash equilibrium if each player has no incentive to deviate, taking the other player's behavior as given. In the one-shot prisoner's dilemma, it is well known that we have only one Nash equilibrium, mutual noncooperation.[15]

In the multiple-period game, a large number of equilibria may exist. Viewing the foregoing game, we see that a Tit-for-Tat strategy, if adopted by both players, comprises another Nash equilibrium. If each player knows that the other will play Tit-for-Tat, neither player has an

[14] On the foundations of multiple equilibria, see Cass and Shell (1983). The concept of economic "noise," developed by Fischer Black (1986), considers other sources of indeterminacy. Black argues that stock prices, exchange rates, and even the price level and money supply are determined by expectations rather than by traditional economic supply and demand equations. A large continuum of random indeterminacy prevents economics from linking initial conditions to a specified final result. Noiselike theories also can be found in the "disequilibrium" or "nihilistic" branch of the Austrian school of economics; see Lachmann (1977) and Shackle (1972).

[15] The Nash concept, although widely accepted, does not command unanimous adherence among game theorists. The alternatives, such as "rationalizable equilibria," are beyond the scope of this chapter, but they typically do not avoid the issue of multiple equilibria and often exacerbate the problem.

incentive to deviate from cooperation, taking the other player's behavior as given, at least if the discount rate is sufficiently low. Yet the number of available equilibria is much larger. Suppose that player one announces that she will alternate between C and NC, but if player two ever plays NC, player one will play NC forever. This provides another equilibrium under the Nash concept. Or player two may make the same threat, with player one held in thrall. The details of these threats and strategies may be changed (e.g., perhaps player one randomizes her strategy with differing probabilities of cooperation), potentially giving rise to an infinite continuum of equilibria.

We cannot generally rule out the equilibrium where everything goes well. According to the well-known "folk theorem," there always exists some set of behavioral conjectures sufficient to sustain a cooperative equilibrium in a noncooperative game, at least provided the discount rate is low enough. Noncooperators must expect that they will be punished for their noncooperation, and that nonpunishers will be punished for their refusal to punish noncooperators, and so on. The cooperative equilibrium exists in the model, regardless of how implausible the implied chain of cooperative relations might be (Kreps 1990, Ch. 14).

According to many critics, game theory has moved beyond looking for mechanisms to a less definite, even nihilistic stance. This criticism, presented in its most extreme form, claims that virtually any economic outcome or mechanism can be rationalized in terms of game theory. Given the initial conditions of the model, almost any result can hold. Game theory rules out nothing and therefore does not present illuminating explanatory or causal chains, according to these critics. Sam Peltzman (1991), for instance, writes of game theory as a "City of Theory," unrelated to explaining the real world or to policy issues. Franklin Fisher (1989, p. 116) writes: "The existence of an embarrassingly large number of equilibria appears to be a fairly general phenomenon. This is a case in which theory is poverty-stricken by an embarrassment of riches."[16] The threat to economic mechanisms is real. If a set of initial conditions can lead to almost any final result, the initial conditions do not seem very important. The relevant "mechanism" might be little more than the theorist's arbitrary choice of which equilibrium to invoke.

[16] For some well-reasoned criticisms of the rational-choice approach from outside of economics, see, for instance, Green and Shapiro (1994).

Refinements and mechanisms

Economists have attempted to resolve the problems with game theory by ruling out multiple equilibria or by developing criteria for choosing one equilibrium over another. Game theorists have developed refinements of the Nash equilibrium concept, such as "subgame perfection," "perfect Bayes equilibrium," "trembling-hand equilibrium," "symmetry," "sequential equilibrium," "Pareto dominance," "Markov perfect," the "Cho-Kreps Intuitive Criterion," and the "Universally Divine" criterion.[17]

Refinements discriminate among equilibria by specifying which beliefs and expectations agents can reasonably hold in the context of a game. To return to the multiple-period prisoner's dilemma, consider the strategy where player one alternates C and NC, and threatens perpetual defection if player two ever chooses NC. Many refinements rule out this equilibrium by various means. The notion of "symmetry," for instance, requires identical players to deploy identical strategies. "Markov perfection" rules out strategies conditional upon an opponent's move from any previous period other than the last one. A player can only look at the immediate past in drawing inferences about what to expect from his opponent. In the multiperiod prisoner's dilemma, Markov perfection eliminates the effectiveness of complex strategies of retaliation contingent on behavior from the distant past. The "trembling hand" requires that the benefits of a strategy be robust to small probabilities that his or her opponent will err or will send a noisy signal. Trembling-hand refinements tend to rule out strategies based on conditional perpetual defection. Players who face some chance of misreading their opponent's signal are unlikely to defect perpetually after one noncooperative signal. Refinements can rule out many of the possible equilibria in a game, leaving us with a smaller set of available solutions or perhaps even a unique solution.

The increasing reliance of economics on refinements of game-theoretic equilibria suggests one of three conclusions. First, economic theory might be moving away from an analysis of mechanisms. Refinements do not refer back to individual maximizing behavior. Rather, the economist provides some *external* standard for which expectations or strategies are more "appropriate" or "reasonable" than others. Refinements provide no ac-

---

[17] For some references and discussions, see Aumann (1985, p. 44), Kreps (1990), and Fudenberg and Tirole (1991).

count of a mechanism through which one set of strategies or expectations will come about, rather than another set.

According to this skeptical view, the theorist's method for solving the game, rather than the model itself, provides the crucial explanatory power. Game theory merely classifies all possible mechanisms, without specifying when a given mechanism is more or less likely. Economics would remain a science that generated and classified mechanisms, but virtually any result could be explained in terms of a mechanism. Even when a given refinement provides for a unique equilibrium (not always the case), we still must choose across the very large number of available refinements. If a large number of possible equilibria are each associated with various refinements, we have not made much progress. The specter of using an external standard to choose among refinements raises the problem of infinite regress.

Second, it may be acceptable for a mechanism to specify arbitrarily a method of solving the relevant game. To place the matter in perspective, we do not typically disqualify social mechanisms for taking preferences and constraints as given. A mechanism is allowed to postulate some initial situation, without explaining where everything came from. Perhaps the expectations and strategies embodied in refinements should be regarded in a similar light, as part of the initial specification of how the real world behaves.[18] Third, we might invoke social mechanisms to solve the problems of game theory. Multiple equilibria represent the incomplete nature of a given model rather than an intrinsic indeterminacy in the real world. Real-world economic outcomes involve no indeterminacy. What happens must have happened, and nothing else could have happened, given the initial conditions. A finding of multiple equilibria shows only that a given model does not represent enough relevant causal features to pin down a unique outcome. If we apply the model to the real world, unmodeled factors must be driving whichever outcome results. Considering further mechanisms might transform these unmodeled factors into modeled factors that can be explained.[19]

[18] I am not convinced by this defense, however. Any model must assume initial conditions, but the purpose of a model is to show a link between the initial conditions and a final result. If the link or process is merely assumed, the model adds little to our understanding.

[19] Alternatively, multiple equilibria might be describing an intrinsic indeterminacy in real-world economic activity, perhaps due to human free will. (Unless economic phenomena are influenced by subatomic indeterminacy at the quantum level, it is difficult to find any alternative interpretation of intrinsic economic indeterminacy.) In this case, the existence of

According to Ken Binmore, we should not solve games by invoking arbitrary specifications of the reasonableness of beliefs and expectations. Rather, we should develop an explicit model of how agents with bounded rationality make decisions, and we should use that model to derive unique strategy choices for each agent. Binmore believes that many of the equilibria in mathematical games require unreasonable degrees of computational ability on the part of agents. Once computational tractability is introduced, the number of equilibria may fall away, perhaps returning us to a manageable number of equilibria, or perhaps even a unique equilibrium.[20]

Evolutionary game theory takes a related approach. Evolutionary models embody agents with different strategies and examine which strategies will persist and flourish over time (Maynard Smith 1982 and Axelrod 1984 made some of the first efforts in this direction). The surviving strategies then provide the appropriate solution concepts and refinements for the analysis of other games.[21] These research programs, if successful, would strengthen the status of mechanism as an explanatory device in economics. As seen earlier, game theory weakens the status of mechanism as an explanatory device. Multiple equilibria were the fundamental problem behind this dilution of explanatory power. If we could specify a mechanism that leads individuals to one equilibrium rather than the others, we would solve two problems at once. The embarrassing multiplicity of equilibria would disappear, and the resulting equilibrium would be determined by a process explicable in terms of mechanism.

Rational-choice sociologists probably are most sympathetic to this third attempt to save game theory from indeterminacies. Yet we should not underestimate the problems involved. First, the tournaments and super-games used to determine the relative merits of solution concepts are unlikely to yield determinate answers. The winning solution concepts will be highly sensitive to how the tournament is constructed (Hirshleifer and

---

multiple equilibria in economic models would simply reflect the limits of any kind of knowledge and should not be considered a problem to be solved.

[20] See Binmore (1990). Consider, for instance, the "folk theorem" discussed earlier. In many contexts, the folk theorem requires that individuals can identify noncooperators, can identify those who do not punish noncooperators, and can calculate the necessary punishments to dissuade those who do not punish noncooperators. Cooperation of this kind presumably would not satisfy Binmore's requirement of calculational tractability.

[21] For surveys of evolutionary approaches to game theory, see Binmore (1992, Ch. 9) and Weibull (1995).

Martinez Coll 1988). Second, even if one solution concept wins most tournaments, we cannot conclude that individuals use that solution concept in real-world decision making. Most likely, our real-world strategies are context-dependent. We cooperate altruistically in some instances but act with a more narrow selfishness in others. No single solution concept comes close to describing the panoply of human strategic behavior. As economic theorists, we cannot replicate the appropriate game-theoretic context without reproducing the specific game in question, which brings us back to a large multiplicity of possible equilibria. The failure of some solution concepts to survive in larger games or tournaments does not imply they are never used.

Concluding remarks

Economic science uses and discovers social mechanisms, albeit in a complex fashion. As we have already seen, economic mechanisms involve different processes (e.g., filters, adjustments, and aggregation effects), explain different aspects of social outcomes (i.e., patterns, real outcomes, or both), rely on the concept of intention to varying degrees, and vary in their universality and their degree of explanatory and predictive power.

Despite the prominence of mechanisms in economics, the status of mechanism in economics is inherently fragile, probably due to the limitations of rational-choice theory itself. Neither pure theory nor empirical work has produced determinate guidelines for translating theoretical constructs into explanations of the real world. One prominent problem is the multiplicity of equilibria in formal game theory, which implies that almost any conceivable economic result can be explained in terms of a mechanism. I do not see any resolution of this methodological difficulty on the horizon.

Rather than rejecting the relevance of economics or the relevance of social mechanisms, I suggest that we reconsider how we evaluate economics. We cannot expect any single social science to provide definitive answers on its own. Rather, our "final theory" of the world is a composite of a variety of methods and disciplines, including economics, sociology, political science, philosophy, cognitive science, psychology, and other fields of research. These approaches often are conflicting or incommensurable. Our "final theory" of social reality therefore resists easy articulation, partly because its component parts are so diverse, and partly because modern social science is so young. Nonetheless we can judge economics, and other social sciences, in terms of their ability to contribute to our final understanding of the world. Using this standard, I would assign high marks to both economics and rational-choice sociology for their success in uncovering and analyzing social mechanisms.

References

Alchian, Armen A. 1950. "Uncertainty, Evolution, and Economic Theory." *Journal of Political Economy* 58(3):211–21.

Aumann, Robert J. 1985. "What is Game Theory Trying to Accomplish?" Pp. 28–76 in *Frontiers of Economics*. Edited by Kenneth J. Arrow and Seppo Honkapohja. New York: Basil Blackwell.

Axelrod, Robert. 1984. *The Evolution of Cooperation*. New York: Basic Books.

Becker, Gary. 1962. "Irrational Behavior and Economic Theory." *Journal of Political Economy* 70(1):1–13.

Binmore, Ken. 1990. *Essays on the Foundations of Game Theory*. Cambridge: Basil Blackwell.

Binmore, Ken. 1992. *Fun and Games: A Text on Game Theory*. Lexington, Mass.: D.C. Heath.

Black, Fischer. "Noise." 1986. *Journal of Finance* 41:529–43.

Boudon, Raymond. 1986. *Theories of Social Change: A Critical Appraisal*. Cambridge, England: Polity Press.

Cass, David, and Karl Shell. 1983. "Do Sunspots Matter?" *Journal of Political Economy* 91:193–227.

Coleman, James S. 1994. "A Rational Choice Perspective on Economic Sociology." Pp. 166–80 in *Handbook of Economic Sociology*. Edited by Neil J. Smelser and Richard Swedberg. Princeton: Princeton University Press.

Cordato, Roy. 1992. *Welfare Economics and Externalities in an Open Ended Universe*. Boston: Kluwer Academic Publishers.

Cowen, Tyler, and Amihai Glazer. 1996. "More Monitoring Can Induce Less Effort." *Journal of Economic Behavior and Organization* 30:113–23.

Cowen, Tyler, and Randall Kroszner. 1994. *Explorations in the New Monetary Economics*. New York: Basil Blackwell.

Dennett, Daniel. 1995. *Darwin's Dangerous Idea*. New York: Simon and Schuster.

Elster, Jon. 1989. *Nuts and Bolts for the Social Sciences*. Cambridge: Cambridge University Press.

Elster, Jon. 1996. "A Plea for Mechanisms." Presented at the "Mechanisms" Conference in Stockholm, June 1996, and revised for this volume.

Fisher, Franklin M. 1983. *The Disequilibrium Foundations of Equilibrium Economics*. Cambridge: Cambridge University Press.

Fisher, Franklin M. 1989. "Games Economists Play: A Noncooperative View." *Rand Journal of Economics* 20(1):113–24.

Fudenberg, Drew, and Jean Tirole. 1991. *Game Theory*. Cambridge: The MIT Press.

Gibbard, Alan, and Hal R. Varian. 1978. "Economic Models." *Journal of Philosophy* 75:664–77.

Green, Donald P., and Ian Shapiro. 1994. *Pathologies of Rational Choice Theory: A Critique of Applications in Political Science*. New Haven: Yale University Press.

Hausman, Daniel M. 1984. "Are General Equilibrium Theories Explanatory?" Pp. 344–59 in *The Philosophy of Economics: An Anthology*. Edited by Daniel M. Hausman. Cambridge: Cambridge University Press.

Hayek, Friedrich A. 1973–9. *Law, Legislation, and Liberty*, three volumes. Chicago: University of Chicago Press.

Hedström, Peter, and Richard Swedberg. 1995. "Social Mechanisms: Their Theoretical Status and Use in Sociology." Department of Sociology, Stockholm University, Working Paper No. 27.

Hirschman, Albert O. 1970. *Exit, Voice, and Loyalty: Responses to Decline in Firms, Organizations, and States*. Cambridge: Harvard University Press.

Hirshleifer, Jack, and Juan Carlos Martinez Coll. 1988. "What Strategies Can Support the Evolutionary Emergence of Cooperation?" *Journal of Conflict Resolution* 32(2):367–98.

Jacobs, Jane. 1961. *The Life and Death of Great American Cities*. New York: Random House.

Kareken, John H., and Neil Wallace. 1980. *Models of Monetary Economies*. Minnesota: Federal Reserve Bank of Minnesota.

Kreps, David. 1990. *A Course in Microeconomic Theory*. Princeton: Princeton University Press.

Lachmann, Ludwig M. 1977. *Capital, Expectations, and the Market Process*. Kansas City: Sheed, Andrews, and McMeel.

Levy, David M. 1985. "The Impossibility of a Complete Methodological Individualist Reduction When Knowledge is Imperfect." *Economics and Philosophy* 1:101–8.

Maynard Smith, John. 1982. *Evolution and the Theory of Games*. Cambridge: Cambridge University Press.

Merton, Robert K. 1936. "The Unintended Consequences of Purposive Social Action." *American Sociological Review*, 1: 894–904.

Merton, Robert K. 1968. *Social Theory and Social Structure*. New York: The Free Press.

Murphy, Kevin, Andrei Shleifer, and Robert Vishny. 1989. "The Big Push." *Journal of Political Economy* 97(5):1003–26.

Nelson, Alan. 1986a. "Explanation and Justification in Political Philosophy." *Ethics* 97:154–76.

Nelson, Alan. 1986b. "New Individualist Foundations for Economics." *Nous* 20: 469–90.

Nozick, Robert. 1974. *Anarchy, State and Utopia*. New York: Basic Books.

Peltzman, Sam. 1991. "The Handbook of Industrial Organization: A Review Article." *Journal of Political Economy* 99(1):201–17.

Posner, Richard A. 1992. *Sex and Reason*. Cambridge: Harvard University Press.

Posner, Richard A. 1995. *Aging and Old Age*. Chicago: University of Chicago Press.

Quine, Willard van Orman. 1960. *Word and Object*. Cambridge: MIT Press.

Reder, Melvin. 1982. "Chicago Economics: Permanence and Change." *Journal of Economic Literature* 20(1):1–38.

Rosenberg, Alexander. 1986. "The Explanatory Role of Existence Proofs." *Ethics* 97:177–87.

Rothbard, Murray N. 1977. *Towards a Reconstruction of Utility and Welfare Economics*. New York: Center for Libertarian Studies.

Schaffer, Mark. 1989. "Are Profit-Maximisers the Best Survivors?" *Journal of Economic Behavior and Organization* 29–45.

Schelling, Thomas C. 1978. *Micromotives and Macrobehavior*. New York: Norton.

Shackle, G. L. S. 1972. *Epistemics and Economics*. Cambridge: Cambridge University Press.

Stinchcombe, Arthur L. 1993. "The Conditions of Fruitfulness of Theorizing About Mechanisms in Social Science." Pp. 23–41 in *Social Theory and Social Policy: Essays in Honor of James S. Coleman*. Edited by Aage B. Sørensen and Seymour Spilerman. Westport, Conn.: Praeger.

Swedberg, Richard. 1994. "Markets as Social Structures." Pp. 255–82 in *Handbook of Economic Sociology*. Edited by Neil J. Smelser and Richard Swedberg. Princeton: Princeton University Press.

Taylor, Curtis R. 1995. "The Economics of Breakdowns, Checkups, and Cures." *Journal of Political Economy* 103(1):53–74.

Ullmann-Margalit, Edna. 1978. "Invisible Hand Explanations." *Synthese* 39:263–91.

Vernon, Richard. 1979. "Unintended Consequences." *Political Theory* 7:57–74.

Weibull, Jörgen W. 1995. *Evolutionary Game Theory*. Cambridge: MIT Press.

7. Social mechanisms of dissonance reduction

TIMUR KURAN

Dissonance and its antidotes

Within segments of the social sciences that are concerned with model building, the individual is commonly portrayed as a pleasure machine incapable of experiencing anguish, regret, guilt, or shame. Exploiting his opportunities to the fullest, this imagined individual suffers no discomfort over unavailable options or bygone choices. The construct has its uses, of course. Ordinarily, we experience no inner turmoil when choosing among restaurants, vacation spots, or investment strategies. Yet to experience anxiety over some of our choices is an essential element of what it is to be human. Many of the participants in the 1978 demonstrations that turned Iran into an economically contracting theocracy continue to question their fateful judgments and actions. Working parents endure persistent anxiety over allocating time between their children and their jobs. Members of ethnic, linguistic, religious, and cultural minorities routinely feel torn between cravings to assimilate and those to retain a distinct collective identity. For yet another example, employees commonly feel frustrated at having to turn a blind eye to the dishonest or unfair actions of their superiors.

What unites these substantively diverse examples is that they harbor choices capable of producing both prospective and retrospective discomfort; initially made with difficulty, the choices are then revisited and critiqued. Individually and collectively, such choices create a demand for discomfort prevention and alleviation. The purpose of this chapter is to

A draft of this paper was presented at the Conference on Social Mechanisms, held on June 6–7, 1996 at the Royal Academy of Sciences in Stockholm. I benefited from the comments of various conference participants, especially those of Andrew Abbott, Thomas Schelling, and Richard Swedberg.

examine some of the major social mechanisms that help meet this demand, with special attention to their interactions.

I use the term *dissonance*, shorthand for "decisional dissonance," to refer generically to the tensions that individuals experience because of their choices. As the foregoing examples indicate, the source of dissonance can vary. I distinguish, in particular, between *expressive dissonance*, which accompanies preference falsification, and *moral dissonance*, which stems from impractical or infeasible values. An example of expressive dissonance is the frustration a college administrator silently incurs over her politically expedient endorsement of an academically questionable curriculum change. And one of moral dissonance is the inner tensions that competing duties instill in a working parent. By no means are the two forms of dissonance mutually exclusive. Immigrants trying to assimilate without losing their ancestral identity can experience expressive dissonance for yielding to conformist pressures, and also moral dissonance for failing to do their share to uphold their cultural heritage.

I argue later that both types of dissonance are inevitable consequences of our social interactions. In living together, producing jointly and consuming collectively, we steadily generate new sources of dissonance and, hence, new demands for dissonance reduction. The demand is met partly as a by-product of efforts to accomplish other ends. Often, however, political, social, and moral entrepreneurs contribute to the process through efforts to make people comfortable with their past and future choices. Such efforts are not, of course, always successful. Depending on factors knowable only imperfectly, they may galvanize events that, while alleviating one form of dissonance, aggravate another. The emergence, operation, and effects of these interrelated mechanisms do not lend themselves to easy prediction. Partly because they involve intrapersonal processes, their dynamics and outcomes are harder to predict than to explain retrospectively. I begin by developing the meaning of expressive dissonance.

Expressive dissonance

In interacting with one another, people routinely encounter situations that place their private preferences in conflict. They respond by trying to reshape each other's private preferences, as when a person seeks to convince his neighbor that she would benefit from a tax hike to finance recreation programs for seniors. He cannot be certain of success, so he will try, in addition, to control his neighbor's relevant public preferences. By proposing that "only the selfish stand in the way of programs for seniors" and hinting that "selfish people get frowned at," he can make her believe that by publicizing her reservations she would tarnish her social standing. In the interest of avoiding negative reactions, the neighbor may choose, therefore, to engage in preference falsification. She can do so by endorsing the planned intergenerational transfers and concealing her misgivings.

In *Private Truths, Public Lies* (1995), I examined, among certain other consequences of preference falsification, the resulting social inefficiencies. A byproduct of hiding one's qualms about a policy is to intensify the social pressures that weigh on others choosing what preferences to communicate. And the induced incentives may produce an equilibrium whereby most people publicly support a policy that few favor privately; they may result, in other words, in a public opinion sharply at odds with private opinion. My interest here is not in the dynamics of this inefficiency-fostering process; it lies in the social mechanisms that lighten the resulting psychological tensions.

As individuals, we derive satisfaction from being our own persons, from pursuing our own goals rather than those of others, from expressing our wishes truthfully. In earlier works, I have referred to such satisfaction as *expressive utility*. If x represents a person's private preference among a set of options and y his public preference, his expressive utility is maximized when $y = x$, in which case he incurs no expressive dissonance. If he picks y to be anything other than x, he fails to maximize his expressive utility, thus experiencing dissonance. For any chosen public preference, then, his expressive dissonance is the absolute value of $D_E = E(x, y) - E(x, x)$, where $E(\cdot)$ is a function declining in the distance between its two arguments.

A person bent on maximizing expressive utility would avoid preference falsification and experience no expressive dissonance. As a practical matter, however, expressive utility forms but a component of the total utility stemming from the choice of a public preference. The chooser will derive *reputational utility* from the reactions of others, and *intrinsic utility* from any substantive effects of the choice itself. In maximizing the *sum* of these forms of utility, the individual may well make a selection that generates expressive dissonance. To revisit an earlier example, if the neighbor being pressured to endorse a tax hike opts to protect her reputation, she will maintain good social relations but only at the expense of expressive utility.[1]

In every society, the extent and distribution of expressive dissonance varies from issue to issue. At one extreme are issues that produce practically no expressive dissonance. An example is the matter of whether highways should be paved: Genuine agreement being nearly universal, people do not feel pressured to conform to a public opinion at odds with their private preferences. Another example is whether the referees of football (soccer) games should return to wearing exclusively black uniforms; sentiments differ, but few of those who care about the matter feel compelled to conceal their preferences. At the opposite extreme are issues that exhibit widespread preference falsification. When a political position gets associated with national honor or survival, there are usually many who mute their contrary views for fear of being considered unpatriotic.

The dissipation of expressive dissonance through internalization

The very social mechanism that produces persistent expressive dissonance on a wide scale generates feedback effects tending to dampen the discomfort. These effects hinge on the important role that public discourse plays in shaping our private understandings and preferences. The distortion of public discourse through preference falsification may lighten expressive resentments by reducing, if not eliminating, people's exposure to facts and arguments in conflict with their private preferences. The corrections would not occur overnight, of course. A person who chooses to hide her reservations about an instituted intergenerational transfer program will not lose her qualms automatically. Especially if the media continue to pay attention to the case against transfers, her private opposition might persist indefinitely. However, the intensity of her ill feelings may well diminish as a result of her greater exposure to arguments favoring the transfers. Al-

---

[1] Whether her intrinsic utility gets affected will depend on the role that her own public preference plays in shaping the forms and magnitudes of intergenerational transfers. Because huge numbers of voters, bureaucrats, media workers, and politicians participate in the relevant policy decisions, her personal influence on the substantive outcome is likely to be negligible. Her intrinsic utility may thus be considered essentially fixed.

though these arguments are unlikely to make her forget the counterarguments, they will at least weaken her preexisting beliefs.

Every society's composition changes over time through births, deaths, and migration. Sooner or later, the individuals inclined to dislike the instituted transfers will be replaced, therefore, by newcomers who were not present at the time of the program's adoption. Insofar as public discourse shapes their private knowledge and preferences – other factors will also play a role – the paucity of arguments against the established program will condition them to accept it unthinkingly. Some of them may not even realize that there is an issue worthy of reflection and debate: They may consider it natural for working generations to subsidize the retired and equally natural for the poverty rate to be higher for children than for seniors. The relative merits of the alternative social arrangements need not concern us here. The relevant point is the existence of a social mechanism tending to make preference falsification self-correcting. At least over the long run, expressive dissonance need not be permanent.

The outlined self-correction mechanism, which is developed in *Private Truths, Public Lies*, does not occur through planning. Although people with insight into the workings of social systems may grasp the long-term effects of preference falsification, the mechanism operates through the decisions that individuals make merely for their own short-term advantages. Ordinarily, it will operate alongside countermechanisms. Higher taxes on workers may reduce their incentives to work and their readiness to bear children; the consequent shrinkage of the tax base may then foster budget deficits, accentuating the competition for government-controlled resources and focusing attention on the proper limits of forced redistribution. Lulled into contentment by years of insincere public discourse, people may one day find themselves awakened, therefore, by its substantive costs. The attention-enhancing effects of this countermechanism may eventually overtake the attention-suppressing effects that operate through public discourse. Accordingly, aggregate expressive dissonance may follow a U-shaped trajectory – falling for some time, then rising.

My illustration should not be taken to mean that the byproducts of preference falsification are necessarily harmful. A common theme in the literature on the Islamic world's economic evolution is that, even as European attitudes toward commerce, profit making, and competition underwent the fundamental changes that culminated in the Industrial Revolution,

Muslim traders tended to remain wedded to the Medieval economic attitudes epitomized by the fraternal, anticompetitive rules of the guilds. The shock waves of Europe's economic transformation eventually made ambitious Muslim traders switch to new ways of doing business. There were initially loud objections to such traders, but as they gained market share from guildsmen, the latter started muting their public complaints. In particular, they began treating as virtues acts that they actually continued to consider vices.[2] The resulting expressive dissonance promoted the Muslim world's economic modernization. Insofar as its effects are measured by economic growth, it produced, then, a major social benefit. In any case, with individuals coming to see aggressive profit seeking as normal, it has self-dissipated.

Reduction in expressive dissonance through revolt

The key point thus far is that the expressive dissonance generated by preference falsification can disappear through the internalization of understandings and sentiments once only feigned. There is another social mechanism capable of overcoming such dissonance: social revolt that exposes knowledge and feelings that had tended to be concealed.

Let us reconsider a self-sustaining distribution of public preferences that rests substantially on preference falsification – a public opinion that differs dramatically from the underlying private opinion. The very existence of individuals privately unhappy with what they profess to want implies the equilibrium's vulnerability to shifts in reputational incentives. Indeed, given the pervasiveness of expressive dissonance, there will be people waiting for the right conditions to make their misgivings public. If such people somehow detect a sufficient decline in the punishments imposed on those making their dislikes public, they will switch sides. In so doing, they will dampen the incentives against displaying public opposition: With the number of vocal opponents growing, members of the public opposition will feel less isolated and possibly less threatened. This change in reputational incentives may encourage others to join the public opposition, whose switches may then galvanize further switches. What I have described is a revolutionary bandwagon process through which public opin-

---

[2] The best source on the Muslim world's preindustrial economic norms is Ülgener (1981); Lewis (1993, Chs. 16 and 27) describes the transformation. See my 1997 piece for additional references and a broader interpretation.

ion shifts dramatically following an intrinsically minor perturbation to reputational incentives.

To the extent that public opinion gets transformed through personal decisions to be truthful, aggregate expressive dissonance will fall. With people who had been pretending to favor the status quo ante now openly supporting change, their expressive dissonance will diminish, thus lowering aggregate expressive dissonance. Sudden overturns in public opinion often generate widespread joy and relief. For example, when a privately hated but long publicly supported government suddenly gets overthrown through a groundswell of public opposition, there is a period of euphoria characterized by vociferous denunciations of the fallen government and exalted forecasts of better days ahead. The same pattern is observed within organizations whose leaders, long quietly resented for their corruption, suddenly resign in disgrace because, say, the authorities overseeing their actions found the moment politically ripe for a crackdown.

In outlining the bandwagon process that propels a major shift in public opinion, I left unexplained the change in reputational incentives that pushes it into motion. A revolutionary bandwagon might get activated by a natural disaster, like a flood that breeds ill will against leaders suspected of negligence. It can also be activated by a coincidence of social events, such as a series of economic decisions that unintentionally produce a recession. But shifts in public opinion can also be driven, at least partly, by the planned actions of astute political activists. Just as an engineer who notices the softness of the soil beneath a house will know that even a moderate earthquake would topple it, so a talented political player might sense the fragility of an apparent near-consensus. Linking up with the declared supporters of change, he may set up a revolutionary organization that seeks both to educate and to lessen the incentives against vocalizing opposition to the status quo. Although no one can know exactly what it would take to activate the revolution, the organization can take steps to increase the status quo's fragility. If its plans bear fruit, the revolution that reduces the expressive dissonance of many individuals will have occurred through a mechanism that was at least partially constructed.

In reducing some people's expressive dissonance, a revolutionary shift in public opinion may well heighten the dissonance of others. In fact, it may well raise aggregate expressive dissonance. This is because the very mechanism that lowers the reputational incentives to support the status quo ante heightens those to oppose it. Accordingly, in the course of a revolution, people genuinely happy with the established arrangements will feel increasingly pressured to feign approval of the ongoing transformation. Their expressive dissonance may increase, therefore, just as that of the sincere supporters of change is decreasing. The net change in aggregate expressive dissonance will depend, then, on the balance of the two effects. But the essential point is that conditions exist under which a revolutionary bandwagon will lower aggregate dissonance.

The two social mechanisms that I have identified as vehicles for dampening expressive dissonance work at cross-purposes. Where internalization involves adjustments that generally reinforce the preestablished equilibrium,[3] revolt entails adjustments that destroy it. The two mechanisms differ also in regard to the variables that they burden with adjustment. Internalization works on private preferences, revolt, primarily on public preferences. The mechanisms differ, finally, in regard to time span. Where internalization often takes generations to run its course, a revolution might occur very quickly and at any time after an equilibrium's establishment.

Insofar as the passage of time fosters internalization, the likelihood of revolution diminishes. This is because a lessening of expressive dissonance lowers the hidden demand for change. The observation raises the question of whether the effects of these mechanisms are predictable and fully explicable. I will offer an answer in the essay's final section, but only after exploring the sources and alleviation of moral dissonance.

Moral dissonance

In addition to the strains that accompany preference falsification, people experience stresses rooted in moral conflicts. The latter form of psychological discomfort, moral dissonance, may occur even in the absence of any expressive constraints.

Moral dissonance arises when one's values are impractical or infeasible. One feels obligated to achieve a goal, satisfy a limit, or abide by a standard; yet one's preferences steer one away from these objectives. Alternatively, the objectives prove unattainable, because one's resources are limited. The values that form a person's moral system or morality rank his preferences, and they judge the actions that his preferences induce. By

---

[3] Under certain conditions, which I have specified elsewhere, the equilibrium will become more extreme.

this account, values are both metapreferences – preferences over preferences – and judges of behavior. They need not be realistic. A devoted mother may feel guilty over the little time she spends away from her children; and she may blame herself for her children's failures. The source of her moral dissonance is that her expectations of herself are too stringent relative to human capabilities. Such *moral overload* can also be generated by values that are incompatible. Consider a shopkeeper who feels obligated, on the one hand, to be strictly honest in his dealings with customers and, on the other, to provide his children certain comforts and privileges. Given his talents and market opportunities, he is able to meet his self-defined parental duty only by overbilling his customers. Were he to keep his business totally honest, his income would fall short of what he requires to give his children the lifestyle he considers essential.

Moral overload is a sufficient but not a necessary condition for moral dissonance. It may be that the shopkeeper is capable of meeting both his values, yet his preferences are such that he overbills his customers anyway. Where expressive dissonance results from failure to express oneself truthfully, moral dissonance thus stems from failure to abide by one's personal morality. The former measures unachieved expressive utility, the latter unachieved moral utility. Let x^m, the individual's *moral base*, represent the action or set of actions that would just satisfy each of the values that form his morality. And let x^c be the choice or set of choices that he reaches by maximizing his intrinsic utility function subject to his resource constraints. In the illustration involving a tradeoff between honesty and standard of living, each of these variables has two dimensions: $x^m = [x^{m1}, x^{m2}]$ and $x^c = [x^{c1}, x^{c2}]$. In terms of this notation, his moral dissonance is $D_M = M(x^m, x^c)$, where $M(\cdot)$ is a function that is increasing in the distances between x^{c^i} and x^{m^i}, for each dimension i for which the moral base is unsatisfied. D_M would be nil for someone whose choice x^c met all his relevant values. It would be positive if, say, x^{c2} fell short of x^{m2}.

In the classical model of decision making, the individual maximizes a unitary utility function subject to a resource constraint. He has no values to satisfy, no inner goals that he must achieve to feel at peace with himself. Accordingly, he does not experience anguish or guilt over his actions. If his resources are very tight, he consumes little and perhaps dreams of having more, but he does not feel that he has failed morally; having tried to derive maximum utility from his resources, he does not feel that he *should* have done better. The framework proposed here superimposes on the classical framework a personal morality – a set of internal standards that the individual must meet to retain a good conscience. Facing a tradeoff between professional honesty and his children's well-being, he need not, having made a choice, feel satisfied that he simply did his best. If his resources are sufficiently limited, he will inevitably feel guilty for behaving dishonestly, failing to meet his parental obligations, or both.[4]

I am thus proposing that the individual has not one but two rankings. Neither ranking has anything to do with how an outside observer might judge them. A father may feel morally obligated to give his daughter a lucrative education, just as he may feel a moral duty to keep her at home as a means of shielding her from what he considers adverse cultural influences; in either case, his feeling constitutes a value that he must meet to keep his conscience clear. Likewise, he may or may not enjoy educating his daughter; whatever we ourselves think of him, his satisfaction, or its absence, points to a preference ordering. The example shows that the distinction between values and preferences has nothing to do with their perceived social advantages. Whatever our own criteria, both preferences and values can be socially beneficial, and both can be socially harmful.

The distinction between the two constructs is not trivial: Although values are never binding, the moral dissonance that they generate can have socially significant repercussions. A morally dissonant person is someone who feels unsettled and, hence, in need of assistance. As the next section will show, this need constitutes a force for social, cultural, and even civilizational change. Moral dissonance is not, of course, the only source of discomfort that we strive to alleviate. We try also to relax our resource constraints, as when a worker, finding her income insufficient to purchase a car, works overtime to raise her income. In contrast to this example, lessening moral dissonance is not a task that ordinarily one achieves unilaterally. We shall see that some major mechanisms for reducing moral dissonance are essentially social rather than personal.

Insofar as we have values that judge our preferences and achievements, they raise the question of why. The most basic probable reason, developed by Robert Frank (1988), lies in human evolution. In the conditions under

---

[4] The notion that human values create inner strains is in itself not new. It was encapsulated by the ancient idea of a Pantheon – a temple housing many gods competing with one another for influence. Over the past century, numerous sociologists have written on what I am calling "moral dissonance," though under different characterizations. For instance, Merton (1968, pp. 348–9) uses the term "ambivalence" to describe the concept. For these observations, I am grateful to Richard Swedberg.

which most of our ancestors lived, personal survival was contingent upon successful cooperation with others, whether in hunting, predation, or defense. Hence, individuals were steadily on the lookout for signs of trustworthiness. A person who appeared guilty upon failing to help a distressed tribe member would, all else being equal, seem a less risky partner than one who gave no indication of having a moral sense. Values involving honesty, sympathy, fairness, and self-control, along with the outer signs of moral dissonance, may thus have become hardwired into the human species because they advanced genetic fitness. Certain specific values, like those associated with parenting, might have gotten disseminated through a similar, yet distinct, genetic mechanism: higher survival rates for the offspring of caring parents relative to those of uncaring parents. This evolutionary mechanism need not, however, have wiped out all values that we would characterize as selfish or antisocial. Because the outward signs of inner turmoil are imperfect, selfish values could have survived, although they would have become less common than altruistic ones.

Ethnographers have documented how the exact content of our values varies across time, across space, and across individuals. Some, like Robert Edgerton (1992), have shown that the dominant values of a society can become dysfunctional, endangering its very existence. But the essential point is that we have a moral sense. The meaning of good parenting may vary enormously, as may interpretations of commercial honesty, fairness among friends, and proper self-control. Yet, as James Q. Wilson (1993) observes, the existence of a moral sense is universal. A contemporary mother might regret placing her children in daycare; her great grandmother might have felt guilty instead for failing to feed her children adequately. Although the perceived failings are different, they both stem from a deep-seated sense of parental duty.

Taking as given the existence of moral dissonance, the next section will turn to the social mechanisms that lessen it. Note that moral and expressive dissonance are not mutually exclusive. They will be present simultaneously if social pressures make it imprudent to vocalize one's values honestly. Consider a person whose chosen action, x^c, leaves x^m unmet, thus generating moral dissonance. He happens to find it prudent, because of social pressures, to pretend that he aspires to no more than x^c. With his *public* moral base, y^m, set at x^c, he will experience both moral and expressive dissonance. It is possible, too, for all three variables to differ. A member of an organization might consider it too risky to express disgust at the corruption of her superiors, pretending that her own standards of honesty are somewhat lower than they actually are. Her own behavior may fall short, however, even of the looser standards that she chooses to articulate; wanting to support her family, she might take bribes in a broader array of cases than even her expressed standards would justify.

Moral dissonance reduction through rationalization and redemption

Moral dissonance results, we have seen, from a combination of biological factors and social forces. We all have an innate capacity to carry values, and some of our specific values are inborn. But social forces influence, and in some contexts determine, how values are interpreted. Behind the social forces lie pressure groups that consider moral education a cheap instrument for achieving their own objectives. Such pressure groups do not coordinate their educational activities; costs of communication and negotiation preclude a comprehensive coordination even in autocracies, and in democracies coordination is not even attempted. Lack of coordination is a leading contributor to moral dissonance.[5] If one pressure group is concerned with parenting, another with professional honesty, and still others with fairness, the social safety net, and professional standards, there will be members of society whose circumstances keep them from satisfying all of the diverse values that they have internalized.

A complementary problem stems from resource inequalities. Although efforts are made to tailor values to individual circumstances, as when a religion teaches that the rich have disproportionate obligations toward disaster victims, the tailoring can never be sufficiently fine to prevent moral dissonance. Inevitably, there will be individuals who develop values that they cannot satisfy fully. Yet another problem is that people's opportunities keep changing even after their values have taken shape. Consider a small-town trader who has adopted standards of fairness and honesty that he can easily satisfy. With changing economic conditions, he moves to a metropolis, where he finds that for economic survival he must conceal the defects of his merchandise and charge what the market will bear – behaviors that he had learned to consider dishonest. The compromises make him experience moral dissonance.

---

[5] This point is developed in my forthcoming paper.

The most obvious way to alleviate this dissonance would be for the former trader's infeasible value to adapt to his new opportunities. Relevant here is a large literature on the personal efforts people undertake to cope with their internal inconsistencies. Leon Festinger's classic, *A Theory of Cognitive Dissonance* (1957), presented evidence that when people hold inconsistent cognitions, the resulting dissonance makes them try to eliminate the inconsistency. One possible remedy is selective exposure to information. Within the context of moral dissonance, our focus here, it would take the form of avoiding information likely to provide reminders of one's moral failures and seeking information about one's successes. Subsequent research, reviewed by John Cotton (1985), has emphasized that, while selective exposure is hardly a spurious phenomenon, its effectiveness is plainly limited. To this day, Cotton adds, we have learned little about why people differ in their abilities to benefit from selective exposure.

In any case, from the fact that moral dissonance can be a widespread problem whose eventual alleviation often comes through social means, one can infer that selective exposure is not always effective. One can also infer that discarding dissonance-generating values is not a simple task. In the spirit of La Fontaine's fox who called the grapes he could not reach sour, the peasant settling in a city might *want* to dismiss his now-infeasible values as old-fashioned. But he may not be able to do so: Migrants commonly experience problems of adjustment, including the feeling that their new conditions make it impossible to live morally. As a practical matter, the ability to change one's own values intentionally is limited. For reasons that Jon Elster (1983) identifies in relation to preferences and beliefs in general, values often change either through social means or as by-products of actions that individuals take for other purposes.

A commonly used personal coping mechanism involves *rationalization*: Remaining committed to upholding one's values, one redefines what the task requires. The small-town trader who moves to the city will not just abandon his commitment to being fair; rather, he will redefine the concept of fair commercial behavior in a way to make the value easier to fulfill. In his initial location, he considered it unfair, say, to raise his prices in response to a shortage; the practice was easy to follow, for it offered him reciprocal benefits in the form of pricing restraint on the part of his own suppliers. With such reciprocal benefits now essentially gone because of the complexity and relative anonymity of metropolitan economic relations, the opportunity cost of restraint becomes too high. So he redefines short-age-induced price increases as compensation for the costs of inventory replacement. Insofar as the rationalization works, his moral dissonance falls.

Our trader's efforts to redefine fairness are more likely to succeed if most other traders respond similarly to their own moral dissonance than if the preponderance continues exercising restraint. Aggressive pricing on the part of others will make it easier for him to justify his own price adjustments as a business necessity.[6] Reasoning that so many people could not all be immoral, he can feel more confident that urban commodity shortages differ qualitatively from rural ones. If it appears, however, that most traders are showing restraint, he will have reason to doubt his judgment. By the logic that his fellow traders would not pass up opportunities for windfall profits unless such gains were immoral, he will endure guilt.

Campaigns to alleviate the moral dissonance experienced by one social group need not be limited to that particular group. Religious, moral, and legal experts may provide new rationalizations or bolster existing ones. In times and places where interest was commonly considered sinful, moral entrepreneurs have devised ruses to enable people to give and take interest in roundabout ways. One such ruse, fashionable in the Medieval Muslim world, allowed a person to lend at interest by buying from the borrower an object for a certain sum and immediately returning it for a larger sum, payable at some future date. The ongoing revival of the Islamic ban of interest has generated a fresh supply of ruses aimed at helping the pious cope with the difficulties of abiding by the prohibition. In the Islamic Republic of Iran, for example, prominent clerics have decreed that when a financial transaction between two government agencies occurs at a fixed rate of return, no interest is involved. The proposed logic is that all government agencies represent the same entity – the people – and an entity cannot lend to itself. The purpose of the rationalization has been to reduce the moral dissonance experienced by devout government employees.[7]

There exist additional mechanisms for lessening moral dissonance through collectively supplied means. One can provide guilt-ridden individuals opportunities to redeem themselves through donations, community

---

[6] This is an application of the heuristic of social proof, discussed in Kuran (1995, Ch. 10).

[7] On this ruse and others, see my 1993 article, pp. 308–17. The article examines also the initial rationale for the prohibition of interest.

service, penance, confession, political activism, and voting, among other possibilities. Redemption mechanisms require its designers to convince the potential beneficiaries of their viability, of course. Specifically, the beneficiaries must believe that failure to satisfy a particular value can legitimately be compensated through the designated means. Accordingly, the developers of guilt-alleviation mechanisms are generally among the important contributors to moral discourse. As Jean Delumeau ([1983] 1990), Robert Ekelund, Robert Hébert, and Robert Tollison (1992), and others, have documented, the Medieval Church promoted the idea that one could make up for sins through generosity and the purchase of indulgences. In the same vein, modern politicians strive to give moral significance to votes cast for them. By presenting issues like racial equality, abortion, and the environment as matters of right and wrong – clashing values as opposed to clashing preferences – political candidates enable morally distressed voters to gain comfort through the act of voting.

The gist of this section is that widespread moral dissonance generates socially provided, supported, and legitimated vehicles for helping individuals achieve inner peace. The prevalence of such mechanisms hardly implies, of course, that societies are able to rid themselves of psychological tension. Just as the tendency for markets to clear does not mean that they always do, so the existence of mechanisms for rationalization and redemption allow the indefinite persistence of moral overload. In any case, there is never a shortage of groups trying to promote new values that conflict with old values or with the prevailing preference orderings. Moreover, changing conditions are always producing new issues that generate clashes among previously compartmentalized values. As a case in point, the ongoing environmental movement is making people feel guilty for activities they once considered perfectly ethical. And it is making people relate their consumption and production choices to the planet's survival; not long ago, nature was considered too vast and too powerful to be vulnerable to human excesses.

Moral reconstruction

Rationalization and redemption make it cheaper to satisfy a fixed set of values. An alternative remedy for widespread dissonance is reconstruction of the moralities that people harbor. Ordinarily, individuals cannot accomplish this task by themselves, for they cannot control public discourse. In practice, the task requires collective action. And, as such, it is vulnerable to free riding: Because its benefits would accrue mostly to others, individuals may find the relevant personal efforts too costly in relation to their own expected benefits. Often, however, there is a mitigating factor stemming from the multiplicity of potential solutions. If there is more than one way to restructure a society's moral system, many of its individual members will have a stake in the particulars of reform.[8] One is likely to observe, therefore, the emergence of multiple pressure groups competing over the content of the moral reconstruction. At odds over the meaning of right and wrong, the groups will endeavor to eliminate values that others are trying to preserve, agreeing only that society is in *moral crisis*.

Europe's moral transformation that culminated in the Protestant Reformation offers an example of a moral crisis solved through intense political struggles over the definition of good and evil. As Nathan Rosenberg and L. E. Birdzell (1986, Ch. 4), Albert Hirschman (1977), and others have discussed, the expansion of European trade in the late Medieval era made it increasingly difficult for traders to live by the economic morality of the Church. They were forming attachments to economic enterprises based less and less on small-group solidarity and increasingly on individual profit; yet the Church continued to define economic virtue in terms of the pursuit of group benefits and to treat economic success as a reflection of character defects. The consequent moral dissonance fueled the political contest that spawned the Reformation. Although certain Reformation leaders fought to strengthen Church dogma on economic matters, it ended up legitimizing the rapidly spreading economic practices, enabling producers and traders to carry on their activities without developing guilt.

European struggles over defining economic virtue did not end, of course, with the Reformation. Even today, all branches of Christianity harbor strains hostile to economic individualism. And pressure groups formed primarily for economic reasons, like socialist parties of the industrial era, have pursued anti-individualist moral agendas as part of their political strategies.[9] With their educational campaigns influencing both economic values and economic preferences, the result has been the aggravation of moral dissonance related to economic behavior – the opposite

---

[8] This mitigating factor exists in other contexts, too. For a general analysis, see Hardin (1982, Ch. 5).

[9] Anti-individualism has taken two forms: communalism and collectivism. Oakeshott ([1958] 1993) contrasts them with individualism.

of what the Reformation achieved. The depiction of capitalists as "blood-suckers" serves to preserve the questionable moral status of individual profit seeking, much like the 16th-century north European proverb that treated usurers, millers, bankers, and tax farmers as "the four evangelists of Lucifer."[10]

For another example of a moral crisis that has occasioned attempts and counterattempts at moral reconstruction, let us move to the Islamic world. Ever since it became clear that the West had overtaken Islamic civilization militarily and economically, efforts to emulate the West's economic productivity have kept Muslims in touch with Western values, including individualism. Given Islam's communalist tendencies, a lasting consequence has been widespread moral dissonance, as in Europe in earlier times. Indeed, for over a century, diverse writers have characterized Islamic civilization as suffering from a moral crisis rooted in incongruities between, on the one hand, certain traditional values associated with Islam and, on the other, some of the new values derived from contacts with the West.[11] The crisis has generated competing attempts to discard one set of values as a means of strengthening the status of the other. Atatürk in Turkey, the Pahlavis in Iran, and Bourgiba in Tunisia sought to lessen inner conflicts through Westernization. By contrast, Iran's Khomeini endeavored to draw Muslims away from the West; when he quipped that "the Iranian revolution was not made to make watermelons more plentiful," he meant that, as far as he was concerned, the revolution's primary mission was moral and cultural rather than economic and political.[12] The struggle between the two camps, Westernizers and Islamists, continues to be fought throughout the Islamic world. The Westernizers accuse the Islamists of suffering from "Orientatis" – the disease of Eastern traditionalism. For their part, the Islamists portray the Westernizers as victims of "Occidentosis" – the malady of blind Westernism.[13]

My final example of moral reconstruction has accompanied the massive rise in the share of women in the paid workforce. This social transformation has unfolded over the past half-century against a background of

[10] I owe the last example to John Montias.
[11] For a statement by a prominent Islamist, see Maududi ([1940] 1985). Shayegan ([1989] 1992) offers similar observations from a Westernizer's perspective. See Ayubi (1991, Chs. 2–3) for a comparative analysis.
[12] This was not an isolated remark. See my 1993 paper, pp. 303–8.
[13] For a spirited polemic against Occidentosis, see Al-Ahmad ([1964] 1982). Published in Iran, this book was banned by the Shah's regime, which correctly saw itself under attack.

values that evolved in times when women tended to stay at home and carried primary responsibility for raising children. Working women have found it difficult to continue satisfying those values along with the new ones that they have acquired as professionals. In particular, they have found it emotionally draining, if not practically impossible, to reconcile the responsibilities of parenthood with those of pursuing a steady and serious career. Feminism has been one response to this moral crisis. Various strands of feminism have promoted moral reconstruction in seeking to legitimize childcare outside the home, calling for husbands to assume greater household duties, trying to make the professions gender-neutral, and seeking to eradicate moral obstacles to abortion. As in previous examples, there have been countercampaigns. Certain conservative religions have tried to reinvigorate traditional values and delegitimize the new ones.[14] Intellectuals who recognize the genetic foundations of human values are cautioning that psychological differences between the sexes, including differences in aggression and cognitive skills, make the feminist agenda infeasible.[15] And within feminism itself, a submovement is promoting the view that women deserve professional advancement not because their abilities are identical to those of men but because they are not.

If several values are jointly causing moral overload, the problem can be lightened by eliminating one or more elements of the system. This form of reconstruction constitutes *uniform simplification*. A less extreme form of reconstruction, *variable simplification*, involves limiting the situations to which each value applies. An extreme form of variable simplification is *moral compartmentalization*, which relegates the incompatible values to separate spheres of activity. Moral compartmentalization can be *contextual*, as when a person feels bound by one set of values at work and another at home. It can be *temporal*, as when one feels obligated to abide by religious precepts on certain days, feeling free to ignore them on others. It can also be *locational*, as when one considers it acceptable to litter the sidewalk when walking in a rundown neighborhood but not when walking in a posh part of town.

For moral compartmentalization to work, a person must be able to par-

---

[14] Focusing on the United States, Hunter (1991, especially Ch. 7) offers many insights into the struggle over gender roles. He makes a convincing case that this struggle has contributed to a major realignment in American politics. See also Haeri (1992) and Hardacre (1992) for complementary observations.
[15] Popenoe (1995) argues that in weakening the father's duty to provide for his family feminism has strained the institution of marriage and harmed children.

tition his choices into mutually exclusive domains that invoke different values or sets of values. The task might be impossible if others are behaving in ways that do not respect one's chosen compartments. If Muslim Cairenes tend to interrupt their work for afternoon prayers, the individual Muslim employee will find it harder to consider his worship obligations met by attending mosque services just once a week on Friday. Encountering daily evidence of his religious lapses, he will experience moral dissonance. By contrast, if his fellow employees are all avoiding public religious displays, he will find it relatively easy to treat his work as free of religious significance. This observation is supported by Daniel Kahneman and Amos Tversky's (1984) finding that the "framing" of choices has consequences. Just as an individual's willingness to pay for a therapy depends on whether its outcome is described in terms of mortality or survival, his perceived religious obligations during work hours will reflect the apparent values of his officemates.

Uniform and variable moral simplifications sometimes serve as complementary, rather than rival, forms of moral reconstruction. One can discard some of the values within a burdensome moral system, relegating the rest to compartmentalized domains. As a case in point, Atatürk's secularization campaign used a combination of repression and education to restructure Turkish Islam. For example, it employed state-approved sermons and manuals to promote an interpretation of Islam compatible with expanding women's rights. At the same time, it treated religion as irrelevant beyond the personal sphere; the workplace, for instance, was to be free of religious displays. Islamists have been disputing both the revisionist interpretation of Islam and the restrictions on its domain of authority.

Implications for social forecasting and explanation

I have not provided a comprehensive account of the mechanisms that alleviate moral dissonance. A morally troubled society could also respond by splitting into several societies with separate moral systems, thus allowing its members to lighten their moral loads in diverse ways. This response, *social segmentation*, might unfold when multiple moral reforms are being advanced and individuals differ in their predispositions toward the form of resolution. For it to succeed, contacts across the new, smaller societies must be minimal; otherwise, individual exposure to dissonance-increasing values would remain substantial. Where subsocieties with different moral systems are already in existence, the segmentation can also be accomplished through individual escape. Morally overburdened people, hoping to simplify their personal moral systems, might move to a subsociety whose dominant values appear more manageable than their own.[16] A fuller analysis of moral dissonance reduction would address such additional possibilities[17] and draw out their implications. One implication is that some forms of structural complexity make it easier to cope with moral diversity; another is that the happiness of a person with a given moral history will depend on the moral discourse to which he gets exposed.

But even the limited analysis of the preceding two sections captures the factors essential to the implications to be drawn in this concluding section. The multiplicity of the mechanisms for lightening moral dissonance complicates the task of forecasting the resolution of moral dissonance. One obstacle to sound prediction is that the mechanisms for lightening moral dissonance can undermine one another, reducing their total effect below the sum of their parts. Campaigns to create redemption opportunities may weaken the effectiveness of moral reconstruction efforts. In particular, individuals subjected to incessant calls to do penance for behaviors characterized as sinful may become resistant to the countermessage that those behaviors are perfectly ethical. Likewise, escape can undermine moral reconstruction by reducing the size of its natural constituency. If individuals most likely to support the elimination of a certain value decide instead to emigrate, the constituency for this moral reconstruction will be that much smaller.[18]

Another obstacle to prediction is that the various determinants of moral dissonance interact with those of expressive dissonance. Mechanisms that reduce expressive dissonance may end up aggravating, even generating, certain forms of moral dissonance, and vice versa. Every society produces abundant issues on which some people's private preferences come into conflict with those of others; attempts to resolve the clashes generate social pressures that result in preference falsification. The falsification produces expressive dissonance, and it also distorts the relevant public discourse, including its moral component. If this public discourse then remains es-

---

[16] Escape is a form of selective exposure predicated on the dependence of personal values on social influences.

[17] Some further observations are made in Kuran (forthcoming).

[18] The argument is analogous to Hirschman's (1970) insight that "exit" often weakens "voice."

sentially undisturbed for a sufficiently long time, the values that it promotes may get widely internalized. These values may well conflict with other common values, so an unintended byproduct of the internalization process might be new forms of moral dissonance. The same outcome could arise, of course, if revolt rather than internalization were the mechanism for alleviating expressive dissonance. The consequent change in public discourse could promote values that clash with preexisting ones.

The moral crisis that results from either internalization or revolt will produce, in turn, a new set of political struggles. To reduce moral dissonance, efforts will be made to reinterpret certain values, even to discard them altogether. Struggles will arise over the form of moral reconstruction, and the consequent social pressures may drive certain values underground. We have now come full circle, with politically induced expressive dissonance fueling moral dissonance, and with attempts to alleviate moral dissonance then generating expressive dissonance. Such a circular process may carry on indefinitely, especially if natural events, innovations, and cross-societal contacts are constantly reshaping individual utility functions. New sources of dissonance will generate reactions that create further sources, even as they extinguish others.

Circularity always complicates prediction. If every element within a system affects other elements, and those others produce feedback effects, the information necessary for knowing the long-term consequences of a given perturbation is enormous. Circularity does not mean, however, that political struggles must remain resistant to analysis. Observers with a good sense of the relevant social mechanisms can identify a society's politically sensitive issues; they can distinguish between public statements that bring rewards and ones that bring punishments; and if a political taboo suddenly vanishes, they can make sense of both the speed and the surprise. Likewise, if large numbers end up internalizing a value that public discourse has long favored, knowledgeable observers will understand the role that public discourse has played. They will also understand the incompatibilities responsible for a moral crisis. From the writings, goals, and pronouncements of the participants in moral struggles, they will be able to determine what is at stake for people's inner lives.

It is one thing to understand the social mechanisms at play, and quite another to make accurate forecasts of a social system's evolution. Many participants in the struggles over Church teachings knew what they were fighting for, and they understood what their efforts could accomplish. But they had no way of knowing how Europe's economic morality would actually evolve. The same point can be made with respect to the ongoing struggles over gender roles and over Islam's domain. The participants in these contests understand the immediate implications of the moral agendas that they are defending as well as those of the ones they are opposing; but none can know how the struggles will be resolved, to say nothing of identifying the chain effects of their own efforts.

In earlier writings, I have pointed to two basic reasons why the outcomes of political struggles are inherently easier to explain than to predict. First, the imperfect observability of people's sensitivity to social pressures suppresses knowledge as to what it would take to change public opinion. And, second, the nonlinearity of the social effects of individual decisions means that changes and their consequences need not be proportionate; minor adjustments in individual behaviors might produce huge social shifts, just as major individual changes can leave social outcomes unaffected. This pair of observations rested on the fact that on politicized issues people commonly protect their reputations through preference falsification. We have limited access to people's inner worlds, yet their hidden motives are capable of producing huge consequences.

When two movements aim to solve a moral crisis in opposite ways, with one seeking to reinvigorate values that the other is trying to eradicate, how will the agendas resonate with any given group of individuals? And to what extent will a movement pursuing rationalization dampen the need for moral reconstruction? As a practical matter, confident answers to such questions cannot be given, because they call for information unknowable, except possibly by the individuals themselves. Even individuals may not have answers until actually presented with alternatives and compelled to make decisions. By definition, to experience moral dissonance is to feel committed to satisfying an infeasible moral system. Individuals may remain in this state indefinitely in the absence of social developments offering ways out. Until the solutions present themselves, they may not even consider ranking their values, hoping against hope to find a way to avoid unpleasant compromises.[19] The multiplicity of the social mechanisms that might come into play makes it all the more difficult to forecast individual responses.

[19] Slovic (1995) reviews a large literature that shows how personal preferences get constructed in the course of social interactions. Although this literature does not make this chapter's distinction between values and preferences, its insights are relevant to both.

The proposition that moral evolution is imperfectly predictable clashes with a large scientific literature that takes human preferences and values as essentially fixed. As a case in point, neoclassical economics treats individualistic profit maximization as an act that individuals universally consider legitimate. While recognizing that the act might get blocked through political means, it also asserts that the drive of profit maximization is constant. This neoclassical view overlooks the social factors shaping interpretations of what constitutes legitimate economic behavior. Moreover, it overlooks the possibility of clashes between the values of economic individualism and other human values. As such, it predicts that movements hostile to profit-oriented economic individualism must be ephemeral.

For another example, some thinkers consider the gender roles with which people feel comfortable to have been determined genetically. On this view, values in conflict with biologically natural gender roles cannot persist; such values will give way to ones sympathetic to the traditional division of labor between the sexes. Once again, the argument sketched here suggests, on the contrary, that poorly predictable social processes help shape individual values concerning proper gender roles. Insofar as the prevailing gender roles produce moral dissonance – or, for that matter, expressive dissonance – they will indeed be vulnerable to removal. But usually there is more than one way to achieve inner peace, so society's moral evolution will depend on the outcomes of struggles among groups with conflicting agendas. Moreover, individuals have a capacity to live indefinitely with some dissonance, whether expressive or moral. There is no sound basis, therefore, for believing that values contributing to inner turmoil must quickly self-destruct.

References

Al-Ahmad, Jalal. [1964] 1982. *Plagued by the West (Gharbzadegi)*, 2nd. ed., trans. Paul Sprachman. Delmar, NY: Caravan Books.

Ayubi, Nazih N. 1991. *Political Islam: Religion and Politics in the Arab World*. New York: Routledge.

Cotton, John L. 1985. "Cognitive Dissonance in Selective Exposure." Pp. 11–33 in *Selective Exposure to Communication*, edited by Dolf Zillman and Jennings Bryant. Hillsdale, NJ: Lawrence Erlbaum.

Delumeau, Jean. [1983] 1990. *Sin and Fear: The Emergence of a Western Guilt Culture, 13th–18th Centuries*, trans. Eric Nicholson. New York: St. Martin's Press.

Edgerton, Robert B. 1992. *Sick Societies: Challenging the Myth of Primitive Harmony*. New York: The Free Press.

Ekelund, Robert B., Robert F. Hébert, and Robert D. Tollison. 1992. "The Economics of Sin and Redemption: Purgatory as a Market-Pull Innovation?" *Journal of Economic Behavior and Organization* 19:1–15.

Elster, Jon. 1983. *Sour Grapes: Studies in the Subversion of Rationality*. Cambridge: Cambridge University Press.

Festinger, Leon. 1957. *A Theory of Cognitive Dissonance*. Stanford: Stanford University Press.

Frank, Robert H. 1988. *Passions within Reason: The Strategic Role of the Emotions*. New York: W. W. Norton.

Haeri, Shahla. 1992. "Obedience versus Autonomy: Women and Fundamentalism in Iran and Pakistan." Pp. 181–213 in *Fundamentalisms and Society: Reclaiming the Sciences, the Family, and Education*, edited by Martin E. Marty and R. Scott Appleby. Chicago: University of Chicago Press.

Hardacre, Helen. 1992. "The Impact of Fundamentalisms on Women, the Family, and Interpersonal Relations." Pp. 129–50 in *Fundamentalisms and Society: Reclaiming the Sciences, the Family, and Education*, edited by Martin E. Marty and R. Scott Appleby. Chicago: University of Chicago Press.

Hardin, Russell. 1982. *Collective Action*. Baltimore: Johns Hopkins University Press.

Hirschman, Albert O. 1970. *Exit, Voice, and Loyalty: Responses to Decline in Firms, Organizations, and States*. Cambridge, MA: Harvard University Press.

Hirschman, Albert O. 1977. *The Passions and the Interests: Political Arguments for Capitalism before Its Triumph*. Princeton: Princeton University Press.

Hunter, James Davison. 1991. *Culture Wars: The Struggle to Define America*. New York: Basic Books.

Kahneman, Daniel, and Amos Tversky. 1984. "Choices, Values, and Frames." *American Psychologist* 39:341–50.

Kuran, Timur. 1993. "The Economic Impact of Islamic Fundamentalism." Pp. 302–41 in *Fundamentalisms and the State: Polities, Economies, and Militance*, edited by Martin E. Marty and R. Scott Appleby. Chicago: University of Chicago Press.

Kuran, Timur. 1995. *Private Truths, Public Lies: The Social Consequences of Preference Falsification*. Cambridge, MA: Harvard University Press.

Kuran, Timur. 1997. "Islam and Underdevelopment: An Old Puzzle Revisited." *Journal of Institutional and Theoretical Economics* 153: 41–71.

Kuran, Timur. Forthcoming. "Moral Overload and Its Alleviation." In *Economics, Values, and Organization*, edited by Avner Ben-Ner and Louis Putterman. Cambridge: Cambridge University Press.

Lewis, Bernard. 1993. *Islam in History: Ideas, People, and Events in the Middle East*. Chicago: Open Court.

Maududi, Sayyid Abu'l-A'la Maududi. [1940] 1985. *Let Us Be Muslims*, ed. Khurram Murad. Leicester: Islamic Foundation.

Merton, Robert K. 1968. *Social Theory and Social Structure*, enlarged ed. New York: The Free Press.

Oakeshott, Michael. [1958] 1993. *Morality and Politics in Modern Europe: The Harvard Lectures*. New Haven: Yale University Press.

Popenoe, David. 1995. *Life without Father*. New York: The Free Press.

Rosenberg, Nathan, and L. E. Birdzell, Jr. 1986. *How the West Grew Rich: The Economic Transformation of the Industrial World*. New York: Basic Books.

Shayegan, Daryush. [1989] 1992. *Cultural Schizophrenia: Islamic Societies Confronting the West*, transl. John Howe. London: Saqi Books.

Slovic, Paul. 1995. "The Construction of Preference." *American Psychologist* 50: 364–71.

Ülgener, Sabri F. 1981. *İktisadi Çözülmenin Ahlak ve Zihniyet Dünyası* [The Moral and Intellectual Dimensions of Economic Decline], 2nd. ed. Istanbul: Der Yayınları.

Wilson, James Q. 1993. *The Moral Sense*. New York: The Free Press.

8. Social mechanisms without black boxes

RAYMOND BOUDON

Introduction

"Explaining" means "finding the causes." Explaining a social phenomenon means identifying its cause(s). In most cases, the explanation takes the form of a more or less complicated set of causal statements. The relations between the elements of the set can be more or less complex; they can be linear, recursive, include feedback loops, and so on. The set is what we usually call a "social mechanism" (SM). A SM is, in other words, the well-articulated set of causes responsible for a given social phenomenon. With the exception of typical simple ones, SMs tend to be idiosyncratic and singular (Boudon 1986).

I am essentially interested here in the discussion of a basic distinction – namely, that some explanations of social mechanisms give the impression of being "final," while others do not. Thus the causal statement "A legal limitation of rents provokes a degradation of housing" arouses the further question "Why is that so?" In that sense, it is not "final." The answer to this question is that the owners, who have the exclusive capacity of repairing the houses, are not incited to do so when this cost exceeds the benefit that they draw from renting their house. With this answer, we have the impression that the explanation is final: It arouses in our mind no additional question. We have this impression because the causes of the social mechanism lie in a behavior of the owners that we easily perceive as understandable: We understand very easily why the owners do what they do. That the ultimate causes have the character of being individual decisions implies that the explanation of the SM in question has been analyzed in terms of the methodological individualism paradigm (MIP).

Theories of SMs that do not belong to the MIP paradigm can exist and

This chapter is a companion to Boudon 1996a,b.

be useful. Thus it can be useful to observe that in given circumstances inflation has a positive effect on employment, or that suicide rates decrease during severe political crises, even if we are not able to make these theories final. They lead, namely, to further questions: Why is that so? Under *which* circumstances do the effects occur, and so forth? But we may be unable to answer them. So SMs and MIP imply each other only to the extent to which final theories are aimed. On the other hand, all theories belonging to the MIP do not give the impression of being final. Suppose that a theory rests upon individual statements of the form "People do so because they have been socialized to do so." This theory would belong to the MIP (the ultimate causes of the social phenomenon would lie in individual decisions), but the explanation arouses further questions, such as: What does the expression "being socialized to behave in a given way" actually mean? Which mechanisms are hidden behind the word "socialization"? Maybe the sociologist would have the impression in this case that he should ask the psychologist or eventually the biologist about these mechanisms, because his own competence does not allow him to put any precise mechanisms under the vague notion of "socialization." In other words, socialization is a black box. "Final" explanations can be defined as explanations without black boxes.

So the MIP does not guarantee the absence of black boxes. Another condition needs to be met before an explanation gives the impression of being final: that individual decisions are "understandable," or in more concrete terms, that they can be described as grounded on strong reasons, briefly as "rational." The fact that the MIP eliminates black boxes as soon as it includes the rationality postulate is certainly one of the main reasons for the appeal of the "Rational-Choice Model" (RCM), a model that can be defined by these two features: MIP and rationality – a "rationality" of a particular type, though, as we will see. More precisely, I will be arguing that the utilitarian concept of rationality is too narrow for sociology and that it should be replaced by one that includes what I will call "cognitive" as well as "axiological" reasons (or, in brief, the Cognitive Model of Rationality).

Reasons, meaning, black-box causes

As recommended by Scheler ([1913–16] 1954) and then by Weber (1922) and Popper (1967), sociologists are entitled to introduce the postulate of rationality, which can be formulated as "Assume that the actions and beliefs of the social actor are inspired to him by reasons." This postulate rests on a main ground: that the actions, beliefs, and the like of the actor are normally perceived as meaningful by himself as well as, in principle at least, by the observer. Although the latter can (as the actor himself) be unclear on the identity of the reasons motivating the actor, he would normally assume that some reasons explain his actions or beliefs.[1]

Obviously, all actions are not inspired by reasons. The causes underlying human behavior can also *not* have the status of reasons. Familiar expressions illustrate these irrational causes: "He behaved the way he did because he was angry, because he was tired, because he was accustomed to do so, and so on." Actions can also, said Weber, be "traditional" or "affective." Also, even the most narrowly rational actions, such as avoiding physical danger, are grounded on basic instincts.

Consciousness can also *occasionally* be "false." I can believe that Mrs. Smith is right while the real cause of my appreciation is actually that I like her. But one cannot accept the idea that consciousness would be false *by essence*, so to speak. Some writers, taking their inspiration notably from the Marxian or Freudian vulgates, introduce easily this assumption. It is exposed to obvious empirical and logical refutation, though. It is extremely strong because it sees action as due to causes that have nothing to do with their meaning to the actor herself. It is moreover obviously self-defeating as soon as it is taken literally.

On the whole, action should be analyzed as grounded on reasons; if not, it should be seen as meaningful; if not *and only if not*, it should be seen as produced by black-box causes. If I see somebody cutting wood, the most natural explanation is that he has reasons to do so, such as getting warmer. If this assumption appears implausible, I may assume that he wishes to show his neighbor the way to cut wood. If he is alone in his yard, he may cut wood to get relieved from some sorrow. If not, he may celebrate a ritual. If he does not belong to any woodcutting sect, and if I have the impression that I have more or less exhausted the possible reasons to cut wood, I will be entitled to assume that he cuts wood, say, under

---

[1] "Nonconsequential normative beliefs" means "statements of the normative type, as "X is good, legitimate," etc., endorsed by the subject because they appear to him as grounded on reasons that have nothing to do with the eventual consequences of X." These nonconsequential reasons are the core of Weber's notion of "axiological rationality." They have nothing to do with affective motivations and should be sharply distinguished from "values." See Boudon (1995a) for a discussion of this notion and Boudon (1996a) for a more sketchy presentation.

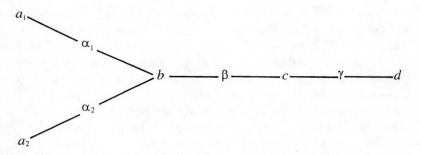

Figure 8.1. Diagrammatic representation of Tocqueville's explanation of the stagnation of French agriculture at the end of the 18th century.

the effect not of reasons but of some irrational cause, such as "compulsion." But "compulsion" will be a "black box" or a mere label covering my ignorance. The same comment could be made of other currently used black boxes, such as "imitation instinct," "magical thinking," "cognitive biases," "primitive mentality," "frames," "habitus," "national spirit," "aversion against risk," "resistance to change," and so forth. A long repertory of such current explanatory black-box factors could easily be produced. One should be very prudent at any rate before attributing to actions black-box causes that are neither rational nor even meaningful to the actor. A main reason for the success of the RCM is that it provides an insurance against black boxes.

This chapter will deal with the question: How can we define rationality to get final explanations of SMs? Should we define rationality as the RCM does? Before answering this question, it is useful to stress the importance of the combination of the two postulates, MIP and rationality.

Importance of the two postulates: Methodological individualism paradigm and rationality

The history of sociology shows that many of the sociological theories that appear as the most convincing meet these two postulates. Consider as an example (Figure 8.1) Tocqueville's explanation of the stagnation of French agriculture at the end of the 18th century (Tocqueville [1856] 1955). Administrative centralization is the cause of the fact that there are many positions of "civil servants" available (statement a_1) in France and that they are more prestigious than in England (a_2); the causes expressed by statements a_1 and a_2 provoke a rate of landlord absenteeism much larger than in England (statement b); landlord absenteeism is the cause of a low rate of innovation (c); and the low rate of innovation is the cause of the stagnation (d). In order to make this nonfinal explanation final, one has to explain further why a_1 and a_2 are causes of b, why b is cause of c and why c is cause of d. The answer will take the form of "individualistic" statements – namely, statements explaining why the ideal-typical individuals belonging to relevant categories behaved the way they did. Why are a_1 and a_2 the causes of b? Because (α_1) landlords see that they can easily buy a position of civil servant and that (α_2), by so doing, will increase their power, prestige, and possibly income. In England, the positions of civil servants are less numerous, less accessible, and less rewarding, while the local political life offers many opportunities of getting interesting social rewards. So the French landlords have reasons (described by α_1 and α_2) to leave their land and serve the King, which their British counterparts do not have. Such statements deal with the question "Why did the relevant category of landlords behave the way they did?" Why does b cause c? Why is landlord absenteeism unfriendly to innovation? Because landowners rent their land (β)? Why is c cause of d? Why don't farmers innovate? Because they don't have the capacity of doing so? Hence they have reasons (γ) to cultivate the land in a routinized fashion. So the theory explains why the relevant social categories, the landlords and the farmers, behaved the way they did. Tocqueville's theory gives the impression of being final – first, because its empirical statements appear as congruent with observational data; second, because it belongs to the MIP of the "rational" type; and finally because its ultimate nonempirical statements (those described by the Greek letters) on the reasons explaining why farmers, landlords, and so on behaved the way they did are acceptable in the sense that we do not feel we should address any objection to the "psychological" mechanisms that they introduce. We perceive them as "evident" not in the logical but in the psychological sense.

Which rationality? The importance of the Rational-Choice Model

James Coleman (1986) has rightly written that the reason why rational action has "a unique attractiveness" as a basis for theory is that it is a conception of action "that we need ask no more question about"; Hollis (1977) has expressed the same idea in other words: "Rational action is its own explanation."[2]

In the language used earlier in this chapter, once a SM is analyzed along the lines of the MIP, provided the rationality postulate is introduced, we get a "final" explanation. When a sociological phenomenon is made the outcome of individual reasons, one does not need to ask further questions. Suppose that we could know exactly how the human brain is wired or, to use Leibniz's metaphor, that we could walk inside the brain as among the wheels of a windmill: This would add nothing to a good MIP-rational theory. In that sense, Tocqueville's theory on French agricultural stagnation is "final." Even if we could know exactly what happened in the brains of the landowners, this would not add anything to Tocqueville's explanation.

The next question to be examined then concerns which theory of rationality we should endorse. Many sociologists who recommend the MIP endorse the theory of rationality used by neoclassical economics. When they speak of the Rational-Choice Model (RCM), they mean that human action should be analyzed as guided by the principle of maximizing the difference between benefits and costs to the subject of alternative lines of action – in other words, choosing the action with maximum expected utility. Let us call this definition of rationality the "utilitarian" one.

Tocqueville's analysis, to which I referred earlier, is a good illustration of this definition of rationality. The French landlords are better off when they leave their ground and become civil servants. This is not true of their British counterparts. This approach raises the question: Should rationality be assimilated to utilitarian rationality?

The success of the utilitarian version of rationality

The first reason for the success of the RCM is that it explains satisfactorily many social phenomena. It is very easy to find in classical and modern sociology many examples illustrating this success. I have taken an example from Tocqueville because he evidently did not belong to the utilitarian school. Still, he uses the MIP systematically and very often the RCM utilitarian version of it. I could have selected many other examples from his *Democracy in America* or from his *Old Regime*. If we correlate this

[2] Quoted by Goldthorpe (1996).

point with the impression of solidity and strength produced by Tocqueville's work, we draw the conclusion that the MIP–RCM model is a powerful one.

The exceptional importance of the presociologist Rousseau can be explained in the same way. He has definitely provided the basic explanation as to why we consider and treat as legitimate all kinds of unpleasant social constraints. The *Discourse on the Origin of Inequality Among Men* as well as *The Social Contract* can be considered as providing an unsurpassed theory as to why we have the collective feeling that these constraints are acceptable and legitimate, though they are unpleasant: They are the only way of protecting ourselves against the suboptimal solution normally produced by the "insurance game," the "prisoner's dilemma" game, and other similar structures. The fact that Rousseau's main intuitions can be expressed in the language of game theory suffices to show that the MIP–RCM is latent in his political work, because game theory belongs obviously to this model. Marx, Sombart and Simmel, and even Durkheim would also provide many examples of classical and solid analyses inscribed in the MIP–RCM model, although none of them belongs properly to the "utilitarian tradition."[3]

Obviously it would be easy to mention many modern works that owe their scientific value to the fact that they use this model. One can think of these writers coming from economics who, from Olson (1965) to Kuran (1995), have produced important theories using the MIP–RCM model normally used by economists. Besides them, sociologists such as Coleman (1990), Oberschall (1989), and others, as well as historians such as Root (1994), have also produced important contributions using the MIP–RCM model. Root's work on the development of the modern state is a work in comparative sociology. Its main aim is to explain a number of differences between France and England in the 17th and 18th centuries. Thus he notes that French and British economic policies tend to be favorable to consumers and to producers, respectively. Another difference is that the French "journées" – episodes of collective urban violence against the political power, which are so frequent in Paris – are much less frequent in London. Why? Because the power in Westminster is held by landowners who are concerned by the interests of the voters who elect them, mostly landowners

---

[3] See Boudon (1993). Obviously, the MIP–RCM model is incompatible with many ideas and analyses proposed by Marx and Durkheim. But it is interesting to note that when they forgot their principles, they sometimes could use this model in an instinctive fashion.

such as themselves, whereas the power in Paris is held by civil servants. The ordinary people in Paris know that they can exert a pressure on the political power with a reasonable chance of getting what they want, whereas in London, they feel that collective action would remain without much effect.

So the main reason for the success of the MIP–RCM model is simply its scientific powerfulness. Another reason often put to the fore by its supporters is that it leads naturally, so to speak, to deductive and predictive theories.

The shortcomings of the utilitarian version of rationality

So there are good reasons to think that the RCM version of the MIP could legitimately claim to be general. But there are also strong reasons to think that this claim is illegitimate.

First of all, a huge number of common, easily observable phenomena cannot be explained within the framework of this model. The paradox of not voting has been christened in this fashion because, against the prediction derived from the RCM according to which people should not vote, they actually vote. The effect of any single vote on any election turnout is so small, claims the RCM, that rational actors should refrain from voting: The costs of voting will always be higher than the benefits. As one of these voters, I should prefer resting, walking, writing an article, or even operating my vacuum cleaner to voting. Still, I vote. The paradox has been "solved" in many ways: People like to vote, says a first theory; as Pascal's Christians, people would have such strong regrets if their ballot would make the difference that they would vote even though they know the probability of this event occurring is infinitesimally small, says a second theory (Ferejohn and Fiorina 1974). Recently a solution was proposed where "reputation" was made the main concern of the voter: If I do not vote, I run the risk of losing my reputation (Overbye 1995). This "solution" of the paradox implies, however, that people would generally be convinced that one should vote – in other words, that people would be "irrational" according to the RCM definition of rationality. So this "solution" of the paradox fails to save the RCM. Other solutions have been or could be imagined easily.

Sometimes the RCM is made more flexible thanks to the notion of "cognitive frames" (Quattrone and Tversky 1987). Applied to the present case, the notion would suggest, for instance, that some "frame" would bring people to overestimate the influence of their ballot. Such "frames" appear often, however, not only as ad hoc, but as typical black boxes.

At any rate, none of these "solutions" has been universally accepted. Some of them, such as Ferejohn and Fiorina's, display a high intellectual virtuosity. Still, they have not eliminated the "paradox of not voting."

Classical "paradoxes" other than voting can be mentioned. Allais's "paradoxes" show that, when confronted with lotteries, people in many circumstances do not make their choice in conformity with the principle of maximizing the expected utility. They are variations on the basic observation that people normally prefer to earn a sum X with certainty rather than play a lottery with a mathematical expectation of X plus H (H being some positive quantity), even if they are allowed to play as long as they wish (Allais 1953; Allais and Hagen 1979; Hagen 1995). So they prefer less to more. This finding was confirmed by experimental psychology. If we want to stick to the RCM, we have to introduce the idea that economic subjects have an "aversion to risk." Such an assumption introduces a typical black box, so that the main benefit of the RCM, avoiding black boxes, is lost.

Psychologists have produced many other observations challenging the RCM. In a classical experiment, subjects play a game called the "ultimatum game" (Wilson 1993, pp. 62–3; Hoffman and Spitzer 1985): 100 Euros are available in the experimenter's pocket. Subject A is allowed to make any proposal he wishes as to the way the 100 Euros should be shared between himself, A, and B. B on his side has only the capacity of approving or rejecting A's proposal. If he rejects it, the 100 Euros remain in the experimenter's pocket. If he accepts it, he gets the sum allocated to him by A. With the RCM in mind, according to which people are exclusively concerned with maximizing the difference between benefits and costs, one would predict that A would make proposals of the type "70 Euros for me, A, 30 Euros for him, B." In that case, B would not refuse the proposal and A would maximize his gains. In fact, the most frequent proposal is equal sharing. This outcome contradicts the utilitarian axiomatics of the RCM.

Sociology also has produced many observations that can be read as challenges to the RCM model. Thus the negative reaction of social subjects against some given state of affairs has in many cases nothing to do with the costs they are exposed to by this state of affairs. On the other hand, actions can be frequently observed whose benefit to the actor is zero or negative. To repair an injustice done to him, Kleist's Michael Kolhaas accepted costs without proportion to the damage. Now, there are many Michael Kolhaas among us.

In his *White Collars*, C. Wright Mills (1951) has identified what could be called the "overreaction paradox." He describes women clerks working in a taylorized firm. They all do the same tasks. They sit in a great room, and all have the same kind of desk, the same work environment, and so on. Violent conflicts frequently occur on "minor" issues, such as being seated closer to a source of heat or light. The outside observer would normally consider such conflicts as irrational, because he would use implicitly the RCM: Why such a violent reaction to such a minor issue? Because the behavior of the women would appear to him as strange in terms of this model, he would turn to an "irrational" interpretation: childish behavior. By so doing, he would confess that RCM cannot easily explain the "overreaction paradox" observed by Mills.

Many observations would lead to the same conclusion: They can be interpreted satisfactorily neither in an irrational nor in a RCM fashion. When I am queuing up at the airport, waiting to show my passport to the immigration officer, I can easily get exasperated by a person who gets checked before me even though she stood after me in the file. The cost she imposes to me is negligible. My exasperation can be high and will likely be approved by others, though. Possibly my exasperation will be greater, the greater the number of people in the file and hence the lower the additional cost imposed to me. Why this lack of proportion between costs and reaction? Why is this relation going in the direction opposite to RCM predictions? On the whole, economists, psychologists and sociologists have produced a tremendous number of observations that can uneasily be explained within the frame of the RCM.

When interferences were observed, Fresnel concluded rightly that they were incompatible with the Cartesian representation of light. In the same way, it is possibly time to try the assumption that the paradoxes generated by the RCM should be solved by using an alternative theory of rationality. This situation raises three questions. I have already answered the first one in a sketchy fashion: Why is the RCM so popular in spite of the objections from social reality? The second one is: Why does the RCM so often fail?

The third one is: Is there a model that would conserve the positive intuitions and the scientific ambition behind the RCM – namely, trying to provide black-box–free explanations of SMs, and get rid of its defects?

The sources of the weaknesses of the Rational-Choice Model

When I cross over a street with heavy traffic, I look on my left and on my right. Why? The RCM provides an immediate explanation of this trivial observation: because the benefits-minus-cost balance of this behavior is heavily positive. The costs are waiting a short while; the benefits, staying in life. Obviously, this RCM account of my action is stenographic. A more complete report would include "cognitive" statements such as "I believe that if I cross over the street blindly, I run the risk of being hit by a car." It would also include "normative" statements, such as "staying in life is a good thing." These statements are trivial, though. For this reason, I do not need to mention them when I explain why I look left and right when crossing over the street.

But in many other cases, these "cognitive" and "normative" statements, far from being trivial, constitute on the contrary the core of the *explanandum*. So when we observe that people in a far tribe execute some ritual to the effect of producing rain, the core of the sociological analysis is not to explain why they want the rain to fall but why they believe that their ritual should facilitate the falling of rain. In this example, the "utilitarian" statements in the global explanation are trivial, whereas the "cognitive" ones are not and constitute on the contrary the main thing to be explained.

The same could be said of normative statements. When the explanation of some phenomenon includes statements of the type "the observed people believe that X is good, legitimate, fair, unfair, etc.," the analyst cannot avoid the task of explaining why the observed people hold the normative belief in consideration, as soon as the belief is not trivial.

RCM has little to say on beliefs. More precisely, it has almost nothing to say on "positive" beliefs. I have already mentioned that when they meet a belief that cannot be ignored, RCMists would evoke the notion of "frame." The observed actors believe so, because they have in mind some frames. Such frames are most often *ad hoc* and, moreover, constitute black boxes.

The situation is more complicated as far as normative beliefs are concerned. Some can be easily explained in RCM terms. In some cases, people consider that "*X* is good" *because* X eliminates undesirable outcomes. Thus traffic lights are unpleasant but good because they make traffic easier. RCM is often adequate to explain normative beliefs of this type – namely, beliefs grounded on "consequential" reasons. But many other normative beliefs cannot be explained in this fashion. RCMists themselves would recognize easily, in congruence with the economic tradition, that while the choice of "means" can be considered as rational, the choice of "ends" cannot.

So my diagnosis is that a major weakness of the RCM is that there are many beliefs on which it has little to say and which are a normal and essential ingredient of many social actions. This weakness explains perhaps more than anything else why its ambition – providing a general paradigm guaranteeing black-box–free explanations of SMs – is generally held as controversial.

Two false ideas

If we accept the idea that the weakness of the RCM derives mainly from the fact that it ignores beliefs or at least is uncomfortable with beliefs, the next question is whether we can develop a rational theory of beliefs. If we can, we are in a better position both to satisfy the main ambition of the RCM, providing explanations of SMs without black boxes, and to analyze SMs including nontrivial beliefs or beliefs that the RCM cannot easily take into account.

Two widely spread though controversial ideas (two "received" ideas in Flaubert's sense) seem, however, to struggle against the assumption that beliefs could be compatible with the rationality postulate. The first one is that it seems impossible to propose a rational theory of *false* beliefs: How can false beliefs be explained rationally? The second one is that, given that *ought* cannot be derived from *is*, it is impossible to propose a rational theory of normative beliefs either. To be more precise on this second point, I mention again here a distinction I introduced earlier: The RCM tradition has no difficulty explaining normative beliefs as long as the explanation takes the form "They believe that X is good because X generates consequences that they will normally consider as good." But it has little to say as soon as a normative belief cannot be analyzed in this "consequential" way. Before we proceed, we have to discuss these two received ideas.

Can false beliefs be rational?

Against the first received idea, false beliefs can be grounded on strong reasons, as familiar examples easily show. Pareto has rightly said that the history of science is the churchyard of all these false ideas that men have endorsed under the authority of scientists. In other words, science produces normally false ideas beside true ones. Nobody would accept the idea that these false ideas are endorsed by scientists under the effect of irrational causes, because their brain would have been wired in an inadequate fashion, or because their mind would have been obscured by inadequate "cognitive biases," "frames," class interests, or affective causes. Scientists believe in statements that often turn out to be false because they have strong reasons of believing them, given the cognitive context.

Aristotelian physicists believed that a sailing ship keeps on moving after the wind has fallen because some force is responsible for its motion: The movement of the ship produces a turmoil that has the effect of pushing the back of the boat. They were not sure of this conjecture. But they were sure that some force explained the movement. Why? Because they had observed that no body at rest can be put into motion without some external force drawing it from its state of rest. Hence, they concluded, there is no movement without a force being responsible for it. So Aristotelian physicists had strong reasons, given the cognitive context, to believe that some force should be responsible for the boat continuing to move after the wind has fallen. At this point, an objection was raised by Jean Buridan (Duhem 1913–59, VIII, pp. 200–18; Brenner 1990, p. 187):[4] If the assumption about the turmoils were true, the straw on a strawheap should fly in different directions depending on the location of the strawheap on the deck of the boat. As this consequence is false, the conjecture about the turmoils became weaker. The discussion went on until the inertia principle was

---

[4] Jean Buridan develops the so-called theory of impetus, according to Duhem a first formulation of the principle of inertia as we know it. Question 12 of Book VIII of *Questions sur la physique* (Jean Buridan, n.d.) in particular criticizes the principles of Aristotelian physics using this example of the strawheap.

formulated in the terms that we know it today: A body at rest needs a force to be moved, a moving body needs a force to be brought to rest. This reformulation solves a number of puzzles that had bothered Aristotelian physics; one could get rid of the turmoils and other undesirable assumptions. On the whole, the reasons to believe that the principle "no movement without a force being responsible for it" were seen as right and hence as strong until the principle was reformulated (Duhem 1913–59, I, pp. 371sq.).

The believers in phlogiston, in ether, or in the many other entities and mechanisms that now appear to us as purely imaginary had also in their time, given the cognitive context, strong reasons to believe in them. It was not immediately perceived as important that when a piece of oxide of mercury is heated under an empty bell-glass, the drop of water that appears on the bell's wall should be taken into consideration: It was not immediately observed that it appears regularly, nor was it clearly perceived that it contradicts phlogiston theory.

Why should not the false beliefs produced by ordinary knowledge be explained in the same fashion as false scientific beliefs – namely, as grounded in the mind of the social subject on reasons perceived by them as strong given the cognitive context in which they move?

I am not saying that false beliefs should *always* be explained in this fashion. Even scientists can believe in false beliefs under the effects of passions and other irrational causes. What I am saying is that beliefs in false ideas *can* be caused by reasons in the minds of the actors, and that they are often caused by reasons in the situations of interest to sociologists. Even though these reasons appear to us as false, they can be perceived as right and strong by the actors themselves. To explain that they perceive as right what is wrong, we need not assume that their minds are obscured by some hypothetical mechanisms of the kind that Marx, Freud, Pareto, Lévy-Bruhl, and their many heirs imagined, nor by the more prosaic "frames" so fashionable today. In most cases, we get more acceptable explanations by making the assumption that given the cognitive context in which they move, actors have strong reasons to believe in false ideas.

I have produced elsewhere several examples showing that the rational explanation of beliefs we consider as normal in the case of false scientific beliefs can also be applied to ordinary knowledge. I have notably explored in an intensive fashion two cases that appeared to me as strategic, given the terms of the present discussion.

The first one is the case of magical beliefs. Although defining magical beliefs is not easy, they can be defined for the sake of simplicity as beliefs in false causal relations. The literature on the subject is immense. But a few typical explanations of magical beliefs can be identified.[5] A first one is the Lévy-Bruhlian one, a causal nonrational one: "Primitives" believe in false causal relations because their brains are wired in a way different from ours, with the effect that they confuse for instance causality with similarity. For this reason, they would think that when they hurt a puppet representing a person, they would hurt the actual person. A second type of theory is the Wittgensteinian one: Magical rituals should be interpreted as having in the "primitive's" mind an expressive rather than instrumental function. A third type of theory says that given the cognitive context, people have strong reasons to believe in false causal relations. This type of theory has the advantage of not introducing strong assumptions. Moreover, it reproduces easily, as I have tried to show, the complex map of the distribution of magical beliefs through time and space. On the whole, it is much more acceptable from the viewpoint of the criteria normally used to evaluate a scientific theory.

I examined carefully a second case: the case of all these false beliefs observed by cognitive psychologists (Boudon 1994, 1995a). The experiments produced by cognitive psychologists are very interesting to sociologists because they produce artificially false collective beliefs in situations where the subjects are affectively neutral with regard to the problems that the experimenters confront them with, so that affective factors can be excluded from the explanation of the false beliefs and, where the subjects are isolated with respect to one another, so that contagion or imitation effects can also be a priori excluded. I have suggested that although the psychologists themselves often explain their findings with the help of Lévy-Bruhlian assumptions (ordinary knowledge, intuition, etc., follow rules that have nothing to do with the scientific rules of inference; subjects would be exposed to "cognitive biases"; etc.), the false beliefs can in most cases be explained by strong reasons.

I will limit myself to one example.[6] When psychiatrists are asked whether depression is a cause of suicide attempts, they would agree affirmatively. When asked why, they would answer that they have frequently

---

[5] See the theories of magic in Boudon (1994).
[6] I elaborate here on a stylized experiment summarizing experiments conducted by Kahneman and Tversky (1973).

Table 8.1

	Suicide attempted	Suicide not attempted	Total
Depression symptoms	a	b	$e = a + b$
No depression symptoms	c	d	$f = c + d$
Total	$g = a + c$	$h = b + d$	$j = a + b + c + d$

observed patients with these two features: Many of their patients appeared as depressed, and they have attempted suicide. Of course, the answer reveals that the psychiatrists use *one* piece of information in the contingency table (Table 8.1): Their argument is, namely, "*a* is high, hence depression is a cause of suicide attempt." Now, every freshman in statistics would know that the argument is wrong: In order to conclude that there is a correlation between depression and suicide attempt, one has to consider not one but four pieces of information, not only *a* but the difference *a/e* − *c/f*.

The answer of the psychiatrists shows that statistical intuition *seems* to follow rules that have nothing to do with the rules of statistical inference considered effectively valid. But it does not prove that we should assume, in a Lévy-Bruhlian fashion, that the physicians' brains are ill wired. The physicians can very well have strong reasons for believing what they believe. Their answer can even suggest that statistical intuition is less deficient than it seems. Suppose, for instance, that *e* in Table 8.1 would be equal to 20% − in other words, that 20% of the physicians' patients have depression symptoms − and that *g* would also be equal to 20% (20% of the patients have attempted suicide). Admittedly, higher figures would be unrealistic. With these assumptions, in the case where the percentage *a* of people presenting the two characters would be greater than 4, the two variables would be correlated, so that causality could plausibly be presumed. So a physician who has seen, say, 10 people out of 100 presenting the two features would have good reasons to believe in the existence of a causal relation between the two features.

In this example, the belief of the physicians is not properly false. In other examples, the beliefs produced by cognitive psychology appear as unambiguously false. In most cases, I found, however, that these beliefs could be explained as grounded on reasons perceived by the subjects as strong. Obviously, these reasons are not of the "benefit-minus-cost" type. They are, rather, of the "cognitive" type. The aim pursued by the actor is not to maximize something but to determine whether something is likely, true, and so forth. So beside its instrumental or utilitarian dimension, rationality has a "cognitive" dimension.

Can normative beliefs be rational?

Many traditions, from Rousseau to the RCM, have recognized that normative beliefs can be rational: Norms often eliminate the unfavorable cost–benefit balance resulting from "prisoner's dilemma," "insurance game," and other situations with suboptimal outcomes. Thus to Rousseau, the social contract and the social constraints that it entails are good and perceived as good by people because they have the consequence of eliminating the suboptimal solution of the "insurance game." We find traffic lights good because, without them, the situation would be worse: They eliminate interaction structures with suboptimal solution of the "prisoner's dilemma" or "chicken"-type games.

But it should also be recognized that social actors can have strong reasons to endorse normative beliefs, without these reasons being of the cost–benefit type, and more generally, without these reasons being of the "consequential" type. An example borrowed from Adam Smith is sufficient to illustrate this crucial point.

A methodologically strategic example from Adam Smith

Although it is recognized that Smith's *Theory of Moral Sentiments* does not rest on the RCM, it is sometimes believed that his better-known work on the *Wealth of Nations* does. The following example shows, however, that this is not the case. Even in this book, which had a tremendous influence on economic theory, Smith does not use the RCM.

Why, asks Smith, do we (i.e., 18th-century Englishmen) consider it normal that soldiers are paid less than miners? Smith's methodology in his answer could be applied to many similar questions of our time: Why do we feel that it is fair for such and such an occupation to be paid more or less than another (Smith [1776] 1976, book 1, Chapter 10)? Why do people consider that TV speakers are too highly paid in France, while they do not consider that football stars get too much, although the latter have much higher incomes than the former (Boudon 1992)? Evidently such normative beliefs are not "consequential": I would be neither better nor worse off if TV speakers were paid less; the nation itself would be neither better nor worse off if many income differentials were different from what they are. Still, we believe that some differentials are fair and others unfair.

Going back to Smith, his answer to the question "Why do we have the feeling that miners should be paid more than soldiers?" is the following:

1. A salary is the retribution of a contribution.
2. Equal contributions should correspond to equal retributions.
3. Several components enter into the value of a contribution, such as the investment required to produce a given type of competence, the risks involved in the realization of the contribution, and so on.
4. The investment time is comparable in the case of the miner and of the soldier. It takes about as much time and effort to make a soldier as to make a miner. The two jobs are characterized by similar risks. The two cases include a risk of death.
5. Nonetheless, there are important differences between the two types of jobs.
6. The soldier serves a central function in the society. It preserves the identity and the very existence of the nation. The miner fulfills an economic activity among others. He is not more central to the society than, say, the textile worker.
7. Consequently, the death of the two men has a different social meaning. The death of the miner will be identified as an accident, but the death of the soldier on the battlefield as a sacrifice.
8. Because of this difference in the social meaning of their respective activities, the soldier will be entitled to symbolic rewards, prestige, symbolic distinctions, and funeral honors in case of death on the battlefield.
9. The miner is not entitled to the same symbolic rewards.
10. Because the contribution of the two categories in terms notably of risk and investment is the same, the equilibrium between contribution and retribution can only be restored by making the salary of the mine workers higher.
11. This system of reasons is responsible for our *feeling* that the miner should be paid a higher amount than the soldier.

First of all, Smith's analysis does not use the RCM. People do not believe what they believe in order to maximize some difference between benefits and costs. They have strong reasons for believing what they believe, but these reasons are not of the cost–benefit type. Not only are they not of the "utilitarian" type: They are not even of the "consequential" type. At no point in the argument are the consequences evoked that would eventually result from the miners not being paid more than the soldiers. Smith's argument takes, rather, the form of a deduction from principles. People have the feeling that it is fair to pay higher salaries to miners than soldiers because it is grounded on strong reasons derived from strong principles, claims Smith. He does not say that these reasons are explicitly present in the minds of all but assumes visibly that they are in an intuitive fashion responsible for their beliefs. Possibly Weber had such cases in mind when he introduced his famous and often misunderstood distinction between "instrumental" and "axiological" rationality (my translation of *Zweck-* and *Wertrationalität*).[7]

A contemporary theorist of ethics proposes analyses of some of our moral sentiments similar to Smith's (Walzer 1983). Why do we consider conscription a legitimate recruitment method in the case of soldiers but not of miners, he asks? The answer is again that the function of the former but not of the latter is vital. If conscription could be applied to miners, it could be applied to any and eventually to all kinds of activities, so that it would lead to a regime incompatible with the principles of democracy. In the same fashion, it is easily accepted that soldiers are used as garbage collectors to meet situations of urgency. But it would be considered illegitimate to use them for such tasks in normal situations. In all these examples, as in Smith's example, the collective moral feelings are grounded on solid reasons but not on reasons of the type considered in the RCM.

A general model

Finally, we come to the idea of a model resting on the following postulates.

1. Until the proof to the contrary is given, social actors should be considered as rational in the sense that they have strong reasons of believing what they believe, of doing what they do, and so forth.
2. In particular cases, these reasons can be realistically treated as dealing with the difference between costs and benefits of alternative lines

[7] See Boudon (1996b).

of action. In other cases, they cannot, in particular, when a decision or action rests upon normative or cognitive beliefs, the reasons may not belong exclusively to this type. This results from the fact that beliefs are not intentional, and normative beliefs are not always consequentially grounded.

3. In some circumstances, the core of some action is constituted by "cognitive" reasons: He did X because he believed that Z is likely or true, and he had strong reasons for believing so. Example: The physician diagnosed depression on the basis of suicide attempt *because* he believed depression is a cause of suicide.

4. In some circumstances, the core of some action is constituted by "axiological" reasons: She did X because she believed that Z is fair, good, or unfair, and she had strong "nonconsequential" reasons of believing so. Example: Smith's example on miners and soldiers.

I propose to call the model defined by these postulates the "Cognitivist Model" (CM).[8]

It follows from the postulates that the RCM is a particular case of the CM. When the reasons in the CM are restricted to belong to the "benefit-minus-cost" type, we get the RCM. Reciprocally, when the restriction that reasons should belong to the "benefit-minus-cost" type is lifted in the RCM model, the CM model is generated.

The CM supposes that actions, decisions, and beliefs are meaningful to the actor in the sense that they are perceived by him as grounded on reasons. Even though he cannot identify these reasons clearly, he has the intuitive impression that they are grounded on reasons.

One important remark can be introduced here. Although it is tautological to define "rationality" by the notion of "strong reasons," it is the only way of getting rid of all these discussions as to "what rationality *really* means," where the discussants expose generally what *they* mean. As with many other tautologies (see, e.g., mathematical tautologies), this tautology would then be very useful. But one should also immediately add that the postulate that beliefs and actions are grounded on reasons is *not* tautological. On the contrary, many traditions and many people start from the idea that actions and beliefs are not the effect of reasons. It can be a

---

[8] Moral philosophers call traditionally "cognitivist" the theories that make moral feelings the outcome of reasons. So the word covers actions inspired by "axiological" as well as "cognitive" reasons.

hard job to find out or reconstruct these reasons, as the previous examples show – for example, why were the French landlords more attracted by civil servant positions than their British counterparts? Why did Aristotelian physicists believe in turmoils? Why did Priestley believe in the phlogiston? Why did Englishmen of the 18th century believe that miners should be paid more than soldiers? Why do we accept easily that football players should have much higher incomes than TV speakers? Why do psychiatrists see depression as a cause of suicide attempts? Why didn't the people of London try to exert pressure on the political power, as did the Parisians? Why are there more magical beliefs in some societies than in others?

Another question can be raised at this point: How can we recognize that we have reconstructed the reasons of the actors in a proper fashion? Answer: the same way we judge that any theory is acceptable. Reconstructing the reasons amounts to building a theory. We judge the quality of this theory with the help of the criteria we normally apply to any theory: The theory generates empirically testable statements that can be confronted with observational data; the nontestable statements should be acceptable; and so on.

The Cognitivist Model has the advantages of the Rational-Choice Model without its shortcomings

Providing final explanations

First of all, the CM has the same *main* advantage as the RCM model: It provides final explanations in the sense that psychology or biology, say, could not possibly contribute to a CM explanation. The CM uses no black boxes. This property derives from the fact that when a piece of behavior can be explained as the effect of reasons, nothing can be added. I believe that two plus two are four because it is true. Once this reason is given, I do not need to know more from psychologists or biologists.

This appealing side of the RCM also characterizes the CM. But the latter model avoids the strong assumption that a specific type of reason ("benefit-minus-cost" reasons) should explain any type of behavior. This leads the RCM to ignore practically all nontrivial beliefs because, being unintentional states of mind, beliefs cannot be explained by considerations of costs and benefits, except in some cases, such as when normative beliefs can be analyzed in a consequential fashion.

So the CM avoids the main shortcoming of the RCM. The latter model would be general only if the positive and normative beliefs put into play by social actors were always trivial or "consequentially grounded."

The capacity of deduction and prediction

As to the argument that RCM has the exclusive advantage of leading to deductive and predictive theories, nothing tells us that it should not be the property of other types of models. Why would there be an exclusive relation between the particular type of reasons used in the RCM model and these features?

The reader will perhaps forgive me if I evoke here an example drawn from my own work. I have used in my *Inequality, Education and Opportunity* model (IEO model) an approach that belongs to the CM rather than to the RCM (Boudon 1974). Still the model leads to a deductive-predictive machinery. Far from making the individual educational decisions a mere effect of cost–benefit calculations, I introduced the idea that they derive, rather, from a system of contextualized arguments. The argument of three ideal-typical students would be described in the following fashion.

The good student from lower class would say: "I am good at school, so that I can have a good prognosis as to my future educational achievement, if I decide to go to the next stage in the curriculum. I know that with the educational level I have already reached, I will almost certainly have a social status somewhat higher than the status of the people around me, etc.; my family will be proud, etc.; still, why not try to go further in the educational curriculum, since I can do it easily?"

The average student from lower class would say by contrast: "I am average. Trying to go to the next stage in the curriculum would be risky. Maybe I will fail or experience a hard school life. On the other hand, I have already reached a school level which insures me that I will have a social status at least equal to the status of all these people I meet in my social environment. So I should not try to go further."

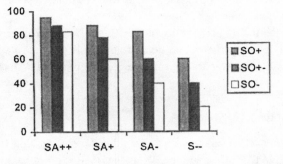

Figure 8.2. Percentage advancing to the next educational level as a function of social origin (SO) and school achievement (SA) (stylized data).

The average student from higher class would have another argument: "I know I am not very good. I know that I may have difficulties in the next class if I try to reach the next educational degree. Still, with my present educational level, I am exposed to the risk of having a social status lower than the status of my orientation family, of the people I have met during my younger years, of all these people in my social environment, so that even if my educational prognosis is not very favorable, I should try to go further."

This IEO theory has been formalized by Fararo and Kosaka (1976). It leads to fine-grained predictions. Thus it tells that an interaction (in the statistical sense) of a very specific structure will be observed between the three variables: "social origin," "level of achievement now," and "probability of going to the next educational level." It predicts that the effect of class origin on educational level will be stronger as the level of educational achievement lowers (see Figure 8.2). Such fine-grained statistical effects are not predicted by the RCM explanation of the same phenomena (Blaug 1968). They are important though: They have been repeatedly observed in many contexts. I am not saying that the theory cannot be made better. Goldthorpe (1996) has developed hints that could make it better. The only point I want to stress by evoking this example is that the capacity of deduction and prediction of a theory, as well as its capacity of being formalized, can be as great with the CM as with the RCM model.

The RCM gives the impression of being a powerful deductive machine because as it uses the axiomatics of neoclassical economics, it is entitled to use the numerous theorems produced by this discipline. This is exactly what happened in the case of the sociology of education inspired by the RCM model. It easily produced a number of theories that were mere applications to the field of education of theorems produced by general economics. But again there is no reason as to why deduction and prediction capacities would be the exclusive property of the RCM, because they do not depend on the nature of reasons mobilized in a model.

The deductive machineries produced by the CM are only less unified. This difference is a direct consequence of the fact that the reasons can be of various kinds depending on the circumstances. The increase in realism from RCM to CM is paid for by a decrease in unity. But scientific theories have to be realistic before anything else.

Of course, I am not sure that the reasons I have put into the minds of pupils and students of my IEO model are realistic in the sense that I could observe them easily and directly with appropriate observational instruments. But as I said earlier, the reconstruction of reasons can be judged along the criteria that are normally used to judge a theory. Thus the reasons evoked in the IEO model reproduce more adequately some statistical data than the RCM. Moreover, they appear as credible.

The paradoxes

A nonnegligible interest of the CM model is that the paradoxes raised by the RCM model become easily solved in the CM framework.[9] A CM solution of Allais's paradoxes can be sketched in the following way. Assume that I am paid a monthly salary of X Euros. The management tells me that I can instead, if I wish, earn a random salary with mathematical expectation of X plus H Euros. Possibly I would accept the deal if H were high enough. But I would not accept it, even for a relatively high H, because accepting a lottery with expectation $X + H$ would in such a real social life situation likely generate all kinds of costs. Thus if I have no savings, or if I want to keep my savings because I regard it as insurance, and if I am indebted, the lottery would expose me to the risk of having to borrow money at a nonzero rate to pay my debts.

Because the experiment creates a closed situation, disconnected from

---

[9] Lévy-Garboua and Montmarquette (1996) propose interesting solutions in terms of "cognitive rationality" of classical "paradoxes."

the real social life of the subject, the analyst assumes that the subject would take into account exclusively the data proposed to him in the context of the experiment, whereas the subject probably generates his answer by "theorizing" the fictitious situation (i.e., by interpreting the experiment by reference to a real-world context). In a real-life situation, however, risk has a potential cost; clearly the subject cannot consider that "maximizing" the immediately visible difference between expected benefits and costs should represent the ultimate principle guiding him or her. In other words, the subjects probably interpret the experimental situation in a fashion meaningful to them, and in a fashion that they have strong reasons to endorse; then, once this interpretation is introduced, they wonder what they should prefer. Utilitarian rationality is guided here by "cognitive rationality." Analysts see here a paradox where there is none because they project on the subject their own interpretations of the experiment.

Incidentally, this example illustrates a point I made earlier. With the RCM in mind, one would predict that the subjects would prefer the lottery for any positive value of H. With the CM in mind, one would predict that they would prefer the lottery when H is greater than some threshold value. The two models lead to "predictions." In this case, the prediction of the latter reproduces the observed data more accurately. Moreover, with the CM rather than the RCM in mind, experimenters would be more curious: They would have more complex hypotheses in mind and would devise more sophisticated experiments. Finally, whereas the CM provides an explanation without black boxes, the RCM has to introduce a black box, "the aversion toward risk." This "aversion" can only be grounded, in a circular fashion, on the effects it is supposed to explain.

On the whole, my guess is that in concrete situations similar to the ones considered in Allais's paradoxes, people would have strong reasons *not* to use the maximization of mathematical expectation as a main criterion. People prefer more to less, but in order to understand their choice, we have to understand why they think they would have more if they do X and less if they do Y. In other words, we have to understand why they theorize the situation the way they do.

The same analysis could be conducted about what can be labeled "Axelrod's paradox" (Axelrod 1990). People choose "Tit for Tat" (TfT) because they theorize the situation created by a repeated "prisoner's dilemma" (PD) game: "My opponent should see that we should cooperate, so I will make the assumption that he will cooperate, and that he will suppose that I will cooperate myself, etc." So when they choose TfT, people do it on the basis of a set of strong arguments.

With the CM rather than the RCM in mind, it becomes much easier to understand why in some circumstances people do *not* actually play TfT but use instead the "defection" strategy. An example – not a minor one – is the arms race between the United States and the USSR during the cold war. For decades the two actors did not play TfT but rather "defection." An end was put to the repeated PD game of the arms race not because the United States and the USSR would have tacitly chosen TfT but because the PD game was destroyed by the big bluff of the "star war," the so-called SDI (Strategic Defense Initiative): With SDI, the USSR could not follow the game any more.

Until this happy end appeared, why did the two nations play "defection" rather than TfT? Basically because they had strong reasons not to take any risk, given the magnitude of the risk involved in being dominated in the arms race. "Defection" is worse than TfT in terms of benefits but better in terms of protection against risk. In technical terms, Axelrod's subjects use Savage's criterion, and the actors of the arms race use Wald's. When people choose a given criterion, we cannot explain their behavior unless we explain why they do so. Generally they have strong reasons for doing so. In the case of the arms race, the strong reasons behind the Waldian choice of the two participants can be formulated in terms of a normative argumentation comparable in its form to Smith's argument, discussed earlier: A government cannot expose the nation it is in charge of to a serious risk if it can avoid it; now, by playing "defection," I, the government, can avoid the risk; so I have to play "defection" in spite of the costs because costs and vital risks are incommensurable. Costs should be made as small as possible, but as long as they can be accepted, they cannot be an argument in favor of TfT. This example shows that when we try to explain why people in some circumstances play TfT and in others not, we have to make the RCM a special case of a more general theory of rationality.

C. Wright Mills's "paradox" can be solved in the same way. The taylorized conditions in which the clerks are placed are such that any departure from a strict equality between contribution and retribution can be immediately and easily perceived. Moreover, it is normally treated as intolerable. The white collars are all equal; they are all devoted to similar tasks. So any minor advantage is perceived as an illegitimate privilege.

From an utilitarian viewpoint, it matters little to me whether I sit a little closer to the window. But as soon as this advantage to the benefit of X results from a decision of the supervisor, I perceive it not as unpleasant but as unfair: I am here to get some retribution from my contribution; I am in a situation of social contract with the firm; any unjustified advantage in favor of X, however minor, is a violation of this basic contract and consequently morally intolerable, even if materially of weak relevance. Any irrational analysis fails to account for the apparent disproportion between cause and effect, but a RCM analysis is not better off here. An irrational analysis does not account for the fact that the conflict occurs independently of the personal idiosyncrasies. A RCM analysis fails to account for the disproportion between the importance of the issue and the strength of the reaction.

I have discussed elsewhere at length the various solutions proposed for the "not voting" paradox (Boudon 1996c). I will leave aside here this critical side of the analysis. It leads to the conclusion that the various "solutions" of the paradox all include strong assumptions and fail to reproduce correctly the observed data. So they are weak on the Popperian and non-Popperian criteria normally used to evaluate a scientific theory.[10] By contrast, a theory taking "axiological rationality" seriously meets the two types of criteria easily. People vote because they have strong reasons to believe that democracy is a good regime. Elections are an essential piece of the democratic system. So they conclude that one *should* vote on the basis of a practical syllogism with strong premises. Even if voting is boring to me, I should vote. Of course, in some cases, people do not know who among the candidates is better, or they can even be convinced that none is very good, and take this into account by refraining from voting. But, on the whole, many people vote.

In its simplicity (why should simple explanations be wrong?), this explanation is much more acceptable than others if one uses the criteria generally used to evaluate a scientific theory. It is congruent with the fact that people do actually vote. It is also congruent with the subjective explanation people usually give of their vote. In most cases, they would feel and say that they vote because one should vote, not that they "like to vote" nor that they "feel constrained to vote," as Durkheimians would maintain. Why should we ignore these subjective facts? Although subjec-

---

[10] See the distinction between the two types of criteria in Boudon (1995b).

tive, they are facts, except to hard-core positivists. A basic rule is that a scientific theory should try to explain all relevant facts without arbitrarily evacuating any. If a theory claims that people "like" to vote or "feel constrained" to vote, it should explain why people feel that they "should" vote. In other words, it should explain the causes of this "false consciousness." Or if analysts take false consciousness for granted, they should explain why it turns out that they themselves have been protected against this fate.

My earlier example drawn from Adam Smith, as well as Mills's "overreaction paradox," "Axelrod's paradox," the paradox of not voting, and others, demonstrate on the whole that as Weber has rightly contended, axiological rationality cannot be reduced to utilitarian-instrumental rationality.

Conclusion

Analyzing social mechanisms requires – at least ideally – making them the outcome of individual beliefs, actions, attitudes, and so on. Consequently, a final account of a social mechanism is reached when these beliefs, actions, and attitudes can themselves be explained. This explanation of course has to take into account the structural features of the social context in which the actors move. I have tried to make two main points: that beliefs, actions, and attitudes should be treated as far as possible as rational – more precisely, as the effect of reasons perceived by social actors as strong – and that reasons of the "cost–benefit" type should not be given more attention than they deserve. Rationality is one thing, expected utility another.

Why should we introduce this rationality postulate? Because social actors try to act in congruence with strong reasons. This explains why their own behavior is normally meaningful to them. In some cases, the context reveals that these reasons are of the "cost–benefit" type. In other cases, they are not: Even if we interpret the notions of cost and benefit in the most extensive fashion, what are the costs and benefits to me of miners being better paid than soldiers if I have no chance of ever becoming a soldier or a miner?

On the whole, to get a satisfactory theory of rationality, one has to accept the idea that rationality is not exclusively instrumental: It also has an axiological dimension and a cognitive one. In other words, the reasons motivating an actor can be strong without belonging to the instrumental species.

Considering the RCM a special case of the CM has the advantage of making possible the extension of the main advantage of RCM (producing black-box–free explanations) to a much wider set of social mechanisms. But I must stress again that if the CM is more general than the RCM, it cannot be applied to all phenomena. Irrationality should be given its rightful place. "Traditional" and "affective" actions also exist. Moreover, all actions rest on a ground of instincts. I look on my right and left when crossing a street because I want to stay alive. Reason is the servant of passions.[11]

Finally, the theory of rationality that I have sketched raises some important questions that I will content myself to mention. Does the fact that behavior and beliefs are normally inspired by strong reasons, even though these reasons can be false, mean that any behavior or belief can be justified? Certainly not. Priestley believed in phlogiston; Lavoisier did not. The two had strong reasons for believing what they believed, and they saw their reasons as valid. The latter was right; the former wrong. So the strength of reasons is a function of the context. Today our cognitive context is such that Priestley's reasons have become weak *to us*, because we know Lavoisier's reasons were stronger. But the latter had to be devised and put on the market before the conclusion could be drawn that Lavoisier was right. It should also be noted that it then became *irreversibly* right against Priestley. So no relativism follows from the contextuality of reasons.

As with cognitive reasons, axiological reasons can become stronger or weaker over time mainly because new reasons are invented. When it was shown that the abolition of capital punishment could not be held responsible for any significant increase in crime rates, the argument "Capital punishment is good because it is an effective threat against crime" became weaker. This provoked a change – an *irreversible* one – in our "moral sensibility" toward capital punishment.

These examples show also that there are no mechanically applicable criteria of the strength of reasons. Priestley's reasons were strong as long as Lavoisier's were not fully developed. Hence it was impossible, looking

---

[11] "Reason is, and ought only to be the slave of the passions and can never pretend to any other office than to serve and obey them" Hume ([1739–40] 1978, book 2, section 3, p. 415).

exclusively at Priestley's reasons, to determine whether they were weak or strong. This analysis can be generalized. Those who look for the criteria of truth, writes Kant ([1787] n.d., I, 2nd. part [Die transcendentale Logik], III [Von der Einteilung der allgemeinen Logik in Analytik und Dialektik], p. 93), are like the two idiots who try to milk a male goat, with one trying to milk while the other holds a bucket under the animal's belly.

References

Allais, M. 1953. "Le comportement de l'homme rationnel devant le risque: critique des postulats de l'école américaine." *Econometrica* 21, 4: 503–46.

Allais, M., and O. Hagen (eds.). 1979. *Expected Utility Hypotheses and the Allais Paradox: Contemporary Discussions of Decisions under Uncertainty with Allais' Rejoinder*. Dordrecht: Reidel.

Axelrod, R. 1990. *The Evolution of Cooperation*. Harmondsworth: Penguin.

Blaug, M. (ed.). 1968. *The Economics of Education*. Harmondsworth: Penguin.

Boudon, R. 1974. *Education, Opportunity and Social Inequality*. New York: Wiley.

Boudon, R. 1986. *Theories of Social Change. A Critical Appraisal*. London: Basil Blackwell/Polity Press.

Boudon, R. 1992. "Sentiments of Justice and Social Inequalities." *Social Justice Research* vol. 5, 2: 113–35.

Boudon, R. 1993. "European Sociology: The Identity Lost?" Pp. 27–44 in *Sociology in Europe. In Search of Identity*, edited by B. Nedelmann and P. Sztompka. New York: de Gruyter.

Boudon, R. 1994. *Art of Self-Persuasion*. London: Polity Press.

Boudon, R. 1995a. *Le Juste et le Vrai*. Paris: Fayard.

Boudon, R. 1995b. "How Can Sociology "Make Sense" Again?" *Revue Suisse de Sociologie*, vol. 21, 2: 233–41.

Boudon, R. 1996a. "The 'Rational Choice Model': A Particular Case of the 'Cognitive Model,' " *Rationality and Society*, 8, 2: 123–50.

Boudon, R. 1996b. Forthcoming. "The Present Relevance of Weber's Theory of *Wertrationalität*" in *Conference "Economics and Ethics in the Historical School of Economics. Achievements and Present Relevance*," 27–31 March, to be published in the series *Studies in Economic Ethics and Philosophy*. Berlin: Springer.

Boudon, R. 1996c. Unpublished. "Au-delà de la rationalité limitée." Séminaire "Transaction et théorie sociologique," FUL d'Arlon, 28–30 March.

Brenner, A. 1990. *Duhem, Science réalité et apparence*. Paris: Vrin.

Buridan, Jean. n.d. *Magistri Johannis Buridam Questiones octavi libri physicorum*. Queritur 12e utrum projectum post exitum a manu projicientis moveatur ab aere vel a quo moveatur. Bibliothèque Nationale, fonds latin, ms. n14723, fol. 106, col. a, to fol. 107, col. b. – *Acutissimi philosophi reverendi Magistri*

Johannis Buridani *subtilissime questiones super octo physicorum libros Aristotelis.* . . . Parisiis, MDIX. Fol. cxx, col b., to fol. cxxi, col b. [Quoted by Duhem (1913–59 : VIII, 201)].

Coleman, J. 1986. *Individual Interests and Collective Action: Selected Essays.* Cambridge: Cambridge University Press.

Coleman, J. 1990. *Foundations of Social Theory.* Cambridge/London: The Belknap Press of Harvard University Press.

Duhem, P. 1913–59. *Le système du monde. Histoire des doctrines cosmologiques de Platon à Copernic.* Paris: Hermann.

Fararo, T. J., and K. Kosaka. 1976. "A Mathematical Analysis of Boudon's IEO Model." *Social Science Information* 15, 2–3: 431–75.

Ferejohn, F. J., and M. Fiorina. 1974. "The Paradox of Not Voting: A Decision Theoretic Analysis." *The American Political Science Review* 68, 2: 525–36.

Goldthorpe, J. 1996. Unpublished. "Class Analysis and the Reorientation of Class Theory: The Case of the Persisting Differentials in Educational Attainment."

Hagen, O. 1995. "Risk in Utility Theory, in Business and in the World of Fear and Hope." Pp. 191–210 in *Revolutionary Changes in Understanding Man and Society, Scopes and Limits*, edited by J. Götschl. Dordrecht/London: Kluwer.

Hoffman, E., and M. L. Spitzer. 1985. "Entitlements, Rights and Fairness. An Experimental Examination of Subjects' Concepts of Distributive Justice." *Journal of Legal Studies* 14: 259–97.

Hollis, M. 1977. *Models of Man: Philosophical Thoughts on Social Action.* Cambridge: Cambridge University Press.

Hume, D. [1739–40] 1978. *A Treatise of Human Nature.* Oxford: Oxford University Press.

Kahneman, D., and A. Tversky. 1973. "Availability: A Heuristic for Judging Frequency and Probability." *Cognitive Psychology* 5: 207–32.

Kant I. [1787] n.d. *Kritik der reinen Vernunft,* Bibliographisches Institüt. Leipzig/Vienna: Meyers Volksbücher, 2nd ed.

Kuran, T. 1995. *Private Truths, Public Lies. The Social Consequences of Preference Falsification.* Cambridge: Harvard University Press.

Lévy-Garboua, L., and C. Montmarquette. 1996. "Cognition in Seemingly Riskless Choices and Judgments." *Rationality and Society* 8, 2: 167–85.

Mills, C. W. 1951. *White Collars. The American Middle Classes.* New York: Oxford University Press.

Oberschall, A. 1989. Unpublished. "Cultural Change and Social Movements." Communication American Sociological Association.

Olson, M. 1965. *The Logic of Collective Action; Public Goods and the Theory of Groups.* Cambridge: Harvard University Press.

Overbye, E. 1995. "Making a Case for the Rational, Self-regarding, 'Ethical' Voter . . . and Solving the 'Paradox of Not Voting' in the Process." *European Journal of Political Research* 27: 369–96.

Popper, K. 1967. "La rationalité et le statut de principe de rationalité." Pp. 142–50 in *Les fondements philosophiques des systèmes économiques*, edited by E. M. Claasen. Paris: Payot.

Quattrone, G. A., and A. Tversky. 1987. "Self-deception and the Voter's Illusion." Pp. 35–58 in *The Multiple Self*, edited by J. Elster. Cambridge: Cambridge University Press.

Root, H. L. 1994. *La construction de l'état moderne en Europe: la France et l'Angleterre*. Paris: PUF.

Scheler, M. [1913–16] 1954. *Der Formalismus in der Ethik und die materiale Wertethik, in Gesammelte Werke*. vol. 2. Bern/München: Francke.

Smith, A. [1776] 1976. *An Inquiry into the Nature and Causes of the Wealth of Nations*. General ed., R. H. Campbell and A. S. Skinner; textual ed., W. B. Todd. Oxford: Clarendon Press.

Tocqueville, A. de. [1856] 1955. *The Old Regime and the French Revolution*. New York: Doubleday.

Walzer, M. 1983. *Spheres of Justice. A Defence of Pluralism and Equality*. Oxford: Martin Robertson.

Weber, M. 1922. *Aufsätze zur Wissenschaftlehre*. Tübingen: Mohr.

Wilson, J. Q. 1993. *The Moral Sense*. New York: The Free Press.

9. Is sociological theory too grand for social mechanisms?

AXEL VAN DEN BERG

Introduction

Nomothesis is definitely *out*. There is, in fact, some question whether it ever existed to begin with, even in principle. Not even Auguste Comte, the original positivist arch-generalizer himself, *really* meant all that stuff about ineluctable "laws" and "stages," it now turns out (Scharff 1995). He was, in effect, a "post-positivist" *avant la lettre*. Talk about being ahead of one's time!

Idiography is all the rage. If there is anything that characterizes the general drift of sociological theory since the eclipse of Parsonian structural functionalism and its *marxisant* challengers, it is the revitalization of all manner of *interpretivist* microsociological approaches, from symbolic interactionism to various forms of phenomenology, from hermeneutics to ethnomethodology.

Against such odds, what is the aspiring social theorist to do? One option is to join the swelling postmodern chorus of denouncers of generalization *tout court*. But once the initial excitement of being up against the nasty establishment and on the side of the downtrodden wears off, such denunciation leaves little to satisfy one's generalizing yearnings.

Another option is once again to attempt the Grand Synthesis. In this chapter, I will argue that this is precisely what the most prominent of the present generation of social theorists have done. They have taken it upon themselves to bridge the gulf between the nomothetic, macrosociological, "structural" traditions of yore and the currently fashionable idiographic,

I would like to thank Peter Hedström, Richard Swedberg, Lars Udehn, Diego Gambetta, Art Stinchcombe, Jon Elster, Andrew Abbott, and the other participants in the session of the Conference on Social Mechanisms in which an earlier version of this paper was presented for their very helpful comments.

microsociological, voluntaristic ("agentic"?) approaches. In the process, so I will argue, a third option, the systematic search for explanatory mechanisms advocated in this volume, never stood a chance.

Let me state at the outset that I will not argue that there are no explanatory mechanisms to be found in the work of these theorists. Indeed, I think their work is replete with such mechanisms. In fact I believe it can be argued – although this is not the place to do so at length – that no account of social events is really possible *without* some recourse, explicitly or implicitly, to at least *some* such mechanisms. But the way in which these theorists treat social mechanisms is, so to speak, consumptive rather than productive. That is to say, explanatory mechanisms figure in an ad hoc, offhand fashion, not to be identified, examined, refined, and tested but in a subsidiary role, in the service of ulterior theoretical motives.

Let me briefly clarify this by reference to Coleman's simple macro-micro-macro model already mentioned in Chapter 1 by Hedström and Swedberg. If we accept that for analytical purposes it is useful to distinguish between macro-structural and micro-individual levels, then the explanatory task of any sociological theory consists of either providing an explanatory mechanism accounting for how structure is converted by individuals into social action, or how such social actions aggregate to constitute social structures, *or* both. My contention, then, is that the main theoretical contributions of the major theorists I will discuss contribute little or nothing to either of these tasks, nor do they hold any promise of doing so.

But why *should* sociological theory contribute to any such hopelessly outmoded, "positivist" program, one might ask. That such a question can be viewed as a reasonable one to put to sociologists – rather than philosophers of science – is itself a reflection of the somewhat alarming shift in the character of "sociological theory" that will be partly documented in this chapter. More and more, it seems, what passes for "sociological theory," or, more ominously, "*general* sociological theory," deals with matters of epistemology, ontology, and philosophy of science, at the expense of the more mundane business of theorizing about the social world. "Sociological theory" nowadays seems to be mostly theorizing about theorizing, not attempting to formulate coherent accounts of things happening "out there." "Theory," in short, has become a subdiscipline in its own right, and one with its own apparent criteria of utility and relevance that seem wholly divorced from the needs and concerns of practicing sociological researchers. In my mind, this is exactly equivalent to the much-lamented autonomization of (mostly quantitative) methodology, and no less absurd or damaging to the discipline as a whole.

Of course, there still are, of practical necessity, lots of sociologists who engage in theorizing with the aim of coming up with better, more coherent, more durable, and/or more encompassing explanations for various phenomena and events in the social world. But in terms of prestige and sheer name recognition throughout the discipline, such "empirical" theorists play decidedly second fiddle to the practitioners of "general" theory. Possibly the last explanatory theorist of the former kind to be recognized widely across subdisciplines and schools of thought was Robert Merton. These days only theorists of the most "general" variety command that kind of respect, or at least recognition.

The four theorists that I will discuss are, without doubt, the most widely recognized practitioners of the *genre*: Jürgen Habermas, Pierre Bourdieu, Anthony Giddens, and Jeffrey Alexander. Few sociologists will claim to be fully conversant with the work of all four, and fewer still can claim to really understand it. But the overwhelming majority will have heard their names and have *some* vague idea of what they are all about.

Of course, I will make no attempt to survey each author's *oeuvre* in its entirety. Such a foolhardy effort would quickly drive the ordinary reader to desperation without ever coming close to satisfying even these authors' most lukewarm admirers. Within the confines of this brief chapter, I can only treat those aspects of their work, and even them rather summarily, that have earned them the status of "general" theorist.

The moral imperative: Habermas

As the foremost heir of the famed Frankfurt School of Adorno, Horkheimer, and Benjamin (see, e.g., Jay 1973), Habermas has never been interested in sociological theory as *merely* a device or foundation for *explaining* things social. An additional and often overriding aim of Habermas's theorizing has been to develop a (basis for) a *critical* theory of society – that is, a theory capable of uncovering and criticizing society's "social pathologies" (Habermas 1984, p. xi). As is well-known, after having given up on the proletariat as the possible material carrier of an *immanent* critique of capitalism, his former mentors ended up losing all hope of ever finding any effective, nonarbitrary antidote against what they increasingly came to see as the all-pervasive and relentless march of "instrumental reason." Habermas's lifework has, in fact, consisted of a sustained effort to somehow recover such hope. His main concern has been, and continues to be, to discover the social (as well as philosophical, linguistic, etc.) bases for an alternative kind of reason that can be effectively used to uncover and counter the deleterious effects of "instrumental reason."

Seen from this angle, sociological explanation has played a decidedly subordinate role in Habermas's work. It has mostly served as an instrument for seeking out *social* (as opposed to "merely" philosophical) sources of, or bases for a form of critical, noninstrumental reason.[1] Nevertheless, particularly in his magnum opus, *The Theory of Communicative Action* (1984, 1987), Habermas quite explicitly sets out to provide a foundation of *explanatory* sociological theory as well, one that integrates "action-theoretical" and "system-theoretical" approaches. Much like his Grand Synthetic contemporaries, Habermas takes up the challenge of *overcoming* the gulf separating micro- from macro-sociology, hermeneutic understanding from causal explanation, and reflective agent from structural compulsion.

In typically Habermasian fashion, he arrives at his "two-level" theory of modern society by means of a series of exceedingly complicated, often downright tortuous, "reconstructions" of the thinking of Marx, Parsons, Weber, Durkheim, Mead, Horkheimer, Adorno, Garfinkel, Goffman, Husserl, Gadamar, Lukács, and Luhmann, to mention but the most prominent. Without exception, these efforts are highly debatable from the exegetical point of view, as a vast secondary literature attests.[2] But the interpretive details need not detain us here. Suffice it to sketch out enough of the outlines of Habermas's Grand Synthesis to assess its promise with respect to the identification and analysis of middle-range social mechanisms.

On the action-theoretic side, Habermas takes his main inspiration from Schutz and Parsons, to posit society as a "lifeworld," a commonly shared, mostly tacitly held "stock of knowledge" consisting of culture, social institutions, and personal identities. This lifeworld is, according to Haber-

---

[1] In this respect, Habermas has remained true to what I have elsewhere argued is the ultimate philosophical core of Marxism (see van den Berg 1988).

[2] As Habermas himself admits: "I make the foreign tongues my own in a rather brutal manner, hermeneutically speaking. Even when I quote a good deal and take over other terminologies I am clearly aware that my use of them often has little to do with the authors' original meaning" (Honneth, Knödler-Bunte, and Widmann 1981, p. 30).

mas, produced and reproduced by symbolic, linguistic means – that is, by *communicative action*. Communicative action, in turn, involves "reaching understanding" under ideal, uncoerced conditions, "a process of mutually convincing one another in which the actions of participants are coordinated on the basis of motivation by reasons. 'Coming to an understanding' refers to communication aimed at achieving a valid agreement" (Habermas 1984, p. 392).

Somewhat notoriously, Habermas has spent half a lifetime trying to establish this, his most fundamental claim, by enlisting a long succession of disciplines and theoretical traditions – suitably "reconstructed" for the purpose, naturally – from psychoanalysis to modern epistemology, from linguistics to systems theory, from speech act theory to hermeneutics, from developmental psychology to historical materialism. From these, Habermas has worked up a massive repertoire of arguments and suggestions[3] purported to show that, in some sense, communicative action, "action orientated to reaching understanding" (Habermas, 1982, p. 227), implies or relies on an "ideal speech situation," a situation that "excludes all force . . . except the force of the better argument . . . all motives except that of a cooperative search for the truth," where participants are "relieved of the pressure of action and experience" so that they can "test with reasons, and only with reasons, whether the claim defended by the proponents rightfully stands or not," with the "aim to *produce* cogent *arguments* that are convincing in virtue of their intrinsic properties" (Habermas 1984, p. 25; see also pp. 272–3, 285–6, 392, 398).

It can reasonably be argued, I think (see van den Berg 1980, 1990), that whatever the specific arguments used by Habermas, in the final analysis they all boil down to the "central intuition" (Honneth, Knödler-Bunte, and Widmann 1981, p. 9; Dews 1986, p. 99) that the "ideal speech situation" is in some way "the inherent telos of human speech" (Habermas 1984, p. 287). There is much confusion and debate about whether Habermas thereby wishes to claim that "communicative rationality" in this sense is logically implied by, inherent in, necessary for, presupposed by, or the necessary means of the reproduction of the lifeworld. At the very least, he would have to concede that real, existing lifeworlds have quite successfully reproduced themselves, and continue to do so, by means of "speech situations" that are considerably short of his "ideal."

---

[3] For a brief, critical review of a number of these, see van den Berg (1990, pp. 163–74).

But in any case, a large part of Habermas's "two-level" theory of society hinges on the notion that there has been a historical tendency for the lifeworld to become *more and more* "rationalized" – his somewhat chilling term for "democratized" – that is, more closely approaching an "ideal speech situation." According to Habermas, with modernization the processes of reproduction of the lifeworld become increasingly "reflexive," increasingly detached from received tradition, increasingly a matter of *"discursive will-formation"* (Habermas 1987, p. 147). "In a rationalized lifeworld the need for achieving understanding is met less and less by a reservoir of traditionally certified interpretations immune from criticism; at the level of a completely decentered understanding of the world, the need for consensus must be met more and more frequently by risky, because rationally motivated, agreement" (Habermas 1984, p. 340).

But not all joint action or interaction is, or can be – particularly in modern societies – coordinated purely by such risky procedures. Some systems of action can be, and in modern societies must be, steered by mechanisms that do not appeal directly to actors' intentions and orientations. To understand this aspect of social reproduction, Habermas claims, we need a functional or systems theory rather than the interpretive, "intentionalist" perspective applicable to the lifeworld just outlined.

Taking his cues from Luhmann and Parsons, Habermas develops the *systems*-theoretic side of his argument to understand, in particular, the functioning of two central societal domains, the economy and the legal-political system. These, he argues, are coordinated through the generalized "delinguistified steering media" money and power (Habermas 1984, pp. 341–2). These steering media do not appeal to or require unwieldy and unpredictable processes of reaching mutual understanding but merely adjustment of individual action in accordance with the pursuit of individual interest. Here Habermas in fact explicitly refers to "systemic *mechanisms* that stabilize non-intended systems of action" (Habermas 1987, p. 150, emphasis added).

Now the fact that money and power can steer the economic and legal-political systems *without* requiring the establishment of consensus by means of communicative action permits these systems to become "uncoupled" from the processes of symbolic reproduction of the lifeworld. This is both the result of the increasing "rationalization" of the lifeworld and a necessary precondition for it. For, as the reproduction of the lifeworld can rely less and less on the automatisms of received tradition in favor of discursive will-formation, this can only be accomplished if *other* spheres of social life can function more or less independently by means of steering mechanism able to *replace* linguistic communication.

Thus the "uncoupling" of system from lifeworld is a necessary part of the overall process of rationalization, according to Habermas. But the process is "contradictory from the start" (Habermas 1984, p. 342). The contradiction arises between a lifeworld in which the communicative reaching of understanding becomes more and more the primary principle of integration, on the one hand, and the increasing complexity of the now unleashed systems of purposive-rational action, on the other (Habermas 1984, pp. 342–3). While the "social-life context" must reproduce "*both* through the media-controlled purposive-rational actions of its members [sic] *and* through the common will anchored in the communicative practice of all individuals" (Habermas 1984, p. 398), there is the persistent danger of a "colonization of the lifeworld" by the subsystems of purposive-rational action (see especially Habermas 1987, pp. 153–97, 301–31).[4]

This is, according to Habermas, the "rational core" (1984, p. 390) of Horkheimer and Adorno's critique of instrumental reason. Once it is formulated in this way, their despair turns out to have been premature since there is an alternative concept of reason available and exemplified by the "mechanism of linguistic communication . . . that emerges in increasing purity from the rationalization of the lifeworld" (Habermas 1984, p. 342). Moreover, Habermas is able to point to a number of recent sociopolitical movements, including feminism, Greens (environmentalists), peace movements, human rights activists, ethnic and geographically based movements, and youth and "alternative" movements, as representatives of the embattled "lifeworld," struggling against the encroachments of monetary and bureaucratic principles of organization (see Habermas 1981, 1986, 1987, pp. 391–6).

As noted by several critics (e.g., Baxter 1987; Schudson 1994), Habermas's stark and largely unmotivated contrast between a "lifeworld" coordinated by democratic consensus seeking and "systems" guided essentially by greed and power has its roots in his need to identify the social bases of good and evil, not in any desire to develop better *explanatory*

---

[4] For two excellent summaries, see McCarthy's introduction to Habermas (1984, pp. xix–xxvii) and Baxter (1987).

resources. Put differently, once again Habermas's *moral* intent wins it, hands down, from his explanatory aspirations.

What is characteristic of the "ideal speech situation," and by implication of the "lifeworld," is precisely the *absence*, or at least decreasing significance, of *any* social mechanism – for all such mechanisms would necessarily "distort" the intent of coming to an unmediated, uncoerced consensus. On the other hand, the social mechanisms that lie behind the developmental trends characterizing the rise and expansion of "systems" are of no real interest to Habermas and can, thus, only be surmised. Presumably they are not unlike those initially posited by Weber to account for the Western trend toward rationalization and disenchantment. At the same time, however, there is a strong element of Parsonian functionalism in Habermas's contention that systems of delinguistified coordination arise *in order to* free the economy and polity from the arduous and cumbersome processes of "discursive will-formation."

On the other hand, there may be some sort of mechanism akin to Simon's "bounded rationality" at work here. That is, Habermas may be assuming that there is some sort of finite limit on the amount of time and energy we can afford to spend on processes of "discursive will formation" and that, when that limit comes in sight, we tend to cast about for ways of coordinating at least some of our joint activities by other more automatic means.

The interaction between the two in the form of "colonization" finally refers vaguely to the intrusion of "alien" elements of purposive rationality into the allegedly communicatively structured "lifeworld." There is some vague resonance here with the currently widespread unease about modernday bigness, impersonal constraints, and materialism, but that is all there is – a vague resonance with equally vague general sentiments. There *may* be some sort of theory of human nature underlying this to the effect that people will resist any encroachments on the processes of democratic, discursive will formation but this is hardly the stuff of solid, explanatory middle-range theory.

My point, then, is not that there are no signs of social mechanisms to be found in the trends and interconnections that Habermas claims to discern in advanced (formerly "late") capitalist societies. To the contrary, his arguments are replete with such mechanisms, albeit in a remarkably unreflective state. There are in fact *countless* hints and implied assumptions running through his labyrinthine exegeses that could certainly furnish the raw materials for quite a repertoire of social mechanisms.

But these would be only incidental by-products of Habermas's massive theoretical project. That project is concerned with identifying the forces for progress in contemporary society and the dangers to which they are exposed, not with carefully formulating and cataloguing the various social mechanisms that might help us better to understand how social systems and individuals' actions mesh. It is also, clearly, this overriding moral-philosophical purpose, rather than any burning desire to sort out the complex causal interconnections between the micro and the macro level of social life, that caused Habermas to pick up the widely circulating action-vs.-system *problématique*. Finally, given his primarily moral purpose and his exceedingly philosophical bent, Habermas's way of dealing with that *problématique* has no doubt greatly contributed to turning it into a matter of abstract epistemology or ontology rather than the middle-level explanation envisaged by Coleman, Elster, and others.

Recursive resolutions: Bourdieu and Giddens

Bourdieu: Habitus

To his credit, of all major Grand Synthesizers, Pierre Bourdieu is the only one who also actively conducts empirical research and who repeatedly and heatedly denies even *being* a "theorist" (see Jenkins, 1992, pp. 66–7).[5] With a dedicated army of followers, Bourdieu has undertaken a vast array of empirical studies of a variety of institutional and cultural sectors – referred to as "social fields" – ranging from the arts to the educational system, from the homeless to the state and politics, from the sociology of taste to marriage and the family (e.g., Bourdieu 1977b, 1984, 1988).

In this empirical work, Bourdieu *does*, in fact, operate with a variety of social mechanisms, although he would not call them that. Behind his notions of various forms of "capital" (social, cultural, symbolic), which are accumulated and monopolized in different forms in the various "social

---

[5] Here is one typical disclaimer on the occasion of a "workshop" with his faithful lieutenant in North America, Loïc Wacquant: "Let me say outright and very forcefully that I never "theorize," if by that we mean engage in the kind of conceptual gobbledygook (*laius*) that is good for textbooks and which, through an extraordinary misconstrual of the logic of science, passes for Theory in much of Anglo-American social science" (Wacquant 1989, p. 50).

fields," according to the rules operative in each, lie, implicitly at least, social mechanisms such as network formation through the systematic exchange of favors and obligations, mechanisms of cultural inheritance, various mechanisms of social exclusion and closure, and so on. But for the invariably pretentious and barely intelligible manner in which these empirical studies are presented,[6] they would seem to be commendable albeit not particularly original efforts.

But if Bourdieu only offered some fairly straightforward handiwork in the more or less Weberian social closure tradition, as he himself occasionally and somewhat disingenuously claims, he would hardly have reached the international intellectual stature he now enjoys. And surely the abstruse presentation is part of a strategy to lay claim to the elevated rank of Grand Theorist far above that to which a merely empirical sociological researcher, however productive, can ever hope to aspire. Moreover, his empirical studies are invariably presented as the product of a revolutionary new theoretical approach and methodology. His own protestations to the contrary notwithstanding, then, it is his alleged *theoretical* genius that is really Bourdieu's claim to international fame (cf. Jenkins 1992).

But for all his alleged originality, Bourdieu is surprisingly similar to his Grand Synthesizing contemporaries in what he claims to accomplish. He, too, professes to have found a way of overcoming the opposition in social science between what he calls "objectivism" and "subjectivism." His approach aims to "move beyond the antagonism between these two modes of knowledge, while preserving the gains from each of them" (Bourdieu 1990a, p. 25). And again, "the sort of philosophy of science that I have tried to develop has, from the first, challenged the Germanic distinction between 'explanation' and 'understanding' which has been a kind of a priori Diktat according to which the human sciences are not the same kind of sciences as the rest" (Bourdieu 1992, p. 46).

The way out of this "ritual choice" (Jenkins 1992, p. 66) is, according to Bourdieu, to realize that "practices can have other principles than mechanical causes or conscious ends. . . . The principle of practices has to be

---

[6] "It cannot be denied that Bourdieu is hard to read," even his admirers concede (Robbins 1991, p. 1). This is a considerable understatement. His prose has been more aptly described as "a veritable *forêt sauvage* of neologisms, sub-clauses, paragraphic sentences and circumlocution" (Jenkins 1989, p. 640). "If anything, Bourdieu is a much worse example of systematically compromised intelligibility than Parsons" (Jenkins 1992, p. 173, fn.30).

sought instead in the relationship between external constraints which leave a very variable margin for choice, and dispositions which are the product of economic and social processes that are more or less completely reducible to these constraints, as defined at a particular moment'' (Bourdieu 1990a, p. 50). Thus Bourdieu's introduction of his oft-cited but little understood notion of *habitus*, his solution to the theoretical dilemma.

Unfortunately, *habitus* is a notoriously difficult notion to pin down. By most accounts, *The Logic of Practice* contains the "most exhaustive theoretical explication of Bourdieu's *habitus* theory" (Broady 1990, p. 228, my translation), with a whole chapter devoted to the concept. Yet one looks in vain for a straightforward definition. The closest thing I was able to find is this: "systems of durable, transposable dispositions, structured structures predisposed to function as structuring structures, that is as principles which generate and organize practices and representations that can be objectively adapted to their outcomes without presupposing a conscious aiming at ends or an express mastery of the operations necessary in order to attain them" (Bourdieu 1990a, p. 53).

Although the foregoing quote is not terribly helpful, I believe what Bourdieu has in mind is something like the following. Social action is to be explained as the joint product of the objective conditions that people face and the preexisting dispositions with which they confront and interpret those conditions. Those predispositions, in turn, are in fact none other than the "practical answers" people had devised to meet *previous* conditions and which are, therefore, "objectively compatible with these conditions and in a sense pre-adapted to their demands" (Bourdieu 1990a, p. 54). As long as these conditions do not change, the *habitus* "tends to guarantee the 'correctness' of practices and their constancy over time" (Bourdieu 1990a, p. 54). Thus "the *habitus*, a product of history, produces individual and collective practices – more history – in accordance with the schemes generated by history. It ensures the active presence of past experiences, which, deposited in each organism in the form of schemes of perception, thought and action, tend to guarantee the 'correctness' of practices and their constancy over time, more reliably than all formal rules and explicit norms" (Bourdieu 1990a, p. 54). If objective conditions do change, however, this will force people to consider new practical solutions which, ipso facto, modifies the *habitus* accordingly.

The following quote confirms my general interpretation.

The lines of action suggested by habitus may very well be accompanied by a strategic calculation of costs and benefits which tends to carry out at a conscious level the operations which habitus carries out in its own way. . . . Times of crises, in which the routine adjustment of subjective and objective structures is brutally disrupted, constitute a class of circumstances when indeed "rational choice" often appears to take over. But, and this is a crucial proviso, it is habitus itself that commands this option. We can always say that individuals make choices, as long as we do not forget that they do not choose the principle of these choices. (Wacquant 1989, p. 45; see also Jenkins 1992, p. 77)

Thus there exists a "dialectical relationship . . . between the regularities of the material universe of properties and the classificatory schemes of the *habitus*" (Bourdieu 1990a, p. 140), with material conditions and *habitus* mutually (re-)producing one another in a seamless "network of circuits of circular causality" (Bourdieu 1990a, p. 97).

Every "social field," Bourdieu declares, requires "agents equipped with the *habitus* needed to make them work" (Bourdieu 1990a, p. 67). The requisite dispositions must be systematically and relentlessly inculcated from early childhood on so as to acquire the character of "doxa," "undisputed, pre-reflexive, naive, native compliance with the fundamental presuppositions of the field" (Bourdieu 1990a, p. 68). The use of the automatisms of language and bodily postures or "hexis" ("body language")[7] is particularly important, Bourdieu maintains (1990a, pp. 68–71; see also Jenkins 1992, pp. 67–84).

These, then, are the elements with which Bourdieu wants to carry out his radical "transformation of scientific practice" (1990a, p. 145) and that will permit us at last to "move beyond the false choice in which social science generally allows itself to be trapped, that between social physics and social phenomenology" (ibid., p. 135).

At first sight, Bourdieu's notion of *habitus* appears to be a promising candidate for a social mechanism or cluster of such mechanisms. It suggests something about people more or less turning existing resources to

---

[7] Broady (1990, pp. 236, 252) claims that Bourdieu uses the term *hexis* simply as an Aristotelian synonym for the Latin *habitus*. While the original meaning of the two terms is indeed very similar and Bourdieu does not bother to define either term adequately, it is quite clear that he uses them in the distinct senses indicated here (cf. Jenkins 1992, p. 75).

their advantage by a combination of strategic and habitual action. Yet, on closer inspection, the role of any specific social mechanisms becomes less and less clear.

It would seem sensible enough, albeit not especially novel, to depict human action as the joint product of objective conditions and preexisting dispositions. This is, in fact, the standard form of most explanations of social action, is it not? But then the question remains where these dispositions come from and how they affect action. Are they more or less freely chosen, or are they deeply inculcated and hence followed more or less blindly? Do they prescribe behavior within very specific limitations, or do they only offer a wide repertoire from which one can choose?

Although "Bourdieu is to the highest degree heedful of the fact that people have intentions, will and a capacity for conscious action," we are told by one devotee, "he never neglects to raise the question of how these intentions, this will and this capacity to act have been implanted" (Broady 1990, p. 233, my translation). "Implanted" seems an apt term for the way Bourdieu insists on the necessity for systematic inculcation from early childhood of the unconscious, prereflexive dispositions of the *habitus* that are a functional requisite for any "social field." But such a process of involuntary "implantation" would seem to leave precious little room for any "intention, will or conscious action." In fact, it would seem to render Bourdieu's notion of *habitus* indistinguishable from the most relentlessly deterministic models of behavior as espoused by structuralists and structural functionalists (cf. DiTomaso 1982; cf. Jenkins 1992, pp. 81–2, 96–7).

Yet Bourdieu forcefully dismisses the charge:

As an acquired system of generative schemes, the *habitus* makes possible the free production of all the thoughts, perceptions and actions inherent in the particular conditions of its production – and only those. ... This infinite yet strictly limited generative capacity is difficult to understand only so long as one remains locked in the usual antinomies – which the concept of the *habitus* aims to transcend – of determinism and freedom, conditioning and creativity, consciousness and unconscious, or the individual and society. Because the *habitus* is an infinite capacity for generating products – thoughts, perceptions, expressions and actions – whose limits are set by the historically and socially situated conditions of its production, the conditioned and conditional freedom it provides is as remote from creation of unpredictable novelty as it is from simple mechanical reproduction of the original conditioning. (Bourdieu 1990a, p. 55; cf. Robbins 1991, pp. 170–3)

This sounds like the fairly commonplace idea of "choice within certain limits" that many consider to be a solution to the determinism-voluntarism problem. But I must confess that I, for one, "locked in the usual antinomies" as I am, have never understood how this solved anything at all. Viewing the *habitus* merely as repertoires that actors may select from simply raises the earlier questions once more: What causes people to choose one alternative within the "permitted set" rather than another? If this really is a matter of choice, then we *are*, in fact, in the realm of "unpredictable novelty." If, on the other hand, the choice of alternatives is predictable on the basis of further dispositions, we are back at "simple mechanical reproduction of the original conditioning." No doubt, dispositions evolve over time as people are forced to adjust their "practical answers" to changing conditions. But here again, one has to ask what makes people choose certain answers as "practical." If it is either some universal pursuit of "practicality" (maximizing utility?) *or* unconscious implementation of preexisting dispositions, we are back once again with the "mechanistic determinism" of economics (Bourdieu 1990a, p. 46) or functionalism. In short, for all his confident declarations to the contrary, I fail to see how Bourdieu's own approach does anything at all to "transcend the usual antinomies."[8]

My point here is not that Bourdieu's solution to this intractable problem is particularly wrongheaded – rather, that it is so surprisingly unoriginal. In fact, the concept of *habitus* – almost *always* italicized, presumably to underscore its immense theoretical significance – has a rather *déjà vu* quality about it. On several occasions, Bourdieu describes it, or perhaps its "doxa,"[9] in terms that are indistinguishable from those used by phenomenologists describing their similarly ill-defined concept of the "lifeworld": "the pre-verbal taking-for-granted of the world that flows from

---

[8] See Jenkins (1992, pp. 79–83) for a whole series of obscure and apparently inconsistent statements by Bourdieu on the relation between external conditions and supposedly evolving *habitus*, showing the lack of any clear mechanism by which its "dispositions" are formed, changed, or maintained in his theory.

[9] I must confess that the relation between the two concepts is not entirely clear to me. Bourdieu's only and rather puzzling indication is that "Doxa is the relationship of immediate adherence that is established in practice between a *habitus* and the field to which it is attuned" (Bourdieu 1990a, p. 68).

practical sense" (Bourdieu 1990a, p. 68). Bourdieu's heated and repeated denials of any such "regression towards intuitionism" (Bourdieu 1990a, p. 269) or of any kinship with the tradition of Dilthey and Husserl (Bourdieu 1990a, p. 19) do little to dispel the striking resemblance (cf. Jenkins 1992, p. 140).

But as a solution to the problem that lies at the heart of the whole objectivism-vs.-subjectivism *problématique* – the problem of which came first, social structures or the people who make them up – this seems entirely vacuous. What such unappealing circumlocutions as "the dialectic of social structures and structured, structuring dispositions" (Bourdieu 1990a, p. 41), "structured structures predisposed to function as structuring structures" (Bourdieu 1990a, p. 53), and a "network of circuits of circular causality" (Bourdieu 1990a, p. 97) seem to have in common is that they simply restate the problem: Obviously, people shape social structures, and social structures shape people. Somehow this does not immediately strike me as the colossal conceptual breakthrough that is going to rescue us from the "spurious alternatives of social physics and social phenomenology" (Bourdieu 1990a, p. 140). It amounts to little more than an obscurantist way of restating Coleman's micro-macro *problem*, without even beginning to suggest anything that might help to address it.

The few further specifics that Bourdieu supplies do not give one a sense of extraordinary insight or utility either. First, there is the principle that similar conditions will produce similar *habitus*, it being "precisely this immanent law, *lex insita*, inscribed in bodies by identical histories, which is the precondition not only for the co-ordination of practices but also for practices of co-ordination" (Bourdieu 1990a, p. 59). This "principle" is also, one might add, rather an indispensable precondition for doing almost any kind of social science since without it relations between people's actions and their social environments would be entirely random. The second feature, presented with the same aplomb, is equally banal. Unless conditions change, Bourdieu tells us, the *habitus* reflects the "tendency of groups to persist in their ways" (Bourdieu 1990a, p. 62). Who would have thought?

Thus even in this, its "most exhaustive theoretical explication," Bourdieu's central concept of *habitus* emerges as neither particularly original nor especially coherent. Rather than helping to overcome the opposition between objectivism and subjectivism, it simply seems to provide a conveniently vague cover for Bourdieu's theoretical drift between the two. It gives the *appearance* of theoretical coherence where in fact there is only incoherence and ambivalence.

At the same time, as many observers have noted (e.g., Jenkins 1982, 1992; Mouzelis 1995, pp. 110–11), *in practice* Bourdieu *invariably* emphasizes how the "rules" of any particular "field," and the *habitus* that fit those rules, *determine* people's behavior, without ever bothering to make even any *pro forma* gestures in the direction of any more voluntaristic, situational aspects. From his early analyses of the "symbolic violence" inflicted upon the dominated classes through the educational system in order to inculcate in them a *habitus* that will effectively prevent them from recognizing their own oppression (Bourdieu 1977b) to his later work on various other "social fields," Bourdieu treats social action as the result of deeply and irrevocably internalized schemes and patterns whose iron grip is all the more inescapable because actors themselves are unconscious of them. Although Bourdieu occasionally vents his deep irritation over this "deterministic misreading" (Wacquant 1989, p. 28; cf. Bourdieu 1990b, pp. 116–19) of his work, his own repeated *practice*, as well as many of his less guarded theoretical *pronunciamentos* (see, e.g., Bourdieu and Eagleton 1992, pp. 111–15), heavily and unmistakeably leans toward the "objectivist" end of the continuum.

Thus Bourdieu's efforts to "transcend" the opposition between objectivism and subjectivism in the end seem to boil down to little more than lip service to the *intention* to transcend it combined with a decidedly objectivistic slant in actual practice. There are at least two reasons why this is perhaps not so surprising. First, notwithstanding his self-assured claims to have reached an unprecedented level of reflexivity with respect to his own methods and philosophical assumptions, Bourdieu still seems fairly helplessly caught in the spell of structuralist objectivism. This is particularly evident in the fact that while he devotes many pages of tortuous, and often, where they are somewhat intelligible, plainly contradictory arguments against the demons of structuralism, it is obvious that Bourdieu has great trouble taking the "subjectivist" perspective seriously at all. He simply rejects Sartre's "ultra-consistent formulation" of "the philosophy of action . . . [describing] practices as strategies explicitly oriented by reference to ends explicitly defined by a free project" (Bourdieu 1990a, p. 42), as unable to recognize durable dispositions or causes of action, and thus forced to view society as a pure creation "ex nihilo" (Bourdieu 1990a, p. 42–6). Economic "rational-actor" theories are summarily dismissed on similar grounds (Bourdieu 1990a, p. 46).[10] Besides this Bourdieu limits himself to the sporadic display of contempt for "the eulogists of 'lived experience' " (Bourdieu 1990a, p. 145).[11]

Second, and more important, whenever Bourdieu does try to explain actual social behavior, he is forced to resort to "objectivistic" mechanisms of explanation because he remains committed to *explanation* rather than empathic description. Although this is not the right place to do so, it can, I think, be convincingly argued that the various "subjectivistic" approaches simply do not possess any conceptual tools for *explaining* social behavior. In fact, the distinctiveness of such approaches (a number of variants of symbolic interactionism, phenomenology, hermeneutics, and so on) consists precisely in their more or less outright *rejection* of any explanatory strategy worthy of the name.

Mouzelis, in an analysis not unlike the foregoing (with the important exception of my last, admittedly underdeveloped point) concludes that "[Bourdieu's] rather megalomaniacal attempts at 'transcending' existing approaches, distinctions or concepts may have more to do with the *habitus* of a certain type of French intellectual (who, by caricaturing or completely ignoring what already exists, is obsessively concerned with the 'new', even where this merely means putting new labels onto old bottles) than with any serious elaboration of a genuinely new theoretical synthesis" (Mouzelis 1995, pp. 110–11). Although many have commented on the Gallic peculiarities of Bourdieu's self-presentation,[12] this seems to be a matter of style (and surely also strategy) rather than content. For the remarkable thing is – and this is a major point of this chapter – that a number of aspiring Grand Synthesizers, hailing from different countries and wildly different theoretical traditions, seem to have arrived at virtually the same conclusion, or, rather, impasse.

---

[10] While, rather curiously, being denounced for their "mechanistic determinism" at the same time (Bourdieu 1990a, p. 46).

[11] Consider, for instance, a recent offhand dismissal of the "Germanic" distinction between understanding and explanation as a basis for distinguishing human from natural sciences: "This unscientific mode is a defensive system, established by certain philosophies of the person, which demands that there are things beyond science, in particular the 'person', 'creation', the 'creators', which is to say, in brief: the narcissistic ego of the intellectuals" (Bourdieu 1992, p. 46).

[12] Including the present author (see van den Berg 1992).

Giddens: "Structuration"

By quite a different route, Anthony Giddens has ended up in a position that is strikingly similar to that of Bourdieu. Coming from the "Anglo-Saxon" tradition that Bourdieu appears to hold in such contempt, Giddens was initially little affected by continental fancies like structuralism, Sartrian subjectivism, or critical theory for that matter. His early work was instead aimed at throwing off the yoke of Parsonian structural functionalism that still carried some weight in Anglo-Saxon sociological theory, if not in actual research. To this end, he initially seemed to lend his voice to a growing chorus of neo-Weberian conflict theorists seeking to replace Parsonian consensualism with a more hard-nosed, yet *not* dogmatically Marxist, "conflict" perspective (Giddens 1971, 1972; cf. Parkin 1971, 1980; Collins, 1975).

An influential work in this general movement was Giddens's *The Class Structure in Advanced Societies* (1973), a wide-ranging *tour d'horizon* of the state of stratification theory and research at the time. There Giddens presents for the first time what was to become his theoretical master concept, "structuration." However, the meaning of the concept has changed quite considerably in the ensuing years, in step with Giddens's rapidly expanding theoretical ambitions.

In the original formulation, the notion of "structuration" sounded remarkably like a social mechanism of the Elsterian variety. Giddens applied the term to the process whereby socioeconomic advantage and disadvantage congeal into certain patterns of social mobility, behavior, and social intercourse, thence producing more or less stable class cultures and consciousness (see especially Giddens 1973, pp. 107–12).

After this, however, Giddens soon became much preoccupied, like his fellow Grand Synthesizers, with what he influentially dubbed the "agency versus structure" problem. In a book modestly entitled *New Rules of Sociological Method*, "structuration theory" was already transformed from a theory highlighting one social mechanism among many to *the* solution to the most intractable dilemma of the social sciences. Some years later, structuration theory received its apparently definitive treatment in Giddens magnum opus to date,[13] *The Constitution of Society* (1984).

---

[13] For one who produces roughly one major book every year, nothing much is likely to remain definitive for very long.

Probably in reaction to the "oversocialized" conception of social action (cf. Wrong 1961) in structural functionalism, and quite unlike Bourdieu, Giddens takes the subjectivist alternative offered by phenomenological approaches such as Garfinkel's "ethnomethodology" very seriously indeed. In fact, he never seems to tire of declaring his firm commitment to "the fundamental significance of knowledgeability of human actors . . . [who] are vastly skilled in the practical accomplishments of social activities and are expert 'sociologists' " (Giddens 1984, p. 26). But although this may be "absolutely essential if the mistakes of functionalism and structuralism are to be avoided . . . it is equally important to avoid tumbling into the opposing error of hermeneutic approaches and of various versions of phenomenology, which tend to regard society as the plastic creation of human subjects" (Giddens 1984, p. 26). In short, Giddens, too, promises to deliver us from the seemingly insuperable dualism of agent and structure, micro and macro, voluntarism and determinism, subjectivism and objectivism.

Much of Giddens's theorizing is preoccupied with the development of taxonomies and schemata, neologisms and redefinitions, which have provoked much exegetical exertion and debate but not much to detain us here. If anything, his grim determination to blanket social reality with a vast conceptual quilt leaving *nothing* exposed reminds one, rather forcefully, of his erstwhile arch-nemesis, Talcott Parsons.

But at the core of Giddens's theory of structuration, lies a deceptively simple idea: the "duality of structure." With this single wave of the conceptual wand, Giddens claims to have simply dissolved the above dualism. Instead of conceiving of actors and structures as external to each other, giving rise to mutually exclusive emphases on the causal effectiveness of either one or the other, Giddens proposes to reconceptualize them as a "duality," as "simply two sides of the same coin" (Craib 1992, p. 3).

Giddens sees the relation between actors and structures as a "recursive" process. Somewhat idiosyncratically, he defines "structures" as consisting of "resources" and "rules" on which variably knowledgeable actors draw to produce and reproduce the recurrent practices that constitute more structures, and so on and so forth. Hence "the theorem of the duality of structure": "The structural properties of social systems are both medium and outcome of the practices they recursively organize" (Giddens 1984, p. 25). In a very real sense, then, there is no social structure influencing and constraining agents' actions from the outside, as supposed by a variety of structuralist approaches. Rather, "structure only exists in and through the activities of human agents" (Giddens 1989, p. 256).

But for all his celebration of knowledgeable agents actively and reflexively monitoring and creating "structures," Giddens has remained notoriously vague on what exactly motivates these agents, or *how* knowledgeable they really are, or *how* constrained they are by the "structures" that provide both the "resources" for their actions and the "rules" whereby to act. He distinguishes between "discursive" and "practical" consciousness on the part of actors, for instance, but has little to say on which is more likely to prevail under what conditions (see, e.g., Giddens 1984, pp. xxiii, 7, 41–5). Following Garfinkel to some extent, he emphasizes the actors' need to retain or repair their "ontological security" by means of maintaining predictable routines (Giddens 1984, pp. 60–4). But then again, he also constantly stresses actors' creativity and innovativeness as a source of social change. Hence the following rather typical summation: "Social life may very often be predictable in its course, as such authors [who take institutional analysis to comprise the field of sociology *in toto*] are prone to emphasize. But its predictability is in many of its aspects 'made to happen' by social actors; it does not happen in spite of the reasons they have for their conduct" (Giddens 1984, pp. 285).

Thus, coming from quite a different original position, Giddens ends up with almost exactly the same theoretical result as Bourdieu did. His "duality of structure," just like Bourdieu's *habitus*, does not seem to imply anything more than that people make or use social structures and that structures affect the way they do this. As Sharrock rightly notes, "Saying that society is both an objective and a subjective reality and involves both structure and agency, may sound like a conciliation of opposed views, but is it anything more than a restatement of Marx's contention that we make history, but not in circumstances of our own choosing?" (Sharrock 1987, p. 154).

Interestingly, while it is virtually impossible to tell Giddens's and Bourdieu's "solutions" to the agency vs. structure problem apart, Giddens is regularly taken to task for being *too voluntaristic* (see, e.g., Baber 1991; Thompson and Held 1989). Contrast this with Bourdieu's allegedly heavy-handed determinism. The fact that these two virtually indistinguishable theoretical positions[14] could prompt such entirely opposite responses is

[14] For arguments leading to the same conclusion regarding the similarity between Bour-

itself, I think, a sure sign of their effective vacuousness. Paul DiMaggio sums it up perfectly, while at the same time suggesting precisely why the serious study of social mechanisms is a far more promising avenue than the proliferation of grand theories claiming to transcend all existing antinomies:

> Such concepts [such as Bourdieu's (1977[a]) definition of the *habitus* as "structuring structure," and Giddens's (198[4]) "structuration"] are solutions only if they are accompanied by sophisticated and detailed accounts of mechanisms of change. Otherwise, they simply deny oversocialization without offering a real alternative. Bourdieu (1977[a]) provides little guidance as to the plasticity of the *habitus* and Giddens (198[4]) hedges the question with even-handed references to "agent knowledgeability" (DiMaggio 1990, p. 123).

Mired in multidimensionality: Alexander

As compared to Giddens, Jeffrey Alexander hails from almost exactly the opposite end of the theoretical spectrum. Beginning with his early four-volume, *Theoretical Logic in Sociology* (Alexander 1982–3), he has set himself the task of rehabilitating Parsons's structural functionalism. But Alexander's *neofunctionalism* was to modify and amend the original Parsonian formulation in light of some of the justified criticisms of it. In particular, neofunctionalism was to have none of the anti-individualism, the antagonism to change and conflict, and the unidimensional reliance on culture as the principal determinant of human action that marred its precursor. Deeply committed to a resolute multidimensionalism, neofunctionalism would avoid the pitfalls of all extant one-dimensional approaches, while incorporating their valid insights. Note, once again, the great synthetic ambition.

In true Parsonian style, Alexander offers nothing less than a "new 'theoretical logic' for sociology" (1982–3, p. xv). Each theoretical approach, he claims, rests on its own set of mostly a priori presuppositions that guide and limit it. The most important of these presuppositions are implicit solutions to the two fundamental theoretical problems that all approaches face: the "problem of order" and the "problem of action." With respect

dieu's and Giddens's attempts to overcome the subjectivism/objectivism dualism, see Mouzelis (1995, Ch. VI) and Jenkins (1982).

to the former, theorists have chosen to focus either on the micro/individual or on the macro/collective level. At the micro level, social order is viewed "as the product of negotiation freely entered into, as the result of individual decisions, feelings, and wants" (Alexander 1984, p. 7). "Individualist theorists . . . [assume] not only that individuals have an element of freedom but that they can alter the fundamentals of social order at every successive point in historical time. Individuals, in this view, do not carry order inside of them. Rather, they follow or rebel against social order – even their own values – according to their individual desires" (Alexander 1987, p. 11). Macro-level approaches, by contrast, are collectivist in that they stress how social order is, "in Emile Durkheim's famous phrase, a reality *sui generis*, [in which] the decisions of those who came before us have become sedimented into institutions" (Alexander 1984, p. 7). "Any individual act, according to collectivist theory, is pushed in the direction of preexisting structure, although this direction remains only a probability for those collectivists who acknowledge that action has an element of freedom" (Alexander 1987, p. 11).

The "problem of action," on the other hand, requires a choice between materialist-instrumentalist conceptions of action, which depict action as rational, instrumental, and self-interested, on one end of the continuum, and nonmaterial conceptions, emphasizing the normative, nonrational, and affective aspects of action.

> The "problem of action," then, is whether we assume actors are rational or nonrational. . . . In social theory . . . this dichotomy refers to whether people are selfish (rational) or idealistic (nonrational), whether they are normative and moral (nonrational) in their approach to the world or purely instrumental (rational), whether they act in terms of maximizing efficiency (rationally) or whether they are governed by emotions and unconscious desires (nonrationally). All these dichotomies relate to the vital question of the internal versus external reference of action. Rationalistic approaches to action portray the actor as taking his bearings from forces outside of himself, whereas nonrational approaches imply that action is motivated from within. (Alexander 1987, p. 10)

A simple cross-classification yields a fourfold typology into which, according to Alexander, all major theoretical traditions can be usefully arranged. Thus, for instance, Marxism tends toward the collective solution to the problem of order but is on the materialist side where the problem of action is concerned. The latter is also true for rational-choice theory, but it adopts the individualist position with respect to social order.

Now, while Alexander repeatedly calls for abandoning these one-dimensional (actually two-dimensional according to his own scheme) approaches in favor of a more thoroughly "multidimensional" alternative, he still favors a basically Parsonian position over the others. That is, he argues, very much in line with the Durkheimian/Parsonian tradition, that it is a "theoretical mistake" to "privilege the arena of micro process" (Alexander 1988, p. 307), as this could never explain the fact of social *order* (also Alexander 1984, p. 9). With respect to the problem of action, Alexander rejects the materialist solution as too deterministic: "[B]y assuming that actors are efficient calculators of their own material environment, the instrumental approach to social structure makes action completely determined by external control . . . [and thus] denies the possibility of individual control" (Alexander 1984, p. 14). With its "narrow, merely technically efficient form of rationality . . . "motives" are eliminated as a theoretical concern. . . . I am arguing, then, that rational-collectivist theories explain order only by sacrificing the subject, by eliminating the very notion of the self" (Alexander 1987, p. 14).[15]

Consequently, "[t]he hope for combining collective order and individual voluntarism lies with the normative, rather than the rationalist tradition" (Alexander 1982–3, p. 108).

The aim of the normative approach to social structure has been to allow for collective order without eliminating the consideration of individual control. This can only be accomplished, however, if the individual is viewed in a manner that is not rationalistic. Only if theorists are sensitive to the internal components of action, to the actor's emotions and moral sensibilities, can they recognize that social structure is located as much within the actor as without. Only with this recognition can social theory make the individual a fundamental reference point without, at the same time, placing him outside of his social context (Alexander 1984, pp. 14–15).

---

[15] Note that the quotation here refers to *collectivist* (w.r.t. to the "problem of order") variants of rationalist theories of action. But in terms of the points at issue here (viz., the *externality* of constraints reducing actors to "mere" calculating robots), there is no difference between the two variants. At the same time, the quote does nicely illustrate a central "conflation," to use one of his own favorite terms, running through Alexander's work generally, as we shall see.

Thus Alexander seems to end up with a "[n]ormative structuralism" (Alexander 1984, p. 18) that is rather difficult to distinguish from the old, orthodox Durkheimian-Parsonian variety. Nor does it seem, at first sight, to be any more "multidimensional" than the approaches he rejects. Just like them, he opts for *one* of the two prototypical solutions to the "problems" of action and order, only *his* happen to be the *right* choices: normativism and collectivism, respectively. These were, of course, exactly the presuppositional choices Durkheim and Parsons are supposed to have made. And, very much like Parsons before him, Alexander justifies these specific choices on the grounds that they allow social theory to account for social order – in contrast to individualist theories – *without* sacrificing voluntarism in the manner done by other forms of collectivism (read: Marxism and Weberian macrosociology). "Normative structuralism demonstrates," according to Alexander, ". . . that a 'social' approach to action does not necessarily have to neglect the contributions of the individual, the nature of his inner emotion, and the extent to which collective order depends upon his voluntary participation" (Alexander 1984, p. 18). This is, we are told, the point of Durkheim's analysis of the modern *conscience collective* in the form of the "religion of individualism," and of Parsons's later demonstration of the interdependence of moral integration and individuation through processes of differentiation and socialization (Alexander 1984, p. 15).

Note that in all this the problem of action seems to take front stage relative to the problem of order. In his earlier work, no doubt faithfully reflecting the theoretical climate of the period, Alexander mostly analyzes and criticizes the other major *macro* approaches, Marxism and Weberianism, apparently not taking the individualist traditions all that seriously yet. Since then, however, his critical focus seems to have shifted to the problem of order and the challenge of individualist theoretical approaches.

Moving with the times, Alexander has become increasingly aware of the need to "more effectively incorporate the important, voluntaristic emphasis of individualistic theory" (Alexander 1984, p. 21). He has devoted much of his recent work to addressing the challenge and limitations of "[the] individualistic theories [that] have permeated contemporary sociology [in the last two decades]: antistructuralist hermeneutic, phenomenological and action theories, symbolic interactionism, ethnomethodology, and models of rational choice" (Alexander 1989, p. 147; cf. 1987, pp. 156–301). It has become clear to him "that the centrality of historical contingency and specificity must be recognized but that the socially structured nature of action can never be overlooked'' (Alexander 1988, p. 2). Thus, exactly like Habermas, Bourdieu, and Giddens, Alexander takes it upon himself ''to bring action theory and structure theory back together, in a post-Parsonian way'' (ibid.).

His most sustained effort to date to lay out ''the framework for a new articulation of the micro-macro link'' (Alexander 1996, p. 123) appears in a long article entitled ''Action and Its Environments,'' the culminating chapter of the eponymous book (Alexander 1988).[16] Once more his approach is resolutely multidimensional in intent. Each of the great postwar microtheories, he argues, highlights a different aspect of Parsons's ''unit act'' and can therefore be synthesized with the latter. Thus, ''Parsons's macro theory may be expanded by making variable what it left as parameter – namely, the contingent element in effort'' (Alexander 1988, p. 311). What the microtheories cannot provide, their advocates' claims to the contrary notwithstanding, is a satisfactory theory of social order, as ''[i]t would be as absurd to deduce norms and conditions from transcendental consciousness and exchange as the other way around'' (ibid.). Rather, microtheoretical insights are somehow to be incorporated *into* the overall Parsonian macro approach, which alone can take care of the structural side of things. Such a ''synthesis of unit act and micro theory demonstrates that the referents of contemporary micro theories are only the fluid or open element in larger, more crystallized units'' (ibid.).

After this ''hermeneutical reconstruction of the micro-macro link'' (ibid.), Alexander proceeds to examine ''the nature of action *qua* action (action in its contingent mode) that was left as a black box by Parsons and filled polemically by his individualist critics'' (Alexander 1988, p. 316). The upshot of his reflections is that microtheoretical approaches remind us of how action is always both ''interpretation'' (i.e., typification and innovation) and ''strategization'' (basically, economizing). Nevertheless, these should always be understood within the ''collective environments of action [which] simultaneously inspire and confine it'' (Alexander 1988, p. 316). These ''collective environments'' turn out to be none other than Parsons's famous threesome: social systems (institutions, roles, norms), cultural systems (symbol systems for interpreting and evaluating

---

[16] Alexander himself recently referred to this essay as ''my most important piece of theoretical work'' (Alexander 1996, p. 123).

reality), and personalities ("a selection of objects introjected from social encounters, a selection dictated by the play of organic and developmental needs" (Alexander 1988, p. 323).

All this, then, leads to the following grand finale:

> Why, then, the great divide in sociological discussion today? Because, I believe, theorists falsely generalize from a single variable to the immediate reconstruction of the whole. They have taken one particular system – the economy, the culture, the personality – as action's total environment; they have taken one action mode – invention, typification, or strategization – as encompassing action in itself.... It seems perfectly appropriate that each of these different elements of micro process and macro process can be viewed as the objects of independent scientific disciplines, as they are in the natural and physical sciences. It is unacceptable, however, for any one of these variables and disciplines to be considered privileged in relation to the others. Rather than being thought of as dependent and independent variables, these elements should be conceived as parameters and variables in an interactive system comprising different levels of different "size." This requires, of course, a common conceptual scheme, one the social sciences do not yet possess. (Alexander 1988, p. 328)

As a major contribution toward narrowing "the great divide," this is, to put it mildly, a bit of a disappointment. What, after all, is Alexander's conclusion? That all the different strands of current sociological theorizing capture some part of the social truth but none captures all of it? That it would be nice somehow to unite them all into one "common conceptual scheme" that respects the contributions of each? Fine sentiments, indeed, but not much in the way of an advance toward that elusive common conceptual scheme.

" 'Reality,' I believe, is multidimensional: there are norms and interests, individual negotiation and collective force. A theorist may ignore significant parts of this complex reality, but he can not [sic] make them go away" (Alexander 1987, p. 178). Only the most doctrinaire partisans in the ongoing paradigm wars could possibly disagree with such a declaration of catholic "multidimensionality." But that is not exactly a recommendation, of course. The hard part is to move beyond such bland statements of good intentions toward some serious thinking about how/when/why norms, interests, negotiation, and force relate to each other. This is, of course, precisely the point of the focus on social mechanisms advocated in this volume. By his own admission, Alexander has yet to begin the journey, for lack of "a common conceptual scheme." But then again, as we have seen, in this respect he is in good company. With the partial exception of Habermas, all four Grand Synthetic Theorists discussed here have responded to the recent reopening of the chasm between interpretivist micro and explanatory macro approaches by declaring that it would be nice to somehow close it again . . . and then leaving it to others to do so.

Another aspect of Alexander's work deserves mention here, as it illustrates a rather curious tendency in recent sociological theorizing more generally. Upon closer inspection, it turns out that Alexander's two basic "presuppositional problems" actually revolve around one and the same issue, viz., how "to preserve both order and volition" (Alexander 1989, p. 148). Although he rejects "individualist" solutions to the "problem of order" as too voluntaristic, he dismisses materialist-instrumentalist (read: rational-choice) solutions to the "problem of action" as *not voluntaristic enough*. Unlike normativist approaches, he says, they deny "the possibility of individual control . . . sacrificing the subject."

For anyone even vaguely familiar with the standard, more or less rational-choice–inspired criticisms of Parsons's normativism, this may come as something of a surprise. Was not Homans's (1964) famous call for "bringing men back in" aimed precisely against the excessive determinism of Parsons's structural functionalism? Was not Wrong's (1961) equally famous broadside at the "oversocialized conception of man" intended to show how Parsons tended to reduce people to "cultural dopes," in Garfinkel's memorable phrase?[17] To say the very least, it is far from obvious in what way a rational-choice approach is inherently more deterministic than an emphasis on norms or culture as the prime motivator of social action.

Things get even murkier when Alexander lumps exchange/rational-choice theory together with other micro-individualistic theories that are, in his view, *too* voluntaristic to be able to account adequately for social order (as, e.g., in Alexander 1987, pp. 172–94; 1988, pp. 308 ff.). The underlying assumption seems to be that a focus on the individual, micro

---

[17] In this connection, recall also Duesenberry's famous quip that economics is all about how people make choices while sociology is all about how they have no real choices to make!

level is somehow inherently connected with a voluntaristic approach to social action. No doubt this particular misconception owes much to the voluntaristic rhetoric and sheer *pathos* typical of symbolic interactionist and phenomenological attacks on macrosociology, especially the Parsonian variety. But it is no less of a misconception for all that. If nothing else, rational-choice theory, as well as the entire body of traditional social psychology, makes it perfectly clear that there is no necessary connection whatever between theories that focus on the individual or the micro level and any kind of "voluntarism."

In perpetrating these two rather odd "conflations," Alexander does, however, reflect the temper of the times with uncanny accuracy. The notion that "culture," the realm of symbols, codes, values, and norms, is somehow more malleable, more subject to human control, than the economy or politics is very widespread indeed. This belief appears to be based on the undeniable fact that "culture" is a peculiarly human creation. Then again, so are "economies," "governments," and "bureaucracies." Yet somehow the latter seem to rule over us while "culture" is produced *by* us. Habermas's celebration of the open, democratic "lifeworld" threatened by rigid, coercive "systems" owes a great deal to this popular notion. Yet the idea itself would seem to make a lot more sense to an intellectual or artist – producers of "culture" who are all too often reminded of the indifference or worse of the worlds of business and politics – than to the ordinary citizen. In fact, the notion appears to have the status of a taken-for-granted piece of the lifeworld of those who subscribe to it. Since it is rarely made explicit, there seems to be little need to supply a plausible rationale for it.[18]

Much the same can be said about the semi-automatic association of micro/individual-level analysis with "voluntarism." Although the association has few explicit or sensible arguments to recommend itself, it certainly seems to be widely held. It also clearly animates both Habermas's and Giddens's attempts to incorporate micro-level phenomenology into their overall schemes. And it certainly has been influential enough effectively to set the agenda for today's Grand Synthetic Theorists, as we have seen throughout.

---

[18] This is all the more remarkable since the *very opposite* notion – that of a sinister Althusserian-Foucauldian *episteme* ruling over, or rather *through*, its hapless human carriers – enjoys at least equal currency among the theoretical avant garde of the moment.

Conclusion: The globalization of Grand Theory

Alexander is surely right about one thing: For much recent sociological theory, "[t]he overriding systematic, or analytic, issue has been to reintegrate subjective voluntarism and objective constraint" (Alexander 1987, p. 376). My review of four of the most prominent sociological theorists in this chapter amply bears this out.

In terms of intellectual origins, these four theorists could hardly have come from more varied and contrasting backgrounds. Yet all four have taken up exactly the same general *problématique*. They have all tried to meet the same challenge: to formulate a Grand Synthesis that somehow closes or narrows the gaping chasm between micro and macro approaches, individualism and collectivism, subjectivism and objectivism, understanding and explanation, voluntarism and determinism, and so on, a chasm that has been opened up by the renewed challenges from various idiographic approaches. Thus a certain "globalization" of sociological theory seems to have taken place in that theorists from widely different traditions and national and intellectual contexts feel called upon to address the same theoretical questions. At first glance, this might appear to be a good thing for the discipline as a whole, a sign of the disappearance of parochial boundaries and preoccupations.

Unfortunately, the *problématique* in question has imposed "globalization" in a second sense as well. The aforementioned antinomies raise a notoriously difficult set of philosophical problems concerning the *very nature* of human action, social structure, and so on. In trying to address such thorny questions, sociological theory has necessarily taken on a highly abstract, philosophical cast. As Giddens has noted with respect to his own work, there seems to have occurred a shift from methodological and conceptual to ontological concerns. Whereas previously at least *some* sociological theory was concerned with developing conceptual and methodological tools for studying matters social, current theory seems to be largely preoccupied with defining "the *nature* of social structures and social actions and their possible interrelation" (Alexander 1988, p. 1, emphasis added) *as such*.

Several commentators on an earlier version of this chapter have pointed out, particularly with respect to Habermas and Bourdieu, that even if one agrees that their efforts at General Synthesis are largely a failure, there may still be much to be admired in the rest of their work.

Be that as it may, it remains the case that it is primarily for their Grand Synthetic pretensions that they are best known and most admired. Thereby they have contributed to the elevation of their *genre* of theorizing to the status of "sociological theory" *tout court*. For anyone still committed to the idea that sociology ought to, *inter alia*, help us improve our understanding and explanations of social life, this is a sad development indeed.

Once upon a time, "sociological theory" might have referred to some more or less coherent effort to explain some social phenomenon like gender stratification or ethnic strife. Today it seems to refer to something quite different, "general" theory of the kind reviewed here. Such "general" theory can lay claim to a certain *grandeur* that eludes plain explanatory theorists. Moreover, while the latter must toil in relative obscurity in search of occasional illumination, the former's ability to claim the limelight is in no way hampered by the obscurity of their products. Quite to the contrary, sheer complexity and incomprehensibility seem to be pure assets in the practice of "general" theory. These are welcomed with much respectful commentary about the great profundity of it all and are the occasion for the expenditure of much critical and exegetical energy – not to mention ink, paper, and time – to figure out what exactly the theorist "really" meant.

If all this could reasonably be expected to yield something of even moderate use to the rest of the discipline, then such a commitment of our scarce, and rapidly shrinking, intellectual and other resources might be defensible. But one major conclusion to be drawn from this chapter is precisely that we can expect nothing of the kind. All the profound ruminations about the ultimate relation between agency and structure, action and order, micro and macro, and so on, have merely gotten us to exactly where we started. In one way or another, each of the Grand Syntheses reviewed here has come no further than to acknowledge that Coleman's macro-micro-macro model poses the great explanatory challenge of our day. It is now time to take *it* up.

References

Abraham, David. 1994. "Persistent Facts and Compelling Norms: Liberal Capitalism, Democratic Socialism, and the Law," *Law and Society Review*, 28, 4, Oct., pp. 939–46.

Alexander, Jeffrey C. 1982–3. *Theoretical Logic in Sociology.* 4 volumes. Berkeley: University of California Press.

Alexander, Jeffrey C. 1984. "Social-Structural Analysis: Some Notes on Its History and Prospects," *Sociological Quarterly,* vol. 25 (Winter), pp. 5–26.

Alexander, Jeffrey C. 1987. *Twenty Lectures: Sociological Theory since World War II.* New York: Columbia University Press.

Alexander, Jeffrey C. 1988. *Action and its Environments.* New York: Columbia University Press.

Alexander, Jeffrey C. 1989. *Structure and Meaning: Relinking Classical Sociology.* New York: Columbia University Press.

Alexander, Jeffrey C. 1996. "Jeffrey C. Alexander: An autobiographical sketch," pp. 122–3 in George Ritzer, *Modern Sociological Theory,* 4th ed. New York: McGraw-Hill.

Andersen, Heine, 1994. "Jürgen Habermas: Faktizität und Geltung," *Acta Sociologica,* 37, 1, 93–9.

Baber, Zaheer. 1991. "Beyond the Structure/Agency Dualism: An Evaluation of Giddens' Theory of Structuration," *Sociological Inquiry,* 61, 2: 218–30.

Baxter, Hugh. 1987. "System and Life-World in Habermas's *Theory of Communicative Action,*" *Theory and Society* 16:39–86.

Bohman, James. 1994. "Complexity, Pluralism, and the Constitutional State: On Habermas's Faktizität und Geltung," *Law and Society Review,* 28, 4, Oct., pp. 897–930.

Bourdieu, Pierre. 1977a. *Outline of a Theory of Practice.* Cambridge: Cambridge University Press.

Bourdieu, Pierre. 1977b. *Reproduction in Education, Society and Culture.* Beverly Hills: Sage.

Bourdieu, Pierre. 1980. *Le sens pratique.* Paris: Éditions de Minuit.

Bourdieu, Pierre. 1984. *Distinction: A Social Critique of the Judgement of Taste.* London: Routledge and Kegan Paul.

Bourdieu, Pierre. 1988. *Homo Academicus.* Cambridge, England: Polity Press.

Bourdieu, Pierre. 1990a. *The Logic of Practice.* Stanford, CA: Stanford University Press.

Bourdieu, Pierre. 1990b. *In Other Words: Essays Towards a Reflexive Sociology.* Cambridge, England: Polity Press.

Bourdieu, Pierre. 1992. "Thinking about Limits," *Theory, Culture and Society,* Vol. 9: 37–49.

Bourdieu, Pierre, and Terry Eagleton. 1992. "Doxa and Common Life," *New Left Review,* No. 191, January/February, pp. 111–21.

Broady, Donald. 1990. *Sociologi och epistemologi: Om Pierre Bourdieus författarskap och den historiska epistemologin.* Stockholm: HLS Förlag.

Casebeer, Kenneth, 1994. "Paris Is Closer than Frankfurt: The nth American Exceptionalism," *Law and Society Review,* 28, 4, Oct., pp. 931–7.

Collins, Randall. 1975. *Conflict Sociology.* New York: Sage.

Craib, Ian. 1992. *Anthony Giddens.* London: Routledge.

Dalberg-Larsen, Jorgen. 1994. "Habermas om retten og den demokratiske retsstat," *Dansk Sociologi*, 5, 4, Dec., pp. 72–85.

Deflem, Mathieu. 1994. "Introduction: Law in Habermas's Theory of Communicative Action," *Philosophy and Social Criticism*, 20, 4, Oct., pp. 1–20.

Dews, Peter, ed. 1986. *Habermas: Autonomy and Solidarity*. London: Verso.

DiMaggio, Paul. 1990. "Cultural aspects of economic action and organization," pp. 113–36 in Friedland, Roger, and Robertson, A. F., eds., *Beyond the marketplace: Rethinking economy and society*. New York: Aldine de Gruyter.

DiTomaso, Nancy. 1982. " 'Sociological Reductionism' from Parsons to Althusser: Linking Action and Structure in Social Theory," *American Sociological Review*, Vol. 47, No. 1:14–28.

Giddens, Anthony. 1971. *Capitalism and Modern Social Theory*. Cambridge: Cambridge University Press.

Giddens, Anthony. 1972. *Politics and Sociology in the Thought of Max Weber*. London: Macmillan.

Giddens, Anthony. 1973. *The Class Structure in Advanced Societies*. London: Hutchinson.

Giddens, Anthony. 1976. *New Rules of Sociological Method: A Positive Critique of Interpretive Sociologies*. London: Hutchinson.

Giddens, Anthony. 1984. *The Constitution of Society*. Berkeley and Los Angeles: University of California Press.

Giddens, Anthony. 1989. "A reply to my critics," pp. 249–301 in David Held and John B. Thompson, eds., *Social Theory of Modern Societies: Anthony Giddens and His Critics*. Cambridge: Cambridge University Press.

Giddens, Anthony. 1994. *Beyond Left and Right : The Future of Radical Politics*. Stanford, CA: Stanford University Press.

Guibentif, Pierre, 1994. "Approaching the Production of Law through Habermas's Concept of Communicative Action," *Philosophy and Social Criticism*, 20, 4, Oct., pp. 45–70.

Habermas, Jürgen. 1981. "New Social Movements," *Telos*, 49:33–7.

Habermas, Jürgen. 1982. "Reply to my critics," pp. 219–83 in John B. Thompson and David Held, eds., *Habermas: Critical Debates*. Cambridge MA: The MIT Press.

Habermas, Jürgen. 1984. *The Theory of Communicative Action, Vol. 1: Reason and the Rationalization of Society*, transl. T. McCarthy. Boston: Beacon Press.

Habermas, Jürgen. 1986. "The New Obscurity: The Crisis of the Welfare State and the Exhaustion of Utopian Energies." *Philosophy and Social Criticism* 11:1–18.

Habermas, Jürgen. 1987. *The Theory of Communicative Action, Vol. II. The Critique of Functionalist Reason*, transl. T. McCarthy. Cambridge, England: Polity Press.

Habermas, Jürgen. 1992. *Faktizität und Geltung. Beiträge zur Diskurstheorie des Rechts und des demokratischen Rechsstaats*. Frankfurt am Main: Suhrkamp.

Habermas, Jürgen. 1994. "Three Normative Models of Democracy," *Constellations*, 1, 1, April, pp. 1–10.

Habermas, Jürgen, and Elsa Collomp. 1995. "Interrelations entre Etat de droit et democratie," *Schweizerische Zeitschrift für Soziologie/Revue Suisse de sociologie*, vol. 21, no. 1 (March), pp. 11–20.

Habermas, Jürgen, and William Rehg. 1994. "Postscript to Faktizität und Geltung," *Philosophy and Social Criticism*, 20, 4, Oct., pp. 135–50.

Homans, George C. 1964. "Bringing Men Back In," *American Sociological Review*, Vol. 29, No. 5, pp. 809–18.

Honneth, Axel, Eberhard Knödler-Bunte, and Arno Widmann. 1981. "The Dialectics of Rationalization: An Interview with Jürgen Habermas," *Telos*, 49, pp. 5–31.

Jay, Martin. 1973. *The Dialectical Imagination*. Boston: Little, Brown.

Jenkins, Richard. 1982. "Pierre Bourdieu and the Reproduction of Determinism," *Sociology*, Vol. 16:270–81.

Jenkins, Richard. 1989. "Language, Symbolic Power and Communication: Bourdieu's *Homo Academicus*," *Sociology*, Vol. 23, No. 4:639–45.

Jenkins, Richard. 1992. *Pierre Bourdieu*. London: Routledge.

McCarthy, Thomas. 1994. "Legitimacy and Diversity: Dialectical Reflections on Analytical Distinctions," *Protosoziologie*, 6, pp. 199–228.

Mouzelis, Nicos. 1995. *Sociological Theory, What Went Wrong? Diagnosis and Remedies*. London: Routledge.

Parkin, Frank. 1971. *Class Inequality and Political Order*. London: Macgibbon and Kee.

Parkin, Frank. 1980. *Marxism and Class Theory: A Bourgeois Critique*. New York: Columbia University Press.

Peters, Bernhard, 1994. "On Reconstructive Legal and Political Theory," *Philosophy and Social Criticism*, 20, 4, Oct., pp. 101–34.

Rasmussen, David M. 1994. "How Is Valid Law Possible? A Review of Faktizität und Geltung by Jurgen Habermas," *Philosophy and Social Criticism*, 20, 4, Oct., pp. 21–44.

Robbins, Derek. 1991. *The Work of Pierre Bourdieu*. Milton Keynes: Open University Press.

Scharff, Robert C. 1995. *Comte after Positivism*. Cambridge: Cambridge University Press.

Schudson, Michael. 1994. "The "Public Sphere" and Its Problems: Bringing the State (Back) In," *Notre Dame Journal of Law, Ethics and Public Policy*, 8, 2, pp. 529–46.

Sharrock, W. W. 1987. "Individual and society," pp. 126–56 in Anderson, R. J., Hughes, J. A., and Sharrock, W. W., eds., *Classic Disputes in Sociology*. London: Allen & Unwin.

Thompson, John B., and David Held, eds. 1989. *Social Theory of Modern Societies: Anthony Giddens and his Critics*. Cambridge: Cambridge University Press.

van den Berg, Axel. 1980. "Critical Theory: Is There Still Hope?" *American Journal of Sociology* 86:449–78.

van den Berg, Axel. 1988. *The Immanent Utopia: From Marxism on the State to the State of Marxism.* Princeton, NJ: Princeton University Press.

van den Berg, Axel. 1990. "Habermas and Modernity: A Critique of the Theory of Communicative Action," *Current Perspectives in Sociological Theory,* Vol. 10, pp. 161–93.

van den Berg, Axel. 1992. "Logiken i Bourdieus praktik. En avvikande uppfattning," *Sociologisk Forskning,* Vol. 29, No. 1, pp. 25–46.

Wacquant, Loïc J. D. 1989. "Towards a Reflexive Sociology: A Workshop with Pierre Bourdieu," *Sociological Theory,* Vol. 7, No. 1 (Winter):26–63.

Wrong, Dennis H. 1961. "The Oversocialized Conception of Man," *American Sociological Review,* Vol. 26:183–93.

10. Theoretical mechanisms and the empirical study of social processes

Introduction

This chapter is about the integration of theory and research. Like other reasonable sociologists, I believe the integration of theory and evidence is important and that sociology will never move up from its humble position in the hierarchy of science unless we achieve a better integration between reliable knowledge and powerful theory. Further, since I am a quantitative sociologist, I believe that although qualitative approaches are important for the development of powerful theory, knowledge produced by qualitative research will never be sufficiently reliable and generalizable to satisfy the requirements for a complete scientific theory.

Contrary to many of my peers, I also believe that most current practices in quantitative data analysis in sociology do a very poor job of integrating theory and research. There has been enormous progress in what we can do with data, and in the sophistication of mathematical and statistical tools for the analysis of data, over the last three or four decades. Nevertheless, quantitative sociology remains very theory-poor. In fact, the mainstream has regressed rather than progressed. Quantitative sociology is now less theoretically informed and less relevant for theoretical progress than it was three decades ago.

The reason quantitative sociology has become theoretically poor is that the enormous progress in methodological power has turned quantitative methodology into a branch of statistics[1] This has led to a fascination, if

This is a revised version of a paper presented at the Conference on Social Mechanisms held at the Royal Swedish Academy of Sciences, Stockholm, Sweden, June 6–7, 1996. I am indebted to Hans-Peter Blossfeld, Mario Bunge, Peter Hedström, Nathan Keyfitz, Peter Marsden, Annemette Sørensen, Richard Swedberg, and Alan Wolfe for valuable comments and suggestions, and to Jill Grossman and Gina Hewes for assistance.

[1] I am not the first to make this diagnosis. More than 20 years ago, one of the main

not an obsession, with statistical models and concerns, and a neglect of the need to develop sociological models mirroring conceptions of mechanisms of social processes. The discipline of statistics is a branch of applied mathematics and has no social theory whatsoever. Statisticians never claim otherwise. It is the sociologists' use of statistics that is at fault. Statistics provides tools for estimating mathematical models representing a conception of social processes. Unfortunately, sociologists over the last decades have become less, rather than more, competent at translating theoretical ideas into models to be estimated by statistical techniques. Sociologists therefore estimate ad hoc statistical models of social processes, usually additive models that often represent poor theories of the phenomena being investigated.

It is quite possible to translate theoretical ideas into quantitative data analysis without the use of mathematics. We have a long tradition for how to do this in cross-tabular analysis of survey data. However, it is not possible to use statistical methods for the analysis of the relationships among variables without specifying a mathematical model of these relationships. Usually this model is a simple additive model for the relationships among the variables. Even if simple, an additive model is still a model and hence a conception of what we believe to be the mechanism governing a social process. It might be a good theory. This is usually not known, for sociologists rarely justify an additive model with sociological reasoning about the process under investigation.

When statistics provides the model to be estimated, sociological theory becomes disassociated from evidence. Simple cross-tabulations and percentages are, in fact, often better able to express sociologists' simple theoretical ideas than the ad hoc models suggested by statistical techniques. Therefore we see regression rather than progress in the theoretical sophistication of quantitative empirical research.

Developing theoretical ideas about social processes is to specify some concept of what brings about a certain outcome – a change in political regimes, a new job, an increase in corporate performance, a gain in status, or an increase in score on an academic achievement test. The development of the conceptualization of change amounts to proposing a mechanism for

pioneers of modern quantitative sociology, O. D. Duncan stated: "Over and over again, sociologists have seized upon the latest innovation in statistical method, rushed to their calculators and computers to apply it, and naively exhibited the results as if they were contributions to scientific knowledge."

240   AAGE B. SØRENSEN

a social process. My definition of "mechanism" is simple: It is an account of how change in some variable is brought about – a conceptualization of what "goes into" a process.[2] These accounts can be very simple. The example I will use to illustrate my argument basically proposes only that change in outcomes desired by most people is a result of people taking advantage of opportunities for change, but varying in their ability to take advantage of these opportunities. I hope to show that even such primitive mechanisms can help improve our understanding of a social process over what we learn from adopting ad hoc statistical models.

The first part of the chapter elaborates the argument about the regression of quantitative sociology through the use of ad hoc statistical models and how we got into this situation. There are two main aspects of the decline in the integration of theory with evidence. One is the manner in which multivariate analysis is conducted, the other the widespread adoption of a practice of inferring theoretical validity from the explanatory power of variables. The second part of the chapter presents an alternative conception of theory as a formulation of mechanisms for change in social processes and demonstrates the utility of the approach through the development of an example.

Computing power and the decline of quantitative sociology

The 1960s and early 1970s witnessed a revolution in quantitative sociology. The revolution was caused by the introduction of high-speed computing. It made it possible for social scientists to carry out multivariate statistical data analysis with many variables and many observations. In sociology, the most notable first products of the revolution were the *Equality of Educational Opportunity Report* by James S. Coleman and associates (1966b) and *The American Occupational Structure* by Peter Blau and Otis D. Duncan (1967). These publications reported on elaborate multivariate statistical analyses using massive data sets. In terms of size, the more

---

[2] Often several mechanisms operate in a process. Thus a mechanism producing a gain in a variable may be counteracted by another mechanism reducing or perhaps eliminating the gain. The net outcome may be no overall change. Many processes reach such equilibria. In this way, mechanisms may account for stability. However, when specifying the mechanisms, the focus should be on how change is produced or counteracted. The mathematical treatment of change and of the negative feedback processes that produce stable outcomes of social processes is discussed by Coleman (1968).

spectacular is the *EEO Report*, which presents analyses involving several hundred variables on a sample of 600,000 students in an attempt to measure school effects by accounting for the amount of variance in achievement tests. Blau and Duncan (1967) had fewer variables and a smaller (though still large) data set, but they had more influence on the practice of quantitative sociology through the introduction of path analysis, which became the first encounter with regression analysis for many sociologists.

With the advent of the high-speed computer, we certainly could study the relationships among many more variables than before. More importantly, we could compute precise quantitative measures of the strength of these relationships. The revolution in quantitative sociology was a revolution in statistical productivity. Social scientists could now calculate almost everything with little manual labor and in very short periods of time. Unfortunately, the sociological workers involved in this revolution lost control of their ability to see the relationship between theory and evidence. Sociologists became alienated from their sociological species being.

The explanation for this wholly unintended outcome of the revolution is that computing became too easy and that statistical models became all important for sociological research. The computing power allowed the sociologist to consider too many variables simultaneously and to ask questions that often are meaningless about the relative importance of variables and groups of variables.

Before the availability of high-speed computers, we had card-sorters, and before card-sorters, we stuck needles through cards with holes in them. The needles or the sorters enabled us to count, typically the number of individuals having the same attribute. Then, by physically subdividing piles of cards with needles or card-sorters, we could construct entries in cross-tabulations. This took a fair amount of time, and there were many constraints on what one could do. The constraints were of two types. First, no variable could easily have more than a dozen values, with the typical punch card, and the investigator had bigger piles to subdivide with fewer values.[3] Second, even with few variables, it was impossible to subdivide more than three or five times, with normal-sized surveys. Even when it

---

[3] Galtung (1967) wrote a very good text in methods of data analysis based on the assumption that no variables would have more than three categories. It may be considered the last hurrah for quantitative analysis trying to develop simplifying conceptualizations of social processes. Duncan's review of Galtung's book in the *American Sociological Review* found the three-category approach a 50% improvement over the use of dichotomies and declared the whole approach outdated (Duncan, 1968).

might be possible, it was not very feasible. It was a chore to manage too many piles, and it is impossible to read very large tables and make sense of them. Thus, the precomputer technology forced the researcher to try to characterize a process with few variables and few categories of these variables.

Social processes are complicated phenomena. The task of theory is to simplify them and characterize them in terms of their essential elements. The technology of cross-tabulation forces one to simplify. Therefore, theory development is facilitated. Further, the simplification is most easily achieved in thinking about how outcomes are brought about – that is, in terms of the mechanisms of the processes under investigation. The results are theoretically rich studies such as *The American Soldier, Union Democracy, People's Choice, The Adolescent Society*, and others. Sociology also obtained a very successful integration of quantitative empirical research and theoretical elaboration in the writings of Robert Merton, most notably in his essays on reference group behavior. These essays are among the very few instances where a sociological theorist, not himself gathering and analyzing data, made creative theoretical uses of the research of others. In recent times, most self-declared sociological theorists neither have any interest in nor any ability to understand the vast majority of published quantitative theoretical research. One of the ironies of contemporary graduate training is that theory sometimes becomes the refuge for students who are unable or unwilling to learn statistics.

Due to the nature of quantitative analysis, it became all important that the new techniques allowed for the simultaneous analysis of large numbers of variables in large data sets. This produced long lists of "control" variables and additive models, and it produced the apparent ability to estimate the relative importance of variables and groups of variables.

Computing power and the use of multivariate analysis for causal elaboration

The simplification and conceptual elaboration that was stimulated by precomputer technology received a codification by Paul Lazarsfeld and his associates. The codification provided a rich language of social research, as reflected in the title of one of Lazarsfeld's books (Lazarsfeld and Rosenberg, 1955). Elements of this codification became extremely widely disseminated. All elementary sociological methodology books still present a version of Lazarsfeld's famous three-variable presentation of causal analysis. One all-important lesson is the warning against the dangers of interpreting spurious relationships as causal relationships. Such spurious relationships are to be detected by the introduction of a control variable.

The concern for and treatment of the problem of spurious relationships carried over into the modes of analysis that were made possible by the new computer technology. Ironically, this continuity became the source of much of the decline of quantitative research. The increase in computational power made the linear regression type of model the favorite model for the relationship among the variables analyzed. One usual justification for these models is that we need to control for other variables. The other justification is that we need to assess the relative importance of variables (to be discussed later in the chapter). Nobody, anymore, bothers justifying these controls by suggesting that there is a reason, either conceptually or empirically, to suspect spuriousness. It is evidently better to be safe than possibly sorry, so we just pile variables into the models. The result is a conceptually meaningless list of variables preventing any kind of substantive conclusion – a problem discussed by Lieberson (1985).

While the wish to control by introducing additional variables is taken over directly from tabular analysis, there is an important, but largely unnoticed, difference between the two modes of analyzing data. In tabular analysis, there are no restrictions on the form of the relationships among variables. In regression analysis, the relationship is assumed to be additive.[4] It is extremely rare that sociological theory justifies the assumption of linearity. The justification for the additive model is almost always statistical parsimony.

Parsimony is important, but sociological parsimony should not be confused with statistical parsimony. There is nothing sociologically parsimonious about a model with 10 to 20 independent variables lined up to control each other. There is no known sociological theory that will justify such a model. Additive models are nevertheless strong theories in the sense that they make very strong assumptions about the process under investigation, as I will show later.

The introduction of independent variables as controls in a multivariate

---

[4] Regression analysis usually is understood to mean estimating a model using least squares. The model can be linear or nonlinear. The estimation of nonlinear (and non-loglinear) models in sociology is extremely rare, so in practice, regression analysis has become synonymous with the estimation of linear models for the level of some outcome variable.

statistical model is not usually seen as specifying a theory. The best evidence for this assertion is that it is extremely rare that any sociologist has a hypothesis about the magnitude of a coefficient, other than it is not zero and, perhaps, its sign. Instead, most researchers seem to think that the use of the controls makes the sociologist able to make inferences about causal effects of something in much the same way as a real scientist, or a psychologist, makes these causal inferences using an experiment. However, the analogy is completely misleading. Very few, if any, additive models used by sociologists mirror an experiment (see Lieberson, 1985, for an extended discussion).

There were other tasks in the Lazarsfeld treatment of the three-variable situation than testing for spuriousness. Another task would be the search for relationships that were different for different values of the third variable. This operation, called "specification," amounts to establishing interaction effects. Statisticians and statistically oriented sociologists do not like interaction effects in regression models. They make things less parsimonious and also demand theoretical imagination for their interpretations. Conventional statistical methods therefore make it difficult to establish interaction effects: They are "marginal" to the main effect. So we get fewer of them, especially as we destroy statistical power with too many variables. The result is that we miss out on sociological stories of great interest – how things differ between subgroups and contexts. I discuss the consequences of this omission further in the next section.

Computing power and the estimation of relative effects

The first users of large-scale computing and multivariate statistical models did not justify their analysis in terms of a wish to provide elaborate tests for spuriousness. Both Coleman et al. (1966b) and Blau and Duncan (1967) were mainly concerned with deciding the relative importance of variables: Coleman wanted to measure the relative importance of family background, student body composition, and school facilities; Blau and Duncan wanted to measure the relative importance of family background and education. Coleman's objective was to see how schools could equalize opportunities, Blau and Duncan's to measure the degree of universalism in American society. In both cases, computing power seemed to permit the posing of questions about the relative strength of variables, questions it was not possible to address in earlier quantitative research.

The question of the relative importance of variables, or groups of variables, has no answer in tabular analysis, for good reason: There is no meaningful answer. However, the multivariate techniques made possible by the new technology seemed to provide an answer: various measures relying on the amount of variance explained. Coleman et al. (1966b) used unique portions of variance explained, because they did not have available a technique for summarizing the effect of a large group of variables in a single measure of relative effect. That single measure was available to Blau and Duncan in the form of what they called "path coefficients," which relied on geneticist methodology. Path coefficients later came to be referred to as "standardized regression coefficients," and they measure the effect in terms of standard deviation of the independent variables. It was and is believed that if variable A has a bigger standardized coefficient than variable B, then A is more important. Somehow standard deviations provided a common metric. These sorts of comparisons became very popular, and presumably they could say something about policy – numerous examples of this use are provided by Jencks (e.g., Jencks et al., 1972).

The use of variance explained and standard deviations to assess relative effects is a peculiar obsession of sociologists not found in economics or psychology.[5] Sociologists have made valiant efforts to explain what these comparisons of standardized coefficients mean. Moving people from one percentile in a distribution to another to see what happens is a popular way to provide meaning to the unsophisticated. This approach suggests that the metric that allows comparison of relative importance is friction or wind resistance encountered when moving people from one end of the distribution to the other. This is probably not a useful image to the statistically naive, and it is certainly without meaning. We came to this not because sociologists posed a question and statistics then provided an answer. Instead printouts gave statistics – amount of variance explained or standardized regression coefficients – that presumably were answers to something, and the sociologist thought it had to do with relative importance of variables in additive models (with no interaction effects or other modifications).

In my opinion, there is no statistical quantity that gives a meaningful general answer to the question of which variable is more important. The

---

[5] Though the path models introduced by Blau and Duncan (1967) are the reason for this obsession, Duncan later recommended against using standardized coefficients (Duncan, 1975: 51).

question must, at best, be given a more precise specification. It is possible
to ask which of two teaching techniques will produce the greatest gain in
academic achievement. The reason is that we can imagine, in this comparison, how an outcome can be produced with two different mechanisms.
However, it is impossible to see how it is generally possible to say how
important schools are relative to students' family backgrounds. They are
both required. It is like asking whether oxygen or hydrogen is more important for water. If it is possible to conceive of a mechanism that produces the outcomes focused upon, it might be possible to say something
meaningful. It is further required that the variables compared are in the
same metric, something already argued by Cain and Watts (1970) in their
critique of the first Coleman Report.

The appearance of being able to compare apples and oranges in the
metric of standard deviations is only that: an appearance. It is only a
meaningful metric for one comparison. This is the comparison of whether
two statistics are different or not. Here standard errors, based on variances
and standard deviations, provide a metric in terms of how likely it is that
the difference will be observed again, in particular a difference between
some quantity and zero. This metric informs not about relative importance
but about whether or not to believe a measure of something. Statistical
significance tests are entirely appropriate for experimental outcomes designed to test a null hypothesis. They are also entirely appropriate when
deciding whether to believe the estimated magnitude of some parameters
and whether, therefore, a theory is being rejected. Statistical significance
is not what tells us how important apples are relative to oranges for status
or income or academic achievement.

Although statistical significance tests only inform about whether or not
to believe an estimate of a parameter, they are nevertheless often taken to
inform about theoretical importance. We often meet statements about
something being highly significant as though this meant that it is very
important. This misuse of statistical significance is not unique to sociologists. Also, economists apparently often misuse significance tests (Mc-
Closkey and Ziliak, 1996).

The advent of high-speed computing then led sociologists into thinking
less about what they were doing and letting statistics govern how they
carried out their analysis. It made sociologists ask questions that had no
meaningful answers and allowed them to control for too many variables.
More is described, but less is known.

The new practices also had serious consequences for the conception of how theory is to be linked to evidence. This is discussed next.

Theory as sums of variables

The new methods made available by the new computing power were thought to provide a way of representing and testing causal theories. Path analysis presumably models the causal influences of variables on each other. Therefore, the use of path analysis appears to be providing evidence about theory. The theoretical pretensions became even greater when path models were incorporated into a wider class of models called "structural models," a term borrowed from econometrics where, significantly, it means models mirroring theory. Thus it appeared that we could both compute and integrate theory and research in new and more powerful ways.

Methodologically interested sociologists now had a set of precise tools for estimating and testing theory on large-scale samples, and the tools seemed as powerful as those used by the mathematically more adept economists. In fact, sociologists at the time had more experience with using large-scale survey data for empirical research than did economists – and had better funding opportunities for large-scale research.[6] The future of scientific sociology looked bright in the late 1960s.

The type of data analysis theory that was represented in the causal models of the early application of the new tools became extremely important for how sociologists have carried out analysis and conceived of the relation between theory and research ever since. The models were, as described earlier, invariably linear; that is, they mirror the conception of the process under study as one where outcomes are produced by the sum of the contributions of a set of causal influences represented by the independent variables.[7] The choice of these variables was said to represent theory, and therefore theory became identified with variables. For example, education is considered to represent human capital theory, as I will show later. I will first discuss the additivity assumption and then the practice of seeing the role of theory as justifying choice of variables.

The early status attainment research was replaced by research on income attainment processes emphasizing the impact of labor market processes on

---

[6] The budget for Sociology in the National Science Foundation was larger than the budget for Economics in the late 1960s.

[7] This conception of causal theory is made explicit and elaborated in Heise (1975).

the process of income attainment. Sociologists of the labor market drew much attention to their criticism of status attainment research as being atheoretical and descriptive. Nevertheless, they continued to consider theory to be represented by variables and their relationships. Therefore, even though status attainment research may seem ancient history, it is instructive to use the tradition of attainment research when discussing the conception of the role of theory in quantitative research.

Additive models

Status attainment models were representations of how family background and education influenced socioeconomic outcomes, but they did not present a conception of how these outcomes were obtained, beyond suggesting that one thing followed another: Schooling followed family, first job followed education, and current job followed the first job. The models developed claim that some of the variables characterizing these events would be relevant for variation in some other variables, and some would not be. The additive or linear model was chosen because it was the easiest to estimate. Blau and Duncan (1967) actually provide a statistical demonstration that the main relationships in fact were reasonably linear, something that has not been seen since. However, there is no theoretical justification for using the linear specification.

Additive models can represent peculiar theories. As an example, consider an earnings attainment model. An additive model suggests that each of the independent variables represents some contribution to a person's earnings. A standard sociological earnings model inspired by class analysis might propose a model with class being one independent variable and other independent variables being education, gender, and family background introduced as "controls." These controls are there to make us believe that class makes a difference. This model, in fact, proposes a theory where each person receives x dollars from education, y dollars from family background, q dollars from gender, and z dollars from class. All of it adds up to the person's yearly earnings. We can imagine people walking around among pumps in a large gas station getting something from each of the pumps. The picture should be completed by specifying hypotheses about how many dollars each pump provides, and this would give us some idea of the relative importance of pumps that we could teach in courses on getting ahead in society. What one could call the "gas station theory'' of earnings has apparently become universally accepted by sociologists, if we infer theories from the models used. However, few sociologists think that the form of a regression model has anything to do with theory.

Regression models are made additive because statisticians tell sociologists that while they will be happy to develop techniques to estimate any model the sociologist desires to estimate, sociological theory should suggest the model. Short of such theoretical models, the statistician proposes an additive model as the best. When the sociologist asks for the rationale for the additive model, the statistician suggests that the linear model is the most parsimonious model. Parsimony is here meant as statistical simplicity, both computationally and mathematically. The sociologist has nothing better to suggest and proceeds with following the statistical advice. The possible lack of sociological meaning in the additive specification is rarely noted in statistics and method classes. Theory classes do not consider regression analysis and causal models to be theory.

Additive specifications may be necessary and useful. They may also be valid. In the example I will present later, linearity is also assumed in one part of the proposed model. Some compromise between theoretical imagination, mathematical ability, and the statistical tools available is often needed to do any quantitative research. However, additive specifications assume properties of the processes being investigated. These properties may make sense, or they may not. When they do not make sense, other specifications should be attempted even though it may prevent the researcher from including a multitude of controls or making statements about the relative importance of large groups of variables.

Theory as variables

We have no suggestions in status attainment research about how a person's socioeconomic status is obtained. To provide such a theory was not the motivation for the research. The goal was to assess the relative importance of ascribed versus achieved characteristics for the socioeconomic status of a person. That question originates in the concern of social mobility research and in the question that motivates most mobility research: How much equality of opportunity is there? I suspect Blau and Duncan thought it was pretty self-evident that education had an effect on the type of jobs people got, and that it was not difficult to understand why low education and status of parents also produced low education of their offspring. In any event, even if it was not self-evident, the explanation for why education has an effect on socioeconomic status did not seem particularly relevant for answering the original question about the relative importance of ascribed characteristics, nor do the mechanisms creating the association between family background and status seem relevant for this question. Whatever these mechanisms are, the things that mattered to Blau and Duncan (1967) are the outcomes they produce.

Although status attainment models were not meant to answer questions about why background and education influenced outcomes, the models were said to represent causal flows of something among variables. It was considered a major achievement of Blau and Duncan (1967) that the path models were able to represent the direct and indirect flows of family background influences through and besides education on the socioeconomic status obtained. This made the task of measuring indirect and direct influences of variables possible and almost as important as the measurement of relative importance of variables. Variables were in any event the actors in the causal images created by these efforts. Variables create variances and therefore have effects. Theories about the processes being studied therefore are ideas about which variables to consider, and the truth of the theories is established by showing that those variables matter.

The task for the theoretical elaboration of status attainment research is seen as finding theories that will justify the variables used. This was never done in the early research. Critics of status attainment research accused the research of an individualistic bias. Consistent with the identification of theories with variables, this bias was claimed to be revealed in the choice of variables. Most of the critics suggested that the original status attainment research had ignored nonindividual, or "structural" variables.[8] A variety of theories, mostly obtained from economic research on segmented labor markets, suggested that so-called structural variables be added to the models. Also inspired by economists was the changing of the dependent variable from status to income or earnings – status, to many, seemed a somewhat suspect functionalist variable. Finally, the critique of neoclassical economic theory gave a rationale for criticizing the exclusive reliance on individual variables in the original status attainment research.

---

[8] For a review of the early work in the sociology of labor markets, see Kalleberg and Sørensen (1979); see also Kalleberg and Berg (1987).

Status attainment research became associated with the main neoclassical economic theory being criticized: human capital theory.

Sociologists adopting the vocabulary of economics might be expected also to adopt the conception of the mechanism of the attainment process suggested by human capital theory. However, the identification of human capital theory with individualistic variables did not come about because sociologists took economic theory to be a serious proposal for how socioeconomic outcomes were brought about. Consistent with the already established research tradition, sociologists thought that they could show the importance of structural variables by showing the superior explanatory power of these variables compared to the individual, so-called human capital, variables. The individual-level variables are named human capital variables not because sociologists believe in or even study economics and human capital theory. Rather, the reasoning is that since causal variables must have a theory associated with them, human capital theory serves the purpose well, being a theory of individual endowments.

The practice of labeling individual resource variables human capital variables has spread in sociology beyond attainment research. We almost always now see that the variables of education, experience, ability, and family background are called "human capital variables." This practice leaves unquestioned the validity of the economic theory of human capital, even for things the theory never claimed to be able to explain and could not conceivably explain, like the effect of family background, ability, and occupational status. It is a most peculiar praxis. Clearly very stringent criteria should be fulfilled for an effect of, say, education to be a return on human capital. This was discussed in detail, with empirical analysis, by Mincer more than 20 years ago (Mincer, 1974).

Ability and family background are definitely not produced by the type of investment behavior focused upon in human capital theory. Education might be a result of an investment, but education obviously can have an effect on something without the help of human capital theory. Both economists and sociological theorists provide reasons for such effects alternative to those provided by human capital theory. So an observed effect of education or any other individual-level variable does not necessarily imply anything about the validity of human capital theory.

While human capital theory became the theory attached as a label to individual-level variables, several different theories became attached to the so-called structural variables. They were derived from ideas about dual economy, internal labor markets, and class analysis. Different measures correspond to the different theories. Dualist theories suggested industry variables, internal labor market theory suggested organizational variables, and class analysis suggested measures of labor power (unions) and of class position (authority).[9]

The validity and importance of the various theories are now demonstrated by showing that the various variables derived from the appropriate theories have an effect, net of whatever "controls" the data provide. In continuation of the tradition established by Blau and Duncan (1967), the issue for the sociologists of labor markets became to establish whether some relationships existed or not. In particular, it became important to ascertain if the various measures of labor market structures have an effect, when "human capital" variables are controlled. Such a relationship presumably demonstrated the importance of "structure." The logic of the procedure is quite dubious. Suppose that there are no structural effects; that is, suppose that the labor market is as homogenous as neoclassical economics allegedly claims. What would then determine the individual effects? In the standard economic scenario, the answer would be supply and demand. But demand is certainly structure, also according to the sociologists of the labor market (see Berg, 1981). Therefore, demonstrating that structural variables have no effect would not show that "structure" was not important, only that everyone was exposed to the same structure. Similarly, had Coleman et al. (1966b) found absolutely no school effects, the implication is not that schools are not important, only that all schools are equally important. Presumably very little would be learned about the matters tested for in the achievement tests used as dependent variables in this research had there been no schools at all to teach the material.

In the usual linear models, structure will have an effect only if it affects all individuals in the same manner. Thus if we find an effect of, say, core versus secondary labor market sector in a standard sociological earnings equation, we presumably would conclude that the core sector adds an amount to the earnings of all, regardless of their education, ability, experience, and the like. This means that labor market sector is an extra gas pump that will provide an extra bonus if you put core in it. There are only two ways in which this can take place. Either the sector pump is a proxy

---

[9] A comprehensive survey of the various theories and their measures is provided by Kalleberg and Berg (1987).

for individual characteristics not measured by the individual variables already included in the equation, or the sector pump adds an economic rent that is an advantage available to all in a structural location. In the latter case, we have identified a genuine structural effect. However, the very existence of the effect of the structural variable suggests nothing about what is the source of the effect – unmeasured individual variables or rents.

The search for structural effects could be extended with the inclusion of interaction effects suggesting that structure determined how individual-level variables affected earnings in different structural locations. This was suggested in the early dual labor market theory in economics for the good reason that the segments of sector were identified with different demand schedules, producing different payments on the individual characteristics. Structure is represented with several gas stations, where one gets different amounts of gas for the same types of pumps. For this reason, early work testing dual labor market theory in sociology tested for these interactions (Beck, Horan, and Tolbert, 1978), and early applications of class analysis to labor market processes also suggested their existence (Wright, 1979).

In recent work, sociologists have not taken the idea of interaction effects very seriously for the reason that interaction effects are hard to establish, even harder to convince statisticians about, and difficult to interpret in the absence of theory. What is most important is that the existence of an interaction between an individual and a structural variable makes it impossible to separate structural from individual effects. Therefore interaction effects defeat the very purpose of the research enterprise as it has been defined by the dominant approach to quantitative research in sociology. In other words, we cannot establish the power of variables and the theories associated with them when we have interaction effects. In the school effects literature, interaction effects also would seem a plausible idea. They suggest that different schools would produce different learning outcomes depending on the combination of characteristics of the students and of their schools. However, neither in the original *EEO Report* ncr in subsequent research have these interactions attracted much interest.[10] The reasons are the same as in labor market research: We cannot ascertain the

---

[10] The recent use of hierarchical models in educational research represents a much richer approach to the study of school effects than the standard linear models used in earlier research (e.g., Raudenbush and Bryk, 1986). The approach invites attention to interaction effects. However, the emphasis has been methodological and statistical so far. A systematic reevaluation of the conclusions from the earlier school effects research remains to be done.

relative importance of schools versus family backgrounds if the two sets of variables interact.

In sum, the idea that theories show their power by having their associated variables demonstrate effects produces ambiguities about what the results mean. This is both because a variable rarely only measures one thing and because relative power of theories becomes a matter of statistical significance and amount of variance explained. Further, the identification of theories with variables and the use of statistical rather than sociological models produce poor models and impoverished analysis. In particular, the wish to separate the effects of groups of variables produces the neglect of interaction effects. We learn very little from such research.

A much different understanding of what governs attainment processes is obtained by modeling the mechanisms that produce change. An example of how this may be achieved is presented next.

Theories as models of mechanisms for change

The proper division of labor between statistics and sociology is one where sociological theory suggests a mathematical model of a social process and statistics provides the tools to estimate this model. The branch of sociology presumed to teach us how to formulate models of social processes is mathematical sociology. There are many varieties of mathematical sociology; some seem like notational exercises, and others are mathematical elaborations with no conceivable empirical reference. However, James S. Coleman presents in *Introduction to Mathematical Sociology* (1964) numerous examples of mathematical models mirroring social processes of various sorts with empirical analysis using these models to study a number of phenomena. Most of these models are reformulations of simple stochastic process models for change in discrete variables, such as party affiliation, friendship formation, adopting of a new drug, and so on. They are models of how change is brought about – that is, of the mechanisms of the social processes under investigation. Thus several models mirror how social influence processes occur in groups or other systems by a process of contagion, where one person carrying out an act influences the likelihood that another person will carry out an act. Almost all of these models can be estimated from available data. Most often the data available to Coleman were cross-sectional, showing the state of a system at a point in time. Inferences about the empirical adequacy of the models with such data are obtained by deriving the properties of the processes in equilibrium. This strategy is standard in economics, where the resulting equilibrium models are referred to as "comparative statics models."

The formulation of the Coleman models translates theoretical ideas into mathematical form. This lends conceptual interpretations to the parameters of the model, and the functional form adopted specifies how change is brought about. For example, the well-known models for diffusion of new drugs among medical doctors present two formulations of how adoption of a new drug comes about. One formulation applies to adoption of a new drug when doctors have little contact with other doctors. The other mirrors how it would occur when doctors primarily rely on colleagues for information about new drugs. The two different formulations provide different predictions about the course of adoption among the two groups of doctors. Empirical tests of the models in turn provide evidence about the validity of the functional form assumed. The parameters of the models measure frequency of contact and exposure. The variation of these parameters with independent variables allow for the empirical analysis of what causes variation in the spread of the drug (see Coleman, Katz, and Menzel, 1966a). Statistical tools provide evidence about the fit of the models and the precision of estimates. Coleman was not much of a user of these tools.

The sociological imagination, embodied in Coleman's numerous examples of how to use mathematical models for conceptual elaboration, did not have a large impact on the discipline. There seem to be several reasons. First, the data limitations and computational limitations that inspired Coleman to enormous creativity and imagination in developing and applying the models were removed. Longitudinal data became widely available. This eliminated the need to derive predictions about equilibrium states of the processes.[11] The advances in computing power made it possible to estimate directly what until then had to be inferred using assumptions about equilibrium outcomes. The facility with which one now could estimate parameters of basic stochastic processes, using statistical models for hazard rate or event history analysis, produced a neglect for the properties of the systems embodied in the assumptions of the model. Since no equilibrium outcomes were needed to test the empirical adequacy of the

---

[11] The superiority of longitudinal data is widely agreed upon, but they have never been of much use for the development and testing of change models in the manner proposed by Coleman. Rather, they usually are treated as series of cross-sections, or change is studied in a regression-like manner using event history or hazard rate analysis.

models with cross-sectional data, there was no need to study how an equilibrium would be obtained and therefore to know the properties of the models.[12]

Second, mathematics was never adopted as a tool for theory construction by those who identify themselves, and are identified by others, as sociological theorists, despite a couple of notable exceptions (Stinchcombe, 1968). Mathematical sociology in most graduate curricula was seen as a branch of methodology, and mathematical sociologists willingly adopted the label "methodologists" since they usually could understand and teach statistics. They also seemed to get more prestige from importing econometric and statistical tools than from developing cute models of small processes. Sociological theory became classical theory, and its modern reincarnations, a bit of philosophy. All of it is devoid of reference to quantitative analysis. Quantitative analysis became viewed as largely atheoretical, and when Grand Theory did enter regression equations, it came as variables – for example, in the type of class analysis presented by Wright (1979). Sociology departments did not require calculus of entering graduate students, and it is difficult to obtain facility with differential equation models that mirror mechanisms for change if one does not understand calculus. But standard statistical techniques can be taught and learned without calculus, from SPSS manuals if all else fails.

Finally, Coleman himself abandoned the enterprise soon after the publication of *Introduction to Mathematical Sociology*. His major empirical analysis of educational processes did not apply any of the principles he had proposed. By the late 1960s, Coleman had also abandoned the type of modeling using stochastic process models as the basis that gave such imaginative examples of formulating models for theories that represent social mechanisms; these models were abandoned in favor of developing a purposive actor theory (Coleman, 1973). Purposive actor theory also requires mathematics and invites the formulation of mechanisms, but here the use of mathematics is without the clear empirical applicability of the stochastic process models.

Mathematical sociology has now almost completely disappeared from our graduate programs and is considered by all but a very small group of

---

[12] I am not claiming that social processes necessarily reach equilibrium. However, making inferences about a model from cross-sectional data forces one to assume that equilibrium has been reached. This has the useful byproduct that one is forced to study the dynamic properties of the model.

aficionados to be a rarefied and wholly irrelevant, if not absurd, activity. Nevertheless, mathematics remains the only tool for representing theory in a manner that will allow the use of statistical methods of estimation, for we cannot estimate relationships without making assumptions about the functional form of the relationship. There is no such thing as a theory-free model, however parsimonious the model is.

Rather than elaborating programmatic statements about the virtue of linking theory and evidence in mathematical models, I will illustrate the strategy with an example that hopefully will show the type of insights that a little bit of thought about the mechanisms that govern social processes can provide. The example is from the study of attainment processes, the topic that originated much of the computational and statistical sophistication already discussed.

Modeling mechanisms of attainment processes

There is a way to understand the attainment process other than the conventional one used in sociological attainment research, where structural variables are believed to add to individual variables in producing outcomes according to separate theories for each of the variables or variable groups. One can obtain ideas about such an alternative scenario by focusing on how change in socioeconomic attainments might come about.

Consider a person with a given set of personal resources in the form of ability, skills, background, and experience in a certain "structural" location, most simply a job. She now moves to a different position. Either she experiences a gain in wage or salary, or in occupational status, or she experiences a loss or no change. The former situation is most likely, for most moves seem to be voluntary, and if she initiated the move, she probably did so because of some advantage of the move. If she was forced to change location, she probably experienced a loss, or at best no gain.

Consider now the situation where a gain is obtained. This gain results from either our worker being more productive in the new position, or it reflects that the new position provides her with an advantage that is located in the position and can be obtained by anyone getting access to this position. If our worker is more productive in the new position, it should be because the position changed her, by providing her with new skills or more effort. If the position provided her with an advantage, not caused by a change in her productivity, then the position presumably provided her with a rent.

If changes in socioeconomic attainment reflect changes in the worker's productivity, the mechanisms for change would be the mechanisms that tie individual productivity to rewards in the labor market. Standard labor market theory is as good as any other proposal. This theory implies a process of socioeconomic attainment where workers increase their productivity by learning on their jobs or by receiving incentives to work harder. The rate of learning will decline with age, for a variety of reasons, and the level of effort will, perhaps, also remain stable. In any event, we predict a career trajectory that will show increases in the early years and then stability. That is what we observe.

If positions provide incumbents with rents, then they create genuine structural advantages and we have a nonindividual source of change in attainments.[13] A different conception of the mechanism for change in attainment than the one relying on change in individual productivity is needed. The needed conception should suggest how individuals can increase their wage or status without changing their productivity. Such a conception would be one corresponding to the idea of how change is produced by individuals taking advantage of opportunities, in the meaning of favorable occasions.

In order to arrive at such a conception, it is useful first to note that if positions provide rents, it clearly is desirable to obtain such a position. The position gives you something for nothing. This means that access to the position will be regulated in some manner – that is, the position will be closed to outsiders. Ordinarily, only when the present incumbent of the position leaves the position, for retirement or for another position, will the position be available. The vacancy then represents an opportunity, and the opportunity structure will be defined by the rate at which vacancies are created and their distribution. In Sørensen (1977), I show that assuming a particularly simple form for the distribution of attainments, the exponential distribution, the rate at which new vacancies will be available will be given by the quantity $b = \beta/h;$ $b < 0$. Here is the parameter that governs the distribution of attainment in such a manner that the larger it is, the more unevenly positions are distributed by whatever measure of attainment

---

[13] See Sørensen (1996a) for an analysis of the role of rents in creating structural advantages.

(status or earnings) is employed to characterize positions. The quantity h is the rate at which new positions become vacant by people leaving the system.

In what I call the "vacancy competition model," gains in attainments are produced by job shifts, or shifts in positions, generated by the vacancies. It can be shown that as each job shift produces a gain, the longer the worker has been in the labor force, the less likely it is that there will be a job to which she can get access given her qualifications. A simple formulation (with empirical support) for the relationship between time in the labor force and the rate of job shift is to assume an exponential decline, implying that the number of shifts a person has undertaken by time t will be:

$$v(t) = \frac{1}{b}(e^{bt}-1) \tag{1}$$

A worker will start out with a level of status $y(0)$ at entry into the labor force. By time t, the attainment of this person will equal $y(0)$ plus a gain equal to the average gain per shift. This average gain will equal the total gain to be made, that is $y(t) = y(0) + y\, v(t)$. The average gain will equal the total gain divided by the total number of shifts $v(\ )$. Denoting the maximum attainment to be obtained as $y(m)$, one obtains:

$$\Delta y = \frac{y(m)-y(0)}{v(\infty)} \tag{2}$$
$$= -b[y(m)-y(0)]$$

The quantity $y(m)$ is both a function of the worker's individual resources and a function of the opportunity structure. It is useful to introduce a measure of a person's resources that is independent of the opportunity structure defined by the relation $y(m) = -z/b$, where z is a comprehensive measure of a person's resources. With this definition, Equation (1) can be written, using (2), as:

$$y(t) = \frac{z}{b}(e^{bt}-1)+y(0)e^{bt} \tag{3}$$

This is then the desired expression for the attainment process in a system where gains in wages or status are obtained as rents provided by closed positions in social structure. It describes a career curve that is concave to the time axis, which is what we observe. The same pattern is predicted from human capital theory, which proposes an alternative mechanism for change in attainment – that is, changes in the level of resources z. The standard linear formulations, typical of sociological attainment research, of course propose no mechanism at all and have no predictions about the career.

To show the usefulness of this approach, we should be able to draw insights from the vacancy competition model that cannot be obtained from the standard approach. Further, to show that this theory has something to offer over human capital theory, we should gain insights that would not have been predicted from the mechanism proposed in that theory. The main interest here is in the comparison to the standard approach, for this is the approach that I would like to show is inferior. The comparison is apparently not straightforward, for the vacancy competition model (3) does not look like the models typically estimated in sociological research. The model proposed has only three variables: $y(t)$, the measure of attainment; time; and z, the measure of resources. There is no variable characterizing structure. The impact of structure is reflected in a parameter of the model, b, the measure of opportunities.

A more familiar form is easily obtained. The quantity z is a comprehensive measure of a person's resources – that is, the characteristics of persons that employers pay attention to when allocating people to jobs. This measure could be conceived of as an additive function of measured resource variables such as education, ability, family background, and so on. Thus we may write z as $z = {}_ic_ix_i$, where x_i are the specific resource variables. Inserting this expression for z gives an expression that can be written:

$$y(t) = c_o^* + b^*y(0) + c_1^* x_1 + c_2^* x_2 \ldots c_i^* + c_n^* x_n \qquad (4)$$

where $c_i^* = c_i/b(e^{bt} - 1)$ and $b^* = e^{bt}$. This has the form of a lagged equation, and the parameters can be estimated from observations on the career at two points in time. From these estimates of the c_i^*'s and b^*, it is straightforward to obtain the estimates of the original parameters. The lagged equation is still not similar to what is used in sociological attainment research. Here typically cross-sectional data are used. The formulation of (4) that will allow for cross-sectional analysis is easily obtained, however. Letting $t \to \infty$ in e^{bt} produces the expression ($b < 0$):

$$y(m) = d_0 + d_1 x_1 \ldots d_i x_i + d_n x_n \qquad (5)$$

where $d_t = -c_t/b$. This is then the equilibrium state of the process. It produces the linear model for how the attainment of the worker depends on the variables forming this person's resources or productivity. In fact, it is the type of model estimated in the old status attainment research, before the addition of "structural" variables.

There are a number of important implications of this result. First, the vacancy competition model originated in a conception of how change in attainment came about by the utilization of structural opportunities for change in position. This provided a precise idea of what structural opportunities are and a measure of these opportunities, the parameter b. This quantity can be estimated from longitudinal data. However, it cannot be identified from cross-sectional data.

The structural forces shaping careers shape the *effects* of individual variables on the observed attainment. They are not represented with variables to be added to the equation in the manner of conventional attainment research.[14] In fact, if the vacancy competition model has validity, then an observed effect of structural variables must be due to the fact that the structural variable is a proxy measure for individual resources. This is perfectly possible and would be consistent with an idea of structure changing people, in the manner suggested by human capital and incentive theory. However, it is a paradoxical conclusion for the conventional research claiming that the goal of the research is to separate the influence of structural and individual variables.

Finally, the cross-sectional formulation clearly shows that the use of cross-sectional data assumes that the career process has reached a stable level or equilibrium. This is evidently not correct in a standard national sample including all age groups. The violation of the equilibrium assumption implies that whatever the estimated parameters mean, they cannot be correct representations of the "structural" model since they are unknown functions of time – that is, age or time in the labor force.

The usefulness of the approach exemplified by the vacancy competition model ultimately hinges on the model providing new insights into empirical processes. That this is possible can be demonstrated with an example. In Sørensen (1979), I estimate simple attainment models for Blacks and

---

[14] The structural effects could be modeled as functions of variables in a multilevel model.

Whites, men and women. The objective was initially to validate the interpretation of b as a measure of opportunities. Using data from the 1970 U.S. Census that provide information on occupation at two points in time (1970 and 1965), I estimate Equation (4) and then derive the fundamental parameters. The results are duplicated in Table 10.1.

It is well known that Black men and women have lower levels of attainment than Whites. It is also well established that the resources of Blacks appear to be less efficacious than those of Whites. In Sørensen (1979), I estimated the effect of education on status as .593 for White men and .475 for Black men,[15] and .458 and .425 for White and Black women, respectively. These differences are highly significant.

I will concentrate here on the race results. Clearly Blacks get less for their education than Whites. There could be two reasons. One is that Blacks suffer from discrimination. The other is that the quality of education is inferior for Blacks, so that they get less out of their schooling. Now, the conventional analysis cannot separate these two explanations, for it does not provide a measure of discrimination, or unequal opportunities, that is separate from the estimates of the contribution of a given resource, like education, to the overall level of resources for Blacks. The vacancy competition model allows one to separate the two components.

It is of interest to estimate discrimination directly, since the lower effect of education for Blacks poses a riddle. It is well known that, net of family background, Blacks have higher educational aspiration, lower rates of dropout, and higher rates of college attendance (e.g., Hauser, 1993). It is strange that Blacks seem to invest more in education than Whites, when they get less out of their investment.

The estimates of the vacancy competition model presented in Table 10.1 provide an answer to the puzzle. The estimates of b clearly show the expected difference in opportunity structures among the four groups, with Black men and women having clearly fewer opportunities available to them than Whites. This provides validation of the ideas about the mechanisms that generate these attainment or career processes in the vacancy competition model. The results also solve the puzzle.

Table 10.1 provides an estimate of z, the comprehensive measure of

---

[15] These results are in a metric that differ somewhat from the ordinary. The new metric is obtained through a monotonic transformation of socioeconomic status measured in the conventional manner and a cohort standardized metric for education. The transformation produces a distribution of attainment that meets the assumption of the vacancy competition model. This transformation has no importance for the substantive nature of the findings discussed here, but it does determine the numerical values of the estimates.

Table 10.1. *Estimates of parameters of the vacancy competition model for Black and White men and women using 1970 PUS*

Parameter	White men	White women	Black men	Black women
b	−.222	−.264	−.282	−.324
c_0	.125	.150	.068	.060
c_1	.125	.109	.152	.189
z	.267	.263	.157	.194
N	28,653	18,986	19,493	18,012

Note: Estimates obtained using Equation (4). The quantity b is a measure of opportunities; c_0 estimates unmeasured resources; c_1 estimates contribution of education to a person's resources; and z is the average level of resources for a person with average educational attainment in the given race/gender category.
Source: Sørensen, 1979: Table 4.

resources. This estimate is obtained by using the expression $z = {}_tc_tx_t$ with the estimates of c_0 and c_1 presented, and the mean level of education for the four groups. The estimates clearly show that Black men and women have lower levels of resources than Whites. However, education clearly makes a larger contribution to these resources for Blacks. In fact, the results imply that had Blacks had the same opportunities as Whites, then the effect of education observed in the conventional models would have been larger. The effect for Black men in equilibrium would be .685, that is −.152/−.222, using the b for White men and the expression for d_t in Equation (5). For White men, it would be .563 when the process has reached equilibrium.

Simple ideas about the mechanisms governing social processes formulated in simple mathematical models show that the conventional approaches of letting variables represent theory and letting statistical analysis dictate model formulation can produce quite serious misrepresentations of social processes. Structure is indeed important for attainment processes, and the denial of opportunities to Blacks, not just their lower level of resources, is indeed operative. It is not at all clear how the conventional approach would have shown this.

Conclusion

This chapter has argued that the theoretical poverty of quantitative sociology was a result of the enormous increase in computational power that started in the 1960s. The new computational power made it unnecessary to economize on concepts and variables and made statistical convenience rather than sociological ideas decide the representation of theories of social processes.

I have proposed that sociological ideas are best reintroduced into quantitative sociological research by focusing on specifying the mechanisms by which change is brought about in social processes. This necessarily means a specification in a mathematical model. However, the model need not be very complicated, as shown. The main requirement is that it focuses on change. The model proposed here can indeed be reduced to a simple linear differential equation (Sørensen, 1977). It may then be argued that we have only moved the "black" box down a level – from the level of variables to the rate of change in variables. However, this step is a fundamental one, for it allows the separation of various sources of change – for example, the separation of structural versus individual sources of change in individual attainment.

The development of mathematical models is not a popular activity among sociologists, and sociologists are not required to know much mathematics. It would be good for the progress of the discipline if there were an alternative approach. Some progress might be made by careful attention to the implications of the statistical model for the conception of the process studied. Further, it may be possible to design data collection so that direct measures of the components governing change process are available. Simple tabular analysis, as was done before the advent of high-speed computing, is often not a bad idea.

The simple models for change suggest mechanisms for processes other than socioeconomic attainment. I chose this area of application because it has been unusually important for the development of statistical methodology in social research, and because it is the area I know best. I have used similar reasoning to formulate models for how individual abilities and opportunities for learning produce differences in learning outcomes among schools, what we call "school effects." These models show that the regression models used by Coleman et al. (1966b) and everyone else in this area of research present unreasonable theories of educational processes (Sørensen, 1996b). The use of additive regression models by Coleman is ironic. In his own empirical research on schools, Coleman never applied the principles for how to model social processes advocated in his 1964 text. I believe the reason was that, for policy research, he thought that the representation of sociological theory in mathematical models would make the research unacceptable to everyone but a few sociologists. However, if the sociological theory requires another representation than the one given by the ad hoc statistical model, then the policy implications of the ad hoc model would be wrong.

It is not likely that any change in how sociologists go about doing quantitative research will take place in the foreseeable future. Very few researchers, other than population ecologists (e.g., Hannan and Carroll, 1992), formulate models of change in sociology. Quite a few researchers now estimate models of change in discrete variables, in the form of event history analysis. However, this has become just another way of doing regression analysis with rich opportunities for controlling for everything.

References

Beck, E. M., P. M. Horan, and C. M. Tolbert. 1978. "Stratification in a Dual Economy: A Sectorial Model of Earnings Determination." *American Sociological Review*. Vol. 43:704–20.

Berg, Ivar. 1981. "Introduction." Pp. 1–7 in Ivar Berg (ed.), *Sociological Perspectives on the Labor Market*. New York: Academic Press.

Blau, Peter M., and Otis D. Duncan. 1967. *The American Occupational Structure*. New York: Wiley.

Cain, Glen C., and Harold Watts. 1970. "Problems in Making Policy Inferences from the Coleman Report." *American Sociological Review*. Vol. 35:228–42.

Coleman, James S. 1964. *Introduction to Mathematical Sociology*. New York: The Free Press.

Coleman, James S. 1968. "The Mathematical Study of Change." Pp. 429–77 in *Methodology in Social Research*, edited by Hubert Blalock and Ann B. Blalock. New York: McGraw-Hill.

Coleman, James S. 1973. *The Mathematics of Collective Action*. Chicago, IL: Aldine.

Coleman, James S., Elihu Katz, and Herbert Menzel. 1966a. *Medical Innovation*. Indianapolis, IN: Bobbs-Merrill.

Coleman, James S., et al. 1966b. *Equality of Educational Opportunity*. Washington, D.C.: U.S. Dept. of Health, Education, and Welfare, Office of Education.

Duncan, Otis Dudley. 1968. Review of *Theory and Method in Sociology*, by Johan Galtung. *American Sociological Review*, Vol. 33:457–8.

Duncan, Otis Dudley. 1975. *Introduction to Structural Equation Models*. New York: Academic Press.

Galtung, Johan. 1967. *Theory and Methods in Sociology*. New York: Columbia University Press.

Hannan, Michael T., and Glen R. Carroll. 1992. *Dynamics of Organizational Populations*. New York: Oxford University Press.

Hauser, Robert M. 1993. "Trends in College Entry among Whites, Blacks, and Hispanics: 1972–1988." Pp. 61–104 in Charles Clotfelter and Michael Rothschild (eds.), *Studies of Supply and Demand in Higher Education*. Chicago: University of Chicago Press.

Heise, David R. 1975. *Causal Analysis*. New York: Wiley.

Jencks, Christopher, Marshall Smith, Henry Acland, Mary Jo Bane, David Cohen, Herbert Gintis, Barbara Heyns, and Stephan Michelson. 1972. *Inequality. A Reassessment of the Effect of Family and Schooling in America*. New York: Basic Books.

Kalleberg, Arne L., and Ivar Berg. 1987. *Work and Industry: Structures, Markets and Processes*. New York: Plenum.

Kalleberg, Arne L., and Aage B. Sørensen. 1979. "The Sociology of Labor Markets." *Annual Review of Sociology*. Vol. 5:351–79.

Lazarsfeld, Paul F., and Morris Rosenberg, eds. 1955. *The Language of Social Research; A Reader in the Methodology of Social Research*. Glencoe, IL: The Free Press.

Lieberson, Stanley. 1985. *Making it Count: The Improvement of Social Research and Theory*. Berkeley: University of California Press.

McCloskey, Deirdre N., and Stephen T. Ziliak. 1996. "The Standard Errors of Regression." *Journal of Economic Literature*. Vol. 34:97–114.

Mincer, Jacob. 1974. *Schooling, Experience and Earnings*. New York: Columbia University Press.

Raudenbush, Stephen W., and Anthony S. Bryk. 1986. "A hierarchical model for studying school effects." *Sociology of Education*. Vol. 59:1–17.

Sørensen, Aage B. 1977. "The Structure of Inequality and the Process of Attainment." *American Sociological Review*. Vol. 42:965–78.

Sørensen, Aage B. 1979. "A Model and a Metric for the Analysis of the Intragenerational Status Attainment Process." *American Journal of Sociology*. Vol. 85:361–84.

Sørensen, Aage B. 1996a. "The Structural Basis of Social Inequality." *American Journal of Sociology*. Vol. 101:1333–65.

Sørensen, Aage B. 1996b. "Educational Opportunities and School Effects." Pp. 207–26 in Jon Clark (ed.), *James S. Coleman*. Falmer Press.

Stinchcombe, Arthur L. 1968. *Constructing Social Theories*. New York: Harcourt, Brace, and World.

Wright, Erik O. 1979. *Class Structure and Income Determination*. New York: Academic Press.

11. Monopolistic competition as a mechanism: Corporations, universities, and nation–states in competitive fields

ARTHUR L. STINCHCOMBE

Mechanisms in competitive social fields with relatively stable rankings

The mechanism developed in this chapter models competitive fields with areas of monopoly controlled by corporate groups. The mechanism is to explain autocorrelation of profits, prestige, and power of highly ranked corporate groups in those fields. To show the generality of such a mechanism, I illustrate it by applying it to profits of large corporations, prestige of distinguished universities, and power of large rich nation–states.

I have defined mechanisms before (Stinchcombe 1991) as bits of "sometimes true theory" (the phrase is due to James S. Coleman 1964, pp. 516–19) or "model" that represent a causal process, that have some actual or possible empirical support separate from the larger theory in which it is a mechanism, and that generate increased precision, power, or elegance in the large-scale theories. Here the combined mechanisms of monopoly power and competitive environments have autonomous theoretical and empirical support, especially in economics. Separate measures of the monopoly power of particular firms have been developed, especially in Tobin's q-ratio.[1] It is crucial of course that not all firms have equal

---

[1] The q-ratio is the ratio of the market value of a corporation (e.g., of its stocks and bonds) to the replacement value of its assets. If there were no monopoly power or differential taxation (or subsidy) of different sorts of capital returns and costs, the equilibrium value of this ratio ought to be 1. Tobin and Brainard (1977) found an average of q for industrial corporations fluctuating around 2 during the boom of the 1960s and early '70s. On average at that time, the ratio of earnings to replacement value was about 0.095, while the market discount rate for expected real earnings on the securities was around 0.05, compatible with a market valuation of about twice assets. The crucial estimating assumption for "replacement cost" was a 0.05 per year depreciation of original cost, with original cost appropriately updated for inflation. There has been considerable development of the measurement process since Tobin's early research. See especially Lindberg and Ross (1981) for alternative esti-

monopoly power, so it is worthwhile for us to theorize about the inequalities of rank derived from differential monopoly power in this chapter. Our argument then is that monopolistic competitive fields with differentiated monopolies that account for the continuity of status of corporations in markets, of universities in prestige systems, or of nation–states in world power systems have mechanisms that are closely analogous.[2] I will

mating procedures and data stretching the Tobin and Brainard series into the 1970s, with a published list of q-ratios of American corporations. Klock, Thies, and Baum (1991) reestimate some of these ratios using better data and extending the time period, giving estimates for some firms for 1977 to 1983. The average q-ratio was much lower, showing no average monopoly power of large corporations, but the substantial variance around that lower mean still reflected differential monopoly. Smirlock, Gilligan, and Marshall (1984) separate two kinds of monopoly power, "superior efficiency" monopoly and "conspiracy" monopoly, and try to estimate them separately, and there are theoretical distinctions between what is usually called "monopoly power" and the mere ownership of lucrative or business-enhancing assets such as favorable location, oil reserves, and so forth. From the point of view of this essay, these distinctions are irrelevant, although they are very relevant in American law and in the economic policy implications of antimonopoly legislation. None of these studies pay special attention to the autocorrelation over time of q-ratios of the separate corporations that is crucial to our discussion, although the large variance of q-ratios averaged over time for separate corporations as listed by Lindberg and Ross indicates that that autocorrelation must be substantial. The original papers were directed mainly to the problems of aggregate equilibrium of investment and related business cycle problems, which is why the mean level of q in different periods rather than autocorrelation structure of inequality has been of interest. An application of q-ratios in sociology is Palmer, Barber, Zhou, and Soysal (1995).

   [2] By "monopolistic competition," I mean competition in which each firm or other corporate group (at least, each corporate group toward the top in profits, prestige, or power) delivers a unique product or dominates a unique territory, but there are more or less close substitutes that make them subject to competitive pressure. Thus in economics my concept is quite close to that of Edward Hastings Chamberlin (1962 [1933]), especially Chapters 4 and 5, pp. 56–116), and quite different from that defined as "imperfect competition" by Joan Robinson (1933). The core difference is that in Robinson's thought, new entrants are assumed to produce the same product, at the same time and place as the industry leaders if that is relevant to the theory, and at the same cost, whereas Chamberlin presumes that every firm has some degree of monopoly. In the long run with new entries, Robinson competition produces (absent conspiracy) the same price results as perfect competition, whereas that of Chamberlin does not; for Chamberlin the price rank order may have a determinate equilibrium, but the price level for any given "unique product," or of the "industry" of near-substitutes competing at the edges of their individual markets, need not. From our point of view, it is more significant that Chamberlin's theory, but not Robinson's, makes it easy to imagine that at any chosen time some firms will be more profitable than others by charging a higher price relative to their costs. In the Robinson approach, there is no reason to expect such stratification by profitability (except ins versus outs), and in particular no reason to expect that stratification to be moderately stable. The sharpest formulation by Chamberlin is perhaps: "To add the demand curve for Fords and the demand curve for Packards gives a total which is a demand curve for neither Fords, Packards, nor 'automobiles in general.' It gives no clew [sic] whatever to the price of anything" (1962 [1933], p. 303n – quoting his 1927 Harvard Thesis, p. 361). The place of Packard Motor Company in the automobile market then and now indicates a relatively low autocorrelation of status of automobile companies over 70 years.

first illustrate that similarity by analyzing competition among corporations for a continuing high status measured by profits, competition among universities for continuity of high prestige, and competition among nation–states for continuity of high power. Then I will develop conceptions of how these mechanisms work in the rest of the chapter, using the illustrations, as convenient, for empirical support or for suggestions for research.

My purpose is in part due to the inherent interest in sociology of the continuity of rank systems in fields that are apparently competitive and where ranks are precarious. It is therefore substantively worthwhile for each of these systems to invent theories of such continuity: Precarious monopolies give advantage, but "time and chance happeneth to them all," as Ecclesiastes puts it. But part of our interest here is to illustrate that mechanisms can look very similar even if the substance (in this case, the kind of status of corporate groups that their leaders try to preserve) varies considerably. Thus mechanisms vary, as do other theories, in their scope and in the variety of the environments in which they work. Not everything is a field in which status is competitive but highly autocorrelated, so this mechanism is a "sometimes true theory." But insofar as the argument of this chapter is valid, I could substitute "true often enough to be widely useful."

The conception of the mechanism is especially guided by John R. Commons's definition of competition *as a special type of appropriation* or property that gives a corporate body (e.g., a firm, university, or nation) rights to the benefits that result from certain legitimate activities and freedom from liability for whatever damage is caused by its legitimate pursuit of those advantages. This flow of benefits, being monopolized by being appropriated, may then be used to maintain the group's rank in the system. But corresponding to that particular form of appropriation is the precariousness of one's flow of benefits and position in the overall system because others also are not liable for damages (from their *own* permitted activities) to that standing. Such a system then can explain both the continuity over time (or positive autocorrelation) of rank in a competitive field, and the ultimate precariousness of that rank (autocorrelation less than 1.0).

But my argument will be that this somewhat evanescent monopoly advantage is a relation between a feature of the field, an "opportunity" to be monopolized, and a feature of the corporate group, a "competence" to monopolize that particular activity. Competitive fields then consist in a mechanism of appropriation that attaches competent organizations to opportunities in their fields; fields have a "granular" structure of opportunities (or "niches") that are relatively distinct, and so monopolizable, and organizations have "specialized competencies" that make them especially efficient or otherwise effective in monopolizing one or more of those granular spaces. As the elasticity of substitution between competing products, services, or national powers slopes upward from the center of an organization's niche, competitiveness increases and monopoly advantage declines. That elasticity at any particular place in that niche often varies over time, and this creates an autocorrelation less than 1.0.

The argument of this chapter will be developed in four sections. The first gives a comparison of granular opportunities and competence of firms in markets, prestige systems of universities, and global power systems of nation–states. Then we turn to the characterization of competitive organizations. The third section looks at opportunities as characteristics of fields. The fourth presents the mechanism itself, competition as a distinct type of appropriation.

Three examples of organizations in competitive fields

The point of these examples

Our purpose in developing the following examples is to show that the phenomena that our mechanism is supposed to explain are to be found in at least three radically different fields: competition among firms in markets, among universities in prestige systems, and among nation–states in the global power system. My first objective then is to illustrate the facts, which will surprise no one, that all three systems are fields of competition, that status within them has a high degree of autocorrelation so that the successful ones in one year (or decade) are quite likely to be the successful ones in the following year (or decade), and that the position is maintained by vigorous activity on the part of leaders to hold their high positions, and by competitors to gain high positions.

But I also hope to show that the central elements of our mechanism are to be found in all three. In all of them, characteristics of the organizations are essential to their success, and top organizations have to be competent to produce the benefits that make them successes in order to maintain their position. In all of them, the field provides a possible flow of benefits, a position of opportunity, that describes what gives competitive advantage (in a niche) in the field in which competition takes place. And in all of them, the relation between the corporate organization and the opportunity is one of *precarious appropriation*, a system in which organizations appropriate the benefits of their competence as long as the opportunity continues to pay off, with possible erosion of status if the field changes so that the opportunity no longer pays, or if competitors develop competitive competencies so that the monopoly is no longer defensible.

In fields of markets, prestige systems, and world systems, some organizations perform better than others, and they always do this not by becoming careful *rentiers* choosing their investments. Instead, they organize networks of collective action, create networks of suppliers, build or buy capital resources, and give people incentives to do all those successful performances. This always means maintaining the competence of those networks by beating out alternative networks to which the members or suppliers might go. And it means meeting the competitive challenges to some of the opportunities that constitute the field.

In each case, I argue that it is a mistake to conceptualize the organization of a system of ranks in competitive fields solely from the point of view of the field (as innovations or conspiracies by firms, prestige niches of universities, or coreness of nation–states), because it is the corporate activities of the firms, universities, or nations that sustain the occupancy of such positions in fields. But conversely one cannot see what is going on in such fields if one only searches for *X-efficiency* or *entrepreneurship*, as Leibenstein (1978) or Schumpeter (1964 [1939], 1942) did, or for cultural capital as Bourdieu does for French universities (both *Distinction* (1984) and *Homo Academicus* (1988 [1984]), or for national power as Davis (1964 [1954]) does. None of these concepts shows us what has to be done to maintain the position and why the top positions are so precarious.[3]

---

[3] A somewhat comparable distinction is that between fundamental niches and realized niches is in Hannan and Freeman (1989); see also Podolny et al., (forthcoming). Roughly a fundamental niche is a characteristic of the organization, such as its technical knowledge, that gives it an advantage of certain kinds in certain kinds of competition. A realized niche is the competitive status that it in fact occupies in the market, or the actual space in the set of opportunities it might be advantaged in that it, in fact, realizes in competition with other firms.

Example 1: Tobin's q-ratio and competition among capitalist firms

Firms in markets very often have a larger "going concern value" than the value of the things they own, as measured by the cost it would take to buy or produce their equivalent. For example, in the 1960s and early '70s, a boom time, the average ratio of the market value of leading firms to asset value was likely around 1.4 to 1.5 (see the sources in footnote 1). Roughly two-sevenths (29%) of the value of the average firm, then, was not due to the value of its capital but instead to its capacity to use that capital to make profits above the discount rate used in the stock market.

That is, the resale value of the assets of the corporation, as estimated by what it would take to replace them, is a valuation of the corporation as a bundle of claims on marketable capital goods. The fact that the stock market valued the average large corporation at a higher value than the resale value of its assets, then, was a measure of the ratio of discounted profits of the corporations as going concerns, to the value of its assets as estimated by using the estimated market price of those assets in the capital goods market. Thus it means that the special combination of capital and human organization to exploit an opportunity in the market produced an expected stream of income higher than the assets could be expected to produce in alternative uses.

When Joseph Schumpeter used the fact that there are profits above the interest rate to show that "innovations" must produce the profits (Schumpeter 1964 [1939], pp. 46–83, 105–150; 1942), he was pointing to the same fact as Tobin's *q*-ratio being higher than 1 for innovating firms. He was saying that the added value of a going concern exploiting an opportunity in the market *that no one else could exploit by buying the same assets* produced profits above the interest rate. By calling the phenomenon that produced the impossibility of others exploiting the opportunity an "innovation," he was pointing to the organization-market relationship that created this special relation between the organization and an opportunity.

The opportunity was exploitable only by one firm because it was a new thing in the market, and inimitable for that reason. Thus he expected the excess profits to disappear, and the disappearance in turn to produce financial panics and business cycle depressions when the value of innovating firms was reduced by competitive imitation. This would reduce the value of firm assets to their replacement value. At that time, the innovation ceases being an innovation. In short, Schumpeter was using "innovation" to describe *any* monopoly position established by any inimitable activity of the corporation that produced value.

Schumpeter pointed out that many of the important innovations were "organizational" innovations, such as arranging the relation between lettuce harvests in the West, express railroad trains with refrigerated cars (originally the lettuce was packed in ice), and auction produce markets in the East so that the lettuce got to stores unwilted at an auction price. Thus the innovation was not the "invention" of ice for lettuce but an organization of ice with railroad cars, lettuce harvests, and wholesale produce markets.

The value added by organizations over and above their assets and the costs of labor is instead attributed to the *organization* by Leibenstein (1978), when he talks about "X-efficiency." He takes the fact that *this* organization can exploit the opportunity *as no other one can* as fundamentally a feature of the organization, rather than of the novelty of the opportunity in the market as Schumpeter did. But obviously it is instead a feature of *the relation of* unique features of the organization to market opportunities that produces the extra profits; one cannot invent a uniqueness out of thin air and expect it to pay off. Either one had to produce electricity that no one else could produce because one was an inventor (the fact that Edison is still in the name of some electrical utilities shows this), or one had to be able to organize better than Edison did (the fact that Edison produced direct current while companies with Edison's name in their name now produce alternating current may show organizing better than Edison's). The corresponding concept describing the relation between an organization and an opportunity as a characteristic of an organization, then, is Leibenstein's "X-efficiency."

My argument here is that when Schumpeter describes the excess profits as the fact that the opportunity the organization exploits is created by the organization's activity being an innovation, and when Leibenstein treats the excess profits as a uniqueness of the organization, they are both right. Both are pointing to the fact that an organization can do something unique, and that this something occupies such a place in the market that the assets earn more than their "normal" or "interest rate" return, even after the stock market takes account of the higher risk of the stream of profits.

But in order for an organization's activity to occupy a distinctive opportunity in a market, it has to manage two network tasks. First, with respect to its potential competitors in the market, it has to exclude them from its distinctive niche by doing better than they do in it. Second, with respect to its employees, stockholders, and suppliers, it has to continuously manage them (and especially their possible commitments to others) so that the network that constitutes the organization can achieve a unique set of activities that exploits that opportunity. If it manages its suppliers of labor, capital, and materials well, it can have a "production function" for that activity or product that can stably exploit its niche, consisting in part of its internal authority networks but also in part of its mutual commitments with workers, suppliers, marketers, and creditors. If that production function characterized the industry's (or society's) "technology" rather than the firm, there would be no monopoly profits (after time for new entries).

Thus corporate action of successful firms in a market as a type of social field: (1) cannot be "rule following," for otherwise others would follow the rules and be equal competitors, and assets would earn only normal or interest rate returns – it must be exploiting its "liberties," as John R. Commons (1974 [1924]) put it, using its social rights to do something unique; (2) is exploiting an opportunity that is always open to challenge, to competition, and (at least so Schumpeter says) can expect to lose its monopoly position as the competition manages to reproduce its unique capacities; (3) must manage the flows of its employees, stockholders, and suppliers so that someone continues to supply this organization rather than any potential competitor with its unique competencies.

The q-ratio is an approximate measure of how far such a sustained relation between an organization and a market opportunity is maintained by the set of practices that constitute the organization's competitive position, because it is a measure of how far an organization is more successful than a *rentier* would be with the same assets. It is crucial to our argument that not all firms need have excess profits by successful monopoly, and that any current position of monopoly advantage will normally erode with time.

Example 2: Competition between universities in reputational systems

To a casual view, an endowment to an institution of higher education is a subsidy to the students, and so students in well-endowed institutions should get their education more cheaply. But in fact, all sorts of measures of an institution's endowment, from financial endowment to the number of books in its library, are *positively* correlated with tuition charges. Well-endowed Ivy League colleges and universities charge higher rather than lower tuitions than other schools. I argue that this demonstrates the same sort of fact as q-ratios of highly ranked firms being larger than 1.

The q-ratio being larger than 1 shows that a firm's capital earns more than its asset value. The endowment of a prestige university also evidently generates more than the income due to its asset value, because besides the market valuation of the endowment (measured by the endowment income), a large endowment enables the university to charge more for its services. If there were a capitalized market value of the university's income, then, prestige universities with high endowments (high capital assets) should show a q-ratio greater than 1 because their revenues are all higher. Being non-profit organizations, nobody but the university as such can appropriate the income, so the going concern value cannot be measured by a market value of the organization.

In addition higher endowments are correlated with other sources of higher income, such as more grants for research and further endowments for distinguished professorships or more beautiful buildings. Further there are nonmonetary forms of compensation such as citations, visits by foreign dignitaries, or column inches in the *New York Times*, that come to well-endowed universities. In short, what universities compete for are rich and bright students who will turn into rich donors and parents of future rich and bright students, distinguished faculties that will recruit those students and justify donations, and column inches in the *New York Times*. Turning these reputations into concrete resources means, especially, locating some fairly large set of students, usually mostly from nearby, whose brightest and richest will pay the higher tuitions to come there.

But it is hardly likely that students and their parents are mainly buying the services of endowments like the least-used 2 million volumes of Harvard's Widener Library, or the million dollars apiece for outfitting the research laboratory of MIT assistant professors of biochemistry. Instead, they are buying the reputability of their own respective degrees in literature or biochemistry. That reputability is partly made up of the general aura of resource-richness of the universities, and perhaps the richness of the students. But it is more made up of the reputability of the faculty because they are recognized as expert by other comparative literature professors or biochemists. That reputability in large measure originally justified the endowment of the libraries and laboratories. This in turn is reconfirmed by the fact that some combination of the brightest and the richest students come to leading universities; it is the kind of environment where future literary lights and Nobel laureates are educated and where sociology professors have to explain to 19-year-old students that indeed it is possible for a family to live on less than $300,000 per year.

The correlation between endowments and tuitions then is created by a self-reinforcing causal circle in which (1) endowments help produce the reputation that brings in high tuitions, (2) rich and bright students in the long run create endowments, (3) leading scientists and deep library collections create reputations that bring in endowments and students, and (4) contributions of leading scientists, scholars, and librarians to scholarly work in other universities maintains the solidity of the reputation of the university among those who know. The whole self-reinforcing circle in turn indirectly convinces the rich donors and bright students.

This self-confirming reputational circle means that a slipping department at a leading university has a reasonably high probability of recovering its reputation. Even when lingering anti-Semitism crippled sociology departments in the Ivy League from 1900 to 1950 (when a disproportionate share of leading sociologists were Jewish – and Chicago forged ahead), many of those departments recovered later (Karabel, 1984; Gleik, 1992, "Of Course Feynman is Jewish," pp. 81–5), often after considering abolishing sociology there altogether.

But here the point is that these reputations are a relation to a field of scholarly reputation, and reputation of the degrees produced by faculty scholarly and student social class reputation. The willingness of donors to give to prestigious universities (and to prestigious departments and schools within them), and the willingness of students and their parents to pay higher tuitions for prestigious credentials, create a competitive field of reputations that can be turned into resources to maintain those reputations. The opportunities for prestigious universities to sell prestigious degrees, and to make a library named after Harry Elkins Widener a prestigious namesake, are out there in society, and those opportunities are contested. The University of California at Berkeley, the University of Michigan, and Stanford all rank higher on some of the reputational criteria than most of the Ivy League schools, though they started a good deal behind. Stanford's financial endowment is comparable to, and the libraries of Berkeley and Michigan have bigger collections than, many colleges and universities of the Ivy League.

Again this distinctiveness of the relation between an organization and an opportunity in a contested field is simultaneously a feature of the organizations and of the opportunities. Harvard can produce prestigious degrees, and many people want to buy prestigious degrees. Active recruitment of the best and richest students supplies a reliable stream of endowing alumni. In short, all the elements we used to describe monopolistic competition among firms, even down to the financial equivalent for nonprofits of the q-ratio, apply to universities' reputations.

Why are there nations and empires in the world system?

Nation–states originally grew in Western Europe out of states that existed only episodically when waging international war. Taxes and forced loans to the royal government in early modern Europe (say the 13th to the 18th centuries) went up dramatically when war or a crusade was declared, to go down dramatically afterward. The predecessors of nation–states then did not really exist for purposes of domestic law making and enforcement in times of peace, and they had to publish "bans" (the French word for it) giving special authority to compel people and goods to be mobilized for war, because ordinary domestic taxes and people's ordinary activities did not suffice (Tilly 1990).

Toward the end of early modern times in commercial states (in the Renaissance in Genoa and Venice, in England and the Netherlands in the 17th century, and with France added in the 18th century), parliaments and courts developed as institutions to consult the urban rich (as well as the aristocracy) before going to war. The obligations generated in wars and approved by parliaments were supported by peacetime taxes after the wars ended (Carruthers 1996). The result was both the rapid expansion of these countries overseas to create commercial empires and a period of intense warfare between these empires in the late 18th century, because "the people" (i.e., the rich) had consented to the wars *and* to the repayments.

Since that time, the penetration of such national governments into the daily life of the population grew, either directly (as in Germany, France, Russia, and Spain [and England by the 19th century]) or indirectly through subordinate provincial governments (in the United States and The Netherlands, and in the quite autonomous colonies of England, France, and The Netherlands). These nation–states with their federally governed colonies and provinces then became "the core" of the world system, as Immanuel Wallerstein (1980) and his colleagues have argued. My argument here will be that "strong" states became empires because they generated more power from their "power assets" in the home country, and so gained hegemony in the world system.

Wallerstein (1980) has emphasized that the world during this time became a system, and national power was a relation among competitive core members. Political-economic relations to the rest of the world, and specifically to the colonies that constituted the empires, were part of the basis of core status. Core status was an opportunity in the system as a whole, because there were "power vacuums" on the periphery (for a development of this concept, see Stinchcombe 1987 [1968], pp. 226–7). Core countries could ship manufactured goods to markets that they could protect and could get cheap materials and semi-finished goods in return. These in turn fueled trade with other core countries.

But core status was also a set of capacities of the core nations as organizations, to raise taxes, to borrow money, to build warships and cannons. Thus whereas it is most obvious that an empire is a specialized network of protected trade ties created by the more powerful nation of the empire, those protected trade ties then also fed back to support core status in competition in Europe.

Mercantilism was a theory of protection of network advantages in the international system. In no country was it ever assumed that all the trade of the country should be within its empire. In fact, the idea was that an empire strengthened the capacity to support navies (see Duffy 1981, pp. 3–37, for England and France; and C. R. Boxer 1988 [1965] for the Netherlands) and other military forces and to have goods to trade with other core powers. For example, in the 18th century, Haiti made France the source of most of the intra-European trade in sugar (Frostin 1975, p. 143).

As Julia Adams (1996), Barbara Tuchman (1988), Anne Pérotin-Dumon (1985), and Charles Frostin (1975) have emphasized, colonials often sought to go outside the empire for more advantageous ties, in the Caribbean especially with the Dutch and New England, and in the Dutch East Indies with England. Colonists of an empire quite often even took the other side in interempire wars; Spanish and French planters were often glad to be conquered by England so they would get more favorable treatment of slavery and provisions trade and freedom of trade in sugar.

Within each nation, smuggling challenged mercantilist policies on a large scale, so southern England and Brittany were chronically undermining the mercantilism of their own countries. In the Netherlands, whole cities (i.e., provinces) refused to respect the mercantilist policies of their country; since mercantilism was valid in a Dutch city only if the city agreed, smuggling was in a sense legitimate. Maintaining mercantilist relations of core countries in trading networks was a continuing achievement against substantial and continuing commercial subversion.

The same is true of military competition. As the transition from early modern to modern took place in the late 18th and early 19th centuries, wars among the core countries took a much larger share of the national income and more years of each decade. Part of this was in turn due to the superior capacity of the partially democratized Dutch and English, then slightly later the United States and Napoleonic France, to mobilize the population and national resources for warfare (Carruthers 1996). So the challenges to any given country's match between national organization and world system opportunity got more expensive and deadly. The Dutch, for example, nearly gave up on defending a sugar empire in Brazil and the Guianas militarily, because it would not profit the dominant elites in the Dutch East India Company (Adams 1994a, pp. 336–42), and declined (as Wallerstein, 1980, argues) from hegemonic to merely another member of the core.

An empire or other trading position in the international system was, then, both an opportunity in the world system and a power of a nation to mobilize a commercial and military collective action and to defend the networks of commerce and politics that maintained that position. Empire governments were intensely conscious that their advantages over their challengers were precarious, both militarily and commercially. National prestige, flows of commerce, and military (especially naval) power were all highly correlated, so that Wallerstein could collapse them all into one variable from core, to semiperiphery, to periphery. But that correlation was by no means an invitation to rest on one's laurels, any more than a Nobel prize is, or IBM's position nearly monopolizing mainframe computers and then dominating personal computers was.

Kingsley Davis has argued (1964 [1954]) that the potential military and diplomatic power of a nation is a function of its population size multiplied by the average productive efficiency (e.g., GNP per capita). Thus large countries are more powerful than smaller countries with the same level of development (e.g., India and China are more powerful than Burma or Thailand). But economically developed countries are more powerful than poorer countries of the same size (e.g., the Netherlands or Australia are more powerful than Cuba or Malaysia, or Japan is more powerful than Indonesia). Otherwise put, national power is a function of total GNP rather than of either total population or GNP per capita. National power then characterizes nations as corporate groups, and national income has power value.

But power works most effectively when applied close to its source (e.g., within the boundaries of a nation) and declines rapidly with distance, with higher transportation costs, and with legal barriers. Mountains and beaches present severe problems in the application of infantry power, so within their boundaries, England and Switzerland are safer than France or Belgium. Alaska was far from Moscow and had both beaches and mountains as anti-Russian barriers. The purchase price for United States possession could thus be extremely cheap, because Russian possession would have been extremely expensive (Stinchcombe 1987 [1968], pp. 216–31).

The general point here is that the "opportunities" of nations, the places vulnerable to their advantages in the field of the world system, are strongly determined by geographical distance and geographical barriers. The "monopoly of legitimate violence" that defines sovereignty therefore tends to be quite sharply limited to a territory. An increase of national power (e.g., with economic development, railroad building, or navigation across water barriers) thus has its first effect within national boundaries. Government stretches right up to the border if troops can be got to the border by rail or by ship and therefore do not have to be recruited near the border.

But such increases of national power with economic and transportation development also create a "sphere of influence" on nearby smaller or poorer nations, because the power potential of the United States (for example) stretches not only from the great plains to New Orleans down the rivers but across to Cuba, the Dominican Republic, Haiti, and the Virgin Islands.

Thus the solidity of national boundaries (for the modern definition of sovereignty of nations in the United Nations, see McNeely, 1993, p. 16) is a reflection of the solidity of the monopoly advantage of large rich nations in the international system. It is a physical measure of the exact niche dominated by the advantage of a nation as a corporate group. Vague boundaries between nations on the maps mark low economic development, sparse population, and transportation troubles – straight lines as boundaries in deserts, Arctic tundra, or glacier country mark much the same condition, and a straight-line boundary is hardly ever well defended.

Monopolistic competition as a mechanism

The first thing to notice about these three examples is that they all concern what Commons (1974 [1924]) called the "going concern value" of a corporate group. A corporate group is a network that can work together, and so can do together the activities that bring in benefits from the opportunities that it exploits. But a network is vulnerable at all its nodes. A firm may lose the inventor of the innovation it monopolizes; a university can lose its Nobel prize winners; a nation can fail to keep its soldiers fighting if it lets them get out of sight. Thus, as Chester Barnard (1946) argued, a corporate group has to maintain a positive incentive balance at each essential point in its network by using the resources it gets from exploiting its opportunity or niche and other incentives generated by being a going concern.

Second, what the going concern appropriates is the flow of benefits to the corporate group that it gets by beating out the competition in its niche. A central part of the appropriation is that the competitive damage it does to others by exploiting its niche is not vulnerable to an action for damages. Clients are free to choose a firm and, more important here, firms are free to be chosen; foundations can endow a high-prestige university without answering to another university for it, and another university can hire away a Nobel prize winner without remedy; nations can tax their populations to keep up a bigger navy than they need and sign only those trade agreements they find rewarding, and the only remedy of another nation is to tax for its own navy or to offer more advantages for a trade agreement.

Conversely appropriating the going concern value is only appropriating those competitive advantages that the corporate group can maintain. The monopoly capitalism of Allis-Chalmers, for example, did not help it when the farm machinery niche it occupied became unprofitable. The 17th-century competitive advantage of the Dutch in colonial commerce had to give way to English hegemony by the end of the 18th century.

The third feature of the mechanism in all three cases is that being competitively advantaged in one period produces resources, maintains incentive balances at essential nodes within the group, and so produces a going concern in the next period with a better chance of maintaining competitive advantage. Status or other monopoly advantage in all these fields tends to be autocorrelated, subject to slow decay over time with an occasional catastrophe.

The fourth feature of the mechanism is that the corporate group's maintenance of competitive advantage in these three fields depends on the capacity to make decisions and implement them faster than consensus on the decision by all the nodes that have to act jointly can form. Or in short, the acting entities in the fields are corporate groups, which can act to exploit an opportunity as well as appropriate benefits.

A fifth feature of the mechanism is the granular structure of the competitive field, so that the niches or opportunities of individual corporate groups can be identified within which they have one or another sort of competitive advantage. One or more innovations can create a granule in a market (Podolny and Stuart 1995; Podolny, Stuart, and Hannan 1996; Schumpeter 1942), an area in which a corporation has a temporary competitive advantage. A few members of the National Academy can make a university prestigious in chemistry, able to recruit students, endowments, and young chemists of promise, and so creating an area of competitive advantage. Control of a relatively militarily invulnerable rich heartland and a largely imported industrial culture gave the United States world hegemony up to the borders of the Soviet bloc after World War II and made Caribbean and Central American countries essentially into protectorates, a large granule of power dominance in the world system, sloping off toward the Soviet areas. The granule's boundaries were, however, not impermeable to the competitive action of nearby competitors (e.g., in Finland, Afghanistan, or North Korea).

The central feature tying all the others together, the working part of the mechanism, is the second one: the appropriation of a competitive opportunity by a going concern.

The functions of competitive organizations

In his famous article on why there are firms, R. H. Coase (1937) assumed that there was a field of buyable goods and productive or marketing services that could be contracted for. He then argued that it was appropriate for a firm to buy or contract for all the things that were cheaper on the market (all things considered – e.g., bad schedules of delivery or firm secrets betrayed would be counted as costs) than the firm could produce it for. Thus in equilibrium, the activities within the firm would be the set of all relevant activities that the firm could do better, or cheaper at equal quality, than the market could. Firms then make profits because there are some goods or services that the firm can make or provide better than anyone in the market. This is precisely the relation between opportunities and corporate groups that I have argued create fields of monopolistic competition.

Schumpeter believed then that he could give a positive characterization of what those unique competencies of an organization were likely to be – namely, one or more innovations. But Schumpeter did not provide a theory of why an innovation should be administered by a firm[4] – that is, by a unified set of contracts all governed by a single balance sheet and with authority to integrate activities. If we think of Coase (1937) as supplying that theory, his answer would be that unified administration saved the costs of the transactions and contracts that would be necessary to create a system of activities to manage the innovation. Presumably the uncertainty of what it will take to create economic value from an innovation is the ultimate source of the transaction costs (Stinchcombe 1990, pp. 159–93).

Thus to answer the question "Why are there organizations?" for firms is to explain what class of activities are likely to be *connected together by a unique network that constitutes an organization*. The very general answer is that being connected together in a corporate group makes those

---

[4] Mansfield et al. (1977) provided evidence that the theory had at least the support that most innovations were exploited by the firm that made them. That is, the exploiters of an innovation ordinarily did not exploit an innovation by means of extensive subcontracts or by marketing the innovation freely to all comers including themselves; innovations are ordinarily not a "commodity." That means in turn that the features of an organization, such as its size or capital reserves and the richness of its market determine what exploitation of an innovation would happen, which in a perfect market system for innovations would not be true. In Nelson and Winter (1982), the theory is built on the assumption that an innovation will be exploited by the firm that makes it. Scherer's study (1964) of the arms industry deals with a situation in which the client pays for the innovation as well as its exploitation. In that industry, therefore, all the transactions between research and development and production ordinarily done within the firm in the private sector are necessarily "in the market" (in the Department of Defense); therefore the transaction costs of relying on the market are more transparent. In practice in the biotechnology and software industries, where innovation itself is a more or less predictable process, the firms making the innovations are not necessarily the ones administering their exploitation in the market, so that Microsoft got rich from a software innovation administered and marketed by IBM with their personal computers, even during the period when IBM got poor. But even in such situations, the innovating firm is quite often acquired by a "friendly" takeover by the administering and marketing firm, especially in the drug industry, where clinical testing of a new drug is a complex and capital-intensive transaction with the government, in which biotechnology innovators have no special expertise and not enough capital nor relevant administrative capacity. Thus Schumpeter's assumption that the innovator gets the monopoly is generally right, but not always, so we still need Coase's theory of why things like innovations producing monopolies tend to be done within the firm to predict when Schumpeter is right.

activities more profitable in the firm's field, its market. This is because organizations are structures of coordinated callable routines, routines lying in wait for contingencies in which they are needed, so that the organization can be quickly mobilized to seize opportunities, and so that internal competition is suppressed by an overarching incentive system, paid for by exploiting the monopoly in the market (Roy 1997, pp. 183–92; see also Petersen 1995).

Similarly it is because a given university is a special kind of network structure, ultimately connecting students and their parents to scientific and scholarly activities that these families would not have been able to judge for themselves, that it can create and market academic reputation. It is because a nation–state can create networks of naval and other military mobilization on occasion, and create trading networks defended by that mobilization, that it can create and maintain an empire or a position in the world system core. In the 18th century, Great Britain as an organization thus could create a set of activities that others could not create or buy and that could make it *the* power of the world system, replacing the Dutch. The Dutch state (basically a set of contracts among commercial cities) in the 17th century had a comparable accomplishment, which they did not sustain to the same degree into the 18th century, and so lost out as the hegemon to the British.[5]

If we start, then, by trying to identify the class of activities that a given firm can do better than other firms in markets, that a prestigious university can do better than other reputable nonprofit organizations, and that a given nation–state can do better than other political organizations, we will have the key to why there are organizations in fields.

The clues we have gleaned so far are that (1) innovations and their uncertainties may advantage firms; (2) firms may save transaction costs that would be involved in getting supplies or services from the market; (3) universities can judge reputability of scholars better than students or parents; (4) universities can sell reputations, and get donations for them, better than individual scholars; (5) powerful nation–states can organize

---

[5] I am not satisfied that the living standard of the Dutch was lower than that of the British during the period of British hegemony. The statement that the Dutch lost hegemony is thus not a statement that this was a bad thing, or that one would not, perhaps, rather have been Dutch than English. A corporate position in the world power system did not necessarily make its citizens better off; the slaves in that corporate group's colonies were no doubt worse off. If one is the object of the monopoly of legitimate violence, one is not advantaged by national power.

logistics, loans, taxes, and organized fighting forces better than other political organizations; and (6) core nation–states can organize and defend monopolies in trading networks ("empires" and their equivalents) better than other ways of organizing cartels can. What all these phenomena have in common is that they create and maintain enclosed webs of relationships that can engage in corporate action, to carry out actions that other networks cannot, can operate in the face of competition, and can appropriate the benefits of exploiting that advantage in corporate action to maintain or enlarge their position against competitive challenges. But of course the degree to which organizations can maintain such advantage is a variable, or bust would not follow boom in Schumpeter's business cycles as innovating organizations drive older organizations into failure, Clark University would still occupy the prestige locus that the University of Chicago got by hiring away its best faculty, and the sun would never set on the Dutch empire.

Corporate groups as sets of callable routines

When one looks at formal organization in its details, say at a departmental level, one sees a set of routines that run more or less automatically, except that they have a few adjustable parameters. Thus an accounts payable department has a set of check-writing routines, except with variations in the amounts, the company name on the invoice, the authorizing department, and its subaccount number within the organization. The sociology department has a fairly stable faculty and advertised curriculum, with varying assignment of teachers to courses, varying schedules, sizes of rooms, and contents of the syllabus.

Such routine accomplishment together with easily authorized adjustability avoids complicated negotiation about how to react to all conceivable contingencies in a market contract, and it allows continual improvement of routines (and increases in the number of options or adjustable parameters built into them) to increase their efficiency and flexibility. This in its turn allows the organization to move quickly to respond to challenges in the field in which the organization operates (e.g., to innovate – see Nelson and Winter, 1982, for a complex analysis of the relation between routines and innovation in firms). A nation–state can develop routines to mobilize men into armies and navies (e.g., the "hot press" of British merchant sailors into the navy in the 18th century), to borrow money

(Carruthers 1996) to pay war expenses, and to negotiate alliances and the ends of wars through an established diplomatic apparatus.

Such routines reduce transaction costs and provide for the possibility of there being a set of activities that an organization can do better internally than others can achieve. But such routines have to be "callable" in a flexible fashion, or competitive challenges will not be met.

A coordinating organizational utility function

A central feature enabling organizations to outperform alternative actors in their fields, or actors that might easily be created, is that they can *act corporately faster than consensus can form*. Short-order drill in an army on a modern parade ground or on an 18th-century battlefield is an excellent example. In the 18th century, one could not trust a soldier not to run away and go home if he were out of the officers' sight. One therefore had to look around for a field flat enough to move troops around on while keeping them in sight. Close-order drill was a technique for moving bodies of men who, first of all, would come to the wrong consensus and go home if one left them to form a consensus, and second, would get hopelessly tangled up while being maneuvered into position.[6]

We argue that the rapid governance of corporate activity by a utility function that does not have to be bargained out at the moment requires organizations (firms, universities, or nations, or for that matter households) to have four features: (1) a common understanding of "the collective welfare," so that each person (especially those in authority) can tell when they are pursuing "their job" and when they are pursuing their "personal affairs"; (2) a flow of information about developing contingencies to employees, partners, patriarchs, or other agents of the group, where the news breaks too fast to communicate to all the stakeholders and to wait for their consensus to form; (3) dedicated resources (a "fund" or an "estate") that can be used or spent for the achievement of that collective welfare, distinct from wages or dividends and from "pocket money," often with a distinct status in property law so that their use for personal purposes is criminal; and (4) a somewhat separate sys-

---

[6] A special problem was created by the fact that one wanted the soldiers with loaded guns in the front rank facing the enemy to shoot, and those reloading in the back ranks. At the beginning of the century, it took quite a while to reload, so that one wanted about five to seven ranks reloading for each rank firing; toward the end of the century, one wanted only about two ranks behind. Altogether it was a complicated thing to arrange, quite aside from the fact that each soldier would rather be in back.

tem for distributing the rewards earned by corporate activity so as to form a corporate incentive system.

A corporate group then has (1) a "government" with a "policy" distinct from the utilities of individuals, (2) information flows relevant to that policy to its agents, (3) a means of production or a dedicated flow of liquid resources under the control of the group, and (4) a way of connecting that policy to the utilities of participants by an incentive system made up of property rights and wages or subsistence.

These conditions are sufficient to make some corporate groups into "maximizers" of measures of the outcome of the policy[7] and, for example, makes firms into the kind of units that can be an element of an economic theory of the market in which firms maximize profits. This is a good thing for a theory of the market to have, since most profits are collected and maximized in the first instance by firms, and if they (as well as individuals) did not maximize, economics would be an elegant irrelevancy to modern economies.

The preceding four conditions then are required for social units to manage opportunities in a field, so that firms can have total returns in the general region of 10% and pay out dividends in the general region of 3%, so that Harvard could have a continuing reputation even if George Homans retired before Amartya Sen arrived, and so that the United States could conquer Puerto Rico a couple of decades before it bought the Danish Virgin Islands. So these four conditions make firms, universities, and nations into the sorts of entities that can appropriate opportunities in a field and derive from that appropriation benefits that secure them an advantage in appropriating those opportunities in the future. Opportunities are appropriated by corporate actors with distinct policies, information, resources, and reward systems – in short, with a socially established utility function.

Corporate suppression of internal competition

Of course the utilities or preferences of individuals or households or departments do not disappear when larger corporate groups come into being.

[7] I mean here "maximizers" in the weak sense that *if* cheaper or more effective actions are known in the organization, they will tend to be chosen. "Known" here is a complex network variable as well as a complex guess about the future, so it is very hard to tell whether an organization is a maximizer in this sense. I argue here that an organization cannot be a maximizer unless these four features are present in the network that "constitutes" the organization.

They are sustained by individuals' continuing participation in network ties within and outside the organization. Some of those individual and small-group utilities are likely to be negatively affected by corporate action and would be increased if the people could act *within* the organization in the light of their own interests. The ideal type of corporate group is one in which the *only* connection of organizational action to personal utilities and to solidarities with people outside the corporate group is through the corporate incentive system. But in the nature of things, no corporate group can quite achieve that ideal,[8] and ordinary corporate groups like firms, universities, or nation–states do not even come close.

This means that corporate groups have to *suppress competition* within the corporate group. Rather than individuals exploiting the corporate group's opportunities, rather than organizing an uncontrolled internal competition for group resources, rather than treating their role and its authority and rewards as personal property to be exploited, people and small groups have to be limited to those activities that do not conflict with corporate goals. The example of the Dutch East India Company, and its powerful elite in Amsterdam undermining the Dutch federation's defense of the West India Company's sugar interests in Brazil (Adams 1996), shows the problem clearly. To a large degree, the Dutch state as a whole did not have a corporate policy separate from the policies of its constituent cities (Adams 1994a, 1994b; Tuchman 1988). It did not have dedicated naval reserves or a budget for the navy separate from the customs tolls of those cities. The incentives of the merchants active in city governments were their profits as merchants and shippers, or their income from positions in the city, and they were not dependent personally on the national state.

If the Dutch state as a whole had had sufficient corporate existence to have a separate corporate policy, we cannot of course know whether they would have decided to defend the plantations in Brazil (Boxer, 1969, pp. 106–27, 150–76; Boxer, 1988 [1965]).[9] But Adams's argument is that they

---

[8] The closest approximation is perhaps in some intentional or utopian communities. For an excellent analysis of the tensions this creates, see Benjamin Zablocki's *The Joyful Community* (1971) pp. 239–85. On the comparison between corporations and cartels in the degree they could control internal competition (partly because of the way the law was interpreted), see Roy (1997, pp. 183–92).

[9] The Dutch were actually defeated by a rebellion by Brazilian Portuguese colonists combined with American Indians and black and colored allies, fighting a land war against the Dutch plantations. It is not clear that the Dutch, with the naval basis of their military advantage over the Portuguese, could have defeated the Portuguese even with metropolitan support. Wise Dutch state policy, had there been one, might have been not to fight. There

could not form a corporate policy, not that they had a policy but decided it should not be to defend the Brazilian Northwest.

The field defined as a set of corporate groups cannot exist unless corporate groups have a distinct utility function that they can mobilize to exploit an opportunity. But defined as a competitive system, a field cannot work unless firms often want profits from exploiting their monopolies and hence to compete with other firms that do not (at least yet) have them, unless universities want prestige, unless nation–states want at least the power to govern themselves and to influence their immediate international environment.[10]

Competition and fields of opportunities

In this section I will develop the notion, suggested by John R. Commons, that competitive fields are systems of liberties (in turn often *secured by* rules). Thus what is appropriated, claimed as property or status or sovereignty, is a set of rights to make decisions (and to have other people put up with them). Opportunities, which we have used previously in an undefined sense, are then monopolizable only by corporate groups that have the liberties to do the sorts of things needed to turn those opportunities into streams of revenue, of scholarly prestige, or of national power.

If a firm, for example, has a set of liberties defined in law and market practice *that includes a subset* more profitable to them than to anyone else, then that granule in the space of liberties is simultaneously an opportunity in a market. Such opportunities are subject to competition not in the sense that someone can abolish the liberties that make up the going concern but in the sense that competitors too can use their liberties to produce competitive pressure that can destroy the revenues, prestige, or national power of the concern. One is not free to destroy a competitor's property, faculty, or sovereignty; one is free to destroy by competition the economic value, the prestige value, or the power value of that property, faculty, or sovereignty.

What turns a subset of a corporate group's liberties into an opportunity, then, is the capacity to use those liberties in a way that no competitor can.

were no Portuguese settlers to oust the Dutch from Surinam and what became British Guiana, so the Dutch stayed until the English drove them out of some parts.
[10] V. O. Key is supposed to have formulated the generalization that the party system cannot work unless some people want to be president. It is the same point.

When a competitor becomes able to use its liberties to outcompete, the going concern's liberties are no longer an opportunity. They can be sold only at their replacement price in the capital market, because the going concern value that made them worth more has been destroyed by competition.

John R. Commons as the unifier of the theory of fields

We have emphasized that the places in a social field are opportunities that people have to manage but that others can invade. They are, then, somewhat different from "property," on whose value one might collect interest at the market rate of return. It is precisely getting a return above the market rate that makes Tobin's q-ratio larger than 1. It is precisely creating reputation with an endowment that allows one to charge higher than average tuition that maintains a university's place in higher education. And it is getting more out of an empire than it costs, and in particular more than it would cost someone else to take it, that makes a nation–state a hegemonic power or a member of the world system core.

John R. Commons (1974 [1924]) is the great theorist here, with a little boost from Coase. Commons pointed out that from a legal point of view, it was central to capitalism that the "going concern value" of a firm (the value created above the value of the assets and the costs of production) be legally defensible. That is, it is the ownership, even to the point of alienability, of a firm's value over and above the value of assets (i.e., it is the ownership of the value that makes Tobin's q-ratio greater than 1) that is defining for the legal foundation of capitalism.

But Commons's great innovation was to conceive the features of the law that gave that added value as a *liberty* rather than as a *rule*. That is, to be in a unique relation to an opportunity (by means other than special access to coercion) could only come about by *something one did* that put one into a unique position. So it was not ownership of property as such that created the going concern value. The core of capitalism for Commons was not that firms owned the capital but that the capital could be worth more because it was owned by a going concern. Ownership of capital is defined by the liberties of what all could be done with the property by the owner. Thus what created the added value for capitalists was the capacity by unique corporate actions to occupy opportunities in the market against challenges, against competition, and thus to create what Commons called "going concern value."

This ability to use liberties to beat the competition entailed, according to Commons, the creation of an *exposure* (for everyone in the relevant field) to the consequences of the competitive advantage gained by the use of the liberties. Competitors are exposed to whatever rigors a firm can subject them to by the use of its liberties. It is a key fact of capitalism as a legal system that one cannot, as the guilds of medieval Europe could, go to court to sue for the damages done by competitors. But that means that one holds onto an opportunity by successful corporate (or individual) action rather than by property rights in the assets used. It is the liberty to do something no one else could do as well with an asset that is the central property right distinctive of capitalism.

And finally, Commons located the rules in the field not in the laws by which liberties or property were defended but in the *working rules* of corporate groups or firms. It is the routines that efficiently do the things that constitute exploiting the opportunity that are worked out, *not* in the law, but inside the firm. If they were worked out in the universalistic modern law, then everyone in the market could do them.[11] Tobin's q-ratio being on average considerably above 1 in the 1960s (see the references in footnote 1) shows that it cannot be assumed.

The liberties of capitalism concretely, then, involve the right to develop the routines that differentiate firms. It is that development of routines to do things others could not and to exploit opportunities with those routines that Schumpeter (1942, 1964 [1939]) called "innovations." It was the monopoly power derived from those routines that others did not have, suitably combined with assets and labor that might be bought on the market for capital goods or labor, that gave such innovating firms the capacity to drive the former occupants out of their niches, so creating the downturn of the business cycle. And, so Schumpeter also argued, this is what made a firm have a set of activities that gave it, as Coase (1937) defined more clearly, a boundary between itself and a market, within which it saved "transaction costs" and gained itself a profit above the prevailing rate of return.

---

[11] An inability of the legal system to produce liberties and defensible going-concern value would create no difficulty for imperfect competition as Joan Robinson (1933) conceived it, with firms with the same production function within an industry, including new entrants. It would be a crucial crippling for Chamberlin (1962 [1933]).

The extension of this reasoning to universities regenerating reputations and nation–states building or losing empires is straightforward. In each case, what the organizations exploit is an opportunity in a field, a field in which their occupation of that opportunity can be challenged exactly because it is a liberty rather than a right defended by a rule. In each case, they develop routines that others do not have (or do not manage as well), routines in which the use of assets is embedded. In each case, then, there is a set of liberties (called "sovereignty" rather than "property" by nations) to do some things better than others can, with a corresponding set of exposures of those others to the effects of competition. In each case, sufficient incentives from the exploitation of opportunities can be created so as to suppress competition within the corporate group, so that professors of sociology do not go off in their spare time to offer better sociological services and superior certificates to those of their employer, and colonial civil and military servants do not set up their own empire by conquering and exploiting other colonies on the side (that this is not unproblematic is shown by Adams, 1996, on Dutch colonial officials serving the British East India Company in some matters). And finally, in each case, it is the capacity to do corporately some set of activities for which they are uniquely advantaged that makes a lucrative space for their action in the field.

The sets of liberties and the accompanying resources that enable exploitation of the liberties for our three examples of fields are generally called "equity" or "ownership" for firms, "reputation" or "status" for universities, and "sovereignty" for nation–states. These can be thought of as spaces within which corporate decisions of the different kinds of entities, taken by approved methods or by approved people, are legitimate in the sense that others must suffer exposure to whatever is decided within that space. We dealt earlier with equity as a claim on going-concern value. A few brief comments on reputation and sovereignty are in order to show that they are the same sorts of concepts of appropriation of liberties within which a subset creates monopolies subject to competition.

Reputations and status

Status in a field is the sociological concept closest to Tobin's q-ratio in economics. Sociologists have been confused by two different meanings of "status" – a set of rights that correspond to a position often earned by a reputation (e.g., the status of professor), and "status" (or "distinction," as Bourdieu, 1984, calls it) as the reputational capital on the basis of which such statuses are awarded. Since there are really no assets with a market value that constitute that capital, and since one appropriates such reputational capital mainly by governing the use of one's name, it is somewhat hard to locate the equivalent of going-concern value. But the fact that one gossips about a professor that "he hasn't done anything since," and then classifies him as "deadwood" for the purposes of evaluating a university department, indicates that the reputational capital that got one the status of professor is status constituting a claim on an opportunity in a reputational field, not status as a position. It is only when that status is actively used to create new reputation for the next round of competition that it creates monopoly advantages in the field. If that opportunity is not effectively exploited, the "rights" of the status of professor within the university then look like a mistake of the appointments and promotions process.

The same sort of distinction applies to university reputations. If Massachusetts Institute of Technology fails to cultivate or recruit people who then earn Nobel prizes by finding new knowledge, its accrued reputation for many past Nobels will decline slowly.

Sovereignty

The core opportunity space within which nation–states exercise their liberties is outlined in color on maps. Nation–states and other kinds of states may have "spheres of influence" outside their cores. Beyond those cores, as Edmund Burke (1895 [1775]) put it, even a Turkish sultan must truck and huckster to get his way.[12] Within their boundaries, nation–states can "act freely." In particular, collecting taxes is much easier within that boundary than elsewhere.

The fact that sovereignty is a set of liberties is indicated by the common use of the phrase, *raison d'état*, in discussing international affairs. There

---

[12] "In large bodies, the circulation of power must be less vigorous at the extremities. Nature has said it. The Turk cannot govern Egypt, and Arabia, and Curdistan as he governs Thrace; nor has he the same dominion in Crimea and Algiers which he has at Bursa and Smyrna. Despotism itself is obliged to truck and huckster. The Sultan gets such obedience as he can. He governs with a loose rein, that he may govern at all; the whole force and vigour of his authority in his centre is derived from a prudent relaxation in all his borders" (Burke, 1895 [1775], p. 25).

would be no call for sovereign bodies to have reasons of their own if they had no liberty to pursue them; if the King's wishes were automatically sovereign reasons, the d'état would be superfluous. Raison d'état is ordinarily that set of motives which determines choices according to the "necessities" of maintaining the state in its rank as a world power in the world system. That is, the definition of what sovereigns do with their reason indicates that the nature of sovereignty is a set of liberties appropriated by the nation–state, that a subset of those can be exploited to maintain the powers of the sovereign, and that one of the effects of raison d'état (a motivating effect) is the regeneration of a field of powers of sovereigns.

Relating monopolistic competition as a mechanism to the macroscopic structure of fields

Structures of opportunities with competitive relations

We have repeatedly emphasized that opportunities are challenged. Because a field is a system of liberties, the area of advantage that can be exploited with the resources and competencies of an organization is constantly open to challenge. England's hegemony in the world system gained in late 18th century wars and in empire development was always challenged somewhere, early by the Ottoman Empire, France, Spain, and The Netherlands, and eventually by Germany, the United States, and Japan. Harvard's supremacy in the university reputational system was always challenged by Oxford and Cambridge, then by some German universities as well, eventually by Chicago, Stanford, Berkeley, and Michigan. General Motors eventually could not everywhere match Toyota, and IBM fell (a long distance if not all the way to the ground) to a swarm of imitators.

If we think of an organization's position in a field as its area of advantage, then it is "exposed" to competition from those whose area of advantage overlaps with its area (Baum and Singh, 1996; 1996; Podolny and Stuart, 1995; Stuart and Podolny, 1996; Podolny et al., 1996). Competition is a property of the market, the status system, and the world power system. It is then a relation among the opportunities of different organizations.

Passenger airlines were in the same opportunity space as luxury high-speed trains in the 1950s and 1960s (and between London and Paris and

London and Brussels, they still are) but not in the opportunity space of railway express until somewhat later. German universities were in the same opportunity space for students and tax money as other German universities but not in the same space as American, British, and French universities for the Nobel prize, the capstone of scientific distinction. Japan as a world power was in the same opportunity space as Russia by 1905 but not significantly in the same space as the United States until the 1930s and 1940s. In each case, the competition then depends on the overlap of areas of potential monopoly between corporate actors. Or in the language of economics, competition depends on the elasticity of substitution of a competitor's production, prestige, or power at various points in the space of a group's "granule" of monopoly power.[13]

Overlap is a matter of degree measured by the size of the advantage. This is most obvious where advantage slopes off sharply with distance, as with military vulnerability (Stinchcombe 1987 [1968], pp. 216–31). But also, the drugstore across the street is the one to whose competition one's drugstore is exposed, not either the filling station's competition on the other corner or that of a drugstore in another city. There are analogies to the decline of overlap with other kinds of distance. For example, although the slang of universities refers to individual professors as "stars," their reputational market is only analogous in structure to that in Hollywood, not actually in competition with it. Similarly while one may be morally concerned with freedom of conscience in Tibet, First Amendment cases are tried in American federal courts, and an American spends his or her moral force on them through the American Civil Liberties Union. Moral concern slopes off with cultural and political distance.

Appropriation as a relation between organizations and opportunities

Because durable things are easily identifiable causes of a flow of benefits, they are the "goods" that are the core of the naive notion of property. Causal unity is what makes the thingness of things, so things are the obvious example of the causal unity that makes a set of liberties a piece of property. Likewise a flow of decisions about how to use a thing to produce those benefits is ordinarily easily identifiable, so the liberties at-

---

[13] This is a dichotomous approximation to what is usually a continuous decline of elasticity of substitution for the competences of the acting corporate body.

tached to a thing are defensible as "owning a thing." But since we started our analysis with Tobin's q, which measures the value of a firm as a ratio to the value of its things, we need to focus here on property in flows of decisions and benefits, of which ownership of things is only the clearest example and hence easily put into the denominator of the q-ratio.

But the clear causal role of things as connections between decisions and benefits provides a useful model for defining property. Property is a flow of uses of things or rights. Which of those uses of what things or rights generated or caused a flow of future benefits has to be clear. Otherwise, those assets cannot be built into going concerns. It has to be clear what causal principle unifies a flow of decisions so that it generates the unity of the flow of benefits, so that one can make property of that unity. A corporation, a university, or a nation unifies a set of uses of things and rights and so can have an equity, a status, a sovereignty that it owns.

We have been distinguishing two broad classes of flows: a flow of corporate action under the control of a corporate group with assets and liberties, and a contestable flow of opportunities in a field yielding a flow of benefits. Only if corporate action lies in an area of continuing advantage does it generate a flow of excess profit, reputation, or national power. Only if there are opportunities in the market, the academic reputation system, or the world system, will those advantaged actions return benefits that sustain the organization.

Thus in the theory, a system of appropriation that stabilizes a field needs to be described by how groups or people appropriate the liberties to make decisions, to claim some part of the beneficial consequences of those decisions, and to disclaim responsibility for other consequences (the "exposures" of others). Without claims on benefits and disclaimers for damages of competition, the liberties are worthless. Decisions and benefits have to have markers attached to them that indicate their socially recognized causal connections. Property then is a common-sense epistemology that connects human action to its beneficial consequences or, equally importantly, detaches human action from its competitive consequences.

For example, the "norm of communism" of scientific knowledge (Merton 1968 [1942] pp. 312–13) is reflected in the legal provision that one cannot patent a law of nature as well as in the academic practice of publication of results. The appropriation of reputation in science is intimately bound up with the norms of "authorship," which is the identity and causal unity of the person who is normatively identified as the author of the originality in the discovery.

Similarly corporate action in a field thus is embedded in an "identity" (White 1992) system so that it can be differentiated from the personal acts of corporate members or agents. A corporate identity, then, is defined by the liberties that the corporate group uses to exploit an area of more or less unique advantage in a field. The automobile at the end of the assembly line belongs to the Ford Motor Company because the corporate liberties and the market niche jointly identify Ford. That deep causal connection between Ford's corporate action and the car is embedded in property law by common-sense epistemology of assembly lines, contracts with suppliers, hiring of labor, and their joint causal effect on the self-motion of a ton or so of steel. The right to put the Ford name on a car is thus the same general kind of causal attribution as the right to put one's name, with one's institution's name attached, as author of a scientific paper. It is valuable because that identity helps exploit an opportunity space where the originating organizations, say Ford and Cal Tech, have some degree of contested advantage.

Such identified outcomes of corporate action then become occasions for sales contracts, graduation certificates, treaties, or other social arrangements that bring a flow of benefits to the corporate actor. The identity of corporation and product, university and degree, nation–state and conquered sugar island, is then a socially recognized causal attribution. That identity links the corporate use of liberties with benefits so derived. It consists of the flow of practical or legal liberties enjoyed by the corporation, the flow of sales or tuition or treaty contracts for the outcomes of such decisions about liberties, and the flow of benefits entailed in those contracts.

Max Weber (1968 [1921–2], pp. 125–50) called such systems for making socially recognized causal attributions, as a basis for claims on benefits, "forms of appropriation." The right to make the decisions associated with a flow of benefits, and the identity that connects decisions to claims on the benefits, may be lodged in workers, in owners of things, in political jurisdiction over territories, in guilds or colleges of peers, or in hierarchical corporations. Such flows may be divided in time (as leaseholds in real estate are), by contingencies (as bequests, mortgage foreclosures, insurance, and bankruptcy are), by constraints on alienation (as entails and restrictive covenants were), by audits according to accounting principles establishing net returns, by votes of boards of directors on the dividends, by federal principles written into political constitutions or into multidivisional organization in firms, and so on.

Forms of appropriation are thus boundaries in causal webs, or channels in flows of causes and effects, that connect decisions to benefits and exposures. Those boundaries then constitute the shifting identities of corporate groups or other owners, defining the actions that socially constitute them and raising claims to the outcomes of those actions. What this means for our purposes is that (1) the appropriation of going-concern value as a monopoly of an opportunity is an identity in a flow of decisions or benefits, and (2) all of them depend on a flow of advantages over competitors, exposures to challenges by competitors, and a flow of accruals of future market, status, or power advantages. The changing "identity" of a corporate group, then, is a slowly shifting place in that flow, a place maintained by a flow of activities using the liberties that constitute the appropriation of a competitive position.

Appropriation of profits, reputation, and sovereignty as governments

Modern sovereignty shows most clearly that what is central to appropriation of the return to liberties is the right to legislate, to spend income according to that legislation, to reorganize the working rules of the administration to make that legislation effective, and to create contracts or other agency relations that are binding. That is, property or other liberties put into a corporate fund are useful because they can be governed. They are more useful in the corporate group than in "private" hands because there they can be used to exploit an opportunity in the relevant field. Thus it is the area of autonomy of national governments as organizations that makes their going-concern value greater than the sum of individual rights to bear arms, that makes them "sovereign," and that allows them to administer and tax the resources within a given territory. It is that going-concern value that makes the authority of the government the last word in social conflicts within a given territory.

Similarly it is because distinguished scientists and scholars can be hired and promoted by the baroque personnel processes of universities, and can organize to train their successors (plus chemists for Du Pont or art historians for the Metropolitan Museum of Art) and give them credible degrees, that the universities have reputations that bring in tuition and endowment money. The crucial monopoly indirectly controlled by this personnel process is the use of the name of the university on degrees, which is what is built up by the creation of the working rules of the university and by its wise use of its reputational assets and of the tuitions of its students.

Many of the forms of appropriation available to corporate groups are also available to individuals. Individual authors are the original owners of the liberties protected by copyrights, and they sign them away to publishers on terms that they can, on rare occasions, influence. Very generally publishers do not want to publish manuscripts that the authors refuse to put their name to, partly because buyers or readers use authors' names as an index to what books they might be interested in. There are therefore reputational values in book or article manuscripts that are appropriated by the authors rather than by their publishers or their universities.

But it is crucial to the point of this chapter that appropriation of the returns from an opportunity in a field does not operate by exclusion of others from the opportunity. Or, rather, the exclusion of others from the opportunity is a continuing achievement rather than a defensible right. Paradigm shifts, for example, can render reputations of scientific departments useless. The growth of the population, economy, and navy of the United States made Spanish tenure in Cuba and Puerto Rico dependent on United States toleration by the late 19th century, and it now makes Russian reconquest of Alaska a fantasy of Russian nationalist parties rather than something to worry about.

Monopolistic competition and the epistemology of mechanisms

I have previously defined mechanisms as a bit of theory about subunits of a larger structure that has independent validity at its level and that generates results not otherwise easily got at the level of the larger structure (Stinchcombe 1991). Thus molecular biology provides mechanisms for cell physiology, or a theory of people's choices provide mechanisms for economics and parts of sociology. Only if mechanisms provide the opportunity to study their operation at the lower level, but provide suppleness, elegance, economy, or validity at the structural level, will they be fruitful for the science concentrating on the structures.

A recurrent subject of sociology is the relatively high autocorrelation over time of positions of individuals or corporate groups in a stratification order. We therefore need mechanisms to explain advantages that are persistent, but challengeable, in stratification orders such as social classes, status and prestige hierarchies of people, or power and authority systems. The study of social stratification is about that autocorrelation, especially for cross-generational ranks of families.

The starting point of this chapter is the presumption that such positional continuity over time in riches, prestige, and power applies to corporate groups such as firms, universities, and nation–states (I believe no sociologist would disagree with that presumption). A mechanism to explain these structures of autocorrelation has to explain the continuity over time of the corporate groups as well as the autocorrelation of group position, and it has to explain how such corporate groups meet the competition of other corporate groups. We cannot assume that anything within a skin is an entity to be stratified, because the skins of corporate groups are not so readily observable. It is autocorrelation over time of many features of a pattern that constitutes the thingness of such abstractions as corporate groups or genes, things without skins. And we need to explain how corporate groups can produce a continuous stream of action over time that maintains corporate income, prestige, or world system power.

Genes, which maintain some of the autocorrelation in lineages of plants, animals, and humans, are themselves extremely complicated mechanisms. This essay is so long because the mechanism of corporate appropriation of opportunities in a competitive field has to explain the thingness of corporate groups, so that autocorrelation can be identified. A stream of corporate environmental adaptation over time maintains that thingness (that "identity"). That adaption to a niche simultaneously maintains (to some degree or other) the position whose continuity was originally to be explained. But it has to explain as well why such fields as markets, prestige systems, or world power systems are all systems in which relative positions can be maintained. To use the language of the essay, the problem is to explain the continuity of the monopoly advantage due to the fact that a corporate group can do some subset of things better than anyone else (its "opportunity"), and so maintain its position. Fields are systems of opportunities that can be monopolized.

But that entails that the environment (that field) must consist of activities that can be done better or worse by different corporate groups. If all exchanges between an entity and an environment took place in a timeless instant, with no continuity in either the environment or in the entity interacting, the phenomenon of autocorrelated position to be explained could not be there to be explained. That is why we need a mechanism of the sort we have designed here; we need to explain the causal unity and continuity of the units of our theory just as planetary orbits required gravitational unity and continuity of the planets to produce ellipses.

The core of the mechanism proposed here is appropriation of going-concern value, as John R. Commons called it. But going-concern value would not be different from the value of any other owner of the same assets unless the concern were free to do something with it that other owners would not or could not automatically do. So for that kind of appropriation to take place, the appropriation has to be of a set of liberties in the environment, some subset of which are better done by the going concern than any other. So the core mechanism that we have to build is one in which corporate groups can be better than their environment, and in which liberties generally available to competitors are differentially well managed by different corporate groups. Insofar as such advantageous management is continuous through time, the autocorrelation of status is explained. This shows that, logically speaking, the mechanism described here is adequate to the sociologist's task in stratified fields of corporate groups: explaining the autocorrelation of stratified positions.

I have illustrated the mechanism in three different sorts of fields: corporate firms ranked by profitability (defined by Tobin's q-ratio), universities ranked by prestige, and nation–states ranked by world system power so that the high end is hegemony and the low end is being a pawn in the world system game. The purpose of the illustrations is to give a hint of how to describe the functioning of the mechanism so that it can generate the ranking phenomena with precarious continuity over time prevalent in the different fields.

Besides I think the mechanism is beautiful, and I made this icon to it to lay at John R. Commons's feet.

References

Adams, Julia. 1994a. "Trading States, Trading Places: The Role of Patrimonialism in Early Modern Dutch Development." *Comparative Studies in Society and History*, 36, 2 (April) pp. 319–55.

Adams, Julia. 1994b. "The Familial State: Elite Family Practices and State Making in the Early Modern Netherlands." *Theory and Society*, 23:505–39.

Adams, Julia. 1996. "Principals, Agents, and Company Men: The Decay of Control in the Dutch East Indies." *American Sociological Review* 61, 1 (February):12–28.

Bales, Robert Freed, and Philip E. Slater. 1955. "Role differentiation in small decision-making groups." In Talcott Parsons and Robert F. Bales, and others, *Family, Socialization, and Interaction Processes*. Glencoe, NY: Free Press, pp. 259–306.

Barnard, Chester I. 1946. "Functions and pathology of status systems in formal organizations." In William F. Whyte (ed.), *Industry and Society*. New York: McGraw-Hill, pp. 46–83.

Baum, Joel A. C., and Jitendra Singh 1996. "Dynamics of Organizational Responses to Competition." *Social Forces*, 74, 4:1261–97.

Bourdieu, Pierre. 1984. *Distinction*. Cambridge, MA: Harvard University Press.

Bourdieu, Pierre. 1988 [1984]. *Homo Academicus*. Stanford: Stanford University Press.

Boxer, Charles Ralph. 1988 [1965]. *The Dutch Seaborne Empire: 1600–1800*. Baltimore: Reprinted by Penguin Books [London: Hutchinson].

Boxer, Charles Ralph. 1969. *The Portuguese Seaborne Empire, 1415–1825*. London: Hutchinson.

Burke, Edmund. 1895 [1775]. *Burke's Speech on Conciliation with America* (ed. A. M. George). London: D.C.

Carruthers, Bruce. 1996. *The City of Capital*. Princeton: Princeton University Press.

Chamberlin, Edward Hastings. 1962 [1933]. *The Theory of Monopolistic Competition: A Re-Orientation of the Theory of Value*. Cambridge, MA: Harvard University Press.

Coase, R. H. 1937. "The Nature of the Firm." *Economica* 4:386–405.

Coleman, James S. 1964. *Introduction to Mathematical Sociology*. New York: The Free Press [of Glencoe].

Commons, John R. 1974 [1924]. *Legal Foundations of Capitalism*. Clifton, N.J.: A. M. Kelley [Originally University of Wisconsin Press].

Davis, Kingsley 1964 [1954]. "The demographic basis of national power." In Morroe Berger, Theodore Abel, and Charles H. Page (eds.), *Freedom and Control in Modern Society*. New York: Octagon Books [originally Van Nostrand], pp. 206–42.

Duffy, Michael. 1987. *Soldiers, Sugar, and Seapower*. Oxford: Clarendon Press.

Frostin, Charles. 1975. *Les révoltes blanches à Saint-Domingue aux XVIIe et*

XVIIIe siècles (Haïti avant 1789) [White revolts in Saint Domingue in the 17th and 18th centuries (Haiti before 1789)] Paris: L'École.

Gleik, James. 1992. *Genius: The Life and Science of Richard Feynman*. New York: Pantheon Books.

Hannan, Michael T., and John Freeman. 1977. "The Population Ecology of Organizations." *American Journal of Sociology*, 82:929–64.

Hannan, Michael T., and John Freeman. 1989. *Organizational Ecology*. Cambridge MA: Harvard University Press.

Hansmann, Henry. 1985. "The Organization of Insurance Companies: Mutual versus Stock." *Journal of Law, Economics, and Organization*, 1, 1:125–53.

Karabel, Jerome. 1984. "Status Group Struggle, Organizational Interests, and the Limits of Organizational Autonomy." *Theory and Society*, 13 (January): 1–40.

Klock, Mark S., Clifford Thies, and Christopher F. Baum. 1991. "Tobin's *q* and Measurement Error: Caveat Investigator." *Journal of Economics and Business*, 43, 3 (August):241–52.

Leibenstein, Harvey. 1978. *General X-efficiency Theory and Economic Development*. New York: Oxford University Press.

Lindberg, Eric B., and Stephen A. Ross. 1981. "Tobin's *q* Ratio and Industrial Organization." *Journal of Business*, (September):1–32.

Mansfield, Edwin, John Rapoport, Anthony Romeo, Samuel Wagner, and George Beardsley. 1977. "Social and Private Rates of Return from Industrial Innovations." *Quarterly Journal of Economics*, 91:221–40.

McNeely, Connie. 1993. "The Determination of Statehood in the United Nations, 1945–1985." *Research in Political Sociology*, 6:1–38.

Merton, Robert K. 1968 [1942]. "Science and Democratic Social Structure." In his *Social Theory and Social Structure*. New York: The Free Press, pp. 307–16.

Nelson, Richard R., and Sidney G. Winter. 1982. *An Evolutionary Theory of Economic Change*. Cambridge MA: Belknap-Harvard University Press.

Palmer, Donald, Brad M. Barber, Xueguang Zhou, and Yasemin Soysal. 1995. "The Friendly and Predatory Acquisition of Large U.S. Corporations in the 1960s: The Other Contested Terrain." *American Sociological Review*, 60, 4 (August):469–99.

Pérotin-Dumon, Anne. 1985. *Être patriote sous les tropiques: La Guadeloupe, la colonisation, et la Révolution 1789–1794* [To be a Supporter of the Revolution in the Tropics: Guadeloupe, Colonization, and the Revolution]. Basse-Terre: Société d'Histoire de la Guadeloupe.

Petersen, Trond. 1995. "Transaction Cost Economics." In Pål Foss (ed.), *Economic Approaches to Organizations and Institutions*. Brookfield VT: Dartmouth Publishing, pp. 17–45.

Podolny, Joel M. 1993. "A Status-based Model of Market Competition." *American Journal of Sociology*, 98, 5 (January):829–72.

304 ARTHUR L. STINCHCOMBE

Podolny, Joel M. 1994. "Market Uncertainty and the Social Character of Economic Exchange." *Administrative Science Quarterly*, 39:458–83.

Podolny, Joel M., and Damon J. Phillips. 1996. "The Dynamics of Organizational Status." *Industrial and Corporate Change*. (November)

Podolny, Joel M., and Toby E. Stuart. 1995. "A Role-Based Ecology of Technological Change." *American Journal of Sociology*, 100, 5 (March): 1224–60.

Podolny, Joel M., Toby E. Stuart, and Michael Hannan. 1996. "Networks, Knowledge, and Niches: Competition in the Worldwide Semiconductor Industry, 1984–1991." *American Journal of Sociology*, 102, 3 (November):659–89.

Robinson, Joan. 1933. *The Economics of Imperfect Competition*. London: Macmillan.

Roy, William G. 1997. *Socializing Capital: The Rise of the Large Industrial Corporation in America*. Princeton, NJ: Princeton University Press.

Scherer, Fred M. 1964. *The Weapons Acquisition Process: Economic Incentives*. Boston: Division of Research, Graduate School of Business, Harvard University.

Schumpeter, Joseph A. 1942. *Capitalism, Socialism, and Democracy*. New York: Harper Torchbooks (paperback edition).

Schumpeter, Joseph A. 1964 [1939]. *Business Cycles: A Theoretical, Historical, and Statistical Analysis of the Capitalist Process* [Abridged by Rindigs Fels]. New York: McGraw-Hill.

Smirlock, Michael, Thomas Gilligan, and William Marshall. 1984. "Tobin's *q* and the Structure-Performance Relationship." *American Economic Review*, 74, part 2 (December):1051–60

Stinchcombe, Arthur L. 1987 [1968]. *Constructing Social Theories*. Chicago: University of Chicago Press.

Stinchcombe, Arthur L. 1990. *Information and Organizations*. Berkeley: University of California Press.

Stinchcombe, Arthur L. 1991. "The Conditions of Fruitfulness of Theorizing about Mechanisms in Social Science." *Philosophy of the Social Sciences*, 21,3 (September):367–87. Reprinted slightly modified in Aage Sørensen and Seymour Spilerman (eds.), *Social Theory and Social Policy: Essays in Honor of James S. Coleman*. Westport, CT: Praeger (1991).

Stuart, Toby E., and Joel M. Podolny. 1996. "Local Search and the Evolution of Technological Capabilities." *Strategic Management Journal*, 17 (November): 21–38.

Tilly, Charles. 1990. *Coercion, Capital, and European States, AD 990–1990*. Cambridge, MA, and Oxford: Basil Blackwell.

Tobin, James, and William C. Brainard. 1977. "Asset Markets and the Cost of Capital." In Richard Nelson and Bela Balassa (eds.), *Economic Progress: Private Values and Public Policy: Essays in Honor of W. Fellner*. Amsterdam: North Holland. pp. 235–62.

Tuchman, Barbara W. 1988. *The First Salute: A View of the American Revolution*. New York: Knopf.

Wallerstein, Immanuel. 1980. *The Modern World-System II: Mercantilism and the Consolidation of the European World-Economy, 1600–1750*. New York: Academic Press.

Weber, Max. 1968 [1921–2 in German]. In Guenther Roth and Claus Wittich (eds.), *Economy and Society: An Outline of Interpretive Sociology*. New York: Bedminster Press.

White, Harrison C. 1992. *Identity and Control: A Structural Theory of Social Action*. Princeton: Princeton University Press.

Zablocki, Benjamin. 1971. *The Joyful Community*. Baltimore: Penguin Books.

12. Rational imitation

PETER HEDSTRÖM

Introduction

A few years ago I traveled by car from Stockholm to Copenhagen. It was a long and rather tiresome drive, and in order to stay alert, I started observing and classifying the behavior of my fellow travelers on the road. After a while, a curious fact caught my attention. While the cars around me on the multilane highway normally drove at some 100 to 105 kilometers per hour, they would all frequently and suddenly reduce their speed, as if instructed to do so by an invisible authority, although nothing prevented the cars from passing one another. Soon thereafter they returned to normal speed, but after a while, the same phenomenon occurred again: The cars suddenly slowed down, only to resume their original speed a short while later.

Having observed this pattern of behavior a number of times – a pattern referred to as "wolf-pack behavior" by American state troopers – it became evident to me that it had nothing to do with the driving conditions as such; it happened just as frequently under good conditions as under bad. Furthermore, the pattern of behavior had a clear social structure. What at first appeared to be an instantaneous reaction of all drivers to an instruction arriving from a central but invisible authority, upon closer examination appeared to be a contagious social process set in motion by one car suddenly reducing its speed. A brief moment later, the cars adjacent to the first car did the same, and soon the behavior had spread to even

I wish to thank Göran Ahrne, Raymond Boudon, Ronald Burt, Olof Dahlbäck, Christofer Edling, Diego Gambetta, Rickard Sandell, Ole-Jørgen Skog, Arthur Stinchcombe, Richard Swedberg, Charles Tilly, and Lars Udéhn for their valuable comments, and Ingrid Hansson and Mats G°ardstad for their valuable programming assistance. The research has been financed by a grant from the Swedish Council for Research in the Humanities and the Social Sciences.

more cars. It was as if the drivers were, indeed, able to communicate with one another, but through a communication system of such limited scope that only adjacent drivers were able to be in contact with one another. These drivers obviously did not have access to any radio communication device that could allow them to reach one another verbally. The mechanism that generated the interdependent behavior therefore must have been of a nonverbal kind; through their *actions*, the drivers gave off signals to other drivers, and the interpretation of these signals generated the social behavior that was observed on the highway. When one driver reduced his speed, this sent a signal to the other drivers that he might have observed something that gave him reason to reduce his speed – perhaps a hidden speed trap – and, given this possibility, the other drivers decided to do the same, only to find out a moment later that they could just as well have continued at their original speed.

I relate this episode because it illustrates a class of social behaviors that I believe are of crucial importance for sociological theory. I will refer to this sort of behavior as "rational imitation." By this concept, I have the following type of behavior in mind. An actor, A, can be said to imitate the behavior of another actor, B, when observation of the behavior of B affects A in such a way that A's subsequent behavior becomes more similar to the observed behavior of B (see Flanders, 1968). An actor can be said to act rationally when the actor, faced with a choice between different courses of action, chooses the course of action that is best with respect to the actor's interests and his or her beliefs about possible action opportunities and their effects (see Elster, 1986; Hedström, 1996). Rational imitation hence refers to a situation where an actor acts rationally on the basis of beliefs that have been influenced by observing the past choices of others.[1] To the extent that other actors act reasonably and avoid alternatives that have proven to be inferior, the actor can arrive at better decisions than he or she would make otherwise, by imitating the behavior of others.

The chapter is organized as follows. First I will situate the type of action considered here by contrasting it with other types of imitative behavior. Imitative behavior has often been portrayed as a rather mechanistic and

---

[1] This sort of behavior is closely related to what Goffman (1966) had in mind with his notion of "expression games" (i.e., interactions where individuals through their actions give off signals that, often unintentionally, influence the beliefs and subsequent behavior of others).

intellectually uninteresting form of social action. This is a misconception, however. Imitative behavior is a common and therefore socially important form of action; it is also a multifaceted type of behavior that exhibits many interesting dynamics. In the second part of the chapter, a simulation model is specified in order to analyze the aggregate dynamics of social systems consisting of rational imitators. As the highway example illustrates, rational imitation is not infallible. One main purpose of the simulation analysis is to isolate conditions under which rational imitation is likely to flourish and conditions under which it is likely to fail.

Social mechanisms of imitative behavior

Imitation, in the sense in which the term is being used here, is central to the diffusion of knowledge and practices in most areas of social life. Despite its importance, little systematic work has been done to assemble and distinguish between different mechanisms that are likely to give rise to this sort of behavior.

One possible reason for this unsatisfactory situation may be that the mechanisms that produce imitative behavior are often unobservable, or only observable in their effects, and that many sociologists, for philosophical or methodological reasons, refrain from speculating about such matters. Given their importance, however, it appears essential to explicate the mechanisms that are likely to explain observed interdependencies, even if there are obvious difficulties in doing so.[2] As have been emphasized throughout this book, satisfactory explanations always entail specifying the *mechanisms* that have brought the relationship between observable entities into existence.

What we usually can observe are the actor interdependencies as such – when actor A observes the behavior of actor B, A's subsequent behavior becomes more similar to the observed behavior of B. From this observation alone, however, we cannot infer the mechanisms that explain the interdependencies, because the same observable outcomes may be the result of entirely different mechanisms. One important reason motivating the search for mechanisms is that the reverse does not hold true; that is to

---

[2] Weinberg (1993) gives numerous examples of how the dictates of positivism to theorize only about observables have hindered and delayed the development of new theories in physics. See Hedström's and Swedberg's Chapter 1 in this volume for related arguments concerning the development of sociological theory.

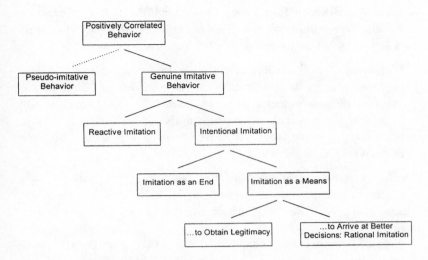

Figure 12.1. Forms of imitative behavior.

say, once we know the mechanisms that are operating, we are usually able to predict with considerable accuracy what observable behavior to expect.[3]

Figure 12.1 distinguishes between different forms of genuine and apparent imitative behavior. On the surface, these different types of behavior appear similar, but the mechanisms that generate and explain the observed interdependencies are strikingly different. In order to clearly distinguish rational imitation from other forms of imitative behavior, the defining characteristic of each form of imitative behavior will be briefly discussed in turn in the next few pages.

A first crucial distinction in Figure 12.1 is between genuine imitation, on the one hand, and apparent imitation, on the other (i.e., between behavior that indeed is directly influenced by observing the behavior of other actors and behavior that only appears to be under such influence). Situations where actors are acting independently of one another, but where their decision-making environments share important components, can often be

---

[3] As a generic example illustrating the asymmetry between mechanisms and observables, consider the problem of explaining the movement of the hands of a clock. From the observation of how the hands move, we cannot infer the mechanisms explaining their movement – digital or mechanical – but once we know the mechanism, we are able to explain the movement fully.

difficult to distinguish from genuine imitation.[4] The following example from Max Weber illustrates the difference between what could be called interdependent but *contingent action* and imitative social action:

Social action is not identical with the similar actions of many persons. ... Thus, if at the beginning of a shower a number of people on the street put up their umbrellas at the same time, this would not ordinarily be a case of action mutually oriented to that of each other, but rather of all reacting in the same way to the like need of protection from the rain. (Weber, [1921–2] 1978:23)

This form of contingent behavior is not explained by imitation or any other sort of inter-personal influence but is exclusively due to an environmental change that makes all actors adjust their behavior in a similar manner.[5]

Genuine imitation thus differs from contingent action in that one actor's behavior is indeed the impetus for another actor's behavior. Early sociological theorists such as Gustave Le Bon ([1895] 1960) and Gabriel Tarde ([1895] 1962) called attention to these types of interdependencies, but they were never able to provide a satisfactory explanation for the important regularities that they observed. Le Bon, for example, made only vague and unsubstantiated references to a "natural tendency to imitate" (p. 126) and to a "law of the mental unity of crowds" (p. 24). As pointed out by Weber ([1921–2] 1978:23) among others, these theorists based their analyses on the rather untenable assumption that action was purely *reactive* and without any meaningful orientation to the actor being imitated. For these reasons, as well as for their inability to distinguish clearly between different forms of imitative behavior, the ideas of Le Bon, Tarde, and others have been discredited in sociology, often on good grounds. Simply postulating the existence of a "natural tendency" to imitate the behavior

---

[4] The difficulties of empirically distinguishing between social contagion and individual adjustments to a common source of influence are well known. See Coleman et al. (1966) for an early and influential study that tries to distinguish between these different types of influences.

[5] One influential organizational theory that is built upon these sorts of explanations is the contingency theory of organizations (e.g., Lawrence and Lorsch, 1967), which assumes that organizations continuously adapt their structures to the changing demands of the environment. An environmental change may thus induce all the actors to adjust their behavior in a similar manner. Unless one is in a position to observe the unfolding of the entire process, the observable behavior may easily give the erroneous impression of being imitative.

of others constitutes a pseudo-explanation that provides no more than a label behind which we can hide our ignorance.[6]

The main alternative to the "reactive" action theory of Le Bon, Tarde, and others is to assume that actors have good reasons for doing what they are doing, or at least that they have good reasons for believing this to be the case. By assuming that actors act *intentionally*, we are forced to probe more deeply into the reasons or mechanisms that explain why actors follow the lead of others. In seeking an intentional explanation of imitative behavior, we must therefore search for possible (good) reasons for individuals to imitate others, and only if this endeavor fails should we resort to explanations which assume that actors act instinctually, randomly, or what not.

In some of the economics literature, *conformity* preferences have been assumed to explain why actors follow the lead of others. Writers such as Leibenstein (1950), Jones (1984), and Becker (1991) assume that imitative behavior is at least partly explained by there being an intrinsic value in not deviating from the behavior of others, and given this theoretical postulate, imitative behavior will arise.

Leibenstein et al.'s analyses are of somewhat limited use in this context because they do not detail any mechanism that is likely to have generated the conformist preferences. In Elster (1983) a useful discussion of mechanisms of subintentional preference change can be found, however. The most important and best understood mechanism generating conformist preferences is undoubtedly the mechanism of dissonance reduction. As Leon Festinger has suggested, if the decisions of other actors point to a different action than the one considered by the actor in question, dissonance is likely to arise, and the more isolated the actor is in his or her opinion, the greater the magnitude of the dissonance is likely to be. The existence of dissonance will, according to Festinger's theory, increase the likelihood that the actor will reconsider his/her choice, since changing

---

[6] Durkheim made a similar point when criticizing Tarde's work for its lack of explanatory mechanisms: "Thus when imitation is mentioned [as an explanation of nonreactive behavior] we are told simply that the fact we reproduce is not new, that is, that it is reproduced, without being told at all why it was produced nor why we reproduce it" ([1897]1951:130). See also Boudon's Chapter 8 in this volume for related arguments. It should be pointed out, however, that while Tarde devoted most of his work to "extralogical" influences on imitative behavior, one chapter in *The Laws of Imitation* explicitly considers the "logical" beliefs and desires that could lead actors to imitate the behavior of others.

one's opinion and adopting the majority point of view is often the most efficient way to reduce the dissonance (see Festinger, 1957, Ch. 8).

Although "hot" mechanisms like these are of considerable importance, the focus of this chapter is on a "cold" cognitive mechanism. The primary focus is not on preferences but on beliefs; imitation is not explained with reference to a preference for conformity or a dislike for being different but with reference to the belief that imitation is a useful strategy for obtaining valued positions or resources.[7]

When imitation is discussed in recent sociological literature, the focus is usually on organizations and on imitation as a vehicle for organizations to obtain *legitimacy*. These sorts of ideas are central to both institutional and ecological theories of organizations (e.g., DiMaggio and Powell, 1983, 1991; Hannan and Carroll, 1992). By imitating already existing and accepted models, these authors argue, organizations reduce the risk of being called into question by customers and important institutional actors, and thereby increase their chances of survival. Thus, the argument goes, other actors in the institutional environment have clearly specified beliefs about the ways in which appropriate and reliable organizations should look. If an organization deviates widely from this preferred ideal, it is likely to be penalized by other actors (e.g., by their avoiding the actor in question). Meyer and Rowan (1977) concisely summarize the core of this argument: "Organizations that incorporate societally legitimated rationalized elements in their formal structures maximize their legitimacy and increase their resources and survival capabilities." One problem with this argument is that it hinges on the postulated existence of very specific and homogeneous beliefs on the part of the actors in the institutional environment. The argument of the new institutionalists makes a great deal of sense as long as one is willing to accept, as a theoretical postulate, that other actors in the environment have clearly specified and largely identical beliefs. Once these beliefs are in place, the rest of the story follows, since the postulated beliefs are rather specific in reference to the sort of behavior they imply. But the problem is that institutional theory does not refer to

---

[7] Empirically, the distinction between means and ends is not always clear cut. As Merton reminds us, means often are transformed into ends: "Adherence to the rules, originally conceived as a means, becomes transformed into an end-in-itself; there occurs the familiar process of *displacement of goals* whereby an instrumental value becomes a terminal value" (Merton, 1968a:253).

any well-specified mechanism that can explain how such beliefs are established, sustained, and diffused, even though these beliefs are supposed to do all the explanatory work.

The type of mechanism considered here avoids the problems confronting institutional theory. The focus is not on the preferences of the actors themselves – as was the case with Leibenstein et al. – nor on the beliefs of those actors in the institutional environment who may determine the fate of other organizations – as was the case with new institutional theory – but on the beliefs of the actors themselves and on how these beliefs are influenced by the actions of others.

Belief-formation processes have not received much attention in the sociological literature. However, some classical works in sociology during the postwar period have worked out the basic principles involved, most notably Robert K. Merton's (1968b) work on self-fulfilling prophecies, James Coleman, Elihu Katz, and Herbert Menzel's (1966) work on network diffusion processes, and Mark Granovetter's (1978) work on threshold-based behavior.

As emphasized in the first chapter of this book, the type of mechanism that gives the analyses of Merton, Coleman, and Granovetter their appeal concerns the specific ways in which they assume individuals' beliefs to be formed. Their proposed mechanism states that one individual's belief in the value or necessity of performing a certain act is partly a function of the number of other individuals who have already performed the act. In an uncertain decision context, the number of individuals who perform a particular act signals to others the likely value or necessity of the act, and this signal will influence other individuals' choice of action. Merton's bank customers based their judgments about the solvency of the bank on the number of other customers withdrawing their savings from the bank; Coleman's physicians based their evaluations of the possible effects of a new drug on the doings of their colleagues; and Granovetter's restaurant visitors based their decisions on where to eat on the number of diners already in the restaurants.[8] In all these cases, individuals imitate the behavior of others not because they are conformists who prefer to be like

---

[8] See Hedström and Swedberg (1996) for a more in-depth discussion of the works of Merton, Coleman, and Granovetter and how their work is related to the notion of social mechanisms. In Hedström (1994a) the same type of belief-formation mechanism is used to account for the spatial patterns of the diffusion of Swedish trade union organizations.

others, or because other powerful actors force them to abide by existing norms, but because imitation is perceived to be a useful strategy for arriving at better decisions.[9]

Robert Cialdini (1984) refers to this heuristic as "the principle of social proof": When in doubt about what to do, always look around at the actions of others for possible clues. This decision heuristic is practiced in the most varied sets of circumstances, from mundane everyday activities, such as being in doubt about which fork to use for the first course of a dinner, to intricate organizational decisions such as those described in Cyert and March (1963).[10]

The prevalence of this heuristic, no doubt, is primarily due to the simple fact that it works well (i.e., by following the lead of others, actors tend to do better than they otherwise would). But there also exists another important mechanism that operates in the same direction as the heuristic of social proof, and which thereby reinforces the same sort of behavior. This is the mechanism of dissonance reduction referred to earlier. In the type of situation considered here, the heuristic of social proof is more fundamental than the mechanism of dissonance reduction, however, because the latter is dependent upon the former, but not the other way around. That is to say, this type of dissonance arises *because* of the belief in the heuristic of social proof and is distinct from whatever other social pressures to conform might be leveled against the deviant actor. Yet while the social-proof mechanism is more fundamental, it is the specific combination of the two – or the specific "concatenation" of mechanisms, to use Gambetta's terminology in Chapter 5 – that makes the behavior so widely observed.[11]

Most of the foregoing examples concern the behavior of human actors, but the logic is the same in the case of corporate actors. That is to say, organizational interdependencies result partly from a mimetic process whereby organizations – or rather key human actors within organizations – believe that they can improve the performance of the organization by

---

[9] As will be discussed more fully later, the self-fulfilling prophecy differs in one important respect from the other two examples in that there is an endogenous change in the true values of the choice alternatives that works in the same direction as the belief-formation mechanism and thereby reinforces the same sort of behavior.

[10] See Kuran (1995) for a range of illuminating examples of the social-proof heuristic.

[11] The prevalence of the behavior is also indicated by the existence of a specific proverb expressing its logic: "When in Rome, do as the Romans do." See Elster's Chapter 3 in this volume for a discussion of proverbs and their relationships to social mechanisms.

imitating others, and in doing so, they also reduce whatever cognitive dissonance might be stemming from unconventional and self-reliant behavior. As John Maynard Keynes once noted: "Worldly wisdom teaches that it is better for reputation to fail conventionally than to succeed unconventionally" ([1936] 1960:158).[12]

Aggregate dynamics: Simulation results

In order to examine how a system composed of actors whose choices are partly or fully oriented toward the actions of others is likely to evolve, a simulation model will be used. The main purpose of the simulation is to examine conditions under which imitation is a reasonable decision strategy.

The core features of the simulation model are the following. The social system consists of N actors. From this group, one actor is selected at random at each point in time, and this actor has to choose one specific action from a finite set of k actions. The values of the outcomes associated with these k alternatives are initially unknown to the actor. The first time the actor is confronted with this choice, the choice is made behind a veil of ignorance: The only information available is information on how other actors have acted in the past when confronted with the same choice situation. Given the heuristic of social proof, actors will take this information into account when making their decisions.

The decision-making model to be used here only includes the minimum number of elements needed to examine the aggregate dynamics of this sort of system. It assumes that actors assign a unique value – what I will refer to as a β – to each alternative, and that the probability of an actor choosing a particular alternative is equal to its β-value divided by the sum of the β-values of all the alternatives.[13] The probability of actor j choosing action i at time t is then equal to

$$P_{ijt} = \frac{\beta_{ijt}}{\sum_{i=1}^{k}\beta_{ijt}}.$$

[12] See Fligstein (1985), Westney (1987), Galaskiewicz and Wasserman (1989), Davis (1991), and Haveman (1993) for empirical evidence of the importance of these kinds of processes among organizations.

[13] See Luce (1959) and Arthur (1994) for related models.

The β-values are assumed to be influenced by the actors' own assessments of the likely utility values of the various alternatives *and* by the past choices of others. More specifically, it will be assumed that the β-values are weighted linear combinations of these two sources of influence:

$$\beta_{ijt} = w_j S_{it} + (1 - w_j) V_{ijt}$$

where

w_j = an actor-specific parameter in the range 0–1 that states how much relative weight the actor attaches to the past choices of others,

S_{it} = alternative i's share of cumulative choices made until time $t-1$, and

V_{ijt} = actor j's assessment of the likely value of alternative i at t.

Actors differ in terms of how much they are influenced by the past behavior of others. Some actors ignore their own experiences entirely, other actors only trust their own judgments, and still others base their decisions on various combinations of the two sources of information. The pure imitators have a w_j-value equal to 1, the "atomistic" or self-reliant actors have a w_j-value equal to zero, and the rest have weights in-between these two extremes.

The simulation results are based on the following sequence of events:

- One of the N actors is selected at random.
- This actor decides on its course of action using the foregoing equations, and this choice is observed by all other actors in the system.[14]
- Once the choice has been made, the true value of the alternative is revealed to the actor, and the actor stores this private information for future use.
- After having made the choice, the actor returns to the pool of the other $N - 1$ actors, and the sequence of events is repeated again.

[14] The choice of action is decided upon by first forming intervals between 0 and 1, where the length of each alternative's interval is proportional to its P_{ijt} value. The limits of the first interval will thus be 0 and P_{1jt}; the limits of the second interval will be P_{1jt} and P_{2jt}; the limits of the third interval will be $(P_{1jt} + P_{2jt})$ and $(P_{1jt} + P_{2jt} + P_{3jt})$; and so on. A random number is then drawn from a uniform probability distribution with a range of 0 to 1. The interval within which the random number falls decides which action will be chosen. To initialize the simulations, all the entries of the S_{it} and the V_{ijt} vectors are set equal to 0.1. In the simulations reported later, actors calculate the S_{it} values on the basis of the last 250 choices in order not to be unduly influenced by the early and erratic history of the system.

Although the model has a simple formal structure, it emulates a social system of some intricacy: An actor makes a decision by observing the choices of other actors, who have arrived at their decisions by observing yet others, and, via the choice of action, the actors in turn influence the future choices of the others.

The results reported in Figure 12.2 refer to a system consisting of 250 actors who have 10 alternatives to choose between. It is a stable system where the true values of the alternatives remain the same throughout the analysis, and where one of the 10 alternatives is far superior to the others.[15] There are five different groups, each consisting of 50 actors. The group that is labeled "Model" in the graph enters the scene first. It is a group of actors who only trust their own experiences, and therefore their w_j-values are equal to zero. Through an individual search process, these "atomistic" actors gradually find their way to the best course of action. At time period 750, when each actor on the average has acted 15 times, the superior action alternative is chosen approximately 60% of the time.[16] Their pattern of choices is observed by the actors in the other groups, and, given the belief in the social proof heuristic, it signals to them the likely values of the various alternatives.

At time period 751, the other actors enter the scene. The main result of these analyses is basically a confirmation of the social proof heuristic: In stable environments like these, pure atomistic learning ($w = 0$) is an inferior strategy to that of pure imitation ($w = 1$). All that the pure atomistic learners can hope to accomplish after a long search process is to perform at best as well as the models. The pure imitators accomplish this "cloning" of the models much faster.

As the results reported in Figure 12.3 illustrate, however, the superiority of pure imitation is restricted to stable environments. This simulation initially is identical to the previous one, and, as was the case there, the models slowly work their way toward the best alternative. But at the moment when the other groups of actors enter the scene ($t = 751$), the "world" suddenly changes, and the actions that worked in the past no longer work. This sudden change is accomplished by reversing the true

---

[15] The true values associated with the 10 alternatives are as follows: .006; .009; .015; .019; .021; .027; .031; .035; .040; and .797.

[16] "Time" in these analyses coincides with the total number of (sequential) choices being made.

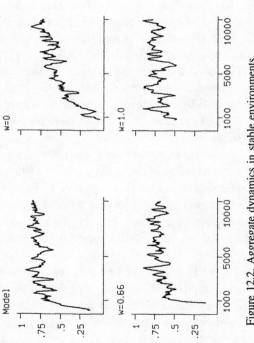

Figure 12.2. Aggregate dynamics in stable environments.

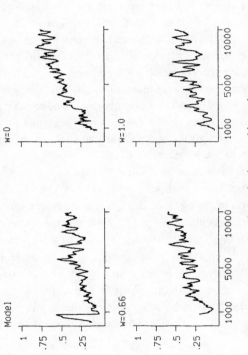

Figure 12.3. Aggregate dynamics in unstable environments.

utility values associated with the alternative courses of action.[17] As can be seen from the figure, the models are unable to recover fully from this environmental shock during the time period being analyzed here, and the more weight that actors attach to the choices of the models, the worse they will do. The moral is this: Assuming that others act reasonably can sometimes lead reasonable actors to act rather unreasonably. This result is understandable once we compare the time trajectory of the models with that of their atomistic siblings, who entered the scene after the change had taken place ($w = 0$). As can be seen, the models are improving their performance at a much slower rate than their atomistic siblings. Strong prior beliefs, built up during a long and eventful history, are usually an advantage in that they lead to decisions with better results for the actors (see Tsebelis, 1990). But in turbulent periods like these, strong priors may, in fact, be a considerable weakness, because they reduce the likelihood that the beliefs and the corresponding actions will be sufficiently modified in the light of new information. That is to say, history introduces an information-based inertia that hinders actors from properly adapting to a changing environment and, through the operation of the social-proof heuristic, this inertia is spread to the imitators as well.[18]

The simulations reported so far assume stable environments or environments that change through exogenous shocks to the system, and therefore they do not capture the type of endogenous dynamics that are at the heart of Merton's notion of a *self-fulfilling prophecy*.[19] Unlike the situations considered so far, self-fulfilling prophecies arise in situations when the value of a particular course of action is an increasing function of the number (or proportion) who have chosen the course of action. The basic idea behind the notion of a self-fulfilling prophecy is that an initial belief, which may be entirely false, evokes behavior that eventually makes the belief come true. The key example that Merton uses to illustrate his ar-

---

[17] That is to say, alternatives 1 to 10 before the change had the following values: .006; .009; .015; .019; .021; .027; .031; .035; .040; and .797. After the change, the order was reversed: .797; .040; .035; .031; and so on.

[18] During turbulent periods, we should thus expect to observe a "liability of obsolescence" rather than the more commonly observed "liability of newness" (Stinchcombe, 1965) in organizational mortality rates. The results also bring to mind Margaret Mead's (1970) distinction between stable "postfigurative cultures," where the elders provide the model for the behavior of the young, and more rapidly changing "cofigurative cultures," where contemporary peers are the models.

[19] See also Schelling (1978) for a most illuminating discussion of self-fulfilling and self-negating processes in social life.

gument is a run on a bank. If a rumor of insolvency somehow gets started, some depositors will withdraw their savings. Their withdrawal will strengthen the belief in the rumor, partly because the withdrawals actually may hurt the financial standing of the bank, and partly because of the social-proof heuristic: The act of withdrawal in itself signals to others that something might indeed be wrong with the bank. This produces even more withdrawals, which further reduces the trust in and solvency of the bank, and so on. Because of the operation of this mechanism, even an initially sound bank may go bankrupt if enough depositors withdraw their money in the belief that the bank is insolvent (see Merton, 1968b).[20]

Another important class of social situations is characterized by *self-defeating processes*, where the value of a particular course of action is negatively related to the number (or proportion) who have chosen the course of action.[21] These types of processes are at the heart of most fads and fashions, but they are also central to many congestion problems (see Schelling, 1978).

In order to examine these sorts of endogenously changing systems, it is necessary to modify the simulation model slightly in order to allow the true values of the action alternatives to be systematically related to the aggregate choices of the actors. In the case of the self-fulfilling process, it will be assumed that the value of an alternative increases proportionately with the number of actors who have chosen the alternative,[22] and in the

---

[20] Processes like this might also arise in situations where only a minority of the actors form their beliefs on the basis of the social-proof heuristic, which suggests that a distinction should be made between the belief in the *usefulness* of the heuristic and the belief in the *truth* of the heuristic. Consider the following situation: (1) I do not believe in proposition A, (2) I know (or believe) that many others believe in A, and their belief in A will have negative consequences for me, (3) these negative consequences will induce me to act as if A were true, and this (4) will signal to others the correctness of proposition A. As I have discussed in Hedström (1994b), the public fear of magnetic fields from power lines exhibits this sort of dynamic. Since this fear threatens to undermine the property values of houses close to power lines, house owners (even those who are convinced that the fear is groundless) are induced to act in the same manner as those who believe that magnetic fields pose a danger to individuals health and to put their houses on the market. This "escape" sends off a signal to others that there indeed must be some substance to the view that living close to a power line is a potential health hazard, which threatens to further reduce property values, and thereby to escalate the process.

[21] Another type of self-defeating process – not considered here – arises in situations where the probability of accomplishing a task is inversely related to the *effort* exhorted. Examples include insomnia and spontaneity.

[22] More specifically, the value of each alternative is multiplied by the proportion that have chosen the alternative, and these new values then are normalized so that they add up to 1.0.

case of the self-defeating process, it will be assumed that the value decreases proportionately with the number of actors who have chosen the alternative.[23]

Figure 12.4 reports the results of two such simulations. The type of system simulated here is simpler than the previous ones in that there are only 50 actors involved who are asked to choose between two alternatives. All actors have w_j-values equal to 0.5 (i.e., they attach as much weight to the actions of others as they do to their own experiences).

The left-hand graph in Figure 12.4 displays the aggregate dynamics of a typical self-fulfilling process. Initially both alternatives are perceived to be equally attractive. Through trial and error, actors realize that one of the alternatives is indeed better than the other, and gradually the frequency with which the better alternative is chosen increases.[24] Because of the simultaneous operation of the social-proof heuristic and the gradual transformation of the true values associated with the alternative courses of action, the system rapidly approaches a state where all actors are acting alike.

The right-hand graph in Figure 12.4 is based on the same set-up, except for the fact that the values of the alternatives here decrease proportionately with the number of actors choosing the alternative. The aggregate dynamics of the system are dramatically different. Whereas the previous simulation generated a stable and homogeneous outcome, this simulation displays the erratic and cyclical time trajectory that characterizes so many fads and fashions. A particular act is valuable as long as it is practiced by a minority. Others will be attracted by the alternative, however. But the more popular the alternative becomes, the less its value. Sooner or later therefore, the tide will change and other alternatives will appear more attractive. The mechanism often generates paradoxical social situations such as the one described in the following statement of the American baseball player Yogi Berra: "That restaurant is so crowded that no one ever goes there anymore."

---

[23] In this case, the values are divided by the proportions, and these new values then are normalized so that they add up to 1.0.

[24] The true values associated with the two alternative courses of action are initially set equal to .66 and .33. But, as in the previous simulations, the actors initially are unaware of these values. It should also be emphasized that other simulations, not reported here, show that the same pattern can arise when the two alternatives are indistinguishable to start with.

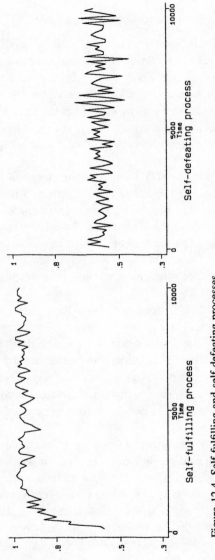

Figure 12.4. Self-fulfilling and self-defeating processes.

Concluding remarks

As argued in the first chapter of this book, we believe that the generality of sociological theory is to be found at the level of mechanisms, and that the future of explanatory sociological theory hinges on our ability to specify and to systematize these sorts of mechanisms. In this chapter, I have focused on one mechanism believed to be particularly important for observed interdependencies in the behavior of actors. This is the mechanism of social proof that systematically links the beliefs of one actor to the actions of others.

The social-proof mechanism results in a form of rational imitation. Through their actions, actors give off signals to other actors, and other actors pay attention to these signals because they provide information about the likely payoffs of different action alternatives. By relying upon the social-proof heuristic and following the lead of others, actors arrive at better decisions than they otherwise would have, and, in addition, they reduce whatever cognitive dissonance might be stemming from adopting an unconventional minority position.

The system of interaction that results from these behavioral principles has an intricate structure in which actors mutually observe, imitate, and influence each other's choices. A simulation model has been used to analyze this structure of interaction. These simulations have underscored that the aggregate outcomes of these types of action systems can vary widely depending upon specific characteristics, such as how much attention actors pay to the actions of others, and whether or not the payoffs are related to the aggregate choices of the actors.

The analyses also underscore the importance of making a clear distinction between ex post and ex ante rationality. Economizing on decision costs by relying upon the social-proof heuristic is a reasonable and useful strategy in most circumstances. In the type of stable environments considered here, for example, imitation clearly is superior to atomistic self-reliant behavior. But as emphasized previously, the strategy is not infallible. In unstable environments that change through unexpected and externally generated shocks to the system, being tied to established and inert actors reduces the likelihood that actions will be sufficiently modified in the light of new information. Also, in so-called self-defeating systems, imitation is less successful, because the rewards in those systems accrue to those who deviate from normal behavior, either by being leaders who perform unconventional acts way ahead of the crowd, or by being laggards who follow far behind the crowd. That even the most rational decision-making strategies can produce actions that are far off the target should not surprise anyone who is even the slightest bit familiar with inferential statistics, however: Even efficient and unbiased strategies often produce actions that deviate considerably from the optimal course of action, ex post.

In real-life situations, the strategies being adopted often are likely to be the result of a social evolutionary process (i.e., actors will realize when a particular strategy is no longer successful and change strategy accordingly). Prevalence and utility, therefore, will be intimately connected, the strategies that flourish in a certain environment – like pure imitation in stable environments – will become more prevalent, and the unsuccessful strategies will gradually vanish.

References

Arthur, W. Brian. 1994. "Path Dependence, Self-Reinforcement, and Human Learning." Pp. 133–58 in W. Brian Arthur, *Increasing Returns and Path Dependency in the Economy*. Ann Arbor: The University of Michigan Press.

Becker, Gary S. 1991. "A Note on Restaurant Pricing and Other Examples of Social Influences on Price." *Journal of Political Economy*. 99: 1109–16.

Cialdini, Robert B. 1984. *Influence: The Psychology of Persuasion*. New York: Quill.

Coleman, James S., Elihu Katz, and Herbert Menzel. 1966. *Medical Innovation*. Indianapolis: Bobbs-Merrill.

Cyert, Richard M., and James G. March. 1963. *A Behavioral Theory of the Firm*. Englewood Cliffs, NJ: Prentice-Hall.

Davis, Gerald F. 1991. "Agents without Principles? The Spread of the Poison Pill through the Intercorporate Network." *Administrative Science Quarterly*. 36: 583–613.

DiMaggio, Paul J., and Walter W. Powell. 1983. "The Iron Cage Revisited: Institutional Isomorphism and Collective Rationality in Organizational Fields." *American Sociological Review*. 48: 147–60.

DiMaggio, Paul J., and Walter W. Powell. 1991. "Introduction." Pp. 1–38 in Walter W. Powell and Paul J. DiMaggio (eds.), *The New Institutionalism in Organizational Analysis*. Chicago: University of Chicago Press.

Durkheim, Emile. [1897] 1951. *Suicide: A Study in Sociology*. New York: The Free Press.

Elster, Jon. 1983. *Ulysses and the Sirens*. Cambridge: Cambridge University Press.

Elster, Jon. 1986. "Introduction." Pp. 1–33 in J. Elster (ed.), *Rational Choice*. Oxford: Basil Blackwell.

Elster, Jon. 1989. *Nuts and Bolts for the Social Sciences*. Cambridge: Cambridge University Press.

Festinger, Leon. 1957. *A Theory of Cognitive Dissonance*. Stanford: Stanford University Press.

Flanders, James P. 1968. "A Review of Research on Imitative Behavior." *Psychological Bulletin*. 69(5): 316–37.

Fligstein, Neil. 1985. "The Spread of the Multidivisional Form among Large Firms, 1919–1979." *American Sociological Review*. 50: 377–91.

Galaskiewicz, Joseph, and Stanley Wasserman. 1989. "Mimetic Processes within an Interorganizational Field: An Empirical Test." *Administrative Science Quarterly*. 34: 454–79.

Goffman, Erving. 1966. *Strategic Interaction*. Philadelphia: University of Pennsylvania Press.

Granovetter, Mark. 1978. "Threshold Models of Collective Behavior." *American Journal of Sociology*. 83: 1420–43.

Hannan, Michael T., and Glenn R. Carroll. 1992. *Dynamics of Organizational Populations*. New York: Oxford University Press.

Haveman, Heather A. 1993. "Follow the Leader: Mimetic Isomorphism and Entry into New Markets." *Administrative Science Quarterly*. 38: 593–627.

Hedström, Peter. 1994a. "Contagious Collectivities: On the Spatial Diffusion of Swedish Trade Unions, 1890–1940." *American Journal of Sociology*. 99: 1157–79.

Hedström, Peter. 1994b. "Magnetic Fields and Cancer Risks: Should Recent Epidemiological Research be a Cause of Concern?" *Occasional Paper Series*. Department of Sociology, Stockholm University.

Hedström, Peter. 1996. "Rational Choice and Social Structure: On Rational-choice Theorizing in Sociology." In B. Wittrock (ed.), *Social Theory and Human Agency*. London: Sage.

Hedström, Peter, and Richard Swedberg. 1996. "Social Mechanisms." *Acta Sociologica*. 39:281–308.

Jones, Stephen R. G. 1984. *The Economics of Conformism*. Oxford: Blackwell.

Keynes, John Maynard. [1936] 1960. *The General Theory of Employment, Interest and Money*. London: Macmillan.

Kuran, Timur. 1995. *Private Truths, Public Lies: The Social Consequences of Preference Falsification*. Cambridge, MA: Harvard University Press.

Lawrence, Paul R., and Jay W. Lorsch. 1967. *Organization and Environment: Managing Differentiation and Integration*. Boston: Graduate School of Business, Harvard University.

Le Bon, Gustave. [1895] 1960. *The Crowd*. New York: Viking.

Leibenstein, Harvey. 1950. "Bandwagon, Snob, and Veblen Effects in the Theory of Consumer Demand." *Quarterly Journal of Economics*. 64: 183–207.

Luce, R. Duncan. 1959. *Individual Choice Behavior*. New York: Wiley.

Mead, Margaret. 1970. *Culture and Commitment: A Study of the Generation Gap*. London: The Bodley Head.

Merton, Robert K. 1968a. "Bureaucratic Structure and Personality." Pp. 249–60 in *Social Theory and Social Structure*. New York: The Free Press.

Merton, Robert K. 1968b. "The Self-fulfilling Prophecy." Pp. 475–90 in *Social Theory and Social Structure*. New York: The Free Press.

Meyer, John W., and Brian Rowan. 1977. "Institutionalized Organizations: Formal Structure as Myth and Ceremony." *American Journal of Sociology*. 83(2): 340–63.

Schelling, Thomas C. 1978. *Micromotives and Macrobehavior*. New York: W. W. Norton.

Stinchcombe, Arthur L. 1965. "Organizations and Social Structure." Pp. 153–93 in James G. March (ed.), *Handbook of Organizations*. Chicago: Rand McNally.

Tarde, Gabriel. [1895] 1962. *The Laws of Imitation*. Second Edition. Gloucester: Peter Smith.

Tsebelis, George. 1990. *Nested Games: Rational Choice in Comparative Politics*. Berkeley: University of California Press.

Weber, Max. [1921–2] 1978. *Economy and Society: An Outline of Interpretive Sociology*. Ed. Guenther Roth and Claus Wittich. Trans. Ephraim Fischoff et al. 2 vols. Berkeley: University of California Press.

Weinberg, Steven. 1993. *Dreams of a Final Theory: The Search for the Fundamental Laws of Nature*. London: Vintage.

Westney, D. Eleanor. 1987. *Imitation and Innovation: The Transfer of Western Organizational Patterns to Meiji Japan*. Cambridge, MA: Harvard University Press.

Author Index

Subject Index

CPSIA information can be obtained at www.ICGtesting.com
Printed in the USA
LVOW082322140312

273119LV00001B/14/P